The Object and Purpose of Intellectual Property

ATRIP INTELLECTUAL PROPERTY SERIES

Series Editor: Graeme B. Dinwoodie, *Global Professor of Intellectual Property Law, Chicago-Kent College of Law, USA*

The ATRIP series presents the fruit of annual meetings held by the International Association for the Advancement of Teaching and Research in Intellectual Property (www.atrip.org). Yielding unique opportunities for IP scholars from a global community to explore together the different facets of one overarching topic, the essence of those meetings is captured in the edited compilation of selected contributions contained in the volumes. Rather than employing a traditional, compartmentalized view of the different areas of IP, the ATRIP series typically follows a horizontal approach, cutting across the usual boundaries of legal categorization, with the aim to uncover hidden commonalities and accentuate the need for differentiation where that is called for. As ATRIP counts among its members leading IP scholars from all parts of the world, and actively encourages the participation of highly talented young researchers, the panel of authors contributing to the volumes not only guarantees excellence, but also represents a full and vibrant picture of contemporary, high-level IP research in an international setting.

Titles in the series include:

Individualism and Collectiveness in Intellectual Property Law
Edited by Jan Rosén

Intellectual Property at the Crossroads of Trade
Edited by Jan Rosén

Methods and Perspectives in Intellectual Property
Edited by Graeme B. Dinwoodie

Intellectual Property and General Legal Principles
Is IP a *Lex Specialis*?
Edited by Graeme B. Dinwoodie

Intellectual Property Perspectives on the Regulation of New Technologies
Edited by Tana Pistorius

Is Intellectual Property Pluralism Functional?
Edited by Susy Frankel

The Object and Purpose of Intellectual Property
Edited by Susy Frankel

The Object and Purpose of Intellectual Property

Edited by

Susy Frankel

Professor of Law and Chair in Intellectual Property and International Trade, Faculty of Law, Victoria University of Wellington, New Zealand

ATRIP INTELLECTUAL PROPERTY SERIES

EE Edward Elgar PUBLISHING

Cheltenham, UK • Northampton, MA, USA

Cover image:

Colin McDiarmid, Victoria University of Wellington
© Victoria University of Wellington

Published by
Edward Elgar Publishing Limited
The Lypiatts
15 Lansdown Road
Cheltenham
Glos GL50 2JA
UK

Edward Elgar Publishing, Inc.
William Pratt House
9 Dewey Court
Northampton
Massachusetts 01060
USA

A catalogue record for this book
is available from the British Library

Library of Congress Control Number: 2019938904

This book is available electronically in the **Elgar**online
Law subject collection
DOI 10.4337/9781789902495

MIX
Paper from
responsible sources
FSC® C013056

ISBN 978 1 78990 248 8 (cased)
ISBN 978 1 78990 249 5 (eBook)

Typeset by Servis Filmsetting Ltd, Stockport, Cheshire

Printed and bound in Great Britain by TJ International Ltd, Padstow, Cornwall

Contents

Contributors

Christoph Ann holds the Chair for Intellectual Property at the School of Management Technical University of Munich. He has law degrees from Germany and the U.S. (LL.M., Duke '88). From 2001–2003, he also served as a judge on the Mannheim Regional Court's renowned IP Infringement Panel with jurisdiction over the technologically eminent German state of Baden-Württemberg.

Margo A. Bagley is Asa Griggs Candler Professor of Law, Emory University School of Law, USA. Her scholarship focuses on comparative issues relating to patents and biotechnology, pharmaceuticals and access to medicines, and technology transfer. She is an expert technical advisor to the African Union in several WIPO matters and is the Lead Facilitator and Friend of the Chair in the WIPO Intergovernmental Committee on Intellectual Property, Genetic Resources, Traditional Knowledge, and Folklore.

Maria Letizia Bixio obtained a PhD in Copyright Law from University 'Parthenope' of Naples; she is now Postdoctoral Researcher at the European University of Rome and contributor for the chair of Commercial Law. She is lecturer of Cultural Heritage Rights at the European University of Rome. She is a Member of CREDA – Innovation & Copyright Excellence Research Centre, ALAI, ATRIP.

Marsha S. Cadogan is a Post-doctoral Intellectual Property Law Fellow with the Centre for International Governance Innovation. Her research includes geographical indications in global consumer markets, trade mark law and policy, intellectual property, trade and development, and the intersections between emerging technologies and intellectual property.

Susy Frankel is a Professor of Law and the Chair in Intellectual Property and International Trade and Director of the New Zealand Centre of International Economic Law, at Victoria University of Wellington. In 2018 she was elected Fellow of the Royal Society of New Zealand.

Jill Klein is a Professor of Marketing at the Melbourne Business School and Professorial Fellow at the Melbourne Medical School. Jill is a distinguished consumer researcher whose work has been published in the Journal of Marketing, Management Science, Journal of Consumer Psychology, British Medical Journal, and more. A particular focus of her research is on decision making biases and how they affect decisions in both business and medical settings.

Jessica C. Lai is a Senior Lecturer of Commercial Law at Victoria University of Wellington, New Zealand. She researches in patent law and the protection of traditional knowledge. She has published numerous articles, chapters, books and edited books in these fields, and is the author of 'Indigenous Cultural Heritage and Intellectual Property Rights' (Springer 2014) and co-author of 'Patent Law and Policy' (with Susy Frankel, LexisNexis 2016).

Valentina Moscon is a Senior Research Fellow at the Max Planck Institute for Innovation and Competition in Munich, Germany. Her research focuses on European and comparative copyright law and information law.

Ana Nordberg is Associate Senior Lecturer at the Faculty of Law, Lund University, Sweden. A former practising lawyer, technology adept and a cross-disciplinary enthusiast, Dr. Nordberg is responsible for IP law courses and researches the legal implications of emerging technology from a broad contextual perspective.

Enyinna Nwauche is a Professor and Head of Department of Private Law at the Nelson Mandela School of Law, University of Fort Hare South Africa where he teaches intellectual property law. He is a member of the African Union Committee on a Model Law on Heritage and Cultural Property. He has also served as Director General of the Nigerian Copyright Commission.

Żaneta Pacud is Assistant Professor in the Institute of Law Studies at the Polish Academy of Sciences, Warsaw, Poland. She specialises in industrial property and life science. Currently she conducts her research on regulatory data protection and biotechnological inventions.

Megan Richardson is a Professor of Law, Director of the Intellectual Property Research Institute of Australia and Co-Director of the Centre for Media and Communications Law at the Melbourne Law School, University of Melbourne. She works across privacy, personality and intellectual property law. Books include 'Fashioning Intellectual Property: Exhibition, Advertising and the Press, 1789–1918' (CUP, 2012), with Julian Thomas, and 'The Right to Privacy: Origins and Influence of a Nineteenth-Century Idea' (CUP, 2017).

Julian Thomas is Director of the Social Change research platform at RMIT University. He works on information law and policy and the histories of new communications technologies. With Megan Richardson, he has published 'Fashioning Intellectual Property: Exhibition, Advertising and the Press, 1789–1918' (CUP, 2012). Books include 'Internet on the Outstation: The Digital Divide and Remote Aboriginal Communities' (INC, 2016) and 'The Informal Media Economy' (Polity, 2015).

Anna Tischner (dr hab.) is an Associate Professor at the Intellectual Property Law Chair of the Jagiellonian University in Krakow, Poland. Anna's main field is industrial property and unfair competition law, and in particular European design law. Her publications include two monographs (in Polish): 'Civil liability for trade mark infringement' (WoltersKluwer 2008) and 'Cumulative protection of designs in the intellectual property law' (C.H. Beck 2015).

Knud Wallberg is a Post-doctoral Researcher at the University of Copenhagen where he teaches in IT law. He is member of the Legal Expert Group established by the EUIPO and holds positions as UDRP panelist with WIPO and expert member of the .dk Dispute Board for Domain names.

Genevieve Wilkinson is a Lecturer in the Faculty of Law at the University of Technology Sydney researching in the fields of intellectual property and human rights. Genevieve holds a PhD from the University of Technology Sydney.

Chongnang Wiputhanupong has a PhD from the University of Nottingham and is a lecturer at the School of Law, Sripatum University, Thailand. Her research focuses on copyright, media and communication. The National Research Council of Thailand is funding her project on the development of originality and creativity in Thailand's copyright system.

Helen Yu is an Assistant Professor and Associate Director of the Centre for Advanced Studies in Biomedical Innovation Law (CeBIL) at the University of Copenhagen, Faculty of Law. Her research focuses on how intellectual property and policy tools can be leveraged to support the responsible transformation of basic research into socially and economically beneficial outcomes. Helen holds a degree in neuroscience and practiced as an intellectual property lawyer and registered patent agent in Canada before obtaining her PhD at the University of Copenhagen.

Acknowledgements

It is an honour to have served as the president of the International Association for the Advancement of Teaching and Research of Intellectual Property (ATRIP) and to contribute this edited volume to further ATRIP's goals of progressing intellectual property research from around the globe.

As president it was a great pleasure to host the 36th ATRIP meeting at Victoria University of Wellington, New Zealand. Thanks to the sponsors of that meeting, including the World Intellectual Property Organization, New Zealand's Ministry of Business Innovation and Employment, InternetNZ and the New Zealand Law Foundation.

I thank all of the authors who have contributed to this volume and Kathleen Henning, LLM student, for her research assistance.

Susy Frankel, FRSNZ
Professor of Law, Chair in Intellectual Property and International Trade
ATRIP President 2015–2017

Introduction

Susy Frankel

Much of the debate around the parameters of intellectual property protection and the extent of how flexible the law should be, at both national and international levels, relates to policies and views about what the law is supposed to achieve. Also relevant to the debate is whether the law reflects its underlying justifications and whether those justifications come to fruition or whether other outcomes are occurring. Put differently, are intellectual property laws and their application achieving their objectives and purposes?

The different objectives and rationales that underpin national regimes are variously reflected in international agreements, which also have their own object and purpose. The international agreements embody many objectives and the various rules for minimum standards for intellectual property protection are the vehicles to achieve those objectives. National regimes, which are collectively called intellectual property, also make up aspects of the 'object and purpose' of international treaties, to quote the words of Article 31 of the Vienna Convention on the Law of Treaties. The object and purpose of intellectual property include copyright's role in encouraging creativity based on utilitarianism and natural rights; patent law's connection to innovation policy and the encouragement of invention; and trade mark law's business and consumer information-supporting functions.

The significance of these broad and often disputed rationales will vary among jurisdictions and may well be reshaped through the operation of the international treaty framework, in particular the Agreement on Trade-Related Aspects of Intellectual Property Rights (TRIPS), which expressly connected intellectual property and trade and placed that relationship at the centre of the international intellectual property regime. Many of the rationales for intellectual property in a trade-related environment are also linked to productivity and competition concerns that are reflected in the World Trade Organization (WTO) and its various parts. The part known as TRIPS explicitly includes a range of objectives and principles. Broadly, TRIPS added explicit trade-related concerns (including both export and development interests) to the existing international and underlying domestic policy rationales of intellectual property. Subsequent to TRIPS, trade and investment agreements have emerged that often aim to increase protection and enforcement and reduce TRIPS flexibilities. In sum this creates a range of objects and purposes that are all relevant to the interpretation of the international regime, in one way or another.

The relevance of intellectual property as a set of discrete rules is arguably both expanding and shrinking. It is practically trite to point out that there are complexities in how intellectual property interacts with changing technologies and other areas of law in many fields. It is, therefore, more important than ever to analyse how the object and purpose of intellectual property applies to new and fast-changing areas such as big data, biotechnology and social media.

The relevance of the object and purpose of intellectual property might be assessed by looking at who is involved in the creation, use and dissemination of intellectual property and the outcomes of rights and uses for those actors. The chapters in this book address these themes and are from scholars based around the world, reflecting the global nature and diversity goals of the International Association for the Advancement of Teaching and Research of Intellectual Property (ATRIP).

The book is divided into four parts. Part I addresses 'Cultural Objectives and Development Goals'. As intellectual property has become a global regime its relationship to cultural objectives, such as protecting local culture and development goals, has become of greater concern. It is well established that a one-size-fits-all intellectual property regime can fly in the face of development and run roughshod over localised cultural concerns. Exactly how to have an effective intellectual property regime that calibrates competing interests remains elusive, for some countries, and can be somewhat inconsistent in the domestic regimes of others. Chapter 1 addresses issues about cultural policy in the Australian trade marks register. The three authors of this chapter, Megan Richardson, Julian Thomas and Jill Klein, bring perspectives from law, media studies and marketing to analyse how the Australian trade marks register shapes cultural policy and makes particular decisions about what is protectable as trade marks and what is not. The chapter argues that the legal treatment of identifying labels for commodities such as wine and coffee in Australia is a product of a cultural trade mark law policy dating back to the height of the British Empire and endorsed in the post-war 'White Australia' period. The authors question whether the Australian trade marks register should passively reflect inherited cultural tensions and propose instead that the rules governing trade mark registration should be part of a thoroughly modern cultural and economic trade mark law policy. In Chapter 2 Jessica

Lai looks in-depth at how Manuka is used in patenting. The chapter uses an empirical analysis of New Zealand registered patents to discuss what has or has not been appropriated from Māori interests and also asks whether the Māori Advisory Committee in the New Zealand Patent Office has served its purpose with respect to those applications. Marsha Cadogan, in Chapter 3, uses a constructivist critique of intellectual property to analyse its relationship with development. Using examples from the Caribbean Cadogan illustrates the issues that divide intellectual property from development. The final chapter in this part, Chapter 4, explores ownership and licensing of traditional knowledge in Africa. Enyinna Nwauche explains the overlapping domestic and regional regimes for the protection of traditional knowledge associated with genetic resources. Together these four chapters demonstrate how the object and purpose of intellectual property is increasingly informed by drivers that arise because of cultural survival and development concerns resulting from the impact of globalised intellectual property rights.

In Part II the international and regional frameworks of design protection are discussed from three different angles. In Chapter 5, Margo Bagley demystifies the complexities of the international design regime. The chapter, 'Designing disclosure: disclosure of cultural and genetic resource utilisation in design protection regimes' shows how the intersection of design and genetic resources is increasing not only because of the allure of exotic cultural expressions, but also because of the burgeoning use of biotechnology in design. The chapter explains how these have become issues in the Design Law Treaty negotiations at the World Intellectual Property Organization (WIPO). There is very little international agreement about the scope for design law and in Chapter 6, Anna Tischner illustrates the variation of approaches to design in the European Union. She analyses how the identification of the object of design protection has become problematic because of the context of communication related to the subject matter of the design protection and the complicated system of both formal and informal protection. In Chapter 7 Genevieve Wilkinson discusses the object and purpose of international trade mark protection. To illustrate her arguments shes uses the plain packaging of tobacco disputes and human rights claims..

Part III focuses on the European Union and innovation and enforcement. In Chapter 8, Żaneta Pacud discusses pharmaceutical protection and analyses the goals of various parts of the law, including supplementary patent certificates and data exclusivity. The chapter shows the complexities of the regime and provides an understanding of how some of the detail reflects competing goals and the differing needs of actors in the regime. Helen Yu, in Chapter 9, examines how regional actors and strategic uses of intellectual property can attract and retain investment and intellectual capital, while optimising socio-economic value from publicly funded research. She debunks the claim that increased innovation will of itself lead to local development and shows how investment in capacity, infrastructure and resources are often needed to achieve development goals. In Chapter 10, Christoph Ann discusses the legal uncertainty that comes with latent patent invalidity. He questions whether European patent law can meet its purpose if patents are unreliable. Drawing on empirical studies from Germany, the chapter discusses particular questions such as if patents are unreliable then why should start-ups, for example, seek them. This part concludes with Chapter 11, where Ana Nordberg and Knud Wallberg map EU-wide enforcement measures. They discuss legal interpretation and the issues about harmonising enforcement rules. The chapter considers whether harmonisation is desirable when a variety of laws address the same subject matter, such as 3D printing and synthetic biology. The discussion reveals a contest between functional pluralism and systemic coherence, which leads the authors to conclude that emerging technologies do not necessarily require legal coherence, but systemic coherence can play an important role in legal responses to global technology-induced business models and social phenomena.

The object and purpose of aspects of copyright law and policy is the focus of Part IV. The digital world has evoked a never-ending discussion about the purpose(s) of copyright law. In Chapter 12, Valentina Moscon uses Europe's debate about online news protection to challenge the utility of using neighbouring rights to address various subject matter issues that arise from copyright's application. The chapter's analysis reveals that neighbouring rights are inadequate to address the concerns relating to news and the author proposes a more holistic approach to capture several purposes. In Chapter 13 Chongnang Wiputhanupong discusses derivative works and their interpretation in the United Kingdom and the United States. She uses this discussion to explain the approach in Thailand. This chapter enlightens readers about the decisions of the courts of Thailand and demonstrates how assumptions about derivative works from one jurisdiction do not necessarily transpose across borders. The final aspect of copyright, which is discussed in Chapter 14, is the variation of collective management goals and structure. Maria Letizia Bixio compares the various models found in Europe and assesses their impacts and effects on competition and the goals of remunerating authors.

Each of the chapters in this volume addresses different aspects of the objects and purpose of intellectual property law. They show how the diversity of goals means that there is always likely to be a diversity of laws. While supporting that diversity is a common theme among the chapters, they also show the problems that too much variety can sometimes cause. By focussing on the object and purpose of intellectual property those who make and interpret law and policy can find ways to progressively develop an understanding of what diversity supports the policy goals of national, regional and international rules and what variations can undermine them. This alone is unlikely to produce international agreement on all aspects of the law, but it provides a set of tools to discuss disagreement in ways that could lead to results rather than polarised positions, which seem to characterise the international intellectual property regime.

PART I

Cultural objectives and development goals

1. From 'Oomoo' to 'Oro': nostalgia labels and cultural policy on the Australian trade marks register*

Megan Richardson, Julian Thomas and Jill Klein**

I. INTRODUCTION

Trade mark law is often thought of as concerned with trade and commerce. But it is also rooted in history and culture and in some instances reflects deeply embedded cultural conflicts as between different imagined communities. In this chapter we focus on two Australian nostalgia labels that demonstrate the point in an especially poignant way. The first lay at the centre of *In the Matter of Burgoyne's Trade Mark*,[1] a case decided at the height of the British Empire, where an English judge held that the trade mark 'Oro' applied to a wine imported from Thomas Hardy's vineyard in South Australia might mean 'choice' to an Australian Aboriginal (in fact it was already noted in colonial records as denoting 'good' to the Dieri people of South Australia) but was 'meaningless' to the 'ordinary Englishman' in Britain.[2] So it could be entered as a trade mark on the nascent United Kingdom trade marks register. A little over a century later, a revived 'Oomoo' label was registered as a trade mark for Hardy's wine in

* All online sources were last accessed on 27 December 2018.

** We are grateful to Henry Biggs, Christine Black, Robert Burrell, Irene Calboli, Jennifer Davis, Graeme Dinwoodie, Che Ekaratne, Susy Frankel, Dev Gangjee, Vicki Huang, Andrew May, Sam Ricketson, Angela Riley, Dan Rosen, Amanda Scardamaglia and participants at the 2017 International Association for the Advancement of Teaching and Research of Intellectual Property Congress in Wellington for helpful information and advice. Research was funded by an Australian Research Council Linkage Grant 'Testing Trade Mark Law's Image of the Consumer' (LP120100249).

1 *Burgoyne's Trade Mark* (1889) 6 RPC 227 (Ch).

2 Ibid 231–2 (Chitty J).

Australia,[3] at the same time that a government-sponsored programme for recovering the endangered Dieri language was under way in the place from which the wine was sourced. The principle that a foreign-language expression without 'ordinary signification' in Australia can be registered as a trade mark was more recently relied on by the High Court in *Cantarella Bros Pty Ltd v Modena Trading Pty Ltd*[4] to hold that 'Oro', meaning 'gold' in Italian and in common use by Italian coffee traders in Australia, was validly registered to Cantarella.[5] Thus, a standard that became entrenched in Australia during the era of its White Australia policy resolves an issue as to a trade mark entitlement to a symbol widely associated with an Italian tradition of coffee in modern Australia.[6] We argue that in these examples the legal treatment of labels applied to wine and coffee in Australia replicates the complicated histories of the products. And we question whether the 'ordinary signification' of language to some 'ordinary' English-speaker should be the measure of a trade mark in a country which prides itself on being both multicultural and respectful of the highly diverse languages and traditions of its Indigenous peoples, proposing instead that the trade mark register should do more than passively reflect the inherited cultural tensions of an earlier period. In short, the rules governing trade mark registration should be treated as part of a thoroughly modern cultural and economic trade mark law policy.

The chapter is arranged as follows. In Sections II and III we trace the roots of the Anglo-Australian inherent distinctiveness standard, arguing that it reflected a cultural policy of (predominantly) English language preservation fashioned in the hands of Victorian judges in Britain, which was then adopted wholesale by Australian judges in post-colonial Australia. In Sections IV and V we consider reforms in other parts of the Anglosphere, including the American doctrine of foreign equivalents and the equal treatment principle applied to Māori in New Zealand – and we conclude that, while introducing reforms modelled on these overseas experiments, for instance adopting a doctrine of foreign equivalents along

---

3 See Trade Mark 1099230, registered to Hardy's Winery in 2006 along with the endorsement: 'The applicant has advised that the translation of the ABORIGINAL word OOMOO appearing in the trade mark is GOOD, NICE, PLEASANT TO THE EYE'.

4 *Cantarella Bros Pty Ltd v Modena Trading Pty Ltd* (2014) 254 CLR 337 (HCA).

5 The trade mark is still registered. See Trade Mark 829098, registered to Cantarella Bros in 2000.

6 As to the White Australia policy, see Gwenda Tavan, *The Long, Slow Death of White Australia* (Scribe 2005). As to the historical as well as modern symbolic character of coffee as a 'regional cultural icon' in Australia, see Andrew Brown-May, *Espresso! Melbourne Coffee Stories* (Arcadia 2001) 75.

with special language protection for Indigenous languages, could be a desirable way to effect change in Australia, the effectiveness of the change will depend on reformist judges and other decision makers of the future creatively interpreting the current law alongside Australian social and cultural aspirations.

II. 'DISTINCTIVENESS' AND VICTORIAN CULTURAL POLICY

The economic idea of a 'trade mark' as an efficient source-signifier – '[a] kind of shortcut to get consumers to where they want to go, and in that way perform a key function in a market economy' – is a central organising principle of Australian trade mark law, which treats the fostering and ordering of efficient trade as its main policy objective,[7] even if it is increasingly accepted that trade marks may serve 'other functions' apart from designating origin,[8] and that the law may also have other 'public purposes' centred around broader social policy concerns.[9] This is not only in Australia. In the large majority of countries around the world in the post-TRIPS era,[10] mainstream legal and economic consensus has it that the statutory language of a 'trade mark' as a sign that distinguishes the goods or services of a trader from those of other traders in the market embodies the trade mark's principal economic function, *viz* of informing and reminding consumers of the trading source of the goods or services, with the implicit message that this can generally also be expected to be the law's main concern.[11] Indeed, the position that trade marks are primarily

---

[7] See *JT International SA v Commonwealth of Australia* (2012) 250 CLR 1 (HCA) [139] (Gummow J) (noting the statement of Binnie J in *Mattel Inc v 3894207 Canada Inc* (2006) 1 SCR 772 (SCC) 788).

[8] Ibid [286] (Crennan J) ('Whilst the prime concern of the Trade Marks Act is with the capacity of a trade mark to distinguish the goods of the registered owner from those of another trader, trade marks undoubtedly perform other functions'), including as an indicium of quality and through their ability to advertise the products.

[9] Ibid [30] (French CJ) ('There are and always have been purposive elements reflecting public policy considerations which inform the statutory creation of intellectual property rights') citing Gleeson CJ et al in *Campomar Sociedad Limitada v Nike International Ltd* (2000) 202 CLR 45 (HCA) [42]–[49] and [35] ('Registered trademarks . . . give rise to, or constitute, exclusive rights . . . created by statute in order to serve public purposes . . .').

[10] Agreement on Trade-Related Aspects of Intellectual Property Rights (opened for signature 15 April 1994, entered into force 1 January 1996) 1869 UNTS 299 (TRIPS).

[11] For instance, James Mellor, David Llewelyn, Thomas Moody-Stuart, David

economic in nature and function continues to be maintained despite a growing body of marketing, sociological, anthropological, cultural, linguistic and legal recognition that these signs may 'represent a variety of ideas and attributes' to the audience.[12]

That it is a long-established position no doubt helps in entrenching its status. It can be traced back to the utilitarianism of the late nineteenth century, when the British trade mark registration system was established over a period of roughly 30 years,[13] serving also as a model for the colonies.[14] It was embodied, for instance, in leading textbook-writer Kerly's statement in 1894 that a 'trade mark' consists of 'a symbol applied or attached to goods offered for sale in the market, so as to distinguish them from similar goods, and to identify them with a particular trader',[15] a statement substantially repeated in later editions throughout the twentieth century.[16] And while the focus in the nineteenth century may have been more on the advantages for traders of being able to efficiently signify the source of their products in a mass-market economy and thus capture benefits from their labours in trade,[17] the assumption was that the

---

Keeling, Iona Berkeley, Ashton Chantrielle, William Duncan, *Kerly's Law of Trade Marks and Trade Names* (16th edn, Sweet & Maxwell 2018) 11–18 (enumerating the trade mark functions, but also identifying the source-signifying function as especially important). See also Graeme Dinwoodie and Dev Gangjee, 'The Image of the Consumer in EU Trade Mark Law' in Dorota Leczykiewicz and Stephen Weatherill (eds), *The Images of the Consumer in EU Law: Legislation, Free Movement and Competition Law* (Hart Publishing 2016) 339, 346 (the source-signifying function 'remains the primary basis for trade mark protection around the world').

12 See *JT International* (n 7) [286] (Crennan J) (the 'advertising function').

13 Trade Marks Registration Act 1875 (United Kingdom); Patents, Designs and Trade Marks Act 1883 (United Kingdom); Trade Marks Act 1905 (United Kingdom).

14 See Lionel Bently, 'The Extraordinary Multiplicity of Intellectual Property Laws in the British Colonies in the Nineteenth Century' (2011) 12 TIL 161; and further, as to Australia, Amanda Scardamaglia, *Colonial Australian Trade Mark Law: Narratives in Lawmaking, People, Power & Place* (Australian Scholarly Publishing 2015) (also pointing to local variations in Australian colonial laws and in some instances the adoption of advanced positions, taking up standards proposed but not yet accepted in the United Kingdom).

15 Duncan Kerly, *Law of Trade-Marks, Trade-Name, and Merchandise Marks* (Stevens and Sons 1894) 25.

16 A typical example is the eighth edition published in 1960, where the statement of Kerly is quoted verbatim: Rhys G Lloyd, *Kerly's Law of Trade Marks and Trade Names* (8th edn, Sweet & Maxwell 1960) 16.

17 See Lionel Bently, Jennifer Davis and Jane C Ginsburg, *Trade Marks and Brands: An Interdisciplinary Critique* (Cambridge University Press 2008) 3 and further as to the colonies, Bently (n 14) and Scardamaglia (n 14).

consuming public would also benefit from their ability to identify traders' products.[18] The basic understanding that the interests of traders and consumers converge in the economic benefits of a system that promotes the adoption, registration and use of trade marks to indicate a trading source thus became established when brands themselves were becoming a central feature of the vast capitalist system of trade stretching across the British world.[19]

Nevertheless, there was one domain in which judges in this period paid close attention to the social and cultural dimensions of trade marks from the beginning, albeit they did so in a rather restricted way. In a series of late nineteenth-century cases British judges treated the law's statutory requirements that a word should be 'fancy', 'invented', non-descriptive (as in 'a word or words having no direct reference to the character or quality of the goods') or otherwise 'distinctive', in order to be registered,[20] as more than simply an attempt to predict a trade mark's ability to distinguish a particular trader's goods from those of other traders through use and without the benefit of registration. That rationale came later. Most notably in *Registrar of Trade Marks v W & G Du Cros* in 1913 Lord Parker said the issue 'largely depends upon whether other traders are likely, in the ordinary course of their business and without any improper motive, to desire to use the same mark, or some mark nearly resembling it, upon or in connection with their own goods'.[21] Rather, using strikingly different language, Victorian judges identified the distinctiveness threshold as a vehicle for protecting 'the great open common of the English language' from the appropriations of traders,[22] drawing on a nineteenth-century linguistic view of the common language of a society as a repository of

---

[18] *The Birmingham Vinegar Brewery Co Ltd v Powell* (1897) AC 710 (HL) 714 (Lord Halsbury LC).

[19] See generally Gary B Magee and Andrew S Thompson, *Empire and Globalisation: Networks of People, Goods and Capital in the British World, c 1850–1914* (CUP 2010) ch 4.

[20] Trade Marks Registration Act 1875 (United Kingdom), s 10; Patents, Designs and Trade Marks Act 1883 (United Kingdom), s 64(1)(c), s 64(d) and (e); Trade Marks Act 1905 (United Kingdom), s 9(3)–(5).

[21] *Registrar of Trade Marks v W & G Du Cros Ltd* (1913) AC 624 (HL) 635 (Lord Parker).

[22] *Dunn's Trade Marks* (1889) 41 ChD 439, 455 (Fry LJ). See also *Eastman Photographic Materials Co Ltd v Comptroller-General of Patents, Designs and Trade-Marks* (1898) AC 571 (HL) 574 (Lord Halsbury LC), 581 (Lord Herschell), 583 (Lord Macnaghten); *Re Joseph Crosfield & Son Ltd* [1910] 1 Ch 130 (CA) 141 (Cozens-Hardy MR).

traditional culture,[23] and using the trope of 'the ordinary Englishman's' knowledge of language as their standard.[24]

Jennifer Davis has noted that 'the ordinary Englishman' was not an average Englishman (or woman) but reflected the judge's 'class assumptions';[25] and his somewhat artificial character allowed considerable scope for him to function as a judicial policy instrument.[26] There is support for this analysis in the observation of Chitty J in *Davis v Stribolt* that 'there are many good English words descriptive of articles which are unknown to an average Englishman, taking rather a high standard'.[27] Indeed the ordinary Englishman's knowledge may well have exceeded that of even the average middle-class Englishman at times, as in that case where the ordinary Englishman's deemed knowledge that 'Bokól' and '*Bokøl*' were Scandinavian words for beer meant these could not be registered as a trade mark for beer in the United Kingdom.[28] Indeed, there is plenty in the cases to support the idea that 'the ordinary Englishman' was a device that enabled Victorian judges to frame and further a policy of protecting a traditional body of English and other languages that judges wanted to treat as available to ordinary – or at least ordinary middle-class – Englishmen from appropriation.

There are other respects in which the Victorian judges' standard relying on 'the ordinary Englishman' seems removed from the way that some groups understood language. That a modern language might develop new significances was still a radical idea put forward by Ferdinand de Saussure in Switzerland and Charles Sanders Peirce in America around the *fin de siècle*.[29] Yet 'the arbitrariness of the sign' would become widely accepted in the twentieth century,[30] and from relatively early on it provided a basis not

---

23 See Megan Richardson, 'Trade Marks and Language' (2004) 26 Sydney L Rev 193, 207–20.

24 Jennifer Davis, 'Locating the Average Consumer: His Judicial Origins, Intellectual Influences and Current Role in European Trade Mark Law' (2005) 2 IPQ 183, pt 2.

25 Ibid 191–2.

26 Cf Chris Dent, 'The "Reasonable Man", his Nineteenth-Century "Siblings", and their Legacy' (2017) 44 J Law & Soc 406.

27 *Davis & Co v Stribolt & Co* (1889) 6 RPC 207 (Ch) 212.

28 Ibid. See also *Philippart v William Whiteley Ltd* (1908) 25 RPC 565 (Ch) ('Diabolo', Italian for 'the devil', as the name of a popular spinning top game based on an ancient game 'Le Diable', or 'Devil on Two Sticks').

29 See Ferdinand de Saussure, *Cours de linguistique générale* (Payot & Cie 1916); Charles Sanders Peirce, 'Letter to Lady Welby' (1904), reprinted in Arthur W Burks (ed), *Collected Papers of Charles Sanders Peirce* (vol 8, Harvard UP 1958).

30 See Damián E Blasi, Søren Wichmann, Harald Hammarström, Peter

only for new thinking about language, but also for a new set of advertising and artistic practices combining language and visual effects in novel forms; for instance, with the playful 'Calligrammes' of Apollinaire,[31] the incongruous word art of Magritte,[32] the 'recurrent references to newspapers' in Picasso's collages,[33] and the expressive line-drawings of Walter Crane, noted British artist and book illustrator, who in 1900 already talked of the line as 'a language, a most vigorous and sensitive speech of many dialects, which can adapt itself to all purposes' in the hands of an artist, unleashing 'a great range of expression'.[34] Nevertheless, the Victorian judges' focus on 'distinctiveness' remained squarely on the traditional meaning of common words 'appropriated' and deployed by traders for their exclusive use, with the only effect the judges were prepared to imagine being that a word previously used to describe a range of things was now being used to describe a trader's products specifically.[35] In the process, 'the ordinary Englishman' becomes not just a middle-class person who was surprisingly knowledgeable in many languages, but also a rather conservative, literal-minded type in his reaction to the treatment of language in some already-becoming-modern advertising and artistic practices.

Indeed, as late as 1909, almost a decade after Crane wrote of language as expressive and adaptable in the hands of the artist, Cozens Hardy MR was still insisting that '[w]ealthy traders are habitually eager to enclose

---

F Stadler, and Morten H Christiansen, 'Sound-Meaning Association Biases Evidenced across Thousands of Languages' 113 PNAS 10818.

31 Guillaume Apollinaire, *Calligrammes: Poems de la Pais et de la Guerre* (Mercvre de France 1918) and Willard Bohm, *Modern Visual Poetry* (University of Delaware Press 2001) (noting the influence of new advertising practices transformed by changes in typesetting, typefaces and photo-reproduction technologies).

32 See Uwe M Schneede, *René Magritte: Life and Work* (Barron's 1982) ch 3; and Roger Rotham, 'René Magritte and "The Shop-Window Quality of Things"' (2007) 3 The Space Between 11 (comparing Magritte's advertising and artistic activities and arguing they were similarly inspired).

33 See Robert Rosenblum, 'Picasso and the Typography of Cubism' in Sir Roland Penrose and John Golding (eds), *Picasso in Retrospect* (Praeger 1973) 33, 34, 36 (noting 'the stimulus of brand names, labels, advertisements, posters was constant in the Cubist millieu').

34 Walter Crane, *Line and Form* (G Bell & Sons Ltd 1900) 21–2.

35 Cf the common law where 'secondary meaning' was accepted as a bulwark against deceptive practices: see *Reddaway v Banham* [1896] AC 199 (HL) 210–11 (Lord Herschell) ('words forming part of the common stock of language, may become so far associated with the goods of a particular maker that it is capable of proof that the use of them by themselves without explanation or qualification by another manufacturer would deceive its purchaser into the belief that he was getting the goods of A, when he was really getting the goods of B').

Source: First author's personal collection.

Figure 1.1 Crosfield's 'Perfection' soap advertisement, Illustrated London News, May 1887

part of the great common of the English language and to exclude the general public of the present day and of the future from access to the inclosure'.[36] Furthermore, 'a mere laudatory epithet' such as 'Perfection', despite its use on 'millions of cakes sold' of Crosfield's soap over many years,[37] was not, in his opinion, 'capable of being registered [as a trade mark]' on the basis that it 'ought to be open to all the world'.[38] The other judges in the case referenced the word's 'ordinary' or 'common' descriptive and laudatory meaning, as denoting literally perfection,[39] to conclude that it should not be allowed to be withdrawn from its 'primary and proper meaning . . . to make it mean "Crosfields" instead of "perfect"'.[40]

36 *Joseph Crosfield* (n 22) 141–2 (Cozens Hardy MR).
37 Ibid 143.
38 Ibid.
39 Ibid 148 (Fletcher Moulton LJ) 151, 153–4 (Farwell LJ).
40 Ibid 153 (Farwell LJ). Note that these judges were not just concerned with protection of the English language as a general matter, but with the 'rights' of other traders to use the language (see for example Fletcher Moulton LJ at 148,

Apparently, the 'ordinary' meaning of 'Perfection' did not take into account the way the word was already being used in advertising (see Figure 1.1) to convey not a precise sense of literal perfection but a more symbolic sense of a wonderful cleanliness in association with Crosfield's soap, in the same way that Crosfield's competitors used 'Matchless Cleanser' and 'Sunlight' to convey a sense of magical cleanliness loosely connected with their soaps.[41]

The growing artistic and advertising reliance on symbolic meaning also helps us to understand the advertising uses of indigenous languages of the colonies in the labels applied to products sourced for British markets around the *fin de siècle*, refashioning their meaning to suit the traders' purposes of communicating their own selected symbolic meanings to their selected audiences. In the same way that leading artists from Van Gogh to Toulouse-Lautrec and Picasso were creatively adapting Oriental and later African and Oceanic symbols, with little regard to their original symbolic meanings,[42] so apparently 'meaningless' indigenous words and imagery were being repurposed by advertisers (sometimes using the same artists) as labels, advertisements and posters in the late Victorian and early Edwardian period – ensuring that 'scenes of empire [entered] into every corner of the home, stamping images of colonial conquest on soap boxes, matchboxes, biscuit tins, whiskey bottles, tea tins and chocolate bars'; or as Anne McClintock neatly summarises it, it was a period of 'imperial kitsch as consumer spectacle'.[43]

We might want to challenge this characterisation of kitschness, although it is a label that more generally has been applied to the art of this period and not without some justification.[44] In fact, the involvement of artists in designing labels, posters and advertisements ensured the artistic quality of advertising could be very high, as with the elegant lines and imagery of

---

Farwell LJ at 151); as such, the case represented a transitional moment between the nineteenth-century language protection cases and the pro-competition focus of later cases such as *Du Cros* (n 21).

41 Ibid 149 (Fletcher Moulton LJ).

42 Many of the most famous artistic works of this period, including Vincent van Gogh's *Irises* (1889) and Henri de Toulouse-Lautrec's *Divan Japonais* (1893) (at the same time an advertising poster), show strong oriental influences. See generally Gabriele Fahr-Becker, *Art Nouveau* (Könemann 1997) 9–11, 14–15, 103.

43 Anne McClintock, 'Soft-Soaping Empire: Commodity Racism and Imperial Advertising' in Nicholas Mirzoeff (ed), *The Visual Cultural Reader* (Routledge 1998) 304–5.

44 As Fahr-Becker (n 42) 7 points out, the Art Nouveau style of this period that many now celebrate as 'the beginning of the Modern Style' has also had its share of detractors, who have dismissed it as 'ornamental hell, kitch, and arts and crafts'.

Toulouse-Lautrec's advertising posters,[45] and the colourful posters, labels and other advertising material produced by commercial lithographer Charles Troedel's company in Melbourne, Australia, which, in the words of Amanda Scardamaglia, demonstrated 'great artistic merit and honoured the style of the French *Belle Époque* in the 1890s'.[46] Nevertheless, the aims and effects of the colonial advertising practices often seemed quite different from the practices of other artist/advertisers whose broader purpose was to create a genuinely 'modern style'.[47] While the latter were at the vanguard of the transition to twentieth-century modernism, colonial advertising practices seemed designed to give consumers the impression that they could enjoy the luxurious experience of living at the centre of a vast colonising enterprise dedicated to providing them with exotic products without having to think too hard about the methods that had been employed in making this possible. Thus we see the beginning of nostalgia labels used to promote and reinforce the idea of the product as 'an unalloyedly blissful substance, except that we wrongfully forget that it is also the product of an expropriation'.[48]

How did the courts treat these practices in the trade mark cases involving indigenous language and imagery that came before them in the last decades of the nineteenth century and the very beginning of the next one? We have already noted how, on the one hand, Victorian and later Edwardian judges treated European languages as within the ordinary Englishman's knowledge, so descriptive words in these languages were precluded from trade mark registration in the same way as English ones.[49] On the other hand, 'the ordinary Englishman's' deemed lack of knowledge of 'barbarous language[s]',[50] meant that traders were left free by the law to pursue their practices of drawing on the languages and imagery of the indigenous peoples of the colonies in their advertising practices. In the case that established the position, *Burgoyne's Trade Mark*,[51] Chitty J held

[45] See, for instance, National Gallery of Victoria, *Japonisme: Japan and the Birth of Modern Art* (National Gallery of Victoria 2018) 56–7, describing Toulouse-Lautrec's *Divan Japonais* as innovatively employing formal qualities of Japanese art in an example of the French Art Nouveau style that many regard as a precursor to modernism.

[46] Amanda Scardamaglia, 'A Legal History of Lithography' (2017) 26 GLR 1, 18.

[47] Fahr-Becker (n 42) 8.

[48] Roland Barthes, 'Wine and Milk' in *Mythologies* (The Noonday Press 1972) 58, 61.

[49] See discussion at n 28.

[50] See Kerly (n 15) 146.

[51] *Burgoyne* (n 1).

Source: Troedel Archive, State Library of Victoria, Image H2000.180/194.

Figure 1.2 Hardy's 'Oomoo' Advertisement, circa 1881

that the word 'Oomoo', applied to an Australian wine made by Thomas Hardy of Adelaide exhibited at the Colonial and Indian Exhibition in London in 1886,[52] which in the label designed by Troedel & Co (see Figure 1.2) was woven into a rural scene featuring Australian flora and fauna to create an impression of unalloyed bucolic enjoyment (notably absent from which were any examples of Indigenous Australians occupying the land), was a 'fancy' word that could be registered as a trade mark by wine importer Peter Burgoyne.

Of course, it was not the Dieri people themselves who objected to the trade mark. Rather the objection that 'Oomoo' meant 'choice' in the 'aboriginal language of Australia' came from a competing wine importer, owner of the 'Emu' trade mark.[53] But Chitty J said that the word,

---

[52] 'Oomoo Red' was Hardy's high-end wine, described as 'light vintage', and selling in bulk at 6*s* per gallon: see Henry Trueman Wood (ed), *Reports of the Colonial Sections of the Exhibition* (William Clowes & Sons Ltd 1887) 215.

[53] *Burgoyne* (n 1) 228. For this as the Dieri language, see George Taplin (ed), *The Folklore, Manners, Customs and Languages of the South Australian Aboriginals,*

'manufactured out of four "o's" and one "m"', was 'meaningless' to 'an ordinary Englishman, or a sufficient number of Englishman in this country', as evidenced by the fact that 'nobody that I know has ever asked for "a glass of Oomoo"'.[54] In this brief passing comment, 'the ordinary Englishman' takes on a further dimension of representing a particular type of English wine-drinking gentleman to be a proper exemplar of public opinion as to what languages should count and which could be dismissed as 'meaningless', with no need to consider apparently the way that the bucolic message of Australian enjoyment has been carefully constructed though the use of Indigenous language combined with Australian imagery. Indeed, the language of 'meaninglessness' adopted in this context, a term evoking an idea of *terra nullius*, serves as another reminder of the difficulty 'indigenous groups faced in negotiating for themselves a place in the British world'.[55]

The reasoning of Chitty J in *Burgoyne* can be contrasted with that of Kay J in *Jackson Co's Trade Mark*,[56] decided earlier in the same year. In this case the onomatopoeic American Indian word 'Kokoko', meaning 'owl' in the language of the Chippewa, was treated as equivalent to the English word 'owl' in signifying the figure of an owl, which, being common in the cotton trade, was accepted to be precluded from registration under the statute.[57] An unusual feature of the case was a clever demonstration of a new technology, a phonograph on which a wax cylinder made by Thomas Edison containing an ethnographic recording of the sound of a Chippewa Indian war-cry imitating the owl's screech was played in court,[58] to the tremendous excitement of those present – and showing, as one newspaper said, 'how valuable and important may be the part which Mr Edison's remarkable discovery may yet play in social and commercial life'.[59] Thus it was already evident to this audience that 'Kokoko' was not just a word in Chippewa language denoting an 'owl', but was also accorded a particular symbolic function in Chippewa culture that could

---

Gathered from Inquiries made by Authority of South Australian Government (E Spiller 1879) 83 ('oomoo' translated there as 'good', and 'oomoomurla' as 'better').

54 *Burgoyne* (n 1) 231.

55 See Magee and Thompson (n 19) 37.

56 *Jackson Co's Trade Mark* (1889) 6 RPC 80 (Ch).

57 It was accepted that 'owl' in English, French, Italian or Russian could not be registered: ibid 82.

58 See, for an account of the demonstration, Patrick Feaster, 'The Origins of the Ethnographic Sound Recording, 1878–1892' (2001) 20 (1/2) Resound: A Quarterly of the Archives of Traditional Music 2, 3.

59 'The Phonograph is Forcing its Way to the Front', Evening Telegraph and Star and Sheffield Daily Times (December 1888) 2. The incident was widely reported in the local and London newspapers.

be preserved and recorded by virtue of the phonograph. Further, responding to the company's argument that 'Kokoko' was a word unknown in the cotton trade in Britain, Kay J held that the possibility of cotton trade with the Chippewa developing in the future could not be ruled out and, for that potential audience at least, the prospect of 'Kokoko' being understood as a descriptive word could not be ruled out.[60] For his part, Chitty J in *Burgoyne* was quick to dismiss such an argument on the basis that 'as to there growing up a trade in "Oomoo" with the Aborigines of the Australian Continent, I think that is far-fetched, and a great deal too fanciful a notion for me, sitting here as a Judge, to proceed upon'.[61]

We have not been able to find any record of the 'Oomoo' label being registered to Burgoyne in the United Kingdom register (although that may have more to do with the hole in the archive than with any actual decision not to register the trade mark, despite his having gone to court to proclaim his entitlement to do so)[62] – and nor was it registered in the name of Hardy in South Australia around the same period, although it seems likely that the 'Oomoo' label in question in the *Burgoyne* case, designed and printed by the Chas Troedel lithographic company for Thomas Hardy's winery, was intended for use also in Australia.[63] But the reasoning of Chitty J that obscure languages from Aboriginal Australia, or 'say, from the centre of Africa',[64] were meaningless to the 'ordinary Englishman' and thus could be freely entered on the register, set the tone for later cases. Six years later, in *Densham and Sons' Trade Mark*,[65] the Court of Appeal upheld the decision of Romer J that 'Mazawattee', a word composed from 'Mazadhar', meaning 'luscious' in Hindi, and 'Wattee', meaning 'garden' in Sinhalese, was a validly registered trade mark for tea imported from Ceylon.[66] One

---

60 *Jackson* (n 56) 83–4.

61 *Burgoyne* (n 1) 232.

62 On the other hand, it is possible that Burgoyne decided not to register the trade mark, which already had achieved the desired goal of making use of Australiana to designate Australian wines imported into Britain, including in the showing at the Colonial and Indian Exhibition. For the use of 'Australian' imagery as a marketing tool see David Dunstan, 'A Sobering Experience: From "Australian Burgundy" to "Kanga Rouge": Australian Wine Battles on the London Market, 1900–1981' (2002) 17 J Aus Studies 179.

63 The 'Oomoo' label along with the 'Emu' label form part of the Troedel archive at the State Library of Victoria.

64 *Burgoyne* (n 1) 231.

65 *Densham and Sons' Trade Mark* (1895) 12 RPC 75 (Ch).

66 The authority of *Jackson* was raised in this case but Romer J said that he was rather inclined to think that 'the Chippeway Indians might have been left to take care of themselves'; ibid 82.

might think that the firm's advertisements of its tea as coming from 'the sweet-scented island of Ceylon, which produces the most luscious tea in the world'[67] might have made the symbolic meaning of luscious colonial cultivation obvious to at least some of the consuming public in Britain, even aside from those who through education or experience might have known the Hindi and/or Sinhalese languages. Nevertheless, Romer J, who as Romer QC had argued for registration of 'Oomoo' before Chitty J in *Burgoyne*, held that 'Mazawattee' was a 'meaningless' invented word; and his decision was upheld without any apparent difficulty on appeal.[68] By the time the House of Lords came to determine the distinctiveness of the Eastman company's trade mark 'Solio' for photographic paper,[69] Lord Herschell could confidently state that the English language was 'common property' and 'no one ought to be prevent the other members of the community from using [it] for purposes of description';[70] although he thought the same might be extended to foreign words – and more generally questioned whether 'meaninglessness' was necessarily the proper standard here.[71] He made an exception for 'words from languages so little known in this country that it would suggest no meaning except to a few scholars'.[72]

III. VICTORIAN CULTURAL POLICY IN MODERN AUSTRALIA

The Victorian distinctiveness standard, culminating in Lord Herschell's judgment in *Eastman Photographic*, found support in Australian cases of the 1940s, 1950s and 1960s, where the notion of distinctiveness protecting 'the common right of the public' to 'the common heritage' is treated as the

---

[67] Ibid 76 (quoting the advertisement).

[68] (1895) 12 RPC 271 (CA). Perhaps Kay J came around to the same view as Romer J; like Kay LJ he agreed with Lindley and Lopes LJJ in the Court of Appeal. The decision's positive reception in the press also suggests that it accorded with views of British traders: see, for instance, 'Letter of Cheesbrough & Royston, Fellows, Chartered Institute of Patent Attorneys' to the Liverpool Mercury (June 1895) (the decision 'shows that [earlier] trade mark cases have now, in the eyes of the law, reached the summit of absurdity').

[69] *Eastman Photographic* (n 22).

[70] Ibid 580.

[71] Ibid (at least for invented words). Thus the 'newly coined' word 'Solio', despite its derivation from the Latin word 'sol' for sun and hint at the process of development involving the use of sunlight, could be registered.

[72] Ibid 581. Cf Lord Macnaghten at 583 ('no objection that [an invented word] may be traced to a foreign source').

principal standard in Australia, supplemented by the economic standard propounded in *Du Cros*.[73] These cases, all decided in a time of the White Australia Policy, are still regarded as authoritative. They provide the backdrop of the 'inherent distinctiveness' standard in section 41 of the Trade Marks Act 1995 (Cth), a standard relied on to allow registration of a trade mark without the benefit of actual or potential use and thus substantially less onerous for a potential registrant than the other standards of 'distinctiveness' permitted under the Act (which require evidence of actual or intended use).[74] In an ironic return to Victorian decision-making, in 2006 'Oomoo' was registered as an inherently distinctive trade mark for a revived brand of Hardy's wine after a lengthy period of disuse.[75] Again registration was not opposed. And presumably it was allowed on the basis that the language, and thus 'Oomoo's' meaning, was little known in Australia – despite a resurgence of interest in the Dieri (or Dayari) language among the Dieri population in South Australia, sponsored by various government programmes,[76] and Australia's support for the United Nations Declaration on the Rights of Indigenous Peoples, including

---

[73] Most notably, *Howard Auto Cultivators Ltd v Webb Industries Pty Ltd* (1946) 72 CLR 175 (HCA) 181 (Dixon J) (citing Lord Macnaghten in *Eastman Photographic* (n 22)); *Mark Foy's Ltd v Coop & Co Ltd* (1956) 95 CLR 190 (HCA) 195 (Dixon J) (referring to 'the probability of ordinary persons understanding the words') 199, 201 (Williams J) (citing Lord Herschell in *Eastman Photographic* (n 22) and adding that 'to say that articles of clothing are "tub happy" [in this case] is in the ordinary use of English meaningless'). The *Du Cros* standard (n 21) (with its emphasis on limiting the prospects of undesirable monopolies) is more the focus in *FH Faulding & Co Ltd v Imperial Chemical Industries Ltd* (1956) 112 CLR 537 (HCA) 555 (per Kitto J, regarding 'barrier' as commonly used in trade). See also *Clark Equipment Co v Registrar of Trade Marks* (1964) 111 CLR 511 (HCA) 513–14 (per Kitto J on the status of 'Michigan' for trucks under s 25 Trade Marks Act 1955 (Cth), permitting registration on the basis of a minimum threshold of inherent distinctiveness combined with actual or potential use, referencing 'the common right of the public to make honest use of words forming part of the common heritage, for the sake of the signification which they ordinarily possess' but also citing *Du Cros* (n 21)).

[74] For s 41 of the Trade Marks Act 1995 (Cth) and the current tripartite 'distinctiveness' standard, see Michael Handler, 'All that Glitters Is Not Gold: A Critical Assessment of Trade Mark Distinctiveness under Australian Law, Part I' (2015) 101 IP Forum 14.

[75] A pictorial label containing the word 'Oomoo' was registered in 2003 and the word 'Oomoo' was registered in 2006 (with an endorsement): Trade Marks 953036, 1099230. See further n 3.

[76] See Peter K Austin, 'And Still They Speak Diyari: The Life History of an Endangered Language' (2014) Ethnorêma 1, for a historical survey and account of the language's revitalisation.

its provision for protection of indigenous 'cultural heritage, traditional knowledge and traditional cultural expressions'.[77]

Likewise, in 2014 in *Cantarella*,[78] the High Court held that 'Oro', meaning 'gold' in Italian, and a common sight on coffee packets circulated by Italian coffee traders in Australia,[79] was validly registered as an inherently distinctive trade mark for Cantarella Bros' Vittoria coffee in 2000,[80] on the basis of the word's 'ordinary [lack of] signification' to the public in Australia – notwithstanding a post-war Italian diaspora which has been active in the coffee industry with the result that coffee is now widely viewed as 'a regional cultural icon',[81] the popularity of Italian language programmes, including in schools and universities, and a long-standing official government policy of non-discrimination on grounds of race extending to 'economic, social and cultural rights'.[82] In assessing knowledge of Italian in Australia, the Court relied on a finding of Emmett J at first instance that only 'a very small minority' understood the meaning of 'Oro' on the evidence available – most notably Census data from 2006 suggesting that those speaking Italian at home in Australia were less than 2 per cent of the Australian population.[83] This demographic fragment was scarcely enough if the purpose was to assess whether 'particular words that are intended to constitute the trade mark are sufficiently well understood in Australia', as Emmett J posited.[84] Indeed, our research conducted after the case suggests the number of those who understand may be nearer 10 per cent of the broader population, around 20 per cent for some quite sizable minority groups *viz* those familiar with Italian language and coffee

---

77 UN General Assembly, 'United Nations Declaration on the Rights of Indigenous Peoples' (adopted 13 September 2007) A/RES/61/295, art 31. See Kristin Carpenter and Angela Riley, 'Indigenous Peoples and the Jurisgenerative Moment in Human Rights' (2014) 102 Cal L Rev 173 (arguing that the Declaration is part of a new invigoration of indigenous rights).

78 *Cantarella* (n 4).

79 Ibid [75] (The High Court disputed whether the evidence of the other trade uses of 'Oro' on coffee packets was sufficient to prove that 'the word "Oro", standing alone, is understood in Australia by persons concerned with coffee products to be to be directly descriptive of the character or quality of the goods').

80 Trade mark 829098; see further n 5.

81 See Brown-May (n 6).

82 International Convention on the Elimination of All Forms of Racial Discrimination (opened for signature 21 December 1965, entered into force 4 January 1969) 660 UNTS 195, art 5(e); Racial Discrimination Act 1975 (Cth) (implementing the Convention).

83 *Cantarella* (n 4) [61] (French CJ et al, citing Emmett J in *Cantarella Bros Pty Ltd v Modena Trading Pty Ltd* (2013) 99 IPR 492 [117]).

84 *Cantarella* (n 4) [113] (Emmett J).

Table 1.1 Significations of 'Oro' – survey results

'Oro' signifies 'gold'		'Oro' signifies 'Italian', 'authentic', 'fancy', 'pure' etc
All respondents	11%	20%
Italian background	56%	33%
Understand Italian	18%	28%
Coffee aficionados	19%	33%

'aficionados' (that is, those serious about coffee as measured by their preference for coffee made from beans/grounds), and more than 50 per cent of the relatively small number of those of Italian background.[85] But, as there was no evidence specifically directed to the latter point put forward in the case itself, the Census data on Italian-speaking became the barometer of public knowledge of Oro's 'meaning' in Australia. The results of the survey are presented in Table 1.1.

At the same time, the Court appeared anxious to distance itself from any suggestion that it was using a standard of an ordinary English language speaker, preferring the neutral-sounding 'ordinary signification' to those 'concerned with' coffee in Australia, 'a familiar beverage consumed by many'.[86] Yet it preferred 'the many' in Australia over other imagined communities – unlike Gageler J, in dissent, who noted that in Australia coffee is 'commonly associated with Italy, often enough imported from Italy and often enough sold to Italian speakers', and supported the 'multicultural' approach of the full Federal Court in taking into account the language of coffee traders as explaining their legitimate choices to use 'Oro' on their packages.[87] At the same time, the Court also made clear that 'allusive or metaphysical meaning' can be disregarded in assessing

---

85 In this research, conducted in September 2015 with the Pureprofile online survey company, we surveyed 250 adult people across Australia, asking questions *inter alia* about their consumption of coffee (around 80% of respondents); whether they bought coffee as beans or grounds (as a measure of coffee aficionado status) or in convenience forms, or did not buy coffee; what they thought the word 'Oro' meant on the package; why they thought 'Oro' was on the package (in other words, the symbolic value they attributed to the word 'Oro'); whether they had an Italian background and whether they understood the Italian language from 'a little' to 'perfectly'.

86 *Cantarella* (n 4) [73], [117] (French CJ et al).

87 Ibid [101]–[113] (Gageler J, discussing the Full Federal Court decision in *Modena Trading Pty Ltd v Cantarella Bros Pty Ltd* (2013) 102 IPR 382).

'ordinary signification'.[88] And so the allusive symbolic meaning that 'Oro' may have for some audiences, which may help to explain its common use to denote pure or authentic Italian quality by Italian coffee traders in Australia,[89] was left out of account on this highly literal analysis.[90] As such, the Court's coded language of 'ordinary signification' fits the observation of Graeme Dinwoodie and Dev Gangjee that 'most efforts by courts [these days] to identify or construct consumers and the marketplace they inhabit are blended exercises that are part-empirical and part-normative'.[91]

IV. TOWARDS A MODERN AUSTRALIAN CULTURAL POLICY

One of the difficulties with the part-normative standard adopted in the *Cantarella* case is that its starting point is a Victorian distinctiveness standard adopted when it was socially acceptable for a British judge to treat 'the ordinary Englishman' as the arbiter of meaning, endorsed without question in Australia during the era of the White Australia policy, and made the measure of the inherent distinctiveness of the 'Oro' coffee label in modern multicultural Australia. As Michael Handler points out, 'expressed at such a high level of generality, and by seeming to treat "anyone concerned with the goods" as an undifferentiated mass, the majority's interpretation of "signification" is not especially helpful in addressing a range of other, more complex situations'.[92] In this chapter we have argued that it was not especially helpful either in addressing the signification to be attributed to a common Italian word, commonly used and applied with respect to coffee products in Australia, to a range of publics. Nor was it especially helpful in addressing the registration of Hardy's 'Oomoo' wine label a few years earlier, relying on the by-then set-

---

88 *Cantarella* (n 4) [73] (French CJ et al).

89 Despite a concerted television advertising campaign launched by Cantarella in 2010, featuring Italian-American actor Al Pacino in a series of vignettes designed to associate himself specifically with a traditional idea of good Italian-style coffee enjoyed by Italian diasporas (an idea reinforced by the old-fashioned sepia-tinged coffee label). The campaign is noted by Emmett J in *Cantarella Bros v Modena Trading* (n 4) [57].

90 For instance, in our survey (n 85), some 20% of respondents, and nearer 30% of the identified minority groups of involved coffee consumers, indicated in response to our question about why 'Oro' was on the Vittoria package that it was used to signify 'Italian', 'authentic', 'fancy', 'pure' etc.

91 Dinwoodie and Gangjee (n 11) 339.

92 Handler (n 74) 22.

tled standard of inherent distinctiveness that privileges the understandings of ordinary English-speaking Australians over minority and Indigenous groups. This standard, construed this way, may represent a more 'correct' reading of a nineteenth-century standard that now appears to be entrenched in Australian law than the 'multicultural' standard espoused by the full Federal Court and by Gageler J in his dissenting judgment. But in terms of modern cultural policy as well as economic policy of limiting monopoly, per Lord Parker in *Du Cros*,[93] theirs seems far superior. And, even then, whether their approach focusing on perceptions of Italian coffee traders without also considering the understandings of consuming and other existing and emerging publics in a rapidly changing modern Australia goes sufficiently far – or indeed whether a focus on an existing coterie of Italian coffee traders who now use 'Oro' leaves out potential other traders of the future who equally may have legitimate interests in using the word to describe their competing products.[94]

So is the answer law reform and, if so, in what direction? Many of those we have consulted in this study have suggested that the American doctrine of foreign equivalents, which is now followed to an extent in current British practice,[95] could provide a solution. This doctrine emerged towards the beginning of the twentieth century in response to the use of Italian, French, Spanish and other languages in vibrant and expanding American trading communities.[96] It allows translation of foreign words into English

---

93 Recall Lord Parker's language of the legitimate desire of other traders to use the same or a similar mark as the standard of distinctiveness, framed in terms of restricting barriers to entry; *Du Cros* (n 21).

94 Bearing in mind that if the focus of the economic standard is whether other traders are 'likely, in the ordinary course of their business and without any improper motive, to desire to use the same mark, or some mark nearly resembling it, upon or in connection with their own goods' (*Du Cros* (n 21) 635 (Lord Parker)), this kind of 'barriers to entry' standard should include not just other traders who now exist, but potential traders in the future.

95 See Ellen Gredley, 'Foreign-language Words as Trade Marks' in Norma Dawson and Alison Firth (eds), *Trade Marks Retrospective* (Sweet & Maxwell 2000) 85 (cited in *Cantarella* (n 5) [97] (Gageler J), although without considering the argument's validity); and further Handler (n 74) 24.

96 For instance, *Roncoroni v Gross* (1904) 92 AD 221 ('Conserva Di Tomate'); *Charles R De Bevoise Co v H & W Co* (1905) 69 NJ Eq 114 ('Brassiere'); *Italian Swiss Colony v Italian Vineyard Co* (1910) 158 Cal 252 ('Tipo Chianti'); *Thermogene Co v Thermozine Co* (1916) 234 F 69 (Fed Circ) ('Thermogene'); *McKesson & Robbin Inc v Charles H Phillips Chemical Co* (1931) 53 F2d 342 (Fed Circ) ('Leche-de-Magnesia'); and authorities noted in *Re Northern Paper Mills* (1933) 64 F 2d 998 (Fed Circ) (a case that itself concerned the Spanish word 'Gazza', meaning gauze, for toilet paper).

for purposes *inter alia* of assessing inherent distinctiveness.[97] It may be feasible to introduce this doctrine into Australian law, whether by legislative amendment or by a more subtle change in judicial approach. Nevertheless, a great deal depends on how it is treated in practice by judges and other decision makers. For instance, some US judges have treated the doctrine as asking simply whether the 'ordinary American purchaser' would 'stop and translate',[98] an approach which seems little different from the current Australian standard of 'ordinary signification'.[99] And even on a more liberal interpretation, 'obscure' languages are generally not accorded protection. In one early case *Selchow v Chaffee*,[100] it was held with respect to 'Parcheesi', a popular game based on an ancient Indian game with a 'very similar' name, that '[b]ecause the foreign name is known here to but a few to-day does not signify it will not be known to hundreds tomorrow and thousands next week and tens of thousands next month', using language reminiscent of the British *Jackson* case.[101] But since then the focus has been more on giving equivalent protection to already common (primarily European) languages. Native American Algonquin have not been accorded the protection.[102] Nor has Arabic, knowledge of which

---

97 The doctrine is also used to determine genericism and similarity of connotation in infringement cases: see *Palm Bay Imports Inc v Veuve Clicquot Ponsardin Maison Fondee* (2005) 396 F 3d 1369 (Fed Circ) 1377.

98 See *Palm Bay Imports*, ibid 1377 (Rader Circ J) ('it is improbable that the average American purchaser would stop and translate "VEUVE" into "Widow"', and thus the doctrine does not apply in this case where 'Veuve Royale' and 'the Widow' were being compared for similarity of connotation in an infringement case).

99 In a later attempt to soften its approach, the US Court of Appeals said the requirement of 'the ordinary American' translating meant 'all American purchasers, including those proficient in a non-English language who would ordinarily be expected to translate words into English': *Re Spirits International NV* (2009) 563 F 3d 1347 (Fed Circ) 1351–2, and note generally Thomas McCarthy, *McCarthy on Trademarks and Unfair Competition* (5th edn, Thomson Reuters 2017) s 11(34).

100 *Selchow v Chaffee & Selchow Mfg Co* (1904) 132 F 996 (Fed Circ).

101 Ibid 999 (Ray DJ). The trade mark was eventually registered in 1918 after ten years' use. Cf *Re Bradford Dyeing Association* (1917) 46 App DC 512, 513 (Van Orsdel J) regarding the relatively obscure French word 'E'clatant' adopted for the applicant's cotton piece goods ('Not only would the meaning soon become known to the public, but the user of the mark would appreciate the advantage of disseminating such information by advertisement or otherwise. Indeed, there would be nothing to prevent the printing of a translation of the word or phrase in direct connection with the use of the mark'); *Otokoyama Co Ltd v Wine of Japan Import Inc* (2001) 175 F 3d 266 (Fed Circ) 270 (Leval Cir J) ('there are (or someday will be) customers in the United States who speak that foreign language').

102 See *Mohegan Tribe of Indians of Conn v Mohegan Tribe & Nation Inc* (1999)

was deemed 'negligible . . . according to Census data',[103] although Swahili on a range of evidence was treated as within the doctrine.[104] Similarly mixed results can be found in the United Kingdom – with, for instance, the Spanish expression 'El Canal de Las Estrellas' treated as equivalent to the English phrase 'The Channel of the Stars' in one decision,[105] but the Japanese word 'Kiku' (denoting 'Chrysanthemum') and a symbol of a globe, said to be 'a common sight' in Saudi Arabia, in other decisions deemed too obscure to be counted on the evidence available when it comes to assessing inherent distinctiveness.[106]

Thus, although the doctrine of foreign equivalents would be a step beyond the current Australian approach (and the approach in some European jurisdictions),[107] it might still end up being a rather modest step, depending on how it is construed. Certainly, as far as 'Oro' in Australia is concerned, a court following the current American or British approach and basing itself on Census data suggesting that less than 2 per cent of the population speaks Italian, might still conclude that Italian is an obscure

---

255 Conn 358, 371–2 (doctrine of foreign equivalents not applicable in assessing genericism of the disputed term 'Mohegan' on the basis that 'no sizable segment of the relevant public is likely to speak the Algonquin languages', and the word was generic as it had 'become synonymous in the English language with the unique Indian people commonly known by that name'). See also *Re Spirits of New Merced LLC* (2007) 85 USPQ2d 1614 (TTAB 2007) (as to 'Yosemite' meaning 'the killers' in the Miwok language and no evidence that the general American public would be familiar with that meaning).

103 *Taza Systems LLC v Taza 21 Co LLC* (US Dist WD Pa, LEXIS 130974, No 2:11-cv-073, 13 September 2013).

104 *S Squared Ventures LLC* (TTAB 86813357, 16 August 2017) (Swahili a 'common modern language' evidenced by university language programmes, clubs, religious and cultural organisations, and broadcasting media).

105 *El Canal de las Estrellas Trade Mark* (2000) RPC 291, 299 (noting also that 'stars' would be understood in the laudatory sense of 'star performers in entertainment' rather than 'celestial stars'). See also Handler (n 74).

106 *Kiku Trade Mark* (1978) FSR 246; Opposition to a trade mark application of Ajlan Bin Arbullaziz Al-Ajlan & Bros Co, Geoffrey Hobbs QC, 11 February 2000 (device of globe).

107 *Matratzen Concord AG v Hukla Germany SA* (2006) ECR 2303 [24] – not following the Opinion of Advocate-General Jacobs, favouring a more liberal approach, as in Britain, Germany, the Netherlands and Belgium (at [52]). See Dinwoodie and Gangjee (n 11), suggesting that in the European Court of Justice empirical considerations of Spanish consumers trumped normative European free trade considerations (although this presupposes that Spanish consumers would not know the meaning of a German word for mattresses that was similar in Dutch, French, Italian and English, and we might also posit an alternative normative nationalist cultural policy here).

rather than a common European language. As to the fate of 'Oomoo', even on the best evidence about language dissemination of Dieri this is not a 'common' language. Indeed, for Indigenous languages something closer to a full equal treatment principle may offer a better guarantee that the language will be protected from appropriation as trade marks.[108] This is the position adopted in New Zealand with respect to Māori, based on the official status of the language under Māori Language Acts, although even then it was decisions of the Assistant Commissioner of Trade Marks that ensured that trade mark law would treat Māori the same way as English in assessing inherent distinctiveness – with the result that 'Kikorangi' and 'Kura', meaning 'blue' and 'red' in Māori, were held not inherently distinctive of blue cheese and yoghurt products (although the first was found distinctive on evidence of 11 years uninterrupted use by the well-known Kapiti Cheeses company).[109] In short, the effectiveness of modelling reform on American and New Zealand language equivalence approaches will depend on how high the threshold of language knowledge is treated by Australian decision makers, how ready they are to accept there may be multiple meanings, and how receptive they are to evidence

---

[108] See Terri Janke and Maiko Sentina, 'Indigenous Knowledge: Issues for Protection and Management' (2018) IP Australia 61 raising the introduction of language protection legislation as one option for reform (the authors note the introduction of the New South Wales Aboriginal Language Act 2017, but state that ideally such legislation could go further in 'empower[ing] Indigenous people to make decisions about [languages'] maintenance and use'). This discussion paper also suggests the establishment of protocols in the Trade Marks Examiners' Manual for examiners to exercise powers of rejection under s 41 of the Trade Marks Act 1995 (Cth) where 'indigenous words and images . . . [are] descriptive' (at 59); and that '[i]t would be an appropriate recognition of cultural protocol for non-Indigenous persons to obtain . . . with the traditional custodians of the language and seek permission to use an Indigenous word or name commercially' and suggesting that the absence of consent could be made an absolute ground of rejection (at 56, 59–60) (with an Indigenous Advisory Committee in IP Australia having an educative role here).

[109] See *Kapiti Cheeses Ltd* [2003] NZIPOTM 21, J Walden Assistant Commissioner of Trade Marks (treating Māori as equal to English in assessing inherent distinctiveness, based on its official status under the Māori Language Act 1987, s 3); *White Cloud Dairy Innovation Ltd* [2017] NZIPOTM 3, Victoria Casey QC Assistant Commissioner of Trade Marks (reaching the same conclusion as to the equal status of Māori under Te Ture mō Te Reo Māori 2016/Māori Language Act 2016, s 5). In the latter decision, the Assistant Commissioner noted also that 'the Māori advisory committee advised . . . that the mark is unlikely to offend' under s 178 of the Trade Marks Act (at [3]), making clear that inherent distinctiveness was a separate issue from cultural offensiveness.

of language knowledge in cases and disputes before them.[110] All we are saying here is that, as the history of the inherent distinctiveness standard has demonstrated, the scope and operation of any future legal standard will be a product not just of design and intention, but of the way that its language is ultimately construed – and construction will almost inevitably be at least partly a function of the policy choices of decision makers.

V. CONCLUSION

In this chapter we have argued that there are a number of reasons, economic and cultural, to question whether a standard about the ordinary signification of language in Australia, a standard whose roots can be traced back to the language of the 'ordinary Englishman' of nineteenth-century colonial Britain, is the best way to determine what should be entered on the trade mark register in modern Australia. We have suggested that Australian law makers, legislators and judges, and other decision makers alike, should now consider how the standard could be updated for a twenty-first-century modern Australia. As to efficiency, an approach that espouses the possibility that a few traders today may become more tomorrow and all should be taken into account in considering the prospect that a variety of traders will have legitimate interests in using certain language expressions for their competing products is surely preferable to one that privileges existing traders. As to culture, a standard that protects the common language of English-speaking people while allowing appropriation of the languages of Indigenous and minority groups fails to give account to the multiple imagined communities in which many people now live in Australia, and the aspirational norms of inclusion that this country espouses. On several counts, then, now is the time to move away from the nineteenth-century idea that a word's 'ordinary signification' should dictate the quality of a sign's trade mark-ness for multiple publics across multiple boundaries.

---

[110] And see for instance, our survey results (n 85). The point is also made more generally by Kimberlee Weatherall, 'The Consumer as the Empirical Measure of Trade Marks' (2017) 80 Mod Law Rev 57.

2. A successful recalibration of patent law vis-à-vis *mātauranga Māori*? A case study of Mānuka (*Leptospermum scoparium*)*

Jessica C. Lai**

I. INTRODUCTION

Patents are theorised to serve a multitude of functions, ranging from incentivising invention and the dissemination of knowledge, to signalling certain capabilities and values, to structuring transactions and the commercialisation process.[1] For all intents and purposes, these functions are misaligned with Indigenous peoples' interests and worldviews. Indeed, beyond failing to serve Indigenous peoples, there is a growing body of literature proclaiming and decrying the appropriation and propertisation of Indigenous knowledge and resources, often referred to under the terms 'traditional cultural expressions' (TCEs), 'traditional knowledge' (TK) and 'related genetic resources' (GRs). This is reflected in the Wai 262 claim in New Zealand, which alleged that the Crown (New Zealand government) had failed in its duty to protect Māori *taonga* (treasures) per the Treaty of Waitangi (signed between the British Crown and Māori in 1840)[2] by allowing (among other things) bioprospecting and third-party

* All online sources were last accessed on 27 December 2018.

** The author would like to thank Susy Frankel and Hai-Yuean Tualima for their invaluable comments on earlier drafts of this chapter. Any errors remain the author's own.

[1] See Jessica C Lai, 'The Changing Function of Patents: A Reversion to Privileges?' (2017) 37(4) LS 807.

[2] The Treaty of Waitangi 1840 is the founding document of modern New Zealand and is a core part of its constitutional law; *New Zealand Māori Council v Attorney General* (1994) 1 NZLR (PC) 513, 516 (Lord Woolf). See also Claudia Orange, *The Treaty of Waitangi* (2nd edn, Bridget Williams Books 2011).

intellectual property relating to sacred species and *mātauranga Māori* (Māori knowledge in a broad sense).[3]

Yet, there is little empirical research measuring the scale of any such appropriation or propertisation.[4] The research and development (R&D) of Indigenous knowledge and related GRs is difficult (if not impossible) to measure, in part because New Zealand does not have a comprehensive regime regulating bioprospecting.[5] The successful use of Indigenous knowledge and related GRs often leads to a patent application for any resultant invention. This chapter presents the results of an empirical search for patents pertaining to Mānuka (*Leptospermum scoparium*) filed through the Intellectual Property Office of New Zealand (IPONZ). One should keep in mind that patent applications are by no means an ideal proxy for R&D of Indigenous knowledge and related GRs. Not all R&D endeavours have positive results or outcomes that are suitable for the patent regime. Patents are, thus, only a measure of R&D that fit within the patent and 'invention' paradigm. Furthermore, as patents are relatively expensive to obtain and maintain, their application and maintenance reflect value, or at least perceived potential value.

The New Zealand Patents Act 2013 introduced a Māori Advisory Committee[6] to assist the Commissioner to determine whether the 'commercial exploitation' of an invention would be contrary to 'public order' or 'morality'.[7] Having the potential to introduce *te ao Māori* (the Māori

---

[3] Report of the Waitangi Tribunal on Claims Concerning New Zealand Law and Policy Affecting Māori Culture and Identity (2011) Wai 262 (Wai 262).

[4] For a general search for biological species in patents around the world, see Paul Oldham, Stephen Hall and Oscar Forero, 'Biological Diversity in the Patent System' (2013) 8(11) PloS ONE e78737. See also Daniel F Robinson and Margaret Raven, 'Identifying and Preventing Biopiracy in Australia: Patent Landscapes and Legal Geographies for Plants with Indigenous Australian Uses' (2017) 48(3) Australian Geographer 311, who searched global patent databases for species with known Australian Indigenous knowledge; and Jessica C Lai and Daniel Robinson, with Tim Stirrup and Hai-Yuean Tualima, 'Māori Knowledge under the Microscope: Appropriation and Patenting of Mātauranga Māori and Related Resources' (forthcoming), who undertook a similar study of species with known Māori uses.

[5] This is despite the fact that New Zealand is a Party to the Convention on Biological Diversity (opened for signature 5 June 1992, entered into force 29 December 1993) 1760 UNTS 79; 31 ILM 818 (CBD). It is not a Party to the Nagoya Protocol on Access to Genetic Resources and the Fair and Equitable Sharing of Benefits Arising from their Utilisation to the Convention on Biological Diversity (opened for signature 2 February 2011, entered into force 12 October 2014).

[6] Patents Act 2013, ss 225–228.

[7] Patents Act 2013, ss 15–16. *Ordre public* and morality are specifically permissible exceptions from patentability under the Agreement on Trade-Related Aspects

world) into a Western legal construct and thereby impact the grant of exclusive rights, the Patents Act 2013 added an extra dimension to existing patent functions. It has yet to be seen if these provisions will truly meet Māori concerns.

This chapter reflects on the applications pertaining to Mānuka filed since the Patents Act 2013 came into force. It analyses whether the creation of the Māori Advisory Committee has served its purpose with respect to these applications.

Leptospermum scoparium is near endemic to New Zealand and Māori have long used the plant for various purposes.[8] These include multiple medicinal purposes, for example the treatment of 'urinary complaints, fevers, colds, burns, dysentery, skin and muscle inflammations, eye and mouth problems, and for pain relief and as a sedative'.[9] Branches from the tree were used as splints,[10] and the wood for canoe decking, poles and weapons.[11] Teas were made from the leaves of the plant to ease fevers,[12] or from the bark to treat dysentery and diarrhoea.[13] The leaves and bark were also used to treat oral infections, open wounds and skin infections.[14] Some uses were more cosmetic, such as the ashes being 'rubbed on the scalp to cure dandruff'.[15]

---

of Intellectual Property Rights (opened for signature 15 April 1994, entered into force 1 January 1996) 1869 UNTS 299 (TRIPS). The Patents Act 2013 uses the term 'public order' rather than '*ordre public*'. There is some debate as to whether 'public order' and '*ordre public*' have the same meaning. However, the Patents Act 2013 specifically states that 'public order' is to have the same meaning as the TRIPS '*ordre public*'. See also IPONZ Patent Examination Manual, 'Section 15: Inventions Contrary to Public Order or Morality not Patentable Inventions' <https://www.iponz.govt.nz/about-ip/patents/examination-manual/current/inventions-contrary-to-public-order-or-morality-not-patentable-inventions/>.

8 To be clear, this author is not Indigenous. The known Māori uses of Mānuka outlined here were located from literature. It might not be exhaustive. There may be uses that have never been published.

9 Te Papa Tongarewa, 'Manuka & Kanuka' <https://collections.tepapa.govt.nz/topic/2988>, citing Stanley G Brooker, Richard C Cambie and Robert C Cooper, *New Zealand Medicinal Plants* (Reed 2002).

10 Rhys Jones, 'Rongoā – Medicinal Use of Plants' *Te Ara The Encyclopedia of New Zealand* <https://teara.govt.nz/en/rongoa-medicinal-use-of-plants>.

11 Wai 262 (n 3) 128.

12 Jones (n 10).

13 Ibid; see also Stanley G Brooker, 'Economic Native Plants of New Zealand' (1989) 43(1) Econ Bot 79, 97.

14 Wai 262 (n 3) 128.

15 Jones (n 10).

Many of these uses took advantage of the essential oil from *Leptospermum scoparium*,[16] which Western science has identified as having antibiotic (including 'nonperoxide' antibacterial activity),[17] anti-fungal, anti-inflammatory,[18] anthelmintic and insecticidal properties.[19] It has also been proven to have anti-viral/cytotoxic bioactivity,[20] and to be anti-oxidant and anti-tumour,[21] and to have enzyme-inhibiting properties.[22] Honey produced from *Leptospermum scoparium* has similar properties, as quantified by the Unique Manuka Factor (UMF).[23] Much of this Western science was undertaken partly based on 'folklore'.[24]

The essential oil from *Leptospermum scoparium* is considered to be highly valuable due to these properties and the fact that it is 'pleasant smelling and could well be used as an inexpensive perfume for soaps, etc'.[25] *Leptospermum scoparium*, particularly its essential oil and Mānuka honey, now has multiple modern applications. Unsurprisingly, these are

---

[16] As *Leptospermum scoparium* is also called New Zealand tea tree, its essential oil is sometimes incorrectly referred to as 'tea tree oil'. Tea tree oil is the essential oil from *Melaleuca alternifolia*. It is possible that there are patents for inventions that use 'tea tree oil', which are actually for the essential oil of *Leptospermum scoparium*.

[17] Victoria L Calder, ALJ Cole and JRL Walker, 'Antibiotic Compounds from New Zealand Plants. III: A Survey of Some New Zealand Plants for Antibiotic Substances' (1986) 16(2) J Roy Soc NZ 169, 170; Elvira Mavric, Silvia Wittmann, Gerold Barth and Thomas Henle, 'Identification and Quantification of Methylglyoxal as the Dominant Antibacterial Constituent of Manuka (Leptospermum scoparium) Honeys from New Zealand' (2008) 52(4) Mol Nutr Food Res 483.

[18] Natasha Old, 'The Medicine of the Manuka' (2013) 31(3) J of Holist Nurs 200.

[19] Brooker (n 13) 95.

[20] Stephen J Bloor, 'A Survey of Extracts of New Zealand Indigenous Plants for Selected Biological Activities' (1995) 33(4) NZ J Bot 523, 533.

[21] Seema Patel and Simon Cichello, 'Manuka Honey: An Emerging Natural Food with Medicinal Use' (2013) 3 Nat Prod Bioprospect 121.

[22] Stephen J Kellam, Margaret H Tisch and John RL Walker, 'Screening of New Zealand Native Plants for Enzyme Inhibitory Activities' (1992) 30(2) NZ J Bot 199, 201.

[23] Wai 262 (n 3) 129.

[24] For an example, see Bloor (n 20) 523. See also Kellam et al (n 22) 199 ('Many of these plants have been used by the Maori people in their folk medicine') and 202 ('It remains to be seen whether or not the observed in vitro enzyme inhibitory effects might correlate with Maori folk medicine usage and, in this respect, isolation of the active compound(s) is essential').

[25] Brooker (n 13) 98.

medicinal (especially in wound management),[26] cosmetic,[27] and in food and beverages. There are commensurately patents in these fields that utilise *Leptospermum scoparium* (whether an aspect of the plant, an isolate, or Mānuka honey).

The following section explains and analyses the patent regime in New Zealand, particularly as it relates to *mātauranga Māori* and GRs. This is vital for understanding why certain patent applications or grants are more dubious than others under existing law. In doing so, it acknowledges that some are questionable with respect to *te ao Māori* and *tikanga Māori* (Māori customary law),[28] regardless of the law. Section II also outlines the relevant recommendations from the Wai 262 Report. Section III describes the methodology used in the empirical search and Section IV discusses the results of that search. The chapter ends with some concluding thoughts, discussing that the Mānuka example arguably reflects that IPONZ is not using the provisions introduced in the Patents Act 2013 for the purpose for which they were introduced.

II. A BACKGROUND IN NEW ZEALAND LAW AND POLICY

A. Patent Law in New Zealand

In New Zealand, patents are statutorily defined as a form of personal property,[29] over 'inventions'.[30] Inventions were classically mechanical in nature but today include chemical compounds and biological isolates.[31]

---

26 For example Algivon (calcium alginate + Mānuka) – taking advantage of antiseptic properties; Anna Coulbourn, 'Algivon: Manuka Honey v Complex Wounds' (2009) 23(6) J Comm Nurs 25; Cheryl Dunford, Rose Cooper, Peter Molan and Richard White, 'The Use of Honey in Wound Management' (2000) 15(11) Nurs Stand 63; and Sylvie Hampton, 'Honey as the New "Silver" Dressing in Wound Care' (2007) 21(11) J Comm Nurs 45.

27 For example, 'Antipodes' Aura Manuka Honey Treatment Mask; 'Antipodes is a range of premium natural and certified organic skin care from New Zealand' (May 2008) Cosmetics International Cosmetic Products Report 5. Or as a surfactant in cosmetics; Valery M Dembitsky 'Natural Surfactants in Cosmetics: From Ancient Times to Present Day' (2008) 19(8) inform 577.

28 Patents Act 2013, s 225(3).

29 Ibid s 17(1).

30 Ibid s 14(b)–(c).

31 See Jessica C Lai, 'The Nebulous "Invention": From "Idea and Embodiment" to "Idea/Embodiment and Observable Physical Effects?"' in Jessica C Lai and

As in most jurisdictions, an invention must be novel, be non-obvious (or embody an inventive step) and have utility.[32] It should not be possible to patent an invention that is not new or is obvious in light of *mātauranga Māori*.

In many ways, patents are considered to be the most controversial form of intellectual property when it comes to Indigenous knowledge. Māori and other Indigenous peoples have multiple concerns, including the cultural and spiritual implications of patenting and owning life forms and things isolated from nature.[33] Aroha Mead has stated that 'nature and living things, tangible and intangible, all are sacred. They are not objects, they are not property, they cannot be owned.'[34] Patents relating to species that are *taonga* and/or with a *kaitiaki* (guardian) relationship are particularly controversial.

During the development of the Patents Act 2013, the Patents Bills 2008 and 2010 were criticised for allowing the patenting of genetic materials, genetically modified organisms and micro-organisms.[35] A move to make all organisms (including micro-organisms) non-patentable was rejected.[36] Concerns relating to biotechnology and life-form inventions are broad and not all of them should or could be dealt with under patent law.[37] However, the Patents Act 2013 does include relevant exceptions from patentability, including explicitly specified biotechnologies and inventions

---

Antoinette Maget Dominicé (eds), *Intellectual Property and Access to Im/material Goods* (Edward Elgar Publishing 2016) 121.

32 Patents Act 2013, s 14(a).

33 Aroha Mead, 'Geneaology, Sacredness, and the Commodities Market' (1996) 20(2) Cultural Survival: Genes, People and Property <https://www.culturalsurvival.org/publications/cultural-survival-quarterly/genealogy-sacredness-and-commodities-market>.

34 Ibid.

35 The decision to allow patentability for such was made after a long review of patentable subject matter; Judith Tizard (former Associate Minister of Commerce), 'Review of the Patents Act 1953 Stage 3: Part 2' (2003) Office of the Associate Minister of Commerce.

36 By the Committee of the Whole House of New Zealand. See Stefan Browning (Green Party), House of Representatives, Supplementary Order Paper No 124 (September 2012); and 'Patents Bill. Third Reading' (August 2013) 693 Hansard (Parliamentary Debates) 12948.

37 Susy Frankel has noted that though patent law is relevant to guiding the ethics of scientific research, patent law is not the correct means by which one can determine the scope of ethical research. Susy Frankel, 'Lord Cooke and Patents: The Scope of "Invention"' (2009) 39 VUWLR 73, 86–87. See also Jacques de Werra, 'Fighting against Biopiracy: Does the Obligation to Disclose in Patent Applications Truly Help?' (2009) 42 VJTL 143, 178–179, who notes that the answer does not only lie in patent law, and other areas of the law must also be explored.

the 'commercial exploitation' of which would be contrary to 'public order' or 'morality'.[38]

The Commissioner 'may' seek advice from the Māori Advisory Committee or any person the Commissioner considers appropriate for assessing whether the commercial exploitation of an invention would be contrary to 'public order' or 'morality'.[39] The Committee advises the Commissioner on whether a claimed invention is derived from Māori TK or 'indigenous plants or animals' (hereinafter referred to as 'derivation') and, if so, whether 'the commercial exploitation of that invention is likely to be contrary to Māori values'.[40] Members of the Committee must, 'in the opinion of the Commissioner', have knowledge of *te ao Māori* and *tikanga Māori*.[41]

If patents incentivise inventive conduct then the Māori Advisory Committee could modulate the patent incentive. For example, disincentivising either R&D of Māori TK and related GRs generally, or such R&D without prior informed consent (PIC), continued consultation, and access and benefit sharing (ABS). The corollary to this is that it could incentivise research by TK holders, those who wish to collaborate with TK holders in accordance with Māori values, or those who want the clarity that PIC and potentially ABS agreements offer. Furthermore, implemented correctly, the provisions could change the signals that patents indicate to investors, business partners and end-consumers. To illustrate, it could result in New Zealand patents and patented inventions embodying certain ethical practices with regard to Māori TK and related GRs. There is also the possibility that this assists in the commercialisation process as investors and business partners might appreciate that the TK holders are less likely to challenge the patents. The marketing potential of such patents could be exploited, selling the story behind the inventions. The development of patent functions depends on how the law on paper is translated into practice.

Before forwarding an application to the Committee, the patent examiner must realise that an invention might be derived from Māori TK, or Indigenous plants or animals, and may be contrary to Māori values. This could be difficult, given that this knowledge is often not well published and may be secret.[42] Even if there is a realisation, the Commissioner is not

---

38 Patents Act 2013, ss 15–16. *Ordre public* and morality are specifically permissible exceptions from patentability under TRIPS (n 7) art 27.2 (see n 7).

39 Patents Act 2013, s 15(3).

40 Patents Act 2013, ss 225–228. See also TRIPS (n 7) art 27.2.

41 Patents Act 2013, s 225(3).

42 As noted in the Wai 262 report, most examiners (who act in the name of the Commissioner) are legally or scientifically trained. They are unlikely to be knowledgeable on Māori TK, culture or values. See Wai 262 (n 3) 200–201.

obliged to seek the Committee's advice. It is worth bearing in mind that the Committee may 'regulate its own procedure, subject to any direction given by the Commissioner',[43] thus raising the possibility that the Committee may informally advise the Commissioner, even if not approached to do so. However, it should be noted that the lack of support from an executive unit could make it difficult for the Committee to make investigations of its own.[44] At the time of writing, the Committee had not assessed any patent applications.[45]

It is not clear what would constitute 'derivation'. For example, is to isolate something from an Indigenous plant/animal to derive something from it? What if there appears to be derivation, but there was in fact independent creation?[46]

The meaning of 'indigenous plants or animals' is also potentially narrow, depending on how strictly IPONZ interprets the three terms. To illustrate, it is not clear if *Leptospermum scoparium* would fall within the definition of 'Indigenous' as it can also be found in south-east Australia. It should, as 'Indigenous' has a different meaning from 'endemic'.[47] Additionally, 'plants or animals' would appear to exclude micro-organisms, otherwise Parliament would have simply used the term 'species'. Notably, Wai 262 refers to '*taonga* species'.[48]

It is up to the Committee to determine the meaning of 'values'. At the time of writing, the Patent Examination Manual did not elaborate on any of these concerns,[49] though it appears that the Committee is in the process of creating guidelines.[50]

---

[43] Patents Act 2013, s 278. This is the same in the Trade Marks Act 2002, s 180.

[44] Wai 262 (n 3) 200.

[45] Email from Simon Gallagher (Trade Marks Manager, IPONZ), 'Request for information about Māori Advisory Committees' (8 February 2017) (on file with the author); confirmed by the Ministry of Business, Innovation and Employment (9 March 2018).

[46] Under the existing patent regime, it is not possible to have independent creation. Existing prior art and the 'common general knowledge' are considered in the assessment of novelty and the inventive step, regardless of what the inventor actually knew. The assessment is objective.

[47] According to the online Oxford English Dictionary <https://en.oxforddictionaries.com>, indigenous means 'originating or occurring naturally in a particular place; native', whereas endemic is defined as 'native and restricted to a certain place'.

[48] For a discussion on the different terminology, see Jessica C Lai, *Indigenous Cultural Heritage and Intellectual Property Rights: Learning from the New Zealand Experience?* (Springer 2014) 265–266.

[49] See IPONZ Patent Examination Manual (n 7).

[50] IPONZ, 'Protecting Intellectual Property with a Māori Cultural Element: User Guide' (2016) 23.

The role of the Committee and the exception to patentability are narrow. This is because the Committee must assess both the conditions of: (1) derivation; and (2) commercial exploitation being contrary to Māori values.[51] Furthermore, it is not enough that the invention is contrary to Māori values – its commercial exploitation must be.

The Commissioner of Patents is not bound by the opinion of the Committee, but must consider the Committee's advice when deciding the broader question of public order or morality. In a way, this makes sense as the Committee's role is more narrowly defined than the scope of public order or morality. It is unclear how much weight the Commissioner would attribute to the advice of the Committee. The Commissioner could theoretically deem the commercial exploitation of an invention not to be contrary to public order or morality, despite the Committee advising that there is both derivation and contravention of Māori values, and notwithstanding the lack of a conflicting opinion.

It is also problematic that the Committee is expected to represent the knowledge and values of all Māori as there is no one *te ao Māori* or *tikanga Māori*. Since the entry into force of the Patents Act 2013, the IPONZ application form has required that patent applicants indicate with yes/no:[52]

> Maori Conflict possible
>
> Traditional knowledge

These terms are not defined.[53] Applicants are not statutorily required to divulge this information. As a result, there are no consequences for failure to answer these correctly or honestly (to the best of one's knowledge). In other words, patent applicants are not disincentivised from answering these questions incorrectly or dishonestly. Instead, they potentially have incentives to be disingenuous and/or untruthful, to avoid issues with novelty/inventive step and the scrutiny of the Committee.

Without a compulsory requirement for patent applicants to disclose

---

51 It seems that IPONZ takes these two requirements as 'either or'. See ibid 25. However, it is clear from the wording of the Patents Act 2013, s 226 that both derivation and commercial exploitation being contrary to Māori values are required.

52 Wai 262 (n 3) 203–205 recommended a disclosure requirement, discussed further in Section V.

53 The IPONZ website states that it is '[o]ptional – select this if the invention is derived from Maori traditional knowledge or from indigenous plants or animals'. See IPONZ, 'Apply for a Patent' <https://www.iponz.govt.nz/about-ip/patents/apply/>.

whether the alleged inventions are derived from Māori TK or 'indigenous plants or animals' and an incentive to disclose this correctly and honestly, it could be difficult for the Committee to identify the relevant interests. A voluntary register of such interests would, thus, be beneficial,[54] as would a requirement that applicants divulge the source of any biological materials used. This would also facilitate PIC and ABS as it would make it easier for the Committee to know the relevant group for PIC and ABS. Together, a disclosure requirement and voluntary register would increase the likelihood that the Committee might, under certain circumstances, advise that the commercial exploitation of an invention is contrary to Māori values in the absence of PIC from the relevant Māori authority.

B. The Wai 262 Report

The Treaty of Waitangi is interpreted chiefly through the Waitangi Tribunal.[55] In 2011 the Tribunal published the Wai 262 Report *Ko Aotearoa Tenei*, 'This is Aotearoa New Zealand'. Filed in 1991 by six *iwi* (tribes),[56] the Wai 262 claim was one of the largest and most complex claims ever heard by the Waitangi Tribunal (between 1997 and 2007). The Tribunal described it as being 'about mātauranga Māori – the unique Māori way of viewing the world, incorporating both Māori culture and Māori traditional knowledge. It is no stretch to describe this claim as being about the survival of Māori culture and its ongoing place in this country.'[57] The claim extended to the 'knowledge system itself, and its internal mechanism for transmission, dissemination, tuition, and development'.[58]

The Tribunal did not recommend that Māori should have exclusive ownership of the genetic or biological resources of *taonga* species[59] as

---

54 Wai 262 (n 3) 201.

55 Treaty of Waitangi Act 1975, preamble. The Waitangi Tribunal is a standing commission of inquiry. It makes recommendations on claims brought by Māori relating to alleged Crown breaches of the Treaty of Waitangi 1840.

56 Namely, Ngāti Kuri, Ngāti Wai, Te Rarawa, Ngāti Porou, Ngāti Kahungunu and Ngāti Koata.

57 Wai 262 (n 3) 1.

58 Maui Solomon (for the Ministry of Economic Development), 'Peer Review Report on WIPO Documents' (2005), appendix to: WIPO, Intergovernmental Committee on Intellectual Property and Genetic Resources, Traditional Knowledge and Folklore, Secretariat, 'The Protection of Traditional Cultural Expressions/ Expression of Folklore: Table of Written Comments on Revised Objectives and Principles' Eleventh Session (2007) WIPO/GRTKF/IC/11/4(b) 358.

59 Wai 262 (n 3) 192.

Māori did not create *taonga* species.[60] The Tribunal found that the *kaitiaki* relationship (as per the guarantee to *tino rangatiratanga* (sovereignty or chieftainship) in the Māori text of the Treaty) needed protection and should be assessed on a case-by-case basis.[61] The greater the effect of the bioprospecting, genetic modification or intellectual property on the *kaitiaki* relationship, the greater the right of involvement in any decision-making.[62]

Regarding bioprospecting,[63] the Tribunal recommended that bioprospecting laws in New Zealand be reformed and that the Department of Conservation (DOC),[64] in consultation with Māori, develop a comprehensive regime that is Treaty compliant.[65] The legislation setting up DOC already required that the Act be 'interpreted and administered as to give effect to the Principles of the Treaty of Waitangi'.[66] To give this teeth, the Tribunal recommended that Māori be given a greater role in applications for bioprospecting.[67] It was also suggested that the role be one of joint decision-making at the regional level.[68] PIC and ABS should not be required for every application for bioprospecting as this would presume that there is an interference of a *kaitiaki* relationship with a *taonga* species.[69] When there is a relevant *kaitiaki* interest, consultation and perhaps even consent might be necessary.

As to patent law, the Tribunal discussed the then Patents Bill 2010 and the creation of a Māori Advisory Committee that would advise the Commissioner of Patents on public order and morality with respect to Māori values.[70] While positive about this, the Tribunal made the following recommendations:

- The Committee should also be able to advise the Commissioner on the requirements of patentability.[71]
- The Committee must be able to advise the Commissioner on any

---

60 Ibid 193.
61 Ibid 193–194.
62 Ibid 194.
63 The law in New Zealand regulating bioprospecting is discussed ibid 144–158.
64 Established by the Conservation Act 1987, s 5.
65 Wai 262 (n 3) 198.
66 Conservation Act 1987, s 4.
67 Wai 262 (n 3) 198.
68 Ibid.
69 Ibid 199.
70 Ibid 202.
71 Ibid 201.

existing and conflicting *kaitiaki* interests, even if the requirements of patentability are satisfied.[72]

- The Committee should maintain an advisory role but should be able to advise the Commissioner as it sees fit (not just when requested) and prepare guidelines and protocols.[73]
- The Commissioner should be required to approach the Committee when an application raises 'Māori issues'.[74]
- IPONZ should create a voluntary registration of *kaitiaki* interests (both in relation to *taonga* species and to *mātauranga Māori* in relation to such, which could also be used for applications for bioprospecting and genetic modification).[75]
- Patent applicants should have to disclose whether any *mātauranga Māori* or *taonga* species contributed towards the invention.[76]

The government has not formally reacted to the Report. Nevertheless, the Wai 262 Report is not going away and it would be a mistake to dismiss it as 'out of mind'. To illustrate, in September 2018 the Ministry of Business, Innovation and Employment (MBIE) released a Discussion Paper on the possible implementation of a disclosure requirement for the origin of GRs and/or TK in the patent regime, largely as a result of the Wai 262 recommendations.[77]

---

[72] Ibid.

[73] Ibid.

[74] Ibid.

[75] Discussed ibid 56, 202–203 and 207. For a discussion on why registration should be voluntary, see Susy Frankel, *Intellectual Property in New Zealand* (2nd edn, LexisNexis 2011) 138; and Graham Dutfield, 'Legal and Economic Aspects of Traditional Knowledge' in Keith E Maskus and Jerome H Reichman (eds), *International Public Goods and Transfer of Technology: Under a Globalized Intellectual Property Regime* (CUP 2005) 495, 515–516.

[76] Discussed at Wai 262 (n 3) 203–205. Frankel has also supported the introduction of a disclosure mechanism into IP laws, with appropriate consequences on failure to comply; Frankel (n 75) 131.

[77] MBIE, 'Discussion Paper: Disclosure of Origin of Genetic Resources and Traditional Knowledge in the Patents Regime' (September 2018) paras 5 and 39–44. The Discussion Paper raised the possibility that applicants have to disclose evidence of compliance with ABS obligations in the country of origin of the GRs and/or TK (paras 75–76). MBIE did not prefer this option as it would increase compliance costs for IPONZ and applicants, and might deter patent application in New Zealand, particularly because such an obligation is not commonly found elsewhere (paras 84 and 105). The Discussion Paper noted that this might be different if New Zealand were to implement an ABS regime in its bioprospecting law, as patent law would then act as a check-point for this (para 106). Submissions to the Discussion Paper closed on 21 December 2018.

III. SEARCH METHODOLOGY

The following explains the search methodology used, including some technical detail. The specificity is important in order to contextualise the results discussed in Section IV. It further explains why certain results were eliminated and are not discussed, and also why some applications might not have been found.

The IPONZ search function allows one to search for terms within the 'Title/Office Title/Abstract' fields. It finds applications and grants, regardless of their status (whether they are expired, abandoned, withdrawn, lapsed, rejected or granted). This was used to search for '*Leptospermum Scoparium*', '*Leptospermum*' and 'Manuka' (without the macron over the 'a').[78] The cut-off date was 31 March 2018.

Data was collected regardless of the status of the applications/grants. Granted patents are clearly of interest as they represent what is or was propertised. Applications (even if they never go to grant) are also significant as they tell us what applicants have sought to propertise. Provisional and complete applications for the same invention were amalgamated. 'Parent' applications and their divisional 'child' applications were also considered together as the subject matter in a child application is also found in the parent application, and they have the same priority date.[79] In contrast, patents of addition were considered separately from their parent patents, as patents of addition embody content not included in the parent application.[80]

The 'claims' of the patent applications found were analysed, where possible, to determine whether the patents were 'of potential concern'. Patent claims are the part of a patent that delimit the subject matter protected by

---

The Wai 262 Report is also present in the review of New Zealand copyright law and plant variety rights. See MBIE, 'Issues Paper: Review of the Copyright Act 1994' (November 2018) at 109–117; MBIE, 'Issues Paper: Review of the Plant Variety Rights Act 1987' (September 2018); and MBIE, 'Māori Engagement Plan: Review of the Plant Variety Rights Act 1987' (September 2018).

[78] A search for Mānuka (with the macron) yielded no results.

[79] Divisional applications are a type of patent application that contain matter from a previously filed application (the parent application). They are often considered to be the remedy for lack of unity of an invention; Jessica C Lai, 'Unity of Invention: The Pre- and Post-Grant Rift in Patent Law' (2017) NZLJ 190. Divisional applications are also used to excise non-patentable material. Patents Act 2013, s 34.

[80] See Susy Frankel and Jessica Lai, *Patent Law and Policy* (LexisNexis 2016) 222–226.

the patent.[81] While most patents have multiple claims, typically only a few are the core claims upon which the others rest. That is, if the core claims lack novelty/inventive step or are contrary to public order/morality, the entire application fails. Claim 1 is always a core claim. Where the claims were not available, the decision was based on the abstract. Patent applications were eliminated as not 'of potential concern' if one of the following applied:

1. the species (or isolate) was mentioned as one of many suitable for the invention;
2. the species or honey (or isolate) was a minor ingredient among many combined to make up a composition;
3. the species or honey (or isolate) was not a component of the invention claimed;
4. the species or honey was mentioned in at least one of the search fields, but did not constitute part of the claimed invention; or
5. there was not enough information provided to make a proper assessment (common when an application was filed, but later abandoned).

The author acknowledges that many Indigenous peoples (including Māori) find the idea of patenting any fauna/flora offensive, and some Māori might find any attempt to patent a part/extract/use of a sacred plant to be offensive, even if what is claimed is remote from any traditional use. Thus, the elimination of patent applications from the search does not necessarily marry up with patents that Māori would be unconcerned about. Furthermore, any categorisation involves some subjective assessment (for example, what is a major or minor ingredient).

The elimination instead represents, first, the reality of limited resources and how many patent applications can accurately be assessed in depth and, secondly, the kinds of applications/patents that could be realistically challenged in New Zealand's Western-based legal system. Regarding the second of these, applications that seem closely connected to (or derivative of) *mātauranga Māori* are more likely (1) to have questionable novelty or inventive step; and (2) to be recognised as something the Māori Advisory Committee should look at. Therefore, a further categorisation of the patents of potential concern was made (as discussed in Section IV.E).

Finally, it must be left to Māori to conduct their own analyses to draw their own conclusions about the relevance of a patent application with

---

[81] The rest of a patent specification is used for the interpretation or 'construction' of the claims; see ibid 247–255.

respect to *mātauranga Māori, te ao Māori* and *tikanga Māori*. The assessment made here of whether a patent application is closely connected to (or derivative of) *mātauranga Māori* depends on a limited understanding of *mātauranga Māori*. It may be that there are failures to identify an invention as being connected to (or derivative of) *mātauranga Māori* because of a lack of knowledge.

IV. RESULTS AND DISCUSSION

A. General

The search for '*Leptospermum Scoparium*', '*Leptospermum*' and 'Manuka' found applications for 36 different inventions. '*Leptospermum Scoparium*' only had one hit, '*Leptospermum*' had seven results,[82] while 'Manuka' had 31 (there were overlaps in the results from the searches).[83] This potentially indicates that applications in New Zealand tend to be made with the everyday name rather than the genus or species name, at least within the 'Title/Office Title/Abstract' field. A further application pertaining to Mānuka was identified while analysing the found applications but did not have any of the search terms in the 'Title/Office Title/Abstract' field. This highlights the difficulties in patent searching and dependency on the search function. The total number of inventions found was 37.

Eight of the 37 inventions were eliminated as not 'of potential concern'.[84] This left 29 patent applications of potential concern.

The most recent filings in New Zealand were six provisional applications from UMF Honey Association Inc.[85] However, on closer inspection, these seemed to relate to just two inventions. No abstract or specifications were available, making this difficult to determine. Presuming that they were related (or eliminating the first four of them simply because there was not have enough information on them and they were all closed or withdrawn), there were then 25 applications of potential concern.[86]

---

[82] '*Leptospermum*' obtained eight results, but one did not pertain to Mānuka (Application No 511191 had the incorrect abstract for Application No 555191, so was picked up in the search).

[83] 'Manuka' obtained 32 results, but one had an incorrect abstract and had nothing to do with Mānuka.

[84] Patent Application Nos 523838; 63321; 584419; 629152; 510267; 542065; 545559 and 570858.

[85] Patent Application Nos 711034; 710257; 728462; 729052; 739964 and 739965.

[86] In chronological order by date of filing, Patent Application Nos 325;

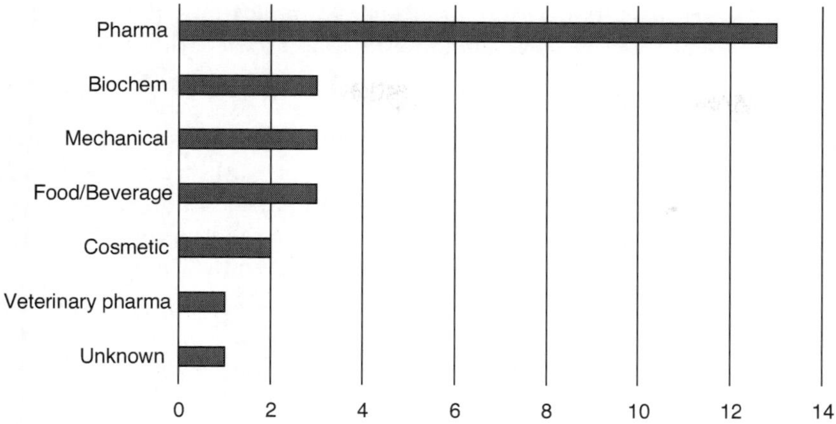

Figure 2.1 Field of NZ Mānuka patent applications

B. Field of Applications

Fifty per cent of the applications related to pharmaceuticals (see Figure 2.1).[87] Including the application for the veterinary pharmaceutical, over half of the applications were in the pharmaceutical industry. Many of these used the antibiotic properties of Mānuka honey and were compositions with the honey or an extract therefrom. Several applied the antibiotic properties of the *Leptospermum scoparium* essential oil.

All three of the biochem applications were for marker compounds to identify Mānuka honey or measure the quality of the same. These were from three different applicants, Healthcare Systems,[88] Comvita[89]

50965; 53035 (Patent of Addition to 50965); #332694; *502158; *519778; # 518044; 533368; 535038; 538828 (parent), 578200 (divisional, child application from 538828), 598644, 598649 (divisional, child application from 578200), 613993 (divisional, child application from 598644), 704841 (divisional, child application from 613993), 724495 (divisional, child application from 704841); *542258; *555191; *573013 (parent), 583333 (divisional, child application); 582246; *570735; *611810; *592091; #615495; ^625099; *630541 (parent), 718249 (divisional, child of 630541), 736274 (divisional, child of 718249); ^624517; *718779; ^722140; ^739964; and 739965.

[87] Twenty-six fields were counted in total rather than 25, as one application was for food and a pharmaceutical.

[88] Patent Application No 625099 (filed 15 Oct 2012, granted 29 Sep 2015).

[89] Patent Application No 722140 (filed 11 Dec 2015, open for public inspection 30 June 2017).

and UMF Honey Association Inc.[90] These applications play into the discourse between New Zealand and Australia around who can use the term 'Mānuka'. The New Zealand Ministry for Primary Industries has developed a scientific definition of 'Mānuka' for export products, including four chemical compounds and one DNA marker.[91] The four chemical markers are different from those identified by Healthcare Systems and Comvita. The UMF Honey Association Inc marker is not yet publicly available. Manuka Honey Appellation Society Inc has filed for a certification trade mark for 'MANUKA HONEY'.[92] The three Mānuka-marker applications, thus, represent the use of patents in a 'war of words' – more specifically a Māori word, 'Mānuka'.

The three mechanical applications were the first three filed in relation to Mānuka, in 1878, 1923 and 1924.[93] These all used the wood or bush of *Leptospermum scoparium* in waterworks. The next patent application was made in 1998, after a 74-year gap. All applications since 1998 have related to the essential oil of *Leptospermum scoparium*, part of the plant, Mānuka honey or chemicals (including amino acids/peptides) extracted from Mānuka honey.

One of the two food applications utilised honey as a sweetener and the other was a food/pharmaceutical application for a honey fortified with a UMF fraction.[94] The beverage application used *Leptospermum scoparium* brush, leaf stem, or a syrup formed therefrom to brew beer.[95] One of the two cosmetic patents employed Mānuka honey as part of a hair-removal formulation,[96] and the other used compounds isolated from Mānuka honey for skincare (loss of skin elasticity).[97]

---

90 Patent Application No 739964 (filed 16 Feb 2018).

91 Ministry for Primary Industries, 'Mānuka Honey' (5 February 2018) <https://www.mpi.govt.nz/growing-and-harvesting/honey-and-bees/manuka-honey/>.

92 Trademark No 1025914; under examination at the time of writing.

93 Patent Application Nos 325; 50965; and 53035 (Patent of Addition to 50965).

94 Patent Application Nos 538828 (parent) and five divisional child applications; and 533368.

95 Patent Application No 519778.

96 Patent Application No 535038.

97 Patent Application No 624517.

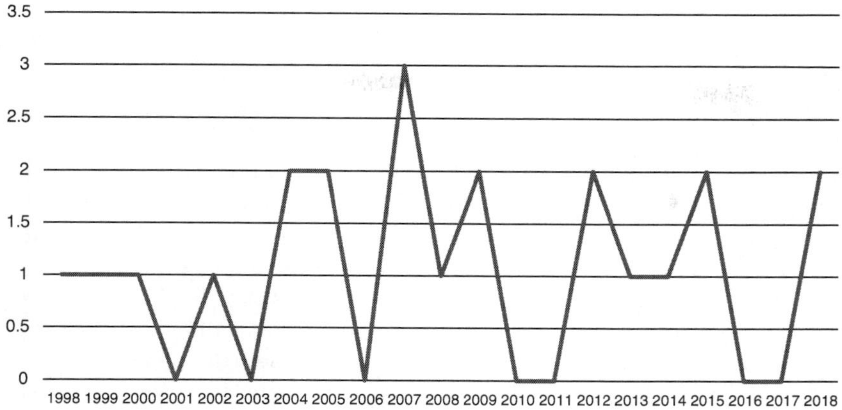

Figure 2.2 Number of applications by filing year since 1998

C. Year of Filing

Since 1998, applications had been steady, between zero to three per year (see Figure 2.2).[98] Only filings from the first quarter of 2018 were identified.

D. Applicants

There were few repeat players. Most applicants had only one application, with the exception of Manukamed Ltd (3), UMF Honey Association Inc (2), Comvita (2) and John James Head (2, though very much related).[99] One should also note that the applicants may not necessarily represent the ultimate owners. For example, Comvita has owned Apimed Medical Honey since 2003 and Medihoney since 2007.[100]

---

98 Divisional applications have not been recorded separately. Where an application had divisional applications, the filing date has been recorded as that of the parent application.

99 Both patents filed by John James Head (50965 and 53035) relate to 'River-Bank Protecting and Channel-Forming Means' and the latter is a patent of addition to the former.

100 Malcolm Burgess, 'Healthcare firm Comvita to buy Medihoney for $6.7m' (April 2017) NZ Herald <https://www.nzherald.co.nz/business/news/article.cfm?c_id=3&objectid=10434938>; Jim Bridges, 'Comvita Acquires Honey Group' (December 2003) <https://www.nzherald.co.nz/business/news/article.cfm?c_id=3&objectid=3541113>.

E. Status

Of the 25 inventions, 19 have been granted a patent (either the main application or a divisional application) at the time of writing. Of the most recent four, two were open for inspection and two were newly filed. Regarding the two that were open for public inspection, this meant that the applicants had not requested examination.[101] Once an application is open for public inspection, any person can require that the Commissioner direct the applicant to request examination.[102] Failure of the applicant to do so constitutes an abandonment of the application.[103]

One application was opposed and withdrawn.[104] This was essentially for different compositions of Mānuka honey in water. It is not difficult to imagine that such an invention could be questioned for want of novelty. Claim 1 was also for a method of medical treatment, which do not constitute patentable subject matter in New Zealand.[105] A divisional child application from this was also opposed and withdrawn.[106]

Two parent applications were abandoned. One of these pertained to use of Mānuka honey in food balanced proportionately in accordance with the Australia-New Zealand Joint Foods Standards Code recommended daily intake.[107] This had six divisional child applications, four of which were abandoned, one of which was granted and one of which was under examination at the time of writing. The other related to the use of Mānuka honey in a wound dressing.[108] This had two divisional child applications, which were also abandoned.

Of the 19 granted patents, the earliest three had long since expired. The rest (16) could still have been within their 20-year patent term.

---

[101] Applicants must request examination within five years of the filing date or the Commissioner can direct that the applicant request examination. Failure to do so results in the application being treated as abandoned. See Patents Act 2013, s 64, and Patents Regulations 2014, s 71.

[102] Patents Act 2013, s 64(3).

[103] Patents Act 2013, s 64(6).

[104] Patent Application No 573013.

[105] This is now statutory; see Patents Act 2013, s 16(2). At the time that the application was assessed, methods of medical treatment were not patentable based on case law; *Wellcome Foundation v Commissioner of Patents* (1983) NZLR (CA) 385, 387; *Pharmaceutical Management Agency v Commissioner of Patents* (2000) 2 NZLR (CA) 529; and *Pfizer Inc v Commissioner of Patents* (2005) 1 NZLR (CA) 362.

[106] Patent Application No 583333.

[107] Patent Application No 538828.

[108] Patent Application No 630541.

However, five were allowed to lapse, leaving 11 still in force at the time of writing.

F. Potentially of Concern

From the analysis of the patent documents available, very few mentioned that Māori have long used Mānuka for a variety of purposes. Specifications often mentioned New Zealand as the source of Mānuka, but not any traditional uses. Indeed, only one specification was identified that did so.[109]

As noted above, the Wai 262 Report recommended a disclosure requirement, including: (1) the 'source and country of origin of any genetic or biological resource that contributed in any material way to the invention'; and (2) 'mātauranga Māori that was used in the course of research, including traditional knowledge that is not integral to the invention but that prompted the inventor to take the course of research that led to the relevant patent application'.[110]

One can imagine that there are situations where an invention might appear to be derivative and be contrary to Māori values, but disclosure might not be necessary. One of the central issues in relation to TK and GRs is the disconnect between Indigenous expectations and worldview, on the one hand, and the ideology behind Western science, on the other hand. It is possible that much of the R&D that led to the patent applications identified in this chapter did not require that the researchers source GRs from Māori land; *Leptospermum scoparium* is found in many parts of New Zealand. It is also conceivable that the researchers considered any *mātauranga Māori* as being in the 'public domain' and, thus, not of any concern.

This also complicates questions regarding PIC and ABS. Without accepting the Western conceptualisation of the public domain, one can nevertheless perceive how Western researchers could view *mātauranga Māori* located in literature, and the use of related GRs, as being no different from any other prior art in their field. It would perhaps (though not necessarily) be different if they got the knowledge directly from a knowledge holder – but there is no evidence of this and traditional uses of *Leptospermum scoparium* are well documented.[111]

---

109 Patent Application No 332694.

110 Wai 262 (n 3) 204.

111 For an example, see Cliff Van Eaton, *Manuka: The Biography of an Extraordinary Honey* (Exisle Publishing 2014) 113–115.

The question then becomes how the patent system can deal with this kind of use or derivation, where there is a break in transmission of the TK and GR. Put another way, how does the system deal with situations where the TK and the GR have entered the Western domains of knowledge and science, and questions about PIC and ABS possibly do not arise? This appears often to be the case with Mānuka, where settlers became aware of related *mātauranga Māori* quite early on, much has been published, and scientific studies on the beneficial properties of the plant have long been performed.[112] It is then interesting to note that the mechanisms in the Patents Act 2013 (outlined above) do not require an unbroken chain of transmission. As patent law is generally objective in nature, whether there is in fact actual derivation does not matter.[113] Similarly, the question of whether the commercial exploitation of an invention is contrary to Māori values (public order/morality) is not necessarily assessed in light of what the inventors knew or did not know; it should be a purely objective inquiry.

Not all of the 25 applications used or were similar to *mātauranga Māori*. Of course, as noted above, one might argue that any inclusion of a *taonga* species in a proprietary structure is offensive and inappropriate. For example, the first three patents for use of the Mānuka wood for waterworks did not (as far as the author is aware) derive from *mātauranga Māori*. They might nevertheless be offensive and contrary to Māori values. It is also possible that the eight applications excluded as not 'of potential concern' would offend. Indeed, any proprietary interest in fauna and flora (or extracts therefrom) might be viewed as contrary to a people's worldview.

Without wishing to detract from these perspectives in any way, the Committee and IPONZ are confined by the nature of the law. That is, assessing novelty/inventive step, or public order/morality. In light of this, the 25 applications of potential concern were analysed for whether they:[114]

- pertain to the plant/honey and appears derivative of a known Māori use
- pertain to an isolate of the plant/honey and a known Māori use
- pertain to an isolate of the plant/honey and a non-known Māori use

---

112 See ibid; Calder, Cole and Walker (n 17); Mavric et al (n 17); Brooker (n 13); Bloor (n 20); and Kellam et al (n 22).

113 See n 46.

114 The categorisation can be seen at above n 86. Application No 739965 could not be assessed due to lack of information.

Realistically, within a Western-based legal system, only applications/patents falling within the first two categories (* and #), of which there were ten and three respectively, could potentially be challenged based on lack of novelty or inventive step in light of *mātauranga Māori*. The latter is more likely as novelty is a relatively low standard to surpass. It is a quantitative rather than qualitative standard, which only requires that the invention being claimed is not in the existing prior art.[115] In contrast, the inventive step standard involves a qualitative inquiry. It asks whether the average person skilled in the art in question would find obvious the steps taken between the common general knowledge and the invention.[116] If that notional person would find the steps obvious, a patent application will be rejected, or a granted patent can be revoked. Both novelty and inventive step are fact-based inquiries. They require evidence about the existing prior art, the common general knowledge and the notional person.[117] Thus, it is not possible here to say whether any of the applications/grants identified in this search are in want of novelty or an inventive step.

It is important to note that of the 25 inventions identified above, one was regulated under the Patents, Designs, and Trade-marks Act 1911 and 20 were regulated under the Patents Act 1953. Only the most recent four came under the Patents Act 2013.[118] This is important because there was no full patent examination under the 1911 and 1953 Acts, and patents were granted solely on an assessment of novelty on a 'benefit of doubt' standard.[119] It is only since the Patents Act 2013 came into force, from 13 September 2014, that patent applications are fully examined for novelty, non-obviousness and utility, under a 'balance of probabilities' standard. In other words, IPONZ did not examine patent applications filed prior to 13 September 2014 with respect to an inventive step. Note, however, that all patent applications can be opposed, and all granted patents revoked, for lack of an inventive step, regardless of which Act they were filed under.[120] At the time of writing, none of the four identified applications

---

115 *General Tire & Rubber Co v Firestone Tyre & Rubber Co Ltd* (1972) RPC (CA) 457, 485. See also Frankel and Lai (n 80) 142–161.

116 *Windsurfing International Inc v Tabur Marine (Great Britain) Ltd* (1985) RPC (CA) 59, 73. See also Frankel and Lai (n 80) 161–198.

117 Patents Act 2013, ss 6–8; High Court Rules 2016, r 22.20.

118 Patent Application Nos 718779; 722140; 739964; and 739965.

119 Frankel and Lai (n 80) 233–235.

120 Patents Act 1953, ss 21(1)(e) and 41(1)(f); Patents Act 2013, ss 92(1)(a), 95(2)(a) and 114(1)(a).

made since 13 September 2014 had gone through examination;[121] two were open for public inspection and two were recently filed.

There were four applications from the third category (^), three relating to marker compounds for identifying Mānuka honey and one for isolates to treat loss of skin elasticity. It is unlikely that these could be challenged for lack of novelty or inventive step based on any known Māori use. However, as *Leptospermum scoparium* is important to Māori,[122] such applications should arguably go to the Māori Advisory Committee. Two of the applications designated ^ were filed after 13 September 2014. Indeed, in the future, the Commissioner should seek the advice of the Committee for all applications that could be deemed *, # or ^.

A possible reason why the Māori Advisory Committee has never been used is potentially the coercive effect of the changes introduced by the Patents Act 2013 outlined in the foregoing. Applicants (or their patent attorneys) might be more careful about seeking patents for inventions that are obvious or that might draw the attention of the Committee. This is an effect that cannot be measured. Notably, since the Patents Act 2013 came into force, three out of four of the applications filed were for isolates from the plant or honey, not directly connected to any Māori TK. It is also possible that the changes brought in by the Patents Act 2013 came too late for *Leptospermum scoparium* or Mānuka honey, and other species with known beneficial uses, where there is enough literature and existing patents to nullify any novelty or inventive step in any invention similar to or derivative of Māori TK, and the research has moved into biotech/biochem, where derivation from TK is less evident.

The failure to consult the Committee might also be due to the Commissioner's narrow interpretation of 'derivation'. Perhaps IPONZ's interpretation of the matter is that to isolate something from an Indigenous plant is not to derive something from the same. It might also be that the Commissioner requires a high degree of similarity to TK for there to be derivation. For example, one application sought protection for a wet wipe made up of a flexible carrier, water and Mānuka (and/or Kānuka) honey.[123] This application seemed ripe to be sent to the Committee (and

---

121 See n 101.

122 Wai 262 (n 3) 128–131.

123 Patent Application No 718779. Two of the Mānuka inventions (Patent Application No 624517 and 718779) additionally related to Kānuka (*kunzea ericoides*), a plant that is often discussed together with Mānuka because of similarities in their appearance. A brief note is thus made here regarding Kānuka patent applications. The IPONZ search function was used to search for 'kunzea ericoides', 'kunzea' and 'Kanuka' (without the macron over the 'a'). The first two yielded the

for being challenged as obvious) as it simply applies the known antibiotic properties of Mānuka honey. However, because Māori may not have had such wipes, perhaps IPONZ considered that there was no 'derivation' from Māori TK. The application was open for public inspection, which means that Committee members could look at it of their own accord.

Furthermore, the Committee's role is limited to assessing derivation from (1) Māori TK, (2) indigenous plants, or (3) indigenous animals. Mānuka honey is not a plant or animal, such that the Committee's role is limited to advising on derivation from Māori TK when it comes to applications using the honey rather than the plant. Comvita's application for marker compounds of *Leptospermum* honeys appeared to be a case in point.[124] The Commissioner would need to have a very broad understanding of derivation to interpret isolated marker compounds from honey as being derived from an Indigenous plant. It is also unlikely that the Commissioner would consider that the Mānuka honey marker compounds constituted derivation from Māori TK. At the time of writing, the application was open for public inspection.

It is similarly possible that *Leptospermum scoparium* was not considered to be 'Indigenous'. Finally, even if the Commissioner believed that an invention had relevant derivation, the Commissioner might have applied the discretion not to seek the Committee's advice.

V. LESSONS TO BE LEARNT?

The numbers presented here are not overwhelming but they are by no means insignificant. Indeed, depending on the perspective, a single granted patent over a *taonga* species (or an isolate or related aspect) might be significant if, for example, that patent affects a *kaitiaki* relationship, or if it forms the basis of a financially noteworthy product/service. It is not difficult to imagine that, were there an example of a large multinational pharmaceutical company patenting a blockbuster drug utilising the antibiotic properties of *Leptospermum scoparium* or Mānuka honey, the issue

---

same three applications (one of which was for *kunzea ambigua*). 'Kanuka' had two hits. There were, hence, four hits in total, two of which had already been identified in the Mānuka search. The additional two were Patent Application Nos 586996 and 629152. Three of the Kānuka applications were in the pharmaceutical industry, while one was cosmetic. Three were granted (though one has since lapsed), and one is open for public inspection. All four applications were filed within the last ten years, by four different applicants.

[124] Patent Application No 722140.

of patenting inventions derived from Māori TK and related GRs might find the limelight.

Perhaps what this empirical research has highlighted is that the Commissioner of Patents should be obliged to seek the advice of the Māori Advisory Committee whenever there appears to be derivation from Māori TK or an Indigenous species, and/or the commercial exploitation might be contrary to Māori values. As recommended in Wai 262, it should not be at the Commissioner's discretion. That it is the commercial exploitation that is assessed results from New Zealand's international obligations. However, it is not apparent why both derivation and commercial exploitation that is contrary to Māori values are required. Sometimes, the latter should be sufficient. Sometimes, the former causes the latter.

The creation of voluntary registration of TK and *kaitiaki* interests (as recommended in Wai 262) would assist IPONZ with knowing when to forward an application to the Committee. It would additionally be helpful for locating prior art. IPONZ's current policy of requiring that applicants disclose whether a 'Maori Conflict [is] possible', or 'Traditional knowledge' was used, is highly commendable. It assists patent examiners in finding prior art and assessing novelty and the inventive step, and would alert the *kaitiaki* and the Māori Patents Advisory Committee to the application.[125] However, the application form should clarify what it means by those two categories, or whatever categories it has. As discussed in this chapter, words like 'conflict' are a matter of perspective, particularly if there is no definition.

Notably, all of the four applications filed after the Patents Act 2013 entered into force indicated that there was neither 'Maori Conflict possible' nor 'Traditional knowledge'.[126] This possibly results from a poor understanding of what 'Maori Conflict possible' or 'Traditional knowledge' mean. It might also be a consequence of the lack of any incentive to answer the questions honestly. Indeed, as discussed above, one has disincentives to do so.

Failure to disclose correctly or honestly should result in statutorily outlined consequences, as also recommended in Wai 262,[127] to ensure that

---

125 Frankel (n 75) 138.

126 As at September 2018, no applicant had indicated yes to either option; MBIE, 'Discussion Paper: Disclosure of Origin of Genetic Resources and Traditional Knowledge in the Patents Regime' (n 77) para 66.

127 It is disputed whether failure to disclose, or incorrectly or incompletely disclosing, can result in the revocation of grant under international law. This is due to the WIPO Patent Law Treaty (adopted 1 June 2000, entered into force 28 April 2005) 2340 UNTS 3; 39 ILM 1047, art 10(1), which states that non-compliance

the law embodies the correct incentives. The Waitangi Tribunal stated that failure to fulfil this requirement should not automatically result in the refusal of a patent application or revocation of a patent as this would be 'draconian' and could have a chilling effect on innovation.[128] Moreover, it may not be in the interest of the source community of the *mātauranga Māori* or *kaitiaki* relationship to have the patent refused or revoked[129] as they might prefer to come to an agreement with the applicant/owner, such as for ABS. The Tribunal recommended that it be up to the discretion of the Commissioner with the Chairperson of the Advisory Committee to decide what the sanction would be. In some situations, no repercussions would be justifiable, such as when the non-compliance has little effect on the relevant *kaitiaki* relationship or when the parties have subsequently come to agreement. However, in other cases, refusal to grant or revocation of a patent may be a valid consequence.[130] Ultimately, proper sanctions would need to be created such that applicants are given an incentive to comply with the compulsory requirement, but an excessively harsh – and possibly pedantic – system should not be implemented.[131]

The Wai 262 Report did not recommend that PIC and ABS should be required for the grant of a patent.[132] It stated that this was not justified and, in any case, PIC and ABS would evolve naturally from the process that applicants would go through, for example when an application is held

---

with formal requirements cannot affect a granted patent. However, New Zealand is not a Member of this Treaty. For discussion, see Lai (n 48) 268–271.

128 The consequences of non-compliance are discussed at Wai 262 (n 3) 205–206. Note that MBIE stated that the Wai 262 approach might not provide sufficient certainty for patent applicants and has recommended that an incomplete or false declaration/disclosure should: if pre-grant, prevent the application progressing until the correct information is provided; or if post-grant, result in the scope of the patent being narrowed, or patent revocation if the provision of accurate information would have meant that the patent would not have been granted. If an applicant knowingly made a false declaration/disclosure, there would be financial penalties. See MBIE, 'Discussion Paper: Disclosure of Origin of Genetic Resources and Traditional Knowledge in the Patents Regime' (n 77) paras 126–129.

129 This was noted by de Werra (n 37) 156.

130 A flexible approach to sanctions was also promoted, ibid 164–165 and 176–177.

131 Christopher Heath and Sabine Weidlich, 'Intellectual Property: Suitable for Protecting Traditional Medicine?' (2003) 1 IPQ 69, 81–82.

132 Wai 262 (n 3) 205. Similarly, in its review of the current Patents Act 1953, the MED stated that questions of ABS would ideally be managed by the parties concerned and not be a matter of legislation, though it acknowledged that this may either not occur or occur inequitably in the absence of legislation; Ministry of Economic Development, *Review of the Patents Act 1953: Boundaries to Patentability* (Regulatory and Competition Policy Branch, MED 2002) para 96.

up by the Committee, or the Commissioner recommends that an applicant consult with the relevant *kaitiaki*. When applicants realise that patents will not be granted because of *mātauranga Māori* or issues with Māori values regarding the use of *taonga* species, industry will slowly adjust to take into account Māori interests prior to application. The patenting process is expensive, such that most applicants would want to clear all hurdles before entering the system.

Whether the Commissioner should be bound by the Committee's opinion is a different and more complicated question. The inquiry into public order/morality is a potentially broad one. Rather than making the Commissioner of Patents bound by the Committee's opinion, the legislation (possibly secondary legislation) could more clearly delineate how it is that the Commissioner is to consider the Committee's opinion, what other factors the Commissioner might consider, and when the Commissioner may decide contrary to the Committee's opinion.

Overall, the enactment of the Patents Act 2013 embodies a unique and positive step towards taking Māori concerns seriously within a predominantly Western legal paradigm. It adds a new dimension to the role of patents, with the potential to modulate any incentive, signal and commercialisation function. But there is room for improvement. If one accepts that the changes brought in through the Patents Act 2013 have some coercive effect, then logically one should also accept that improving the law should enhance that effect. This can be through introducing a voluntary register of interests and TK, having a mandatory disclosure requirement with legal 'bite', requiring that the Commissioner consult the Māori Advisory Committee when there might be Māori concerns, and stipulating how the Commissioner is to use the Committee's advice. This would potentially nudge researchers in the direction of PIC and possibly ABS, and towards inventions that are unquestionably new and non-obvious, and consistent with *te ao Māori* and *tikanga Māori*. In the absence of these, the Committee and related provisions of the Patents Act 2013 might not have the right tools and supporting regulatory measures to affect the functions of patents in a real and observable way.

3. A TWAIL-Constructivist critique of the IP and development divide in the age of innovation – has the protection of place-based goods changed the narrative for the Caribbean?*

Marsha S. Cadogan

I. INTRODUCTION

Many countries in the global south ratified the TRIPS Agreement[1] because of the promise of social and economic development within their territories. Almost half a century after TRIPS, the role of intellectual property (IP) in development policy is still relevant and debatable.[2] As much as the age of innovation brings promise to the field of IP, it also calls for reflective pause to ascertain where the ambitious goal of IP and development stands. This is especially relevant given renewed focus on development using sustainable development goals.[3] Debates about geographical indications (GIs) are usually not posited as a north–south issue although the rural development potential in some developing countries has been questioned.[4] This chapter brings out the north–south dynamics

* All online sources were last accessed on 27 December 2018.

1 Agreement on Trade-Related Aspects of Intellectual Property Rights (opened for signature 15 April 1994, entered into force 1 January 1996) 1869 UNTS 299 (TRIPS).

2 Peter Yu, 'Five Decades of Intellectual Property and Global Development' (2016) 8 WIPJ 1.

3 David Lamber, 'Testing the Global Challenges to the Global Community's Sustainable Development Goals (SDGs) Against Professional Standards and International Law' (2017) 18 JSD 111.

4 See Irene Calboli (ed), *Geographical Indications at the Crossroad of Trade, Development and Culture – Focus on the Asia Pacific* (Cambridge University Press

which can shape and define the contours of GI engagement by the south, specifically the Caribbean. The chapter queries the significance of the concept of an IP and development divide in the age of innovation when refined ways of thinking about and doing IP may create new horizons in intangible proprietary rights. Compared to developed economies, developing countries often lack the resources to create and mobilise IP resources in their domestic jurisdictions to a far greater extent. These constraints include financial hindrances, challenges in developing and commercialising IP, and the tendency for local IP ownership and mobilisation to be concentrated in the hands of local elites. The IP development divide, then, is a positional interjection into the notion of IP as a positive narrative, and instead identifies and problematises why the south's experience with IP as a growth-oriented asset may be compromised. The chapter discusses the development divide in the context of interest in GIs by the south and the prospects for fruitful outcomes given specific dynamics.

The Caribbean identity[5] and its experience with place-based goods is used to make the point that hegemonic actors create obstacles to envisioning GIs as IP assets of development. The chapter then discusses whether IP counterhegemony in the south can produce positive developmental impacts, by viewing GIs through an innovative lens. Third World Approaches to International Law (TWAIL)[6] and Constructivist theory are used as frameworks to investigate the socio-legal construction of the concept of IP and development. This legal framework is also used to address who and what interests it takes to bring counterhegemonic principles to the forefront of developmental objectives in IP. The chapter is divided into four sections. Section II discusses the notion of development gaps between the north and south in the 21st century and analyses who, how and what influences global IP norms in the south. In addressing the development divide from a practical angle, Section III makes linkages between IP and development using specific United Nations Sustainable Development goals. This section concludes that actor interests and identities are crucial

2017); Dev Gangjee, *Relocating the Law of Geographical Indications* (Cambridge University Press 2012).

5 Anthony Payne, *The Political History of CARICOM* (Ian Randle Publishers 2008); Dennis Pantin, *The Caribbean Economy: A Reader* (Ian Randle Publishers 2005); Michael Manley, *Up the Down Escalator: Development and the International Economy* (Howard University Press 1987).

6 Antony Anghie, *Imperialism, Sovereignty and the Making of International Law* (Cambridge University Press 2014); James Thuo Gathii, 'Rejoinder: Twailing International Law' (2000) 98 Mich L Rev 2066; See also Gus van Harten, 'TWAIL and the Dabhol Arbitration' (2011) 3 TDL 131.

considerations in how successful and attainable sustainable development goals can be through IP in the global south. In narrowing the focus of the chapter, Section IV critically discusses the prospects of GIs as innovative IP assets in the Caribbean, and its ability to narrow the IP development divide. Is greater innovation possible by also focusing on producing clean energy products from GI manufacturing wastes? Section V critiques whether capacity building and policy cohesion, as aspects of sustainable development, are possible by conceptualising place-based goods as products that need the right partnerships to flourish globally. The chapter concludes that unless the Caribbean makes innovative uses of its GI rules, its countries and the region will encounter difficulties in establishing GI industries as influential development assets. In this context, the ability of GIs to narrow the development divide is questionable.

II. IP AND DEVELOPMENT IN THE AGE OF INNOVATION: TWAIL-CONSTRUCTIVIST CRITIQUE

The TWAIL scholarship researches international law from the perspective of those at the margins and identifies as critical and systemic the west's authoritarian role in the composition and execution of international law.[7] The notion of the 'Third World' is aptly described by TWAIL scholar Makua:[8]

> TWAIL is driven by three basics, interrelated purposeful objectives: The first is to de-construct, understand and unpack the uses of international law as a medium for the creation and perpetuation of a racialized hierarchy of international norms and institutions that subordinate non-Europeans to Europeans. Second, it seeks to construct and present an alternative normative legal edifice for international legal governance. Finally, TWAIL seeks through scholarship, policy and politics to eradicate the conditions of underdevelopment in the Third World.

I define the Third World as a plundered space,[9] historically subjugated in international law and international relations by influential western actors,

---

[7] But see John D Haskell, 'TRAIL-ing TWAIL: Arguments and Blind Spots in Third World Approaches to International Law' (Mississippi College School of Law, Legal Studies Research Paper No 2014-07) (where the author suggests TWAIL is not reformist).

[8] Makua Mutua, 'What is TWAIL' (2000) ASIL 94th Annual Meeting.

[9] Balakrishnan Rajagopal, *International Law from Below: Development, Social Movements and Third World Resistance* (Cambridge University Press 2003); Jean Grugel, *Politics and Development in the Caribbean* (Palgrave 1995).

often resulting in repressive governance structures and ways of life.[10] Historically, the Third World has been the underdog in international law, with more powerful western actors influencing domestic legal norms in the south. In recent years, TWAIL has taken on a reformist lens and so, in bringing to fore the prejudices of international law to the global south, also directs the dialogue to focus on how to create and sustain reform of international law in the Third World.

The Third World stretches across continents and includes Latin and Central American countries, certain countries in the Asia Pacific, the Caribbean, Africa and India. Throughout this chapter, I use the term south interchangeably with the Third World, in the context of the definition of Third World adopted in the chapter. This contested post-colonial space is heterogeneous in cultural experiences, economic vibrancy and political leanings and, as TWAIL scholar Balakrishnan Rajagopol[11] points out, includes states that are overcoming imperialistic burdens by strategic resilience to international law.

Constructivism[12] complements TWAIL by explaining why international IP law lacks traction in many Third World countries. Constructivism is an international relations theory that posits that actors, their identities and interests are influential in defining and shaping global norms.[13] To the Constructivist, knowledge is a social construct of norms. Norms are created when there is shared understanding and acceptance among or within a group about specific ideas or types of behaviour. How influential actors define and relate to rules is in turn reified or altered by other key actors in the international fora. This makes power and language more significant. Power is a central focus point in Constructivist reasoning.[14] What power does and who wields it are questions that give an understanding of the effect of norms on communities and societies. Language directs actions by shaping collective meanings and actors' perceptions and responses to collective meanings in interactions. As such, language used by influential

---

10 Arturo Escobar, *Encountering Development: The Making and Unmaking of the Third World* (Princeton University Press 1994); James Thuro Gathii, 'The Neo-Liberal turn in Free Trade Agreements' (2011) 86 WULR 421.

11 Balakrishnan Rajagopal, 'Right to Development and Global Governance: Old and New Challenges Twenty-Five Years On' (2013) 25 HRQ 893.

12 Jeffrey T Checkel, 'The Constructivist Turn in IR Theory' (1998) 50 WP 324.

13 Emmanuel Adler, 'Seizing the Middle Ground: Constructivism in World Politics' (1997) 3 EJIR Relations 319.

14 Stefano Guzzuni, 'The Concept of Power: A Constructive Analysis' (2005) 33 MJIS 495; Alexander Wendt, 'Anarchy Is What States Make of It: The Social Construction of Power Politics' (1992) 46 IO 391.

actors can push forward agendas that are favourable to their interests.[15] With these measures, Constructivism 'stresses the reflexive relationship between the social construction of knowledge and the construction of social reality. In other words, it focuses on reflexivity; that is, on how the social construction of knowledge can itself affect the construction of social reality and vice versa.'[16]

Early works on the integration of international relations with international law assert that the interest in analysing international law from spheres outside the legal lens is to diagnose, to make policy prescriptions and to re-engage with international law from a more integrated cross-sectoral perspective.[17] A TWAIL-Constructivist critique of international IP rights pinpoints how actors' identities and interests impact how IP functions in the global south.[18] The framework is also relevant in understanding whether reform of IP rules can be aligned with sustainable development goals and vice versa. This chapter defines development as improvements in the social, economic and human capacities of people's lives[19] brought about by actor interventions, whether legal, political, economic or a combination thereof.[20]

---

[15] Geneva Act of the Lisbon Agreement on Appellations of Origin and Geographical Indications, (adopted 20 May 2015) (Lisbon Agreement); Paris Convention for the Protection of Industrial Property (signed on 20 March 1883, revised on 14 July 1967, last amended 28 September 1979) 21 UST 1583, 828 UNTS 305 (Paris Convention), art 10bis. See also Jutta Brunee and Stephan Toope, 'Constructivism in International Law' in Jeffrey L Dunoff and Mark A Pollack (eds), *Interdisciplinary Perspectives on International Law and International Relations: The State of the Art* (Cambridge University Press 2012).

[16] Guzzuni (n 14) 499.

[17] Anne Marie Slaughter, Andrew Tulumello and Stepan Wood, 'International Law and International Relations Theory: A New Generation of Interdisciplinary Scholarship' (1998) 92 AJIL 367.

[18] Caroline B Ncube, 'Decolonising Intellectual Property Law in Pursuit of Africa's Development' (2016) 8 WIPJ 34.

[19] Michaeline Crichlow, *Negotiating Caribbean Freedom: Peasant and State in Development* (Lexington 2005). Crichlow (discusses how the state and the practice of governmentality failed Caribbean peoples' quest to become economically mobile through social welfare initiatives such as development programmes); Brian Meeks, *Envisioning Caribbean Freedom* (Ian Randle Publishers 2007). One of the points raised in Meeks' book is the use of agricultural development to foster growth in Jamaica's rural economy. In the later segments of this chapter, I approach the issue of innovations in agriculture through GIs and whether this is capable of fostering development.

[20] Escobar (n 10); Dean Baker, Arjun Jayadev and Joseph Stiglitz, *Innovation, Intellectual Property and Development, A Better Set of Approaches for the 21st Century* (Shutterwood Foundation 2017).

Innovation is increasingly relevant to an understanding of the direction of IP and trade in the global south.[21] Innovation can be described as a process or an outcome.[22] Innovation also occurs by necessity. The process of innovation involves the use of new or reworked ideas to produce better-performing products, services or more relevant policy frameworks. For example, driven by state taxes on sugary drinks in Scotland, the country's most popular fizzy drink, produced by an almost 200-year-old company, recently changed its ways of processing the drink to lower its sugar content.[23] The action was innovative as it represented a momentous change in traditional processing practices. As an outcome, innovation is not just the creation of new and often technologically advanced products[24] or ways of doing things.[25] Throughout the chapter, I reason that the repositioning of IP to be more relevant to global communities is also a form of innovation.

The primacy of innovation to the knowledge economy is in the prospects of finding new ways of conceptualising the old, and in creating or adding value that transcends the firm and reaches to consumer markets.[26] The notion of IP and development is premised on the reasoning that development is in reaction to IP policy. An eco-system that encourages the growth of IP-intensive industries also fosters development. In the global south, attempts to affiliate IP with development is a complex trajectory and is not always successful because of differences in political, legal and social norms, economic stature, and ability to access resources to build capacity.[27] That the north obtains more positive benefits from IP that

---

[21] See Ruchi Sharma, Audhesh K. Paswan, Sunil K. Ambrammal, Madan Dhanora, 'Impact of Patent Policy Changes on R&D Expenditure by Industries in India' (2018) 21 JWIP 52; Baker et al (n 20).

[22] Yang Lihau, 'Implementation of China's Rejuvenation Through Knowledge' in Ken Shao and Xiaoqing Feng (eds), *Innovation and Intellectual Property in China* (Edward Elgar Publishing 2014).

[23] Peter Kenyon, 'Och, No! Some Scots Cry as their Beloved Sugary Soda Gets a Revamp' National Public Radio (April 2018).

[24] Matthew Rimmer, 'Intellectual Property, Open Innovation and the Carbon Crisis' (August 2014), https://www.law.berkeley.edu/files/Tesla_Motors_IP_Open_Innovation_and_the_Carbon_Crisis_-_Matthew_Rimmer.pdf.

[25] Jeremy De Beer, *Open Innovation Policy Frameworks Intellectual Property, Competition, Investment and Other Market Governance Issues* (Industry Canada 2015).

[26] Clayton Christensen and Michael Raynor, *The Innovators Solution: Creating and Sustaining Successful Growth* (HBSPC 2013); RP Jayani Rajapathirana and Yan Hui, 'Relationship between Innovation Capability, Innovation Type, and Firm Performance' (2018) 3(1) JIK 44.

[27] Ruth Okediji, 'TRIPS and Its Methods: The Resilience of Developing Country Implementation of Intellectual Property Norms' in Daniel Gervais (ed),

implicate social and economic growth and human development is an axiom, and is well documented.[28]

III. HEGEMONY IN NORTH–SOUTH IP RELATIONS

In this chapter, hegemony is construed from a Gramscian perspective,[29] imbued with Constructivist reasonings.[30] In hegemony, control over how knowledge is construed comes by power. However, power is not forced, but rather is legitimated because those at the receiving end of power accept the 'control' by consent.[31] This consent may be driven by an interest in becoming more central actors in global trade communities,[32] tapping into crucial international markets, or the goal to attain sustainable development across sectors.[33] In effect then, power politics works in a hegemonic atmosphere because there is state or citizenry consent. In the politics and play of IP, powerful actors transfuse their preferred IP rules within and

---

Intellectual Property, Trade and Development: Strategies to Optimize Economic Development in a TRIPS-Plus Era (Oxford University Press 2014); Adebambo Adewopo, 'The Development Imperative in the Global IP System: Some Reflections on Developing Africa' in Graeme B Dinwoodie (ed), *Methods and Perspectives in Intellectual Property* (Edward Elgar Publishing 2013) 245; Ruth Okediji, 'The International Copyright System: Limitations, Exceptions and Public Interest Considerations For Developing Countries' (2006) UNCTAD-ICTSD, <https://unctad.org/en/Docs/iteipc200610_en.pdf>.

[28] Antony Anghie, Bhupinder Chimni, Karin Mickelson and Obiora Okafor, *The Third World and International Order: Law, Politics and Globalization* (BA 2004); Antony Anghie, 'Legal Aspects of the New International Legal Order' (2015) 6 HIJHRD 145; Brian Meeks, *Envisioning Caribbean Futures* (University of the West Indies Press 2007); James Thuo Gathi, 'Imperialism, Colonialism and International Law' (2007) 54 BLR 1013.

[29] Antonio Gramsci, *Selections from the Prison Notebook of Antonio Gramsci* (International Publishers 1971).

[30] Deborah D Avant, Martha Finnermore and Susan K Sell, *Who Governs the Globe* (Cambridge University Press 2010); Ted Hopf, 'Common-Sense Constructivism and Hegemony in World Politics' (2013) 67 IO 317.

[31] Wendt (n 14) 391.

[32] Syed Akhter and Paul Pounder, 'Economic Globalization and Caribbean Economies: Competitive Development, Strategic Response and Performance' (2008) 1 GSJ 69; See also Jean Frederic Morin and E Richard Gold, 'International Socialization at the State and Individual Levels: Mixed Evidence from Intellectual Property' (2016) 29 CRIA 1375, (where the authors establish that institutional facts on IP in developing countries are also influenced by the foreign education of some of their citizenry).

[33] Wolfgang Sachs, 'The Sustainable Development Goals and Laudato si: Varieties of Post-Development?' (2017) 38 TWQ 2573.

across jurisdictions, which the south, in turn, in finding a discursive fit with their ideas,[34] accepts, and legitimates.[35] Many IP laws are accepted in the global south without rational consideration of the practical workings of the rules in the domestic jurisdiction.[36] As I later explain in the context of GIs, the notion of GIs as assets of rural or economic development is a European-designed construct that is *accepted* in many Third World countries, but is not guaranteed to work in the south.

In problematising the IP and development divide from TWAIL-Constructivist reasonings, three dynamics stand out. The first is that international IP is a western construct[37] that has been transplanted in the Third World through colonisation, and legitimated, including through the process of decolonisation.[38] The positions of powerful actors are internalised to the global south through multilateral, bilateral and regional trade agreements, and knowledge transfusion mechanisms such as the foreign education of locals.[39] These mechanisms of diffusion[40] position Third World regions as recipients of IP rules and norms. Increased representation of the Third World in international IP and trade fora has been noticeable in recent years[41] but not in a way that impacts the development and construction of the scope of IP rules. The TRIPS negotiation was

---

[34] Margaret E Keck and Kathryn Sikkink, 'Transnational Advocacy Networks in International and Regional Politics' (1999) 51 ISJ 89; Martha Finnermore and Kathryn Sikkink, 'International Norm Dynamics and Political Change' (1998) 52 IO 887.

[35] E Richard Gold and Jean Frederic Morin, 'An Integrated Model of Legal Transplantation: The Diffusion of Intellectual Property Law in Developing Countries' (2014) 58 ISQ 781.

[36] Ikechi Mgbeoji, 'The Comprador Complex: Africa's IPR Elite, Neo-Colonialism and the Enduring Control of African IPR Agenda by External Interests' (2014) 26 IPJ 26.

[37] Martii Koskenniemi, 'The Politics of International Law 20 Years Later' (2009) 20 EJIL 7; Martii Koskenniemi, 'Histories of International Law: Significance and Problems for a Critical View' (2013) TICLJ 215.

[38] James Thuro Gathii, *War Commerce and International Law* (Oxford University Press 2009).

[39] See Gold and Morin (n 35) 1375 discussing the formation of institutional facts on IP in developing countries and how this can be shaped by local individuals who were schooled in western institutions); see also Mgbeoji (n 36) 313.

[40] Gregory Shaffer, 'Transnational Legal Process and State Change' (2012) 37 LSI 229.

[41] For example, there is marked representation from several developing countries in WIPO's Intergovernmental Committee on Intellectual Property and Genetic Resources, Traditional Knowledge and Folklore and in the Standing Committee on the Law of Trademarks, Industrial Design and Geographical Indications.

an example of this[42] and is now reflected in negotiations of IP provisions (or lack thereof) concerning many Third World countries in regional and bilateral trade agreements.[43] Although current participation of Third World groups in World Intellectual Property Organization (WIPO)-based fora on IP's structure and relevance in their economies has added a new horizon to this narrative, it has not changed the hegemonic paradigm.

Another dynamic is that many Third World countries have small and vulnerable economies.[44] In addition, they are net importers of IP[45] and they have a historically subjugated status in international relations. In many Third World economies, the domestic relevance of IP and innovation is still developing, and the major forms of IP laws are predominantly used by local elites and foreign entities.[46]

Finally, the Third World's ability to use IP effectively is often challenged by resource capacity issues and the inability to protect IP in international consumer markets. For example, high external debt loads, a sluggish economy, elevated levels of unemployment and low interest in innovation affect many Caribbean countries' ability to develop and commercialise IP.[47] The influential actors that shape IP rules also determine how and to what extent norm recipients (in this case the Third World) can use, create and benefit from IP. To many Third World countries, social and economic benefits from IP are one-sided gains in favour of the south.

---

42 Carolyn Deere, *The Implementation Game, The TRIPS Agreement and the Global Politics of Intellectual Property Reform in Developing Countries* (Oxford University Press 2009).

43 Note that the Caribbean had no significant input in the IP provisions of the Cariforum-EU Economic Partnership, a free trade agreement between 15 Caribbean countries and the European Union. The Caribbean also conducted no regional consultations on what these IP provisions would mean for the region. See Norman Girvan, 'Technification, Sweetification, Treatyfication: Politics of the Caribbean-EU Economic Partnership Agreement' (2010) 12 IJPS 100.

44 Indiana D Minto-Coy, 'Diasporas and Development: An Assessment of the Irish Experience for the Caribbean' (April 2009) The Caribbean Papers, Centre for International Governance Innovation <https://www.cigionline.org/sites/default/files/caribbean_paper_07-apr3.pdf>.

45 Gold and Morin (n 35).

46 Raj Bhala, 'Competitive Liberalization, Competitive Imperialism and Intellectual Property' (2007) 21 LLR 77; Miranda Forsyth, 'The Need for a Pluralist Approach to the Link between Intellectual Property and Development: A Pacific Island Case Study' (2016) 8 WIPOJ 123.

47 WIPO, 'Integrating Intellectual Property into Innovation Policy Formulation in Trinidad and Tobago' (May 2015) <http://www.wipo.int/edocs/pubdocs/en/wipo_report_inn_tt.pdf>.

A. The Space for the South in the IP and Development Debate

I use the term counterhegemony in this chapter to describe two different dimensions of change. The first concerns north–south relations. In that context, counterhegemony is defined as the capacity of the south to successfully push back against imperialistic[48] IP laws from the north. As such, successful counterhegemony enables the south to reshape hegemonic IP rules to be inclusive of social, economic and cultural interests, impacting local development. Where hegemonic rules widen the north–south gap, IP counterhegemony from the south upsets western constructed conventions of IP in practice, presenting instead an altered but reasoned perspective on IP.

The second dimension of IP counterhegemony is informed by TWAIL scholar Rajagopal's development from below, in which 'resistance'[49] by the south to how international law works is instrumental in overcoming challenges to the use of IP and innovation as agents of developmental goals. Counterhegemony from the south concerns tackling local political, cultural and economic mindsets of local elites and governing bodies that have perpetuated uneven distributions in income and social benefits. The chapter therefore recognises that several domestic actors and conditions, such as a country's ability to deal with the effects of climate change, the presence of corruption, and global economic crises impact local development.

The TRIPS Agreement recognises a correlation between IP rights and development,[50] cautioning World Trade Organization (WTO) members to consider the public policy implications of IP systems on socio-economic and technological development. Also, the WIPO Development Agenda[51] sought to position IP as a social and economic developmental tool for developing and least developed countries. WIPO's Development Agenda was an initiative with 45 recommendations[52] on how it could produce

---

48 Christopher May and Susan Sell, *Intellectual Property Rights, A Critical History* (Lynne Rienner Publishers 2005).

49 Rajagopal (n 9).

50 TRIPS, art 8(1) ('Members may, in formulating or amending their laws and regulations, adopt measures necessary to protect public health and nutrition, and to promote the public interest in sectors of vital importance to their socio-economic and technological development, provided that such measures are consistent with the provisions of this Agreement').

51 WIPO, 'WIPO Development Agenda' (2007) <http://www.wipo.int/ip-development/en/agenda/recommendations.html>.

52 The 45 recommendations are grouped into six clusters. Cluster A: Technical Assistance and Capacity Building; Cluster B: Norm-Setting, Flexibilities, Public

advantageous results for economies that would otherwise be challenged in accessing and developing IP.[53] Other development-based initiatives are used as platforms to integrate IP with development goals such as the United Nations Millennium Development Goals (MDGs).[54] The United Nations Sustainable Development Goals (SDGs) are the successor to the MDGs.[55] The SDGs represent the United Nations 2030 Agenda for Sustainable Development, encompassing several people-centred objectives to end global human and economic deprivation over the next 12 years.

There are three pillars of the SDGs that are pertinent to IP counterhegemony in the south. TRIPS created norms and rules for the protection and enforcement of various forms of IP in WTO member countries. Over time, some rules governing the workings of IP have changed[56] although the majority have not. Since global IP rules do change, it is possible that rules may at some point reflect counterhegemonic attitudes towards how IP works in the Third World. The prospects of counterhegemony by IP's integration with development may be realised through the SDGs of decent work and economic growth,[57] fostering industries, innovation and infrastructure,[58] reducing inequality within and among countries and by building strategic partnerships.[59] Who and what informs the policies of SDG objectives are important in determining whether they are beneficial to Third World countries.[60] Development strategies that

---

Policy and the Public Domain; Cluster C: Technology Transfer, Information and Communication Technology and Access to Knowledge; Cluster D: Assessments, Evaluation and Impact Studies; Cluster E: Institutional Matters including Mandate and Governance; and Cluster F: Other Issues.

[53] Jeremy de Beer (ed), *Implementing the World Intellectual Property Organization's Development Agenda* (Wilfrid Laurier University Press 2009).

[54] See Mac Darrow, 'The Millennium Development Goals: Milestones or Millstones? Human Rights Priorities for the Post-2015 Development Agenda' (2014) 15 YHRDLJ 55.

[55] UN, 'United Nations Sustainable Development Goals' (January 2016) <http://www.undp.org/content/undp/en/home/sustainable-development-goals.html>.

[56] For example, amendments to TRIPS compulsory licensing rules to recognise greater latitude for least developing countries in accessing essential medicines. WTO, 'WTO IP Rules Amended to Ease Poor Countries' Access to Affordable Medicines' WTO News (2017) <https://www.wto.org/english/news_e/news17_e/trip_23jan17_e.html>.

[57] UN (n 55) Goal 8.

[58] Ibid Goal 9.

[59] Ibid Goal 10 and Goal 17. IP is implicated in other SDGs but the chapter focuses on these specific development goals.

[60] Per Bergling and Sophie Jin, 'The New Black on the Development Catwalk: Incorporating Rule of Law into the Sustainable Development Goals' (2015) 24(3) WILJ 435.

are designed from a western perspective are unlikely to meet SDG objectives. Neither can development-oriented strategies, designed in the Third World, but from a local-elite perspective.[61] If the policies geared towards SDGs bear little actual relevance to development concerns in most Third World communities it will be very difficult for SDG objectives to be met. Theoretically, finding common ground between IP and SDGs is not difficult. The promotion of 'sustained, inclusive and sustainable economic growth, full and productive employment and decent work for all'[62] is an ideal that is implicitly reflected in TRIPS governing principles, and in work done by WIPO's Standing Committee on Development and Intellectual Property.[63] In the context of TRIPS, one of its guiding principles recognises the public policy objectives served by IP rules that promote development objectives.[64] These principles are reflected in specific activities of the TRIPS Council,[65] such as extending the transition of least developed countries' transition to TRIPS to 2021,[66] and in promoting interest in IP and innovation among firms in WTO countries.[67] Development-oriented objectives are also stated as a guiding principle in regional trade agreements such as the Cotonou Agreement between African Caribbean and Pacific countries and Europe, including in its IP chapter.[68] Similar assertions of an IP link with SDG objectives relate to the goal of building resilient infrastructure, promoting inclusive and sustainable industrialisation and fostering innovation.[69] Since an IP-intensive society promotes the conceptualisation of IP from an innovative perspective,[70] finding theoretical intersections between this SDG objective and IP is not far-fetched.

The real issue lies in whether commitment by the south to SDG

---

61 Escobar (n 10).

62 UN (n 55) Goal 8.

63 WIPO, Committee on Development and Intellectual Property, 'Twenty-First Session' (2018) CDIP/ 21.

64 TRIPS, preamble.

65 The TRIPS Council is the body that administers TRIPS.

66 WTO, 'Responding to Least Developed Countries' Special Needs in Intellectual Property' (2013) <https://www.wto.org/english/tratop_e/trips_e/ldc_e.htm>.

67 WTO, 'Extract from Minutes of Meeting of the Council for Trade-related Aspects of Intellectual Property Rights', (1–2 March 2017) <https://www.wto.org/english/tratop_e/trips_e/14_ip_and_innovation_inclusive_innovation_and_msme_collaboration_ip_85a1.pdf>.

68 Cotonou Agreement (signed 23 June 2000, revised 25 June 2005).

69 UN (n 55) Goal 9.

70 Ibid Goal 10.

goals through IP can narrow the gap in how IP rules have worked in its economies. SDG goal 10 brings the political, cultural, legal and economic differences between the north and south into perspective, calling for the reduction of inequality within and between countries.[71] Inequality between the north and south is a crucial consideration in whether narrowing the gap in the IP and development divide is even possible. Although there is interest in[72] and domestic use of some aspects of IP in the Third World, the south remains a vast receptacle for the protection of foreign-based and local elite-interests IP. In this context, IP is inherently biased against the south, whether based on capacity issues or jurisdictional ill-fit.[73] For example, a Third World country may have a policy that permits patent applicants one year to file a patent after public disclosure. However, lacklustre domestic business interest in inventions, or an inefficient IP eco-system may prevent domestic participants from filing patents.[74] Finding synergies between IP and SDG goals is far from the conclusion of the whole matter. Accessing and developing IP on terms amenable to Third World countries' interests, socio-economic and legal capacity may help to reduce inequalities between the north and south. In the context of IP, these inequalities may be related to income, gender gaps, number of viable domestic IP industries, and capacity to create and innovate. The goal of reducing inequalities within and among countries[75] is best integrated with objectives of promoting decent work and economic growth[76] and building industries, innovation and infrastructure,[77] and incorporated with meaningful representation from Third World groups.

The prospects of IP working for the south in a TRIPS-Plus charged global order is only possible when the south owns IP and has sustainable international markets for its commercialisation.[78] As a potential aid to development, IP counterhegemony implicates the involvement of internal

---

71 Ibid.

72 Graham Dutfield, 'TK Unlimited: The Emerging but Incoherent International Law of Traditional Knowledge Protection' (2017) 20 JWIP 144; Margo A Bagley, 'Illegal Designs? Enhancing Cultural and Genetic Resource Protection through Design Law' (2017) Centre for International Governance Innovation, Paper No 155.

73 Srividhya Ragavan, 'Drugs, Drugs Everywhere but not just for the Poor' (2016) 8 WIPO 41; Mgbeoji (n 36).

74 WIPO (n 47) 33.

75 UN (n 55) Goal 10.

76 Ibid Goal 8.

77 Ibid Goal 9.

78 See Susy Frankel, *Geographical Indications and Mega-Regional Trade Agreements and Negotiations* in Calboli and Ng-Loy (n 4).

and external actors and interests. As the next sections of the chapter show, the actors that influence the direction of a set of IP rules may also influence the extent of Third World engagement with IP. In some instances, IP engagement is of little significance on a domestic level and used mostly by foreign firms or local elites. In this setting, IP is compromised and does little to meet SDG development objectives.

Below, the prospects of counterhegemony upsetting the IP–development divide is evaluated in the context of the move to make GIs a mainstream form of IP in developing countries that is closely associated with developmental objectives.

IV. THE SOCIAL AND LEGAL CONSTRUCT OF GEOGRAPHICAL INDICATIONS AS ASSETS OF IP DEVELOPMENT

A. GIs: What They Are

The politics and play of the international law of GIs places a practical dimension on the theoretical assertions made in the earlier segments of the chapter. GIs are signs or symbols used on products to convey a special relationship between the product and its territory of origin.[79] GIs embody a relationship with the product's territory that is inseparable from the product itself. The distinctiveness of the product, whether its taste or style, are imbued with know-how that is not easily replicated elsewhere, based on natural or human characteristics specific to the territory or region.[80]

The chapter's discussion is concerned with non-wine and spirit GIs. Since TRIPS mandates for extensive protection to wine and spirit GIs, there is greater protection and global consensus for these types of products.[81] Non-wine and spirit GIs include food and agricultural products, fisheries, forestry items, furniture and artisan items such as handicrafts. As such, Café de Colombia (coffee) from Colombia, Jamaica Jerk from Jamaica, Prosciutto di Parma (Parma Ham from Italy), Kashmiri

---

79 TRIPS, art 22.1; Calboli and Ng-Loy (n 4); Michael Blakeney, *The Protection of Geographical Indications: Law and Practice* (Edward Elgar Publishing 2014); Gangjee, (n 4).

80 Blakeney (n 79); Tarim Kumar Datta, 'Darjeeling Tea, India, Food and Agriculture Organization'<http://www.fao.org/docrep/013/i1592e/i1592e03.pdf>.

81 See Justin Malbon, Charles Lawson and Mark Davison, *The WTO Agreement on Trade-Related Aspects of Intellectual Property Rights, A Commentary* (Edward Elgar Publishing 2014).

pashminas from India are all examples of GIs. GIs are a European construct, originating in France's aim to prevent the usurpation of specialty wines in its territory.[82] Various strands of protection have developed for GIs under instruments such as the Stresa Convention on Cheese, and internationally with treaties such as the Madrid Agreement,[83] the Paris Convention[84] and the Geneva Act of the Lisbon Agreement.[85] Article 22 of TRIPS lays out legal safeguards which all WTO members should incorporate into their domestic laws for the protection of GIs.

The provision to which agricultural and food-based GIs look for basic protection specifies that GIs should be protected against acts of unfair competition, and against actions which mislead the public as to the true geographical origin of goods.[86]

Geographical indications relating to neither wine nor spirits are protected in WTO countries through various legal means. Certification or collective marks, unfair competition laws or a *sui generis* system of protection are means that different legal regimes use to recognise non-wine and spirit GIs.[87] Except for a *sui generis* GI system that allows for a targeted approach to the rules and laws on GIs, certification and collective marks, unfair competition laws, or the common law are inadequate tools to promote GIs as developmental assets in the Third World. Certification and collective marks are trademark rights that are limited in duration, usually renewable every 10 or 15 years.[88] By their definition and classification as trademark rights, certification and collective marks are limited forms of protection for GIs. Although when GIs are registered as certification marks, the mark conveys that the product is produced, based on specific processing methods, or bears some significance to its place of origin, there are limitations to its protection.[89]

---

82 Valdim Mandrov, *European Union Law on Indications of Geographical Origin* (Springer 2014); Marsha Echols, *Geographical Indications for Food Products* (2nd edn, Wolters Kluwer 2014).

83 Madrid Agreement for the Repression of False or Deceptive Indications of Source on Goods (adopted 14 April 1891).

84 Paris Convention (n 15).

85 Lisbon Agreement (n 15).

86 TRIPS, art 22.2.

87 See Christine Haight Farley, 'Looking Beyond the Known Story: How the Prehistory of Protection of Geographical Indications in the Americas Provides an Alternate Approach' in Calboli and Ng Loy (n 4).

88 See Trade Mark Act 1985 (Canada), s 46(1); European Commission, Regulation (EU) 2017/1001, art 52.

89 *Ontario Dental Assistants Association v Canadian Dental Association* 2013 FCA 279; Trade Marks Act 1985 (Canada), s 23; David W Barnes, 'Classification

Ownership of certification marks is restricted to a single entity or person who has responsibility for monitoring the mark but cannot be involved in commercialising the mark.[90] Collective marks are used by associations or cooperatives to identify their products or services. For example, a real estate association may use a collective mark that enables members of the association to use the mark in their business dealings. If GIs are registered as certification or collective marks, the division of responsibilities between the user and owner of the mark may frustrate the success of business ventures, especially for small-sized enterprises. For example, if the owner of the mark is interested in exploring global markets or brand development initiatives that differ from its licensees' choices, the licensee may have limited ability to change such course of action.[91] Trademarks can be cancelled, declared invalid or used as parts of competitors' marks if there is no likelihood of confusion between both products.[92] If there are qualified terms that differentiate a competitor's trademark product from the place-based product, the competitor cannot be prevented from using the same name on its products, though both products are in the same product class. For example, Gorgonzola is registered as an Italian-oriented GI cheese in the European Union.[93] In the United States and other jurisdictions without similar expansive frameworks or agreements for safeguarding GI rights,[94] it is possible for cheese producers to use name derivatives of 'Gorgonzola' without any successful claims of infringements.[95] When GI-intensive industries have few or no established markets locally or internationally, registration of products as certification or collective marks is likely to prevent the product from distinguishing its presence in the consumer markets.

---

of Marks' in David W Barnes, *Trademark and Unfair Competition Law: Cases and Problems in an Intellectual Property Context* (Wolters Kluwer 2014).

[90] See the Lanham Act (US); *Board-Tech Elec Co v Eaton Elec Holdings LLC* (2017) 1:17-cv-5028 (SDNY).

[91] An example of this is Blue Mountain coffee's registration in its domestic jurisdiction as a certification mark, governed by a state-controlled coffee board. This body, along with the other government agencies, makes exclusive regulation and policies for the use of the mark by licensees.

[92] Teresa Scassa, *Canadian Trademark Law* (2nd edn, Lexis Nexis 2015).

[93] EC, 'Agricultural and Rural Development DOOR database' (1996) <http://ec.europa.eu/agriculture/quality/door/registeredName.html?denominationId=331>.

[94] In the United States, certification and collective marks are trade mark rights and governed by the Lanham Act.

[95] For example, Belgioioso Gorgonzola is a registered trademark of a cheese manufactured in the United States.

Another distinguishing characteristic concerns the purpose of trademark rights versus the objectives of GIs. Trademarks are indications of source and are highly commercial in nature, providing IP protection for goods or services used in the course of trade. GIs may have objectives that cannot be met by their classification as certification or collective marks. These objectives include preserving manufacturing methods passed down through generations[96] or preserving unique plant and land sites used in the production of distinct products. Although these objectives may have economic significance, they are centred on cultural preservation or nation branding through commercially exploiting traditional products.

Owners of GI rights cannot be precluded from commercialising their designations. GIs are collective rights which must be owned by a group of firms, producers or entities, usually called a collective. Similar to certification or collective marks (trademark rights), the users of GI designations are entitled to make, advertise and sell GI products. Unlike trademark rights, GI rights that are protected either by a *sui generis* system or recognised on an expansive basis allow rights holders considerable latitude in the safeguard of their products. These expansive rights may include the right to exclude competitors from using any translation of the product name on their products, and the right to prevent competitors from using terms such as 'similar to', 'styled', 'like' and other such references on their products. Other fully fledged rights that may be given to GIs include indefinite protection against generic-ness and cancellations.[97] In terms of unfair competition, the safeguard provided by unfair competition laws to GIs is very limited. If the consumer is liable to be misled by the GI competitor's product, the GI rights holder may find protection under unfair competition laws. Unfair competition provisions in domestic legislation also cover GIs if a competitor's product uses a designation to falsely indicate that its product is from the GI territory. On the multilateral level, the expanse of protection that is conferred upon wine and spirit GIs is not available to those which are not of the vinicultural variety.[98]

---

96 The domestic-focused French law on Geographical Indications Protecting Industrial Products and Crafts aims to protect traditional products that have high cultural values that are linked to their specific place of origin in France.

97 See WIPO, 'China: Measures for the Administration of Geographical Indications' (2007) <http://www.wipo.int/wipolex/en/text.jsp?file_id=182476>.

98 Malbon et al (n 81).

B. Why GIs Matter to the IP and Development Narrative

The concept of GIs has as much to do with the product–place connection as it does with the identities and interest which influence GI norms within and across jurisdictions. To many Third World countries, GIs have the potential to become development assets.[99] An IP development asset is an intangible commodity that rights holders have commercialised to produce socio-economic returns that have more than minimal spill-over effects on more than one sector of the economy.[100] If the commercialisation of GIs positively impacts producer communities and has more than a *de minimis* cross-sectoral effect on the Third World, then GIs could be IP development assets. But is this the case?

The European Union is relevant to the knowledge paradigm of GIs as IP assets of development. The European Union was among the main supporters for the inclusion of GI protection in TRIPS negotiations. The Doha Development Agenda among WTO members[101] on GIs, to increase the protection level of non-wine and spirit GIs was prolifically supported by the European Union.[102] The initiative failed, and the European Union sought non-multilateral means of GI norm diffusion, including to the south. Over the past ten years, the European Union has defined and packaged GIs to the south as an IP development mechanism. France invented the forerunner to the term 'geographical indications' by enacting a law that recognised and protected place-based wines that were renowned for their quality based on their territory of region.[103] The region, under the Paris Convention, later recognised as protectable place-based products, although no definition for these products was provided in the Convention.[104] Although WIPO and Paris Convention negotiations in the mid 1970s sought to create a legal system for the protection of GIs, there

---

[99] This perspective is under scrutiny in Canada, a developed country but with recent introduction to GIs. Marsha Simone Cadogan, 'Making Agricultural and Food based Geographical Indications Work in Canada' (2018) Centre for International Governance Innovation, Policy Brief 125.

[100] Daniela Benaventa, *The Economics of Geographical Indications* (Graduate Institute Publications 2013); World Intellectual Property Report, 'Intangible Capital In Global Value Chains' (2017).

[101] WTO, 'TRIPS: Geographical Indicators – Background and the Current Situation' (2008) <https://www.wto.org/english/tratop_e/trips_e/gi_background_e.htm>.

[102] Mandrov (n 82); Echols (n 82).

[103] Paul Roubier, *Le Droit de la propriete industrielle* (2nd Vol, Librairie du Recueil Sirey 1954) 722, 753.

[104] Mandrov (n 82).

was no success in the negotiations because of lack of consensus among the parties.[105] TRIPS adopted the WIPO's suggested name for GI products, incorporating that GIs are 'indications that identify a good as originating in a WTO country, where a given quality, reputation or other characteristics of the good is essentially attributable to its geographic origin'.[106]

The European Union has over 700 registered protected GIs on file, for which it has obtained, and continues to seek, international market access and reciprocity of protection in foreign markets.[107] Of this number of European Union GIs, at least 170 are currently seeking protection in the Caribbean via the Cariforum-EPA preferential free trade agreement.[108] GIs are economically valuable IP resources in the European Union, valued at more than 54 billion Euros.[109] The products that are recognisable as GIs in the European Union include dairy, sausages, nuts, fruits, baked goods and beer.[110] Many of these products have gained worldwide recognition including Feta cheese from Greece, Prosciutto di Parma from Italy and Ravioli di Dauphine (pasta) from France.

The EU governance model regulation seeks to create agricultural and economic development for EU producers and communities through GIs.[111] EU GIs are promoted as valuable products with distinctive qualities traceable by their connection with the culture, history and know-how of EU peoples. The European Union's GI Regulation contains several development-oriented goals aimed at achieving a strong GI policy. These include improvements in employment targets for farmers, better incomes, and rural development objectives. Innovative and creative ways of linking the product–place connection with IP are noticeable in the European Union's GI Regulation. As an example, registered GI products cannot become generic.[112] A generic name is one which is regularly associated with a class of product, such as ketchup for all types of sweetened tomato sauce. If a GI cannot become generic it is accorded a premium status in

---

105 TRIPS, art 22.1.

106 Ibid.

107 Frankel (n 78).

108 EC, 'Overview of Economic Partnership Agreements' (March 2018) <http://trade.ec.europa.eu/doclib/docs/2009/september/tradoc_144912.pdf>.

109 EC, 'Value of Production of Agricultural Products and Foodstuffs, Wines, Aromatized Wines and Spirits Protected by a Geographical Indication' (October 2012) <http://ec.europa.eu/agriculture/external-studies/value-gi_en.htm>.

110 Agricultural and Rural Development DOOR Database (n 93).

111 EU Regulation (EU) 1151/2012 on Quality Schemes for Agricultural Products and Foodstuffs [2012] OJ L 343/1 (EU Regulation on Quality Schemes for Agricultural Products and Foodstuffs).

112 Ibid art 13(2).

consumer markets and in the eyes of competitors. Essentially, to be non-generic is a value-advantage for EU GI products, which helps to increase revenue share in domestic and foreign consumer markets.

The European Union's perspective on place-based foods and agricultural products surfaces in various initiatives such as its Common Agricultural Policy (CAP). The CAP aims to promote agricultural innovation among farmers and provide sustainable income means.[113] These ideas on GIs are reflected in how the European Union presents GIs to the south. Influencing how GIs are conceptualised by the south is also a mandate of the European Union's GI policy.[114] Attempts to secure GIs as lucrative IP assets is evidenced by their inclusion in the European Union's foreign trade policy. Expansive EU-GI provisions in bilateral and regional trade agreements are more evident in EU agreements with the Third World than they are with other regions. As an example, the Cariforum-EC-EPA (the EPA) required Caribbean countries to implement domestic GI legislation by 1 January 2014.[115] This was not a requirement of the European Union's preferential free trade agreement with Canada, neither could it have been, given that fewer power differences exist between the two parties.

Some Third World countries are provided technical assistance in incorporating GIs with rural development goals, or in the drafting of GI regulations. In this direction, Switzerland and the European Union have been instrumental facilitators.[116] To Third World countries that have accepted GIs,[117] they are imagined as opportunities for 'owning IP', thereby placing a noticeable dent in the imperialistic culture of the foreign ownership of IP in domestic markets. As much as GIs have been accepted by many Third World communities as IP assets of development, the challenges of establishing sustainable GI markets for Third World products creates a hurdle to developmental goals.

---

[113] For a critique of the CAP, see Apostolos G Papadopoulos, 'The Impact of the CAP on Agriculture and Rural Areas of EU Member States' (2015) 4 J Pol Econ 22.

[114] See EU and AU Commission, 'Creating Value through Geographical Indications: The Power of Origin – Workshop on Geographical Indications' (2011) <https://ec.europa.eu/agriculture/events/gi-africa-2011_en>; Go-Jamaica, 'EU Supports use of Geographical Indications in Jamaica' (2015) <http://go-jamaica.com/pressrelease/item.php?id=5089>.

[115] EU Economic Partnership Agreement [2008] OJ L 289/I/3 (EU Economic Partnership).

[116] Jamaica Intellectual Property Office, 'Geographical Indication Manual' (April 2015) <https://www.jipo.gov.jm/sites/default/files/PDF_Files/MANUALS/gimanual.pdf>.

[117] Go-Jamaica (n 114).

C. Narrowing the Development Divide in IP: The Caribbean's Experience with GIs

The EPA led several Caribbean countries to enact domestic GI laws.[118] This has not created a GI culture as significant gaps remain in envisioning GIs as IP assets of development in the region.

Three Caribbean countries have local GI legislation. Guyana's Sugar Company has applied for the registration of Demerara sugar; in Trinidad and Tobago, a group of cocoa producers filed an application for the GI registration of cocoa; and in Jamaica several jerk seasoning producers have registered Jamaica Jerk as a GI.[119] So far, Jamaica Jerk is the first and only food-based product to have secured GI registration in the Caribbean. The Caribbean region is still in the process of finalising which EU-based GIs to protect as part of the EPA agreement.[120] Based on the vast difference in numbers between EU- and Caribbean-based GIs, the region will likely continue the trend of being (at least for the short and medium term) a protector of foreign-based rights.

To do well as an IP asset of development, GIs need the right eco-system.[121] Fostering decent work and economic growth are the focus points of SDG 8. Whether GI industries can foster decent work and economic growth in the south depends on several factors. GIs can also be a development-oriented query under SDG 9 and 10, fostering innovation and reducing inequalities through infrastructure and cross-sectoral interventions to deal with disparities. Low domestic stakeholder involvement in the sustenance of GI designations, a registered product that does not resonate well with consumers, corruption, climate change, difficulties in penetrating foreign markets, and financial constraints in monitoring GI designations in global consumer markets are all real risks to GI industries.

---

118 Girvan (n 43) 100.

119 Stabroeknews, 'Guyana seeking to register Demerara as geographical indication' (December 2016) <https://www.stabroeknews.com/2016/news/stories/12/02/guyana-seeking-register-demerara-geographical-indication/>; Loop, 'Local Cocoa Farmers File Geographical Indication for T&T Cocoa Beans' (February 2017) <http://www.looptt.com/content/local-cocoa-farmers-file-geographical-indication-tt-cocoa-beans>.

120 EC, 'Overview of Economic Partnership Agreements' (2018). <http://trade.ec.europa.eu/doclib/docs/2009/september/tradoc_144912.pdf>.

121 Teshager Dagne, *Intellectual Property and Traditional Knowledge in the Global Economy: Translating Geographical Indications for Development* (Routledge 2014); Calboli and Ng-Loy (n 4); Bassem Awad and Marsha S Cadogan, 'CETA and the Future of Geographical Indication Protection in Canada' (2017) Centre for International Governance Innovation Paper No 171.

Who constructs GI rules impacts how GIs work in domestic jurisdictions. Data on the Caribbean's first GI, Jamaica Jerk, is new and incomplete. I compiled the Blue Mountain coffee data between 2011 and 2016 as empirical research conducted on the feasibility of using Blue Mountain coffee as a GI asset of development in Jamaica and the Caribbean.[122] Blue Mountain is often associated with a distinct characteristic, and history positions the product as a product–place connection of the Caribbean.[123] The coffee is cultivated and produced across three territorial zones in Jamaica and is exported predominantly to Japan.[124] Over the past decade, the Coffee Industry Board (CIB), the governing body for the coffee industry in the country, has secured new export contracts in coffee markets in China and the United States. Its premium price, tradition of distinct taste in foreign markets and established characteristics sourced from its *terroir* are all tenets of what GIs should embody.

However, domestic and international barriers constrain the ability of Blue Mountain coffee as an IP asset of development in Jamaica.[125] Although there is interest in GI registration, the actors that stand to benefit from the registration are not coffee farmers, but the coffee processors and distributors. Most of the 6,000 coffee farmers involved in the cultivation of Blue Mountain coffee in Jamaica are small farmers and receive fluctuating but steadily low income from its cultivation.[126]

The main actors in the Blue Mountain coffee chain are the CIB, farmers, licensed dealers and coffee distributors. Small farmers often complain of difficulty in clearing fields after droughts, hurricanes and bush fires as major environmental challenges that affect crop yields.[127] Low levels of government assistance to purchase fertilisers impact the quality and quantity of coffee beans. Complaints of favouritism in how subsidies are distributed is also a concern of farmers. Several coffee cultivators have abandoned their fields because of these difficulties. Knowledge of IP,

---

[122] Marsha S Cadogan, 'Geographical Indications and Development in the Third World: Towards a Functional Approach of Intellectual Property Rights in Jamaica – The Case of Blue Mountain Coffee' (Doctorate Dissertation, York University 2016). This chapter visits the issue from an innovative lens and queries whether non-tourism-based industries can foster growth in GI industries in the Caribbean.

[123] WIPO, 'In Search of a Perfect Cup' (2010) <http://www.wipo.int/ipadvantage/en/details.jsp?id=2612>.

[124] The Jamaica Agricultural Commodities Regulatory Authority, 'Industry Statistics' <http://www.ciboj.org/index/industry-statistics>.

[125] The product is registered as a trademark in its domestic jurisdiction.

[126] Cadogan (n 122).

[127] Ibid.

investments in development and of how IP drives innovation in agriculture and commerce are significant aids to development. Many small-scale Blue Mountain coffee farmers are not knowledgeable about GIs. There are also integration and communication gaps between the CIB, small-scale farmers and the Jamaica Intellectual Property Office (JIPO), which makes a sustainable development target and coherent policy difficult.[128]

Three crucial points need to be addressed before Blue Mountain coffee (Jamaica's strongest candidate for GI protection) can become an asset of development with real potential of narrowing the IP and development divide. The first concerns the sale of small leased coffee plots to mega-coffee entrepreneurs, who, through denationalisation, now account for most of the preferred Blue Mountain coffee land holdings in Jamaica. In effect, many small farmers can no longer use the land to earn or complement their income from coffee cultivation. Second, licensed dealers earn more than small-scale Blue Mountain coffee farmers. If small farmers become licensed dealers, the potential for earning more would significantly increase. However, according to the Act governing Blue Mountain coffee cultivation (Coffee Industry Regulation Act),[129] a licensed dealer must produce 6,000 boxes per year, verifiable by three years of records.[130] The obstacle is clear. Lack of capital to maintain coffee fields and environmental disasters hinder many Blue Mountain coffee farmers from scaling up to meet this target.[131] Third, the lack of interaction between small-scale coffee farmers and medium- and large-scale farmers suggests that the prospective GI scheme will not be inclusive. Most small-scale Blue Mountain coffee farmers prefer to work independently.[132] There is also the perception that the large-scale farmers have no interest in collaborating with low-level farmers. With this socio-political mindset, membership of a Blue Mountain coffee GI producer group will likely be heavily concentrated with local elite coffee entrepreneurs setting norms that impact the entire industry.[133]

The Caribbean's ability to use GIs as a developmental tool also depends on GI reciprocity in global markets, domestic innovation, and its financial ability to defend designations in domestic and international jurisdictions. An integrated approach to GI market and product development may help to diversify domestic GI strategy towards international consumer markets

---

128 UN (n 55) Goal 17.
129 The Coffee Industry Regulation Act 1948 (Jamaica).
130 Ibid s 2.
131 Cadogan (n 122).
132 Ibid.
133 Ibid.

that offer reciprocal protection for GIs. GI reciprocity does not guarantee GI registration in foreign markets.[134] However, there is greater potential for success for GI products in jurisdictions that offer similar levels of protection than for those that enter global markets as trademarks. The treatment of Basmati rice in the United States exemplifies this point. India's GI registration of Basmati rice does not prevent US businesses from using the name, its translations or extensions thereof on labels and packaging.

With innovation and full recognition of GI rights in the region's major consumer markets for GI products, GIs are more likely to become established internationally. CARICOM's[135] major consumer market for its products include the United States, Canada and the United Kingdom.[136] GIs are not treated uniformly in these markets. The Comprehensive Economic and Trade Agreement between Canada and the European Union led Canada to protect GIs under its Trade Marks Act.[137] Despite this there are still hurdles to cross for foreign GI holders, including those from Jamaica and the Caribbean. A Caribbean GI rights holder will find that its product cannot become generic in EU markets[138] but can be cancelled in Canada; if it has little or no popularity in foreign markets as a GI, the product will have to pass the likelihood of confusion test with prior or pending trademarks.[139] Among the factors to be considered are the length of time the GI is associated with the product in the Caribbean and the extent to which it is known in Canada. These are real barriers to newly established GIs in Canada, including prospective foreign rights holders. This does not prevent the registration of the product in Canada as a certification trademark.[140]

The United States offers limited protection for products with place-based connections as certification or collective marks. It follows that full-scale protection of GI names is not available in the United States, and, like trademarks, they are susceptible to opposition, including cancellations.[141]

---

134 Frankel (n 78).

135 CARICOM is the acronym for Caribbean Community. It is a regional body that represents 20 Caribbean countries that work together on economic integration, foreign policy, human and social development and security.

136 CARICOM, 'CARICOM's Top 10 Trading Partners' (2014) <http://caricomstats.info/tradsysonline/PDF_Reports/report8.pdf>.

137 Trade Marks Act, R.S., 1985, c. T-13 (Canada).

138 EU Regulation on Quality Schemes for Agricultural Products and Foodstuffs.

139 Trade Marks Act (Canada), s 11.3–11.4.

140 Ibid ss 23–25.

141 See Farley (87).

A post-Brexit[142] United Kingdom will be an interesting jurisdiction to watch for GI reciprocity as nationally, the United Kingdom protects GIs through trademark rights[143] or by passing-off legislation.[144] Unless domestic GI laws are put in place on the same level as the European Union's GI regulation in the UK, prospective GI rights holders seeking registration in the United Kingdom will have limited protection in that jurisdiction. A GI market penetration strategy for Caribbean products may be constrained by established trademarks in Canada[145] and the United States or in markets where the name is not known.

Differences in the definitions of GIs among the Caribbean and major international jurisdictions is another area of concern. GI reciprocity not only means that there is similar protection of GIs between countries, but also that there is agreed consensus as to what products can be protected under the designation. Using examples from Trinidad and Tobago,[146] Jamaica,[147] Canada[148] and the European Union, variations in what constitutes a GI are shown. In Trinidad and Tobago, a GI good is a natural or agricultural product, or any product of handicraft or industry.[149] Jamaica describes GIs in the same manner.[150] These definitions allow for products from the nutraceutical industry such as cannabis-derived medicines, other products derived from herbs, and artisanal items such as handicrafts to obtain GI designations. However, unless the markets for these products are regional (CARICOM), there is limited success for these products if marketed as GIs in many jurisdictions. The European Commission's GI Regulation represents one of the most progressive regulatory frameworks for the protection of GIs.[151] However, the Regulation, though

---

142 Mark Mimler, 'The Effect of Brexit on Trademarks, Designs and Other "Europeanized" Areas of Intellectual Property Law in the United Kingdom' in Oonagh Fitzgerald and Eva Lein (eds), *Complexity's Embrace: The International Law Implications of Brexit* (McGill-Queens University Press 2018).

143 Trade Marks Act 1994 (UK), ss 49–50 and schs 1–2. See also *Robyn Rihanna Fenty v Arcadia Group Brands Ltd* [2013] EWHC 2310 (Ch).

144 Luke McDonagh, 'Where Brexit's Bold Slogan Falls Flat' (2018) Centre for International Governance Innovation <https://www.cigionline.org/articles/where-brexits-bold-slogans-fall-flat>.

145 *MC Imports v AFOD Ltd* (2016) FCA 60.

146 Trinidad and Tobago Geographical Indications Act 1996, s 2.

147 The Protection of Geographical Indications Act 2004 (Jamaica).

148 Trade Marks Act 1985 (Canada).

149 Trinidad and Tobago Geographical Indications Act 1996, s 2.

150 The Protection of Geographical Indications Act 2004 (Jamaica), s 2(1).

151 EU Regulation on Quality Schemes for Agricultural Products and Foodstuffs.

broad, covers only agricultural products and foodstuffs.[152] In Canada GIs for non-wine products are restricted to agricultural products and foodstuffs.[153] Herbs, artisanal goods and other non-food- and wine-based products would be unprotectable as GIs in these markets, including in the United States, and covered under trademark laws (if registrable). If a diversified market penetration strategy is followed, these jurisdictions may consider developing export markets in countries such as Switzerland and India. Switzerland and India's GI laws have one thing in common: products other than food, agricultural products or wine and spirits are GI registrable.[154] These include items such as furniture, silk and pharmaceutical products, which have strong linkages to their place of origin.

D. TWAIL is also Reformist – IP Counterhegemony from the South

TWAIL-Constructivist reasoning recognises that the domestic impact of international IP laws may be positive if local game changers are representative of a diversified and inclusive group that are resilient in their actions.[155] This reformist tenet impacts who is involved in GI industries and how GI rules work in local communities. If GIs are to change who benefits from IP in the Caribbean and narrow the development divide, a lot more work needs to be done. Some issues are more easily dealt with than others. On the domestic level, involving actors at the lower end of the supply chain in both GI governance and product development may help create jobs with improved incomes. As an aspect of sustainable development, work includes the security of adequate wages and good working conditions. Restrictive GI rules may limit the ability of farmers to earn better incomes by excluding them from participating in GI schemes. Additionally, Blue Mountain coffee farmers affected by climate change endure severe hardship in crop management and are unable to participate in GI schemes.

When influential global actors, such as the European Union and

---

152 Ibid. This EU-wide Regulation is limited to foods and agri-products. Some EU countries may have national systems that recognise non-agricultural products as GIs, see Geographical Indications protecting Industrial Products and Crafts 2014 (France). Talks to expand the EU's GI Regulation to non-food and wine products started in 2011 but have not led to changes in the legislation.

153 Trade Marks Act 1985 (Canada), s 11.

154 Geographical Indication of Goods – Registration and Protection Act 1999 (India); Federal Act on the Protection of Trade Marks and Indications of Source 1992 (Switzerland).

155 Rajagopal (n 9).

Switzerland, position GIs as innovation, impactful outcomes may ensue.[156] These outcomes represent investments in development. For the global south, and specifically countries that are new to the concept and its practice, innovation should be at the forefront of national IP strategies. Domestic key stakeholders should consider how GI engagement can change the north–south dialogue from a fourth industrial revolution[157] perspective. If GIs are positioned as innovations in IP, the Caribbean can create GI synergies across various sectors therefore, capitalising on the region's unique natural, cultural resources and human talent. For example, integrating Trinidad's cocoa industry (GI) with initiatives such as tourism (service industry) and energy-inspired sports drinks (manufacturing industry) may create spill-over effects on at least three different industries in its economy. Besides tourism initiatives, a more integrated Blue Mountain coffee GI model in Jamaica should look to manufacturing environmentally friendly products from coffee wastes.

In promoting GIs as IP assets of development, the Caribbean should invent ways of using the by-product from the processing of GI products as advanced manufacturing materials for other products. For example, what is the feasibility of establishing a bio-fuel industry in Jamaica from its Blue Mountain coffee?[158] The biol-fuel[159] industry is an emerging vibrant market, which, as an alternative to traditional oil and gas industries, may be a valid investment. Can Guyana's quest to register Demerara sugar as a GI foster innovation if there is also a focus on developing sugar ethanol industries?[160] This may be helpful to include as a GI and IP strategy for Guyana since it will not be able to use the designation in the United States,

---

[156] Switzerland has strategically used its indication of source framework to foster the growth and recognition of various GI designations globally. Switzerland's GIs include the registration of indications of source, which broadens its protective base to include even pharmaceutical products that have a strong connection to its place of origin.

[157] Klaus Schaub, *The Fourth Industrial Revolution* (World Economic Forum 2016).

[158] The Guardian, 'Waste coffee grounds set to fuel London with bio-diesel and biomass pellets' (February 2014) <https://www.theguardian.com/sustainable-business/waste-coffee-grounds-fuel-london>.

[159] Mebrautue Haile, 'Integrated Volorization of Spent Coffees to Biofuels' (2014) 65 Biofuel Research Journal 2.

[160] Sugar cane ethanol is an alcohol-based fuel produced by the fermentation of sugarcane juice and molasses. Amir Zanca, Renato Vicentini, Fausto A Ortiz-Morea, Luiz EV Del Bem, Marcio J da Silva, Michel Vincentz and Fabio TS Nogueira, 'Identification and Expression Analysis of microRNAs and Targets in the Biofuel Crop Sugarcane' (2010) 10 BMC Plant Biology 260.

Canada or Mexico.[161] The Guyana Sugar Company (Guyana Sugar) was unsuccessful in registering 'Demerara sugar' as a trademark in Canada on the grounds that a Canadian-based business had already registered a trademark for a product of the same class. Guyana Sugar conceded to not use the name on its exports to the whole of North America.[162]

Another potential development is Jamaica's emerging nutraceutical industry. The Switzerland-Jamaica GI agreement[163] lists a number of GIs 'protectable' between the two countries, including Jamaican Bissy (a medicinal herb) and Jamaican cannabis. Whether Jamaican entrepreneurs will seek the registration of specific nutraceuticals as GIs in domestic and international markets, especially Switzerland, remains to be seen.

A focus on innovative approaches to GI helps to create resilient infrastructure to support the growth of IP-intensive and other industries in the region. Diversified and inclusive approaches to GIs in domestic markets call for collaboration among several government and industry players. This includes domestic IP offices, foreign affairs ministries, rural development agencies, tourism ministries and standard-setting bodies. These are relevant synergies and all relate to the SDG target of building resilient infrastructure, promoting inclusive and sustainable industrialisation and fostering innovation.

E. Building Partnerships and Making Voices Heard as an Aspect of Development

Since legal norms are a social construct shaped by influential players and networks,[164] active participation in norm-setting fora is integral to changing the IP and development game for the Caribbean. Building norm-changing partnerships with domestic and international key players contributes to capacity building,[165] an essential aspect of development. In changing the tone and effect of current GI dialogues, Caribbean countries should consider participating in GI and IP epistemic[166] communities. GI

---

161 Stabroeknews (n 119).

162 Ibid.

163 Agreement on the Mutual Protection and Recognition of Geographical Indications between the Federal Council of the Swiss Confederation and the Government of Jamaica (2013) RS 0.232.111.294.58.

164 Hopf (n 30) 317.

165 Daniel Berliner, 'Building Capacity, Building Rights? State Capacity and Labor Rights in Developing Countries' (2015) 72 WDJ 127.

166 Mai K Davis Cross, 'Rethinking Epistemic Communities Twenty Years Later' (2013) 3 9 Rev Intl S 137; Peter M Haas, 'Epistemic Communities and International Policy Coordination' (1992) 46 IO 1.

and IP epistemic communities are networks that share common knowledge and goals and are influential in the creation and dissemination of legal norms and rules. These networks impact how IP works in global societies. For example, the World Intellectual Property Organization's Standing Committees are a type of epistemic community.[167] The actors that create GI rules in preferential free trade agreements are also a type of epistemic network as cumulatively they create language which either extends or retracts the progression of non-wine and spirit GIs in global markets.

Because of jurisdictional differences in GI laws, the Caribbean should seek to fully participate in the dialogue about GI protection in global consumer markets. Like other small vulnerable economy initiatives,[168] these are not easily achieved and takes the commitment of human and capital resources. There is noticeable participation of Caribbean country representatives in WIPO norm-setting committees;[169] the region could better use this to its advantage.

The Lisbon Agreement protects all forms of GIs and appellations of origin. This agreement was amended in 2015 to include the recognition of extensive rights for GIs. Prior to 2015, only appellations of origin, where all stages of the production process occur within one territorial zone, were covered by the agreement. An example of an appellation of origin is 'Hånnlamb' a designation referring to 'lambs and sheep of the "gutefår" breed that are born, reared and slaughtered within the defined geographical area of Gotland' in Sweden.[170] With the inclusion of GIs in 2015, the Lisbon Agreement[171] now makes it possible for goods that have place-based connections that cover more than the defined geographical area to be registered as GIs. The Lisbon Agreement has only 29 members, with Haiti and Cuba as the only Caribbean countries party to the Agreement.[172]

---

167 See also Ruth Okediji, 'WIPO-WTO Relations and the Future of Global Intellectual Property Norms' (2008) 39 Netherlands Yearbook of International Law 69.

168 Cyrus Rustomjee, 'Developing the Blue Economy in Caribbean and Other Small Economy States' (2016) Centre for International Governance Innovation (CIGI) Policy Brief No 75; Cyrus Rustomjee, 'Debt Sustainability in African Heavily Indebted Poor Countries' (2017) CIGI Policy Brief No 133.

169 This point is discussed below.

170 EU Regulation on Quality Schemes for Agricultural Products and Foodstuffs.

171 On the practicality of more countries using the Lisbon Agreement, see Daniel Gervais, 'Irreconcilable Differences: The Geneva Act of the Lisbon Agreement and the Common Law' (2015) 33 Houston L Rev 339.

172 USDA Foreign Agricultural Service, 'EU Prepares to Join Lisbon Agreement on Geographical Indications' (2018) GAIN Report E18015.

For the purposes of this chapter two aspects of its protection are relevant.[173] First, GIs from member countries are protected against uses on products that are not of the same kind if this would suggest a connection between the GI and the other product, would likely damage its interests or unfairly dilute the designation.[174] Second, GIs cannot become generic in contracting parties' jurisdictions.[175] These create stability for GIs by recognising indefinite and expansive protection in member countries.

Under the Lisbon Agreement, GI protection is greater than the rights that may be agreed upon in preferential free trade agreements that prioritise trademarks over GIs. For Caribbean countries, membership of the Lisbon Agreement may run counter to IP protection commitments made in their Caribbean Basin Initiative Partnership Agreement with the United States.[176] The Caribbean Basin Initiative Partnership Agreement has a relatively long history (1983) and provides preferential trade and aid to Caribbean countries, referred to as 'beneficiaries'.[177] Under the Act creating the agreement, duty free and other preferential treatments can be forfeited if a Caribbean country does not 'provide under its law adequate and *effective* [emphasis added] means for foreign nationals to secure, exercise, and enforce exclusive rights in intellectual property, including patent, trademark, and copyright rights'.[178] Since the United States opposes the global expansion of GI rights, it is possible that the Caribbean's alignment with EU-style GI rights may trigger challenges from the United States, on grounds of being IP protection that is ineffective. This may arise if recognition of food-based GIs in the Caribbean prevents the United States from exporting similarly named trademarked goods to Caribbean countries. The EPA (Caribbean free trade agreement with the European Union) specifies that border measures apply to goods that infringe GIs.[179] Therefore, once negotiations on the number of EU products to be protected in Caribbean countries are concluded, each Caribbean country must ensure that infringing GI goods do not enter their countries. Capacity building is disrupted when partnerships with specific GI norm-setting groups fall foul of trade interests with other countries.

In the context of IP recognition of place-based goods in WIPO

---

173 See Daniel Gervais, *A Look at the Geneva Act of the Lisbon Agreement: A Missed Opportunity?* In Calboli and Ng-Loy (n 4).

174 Lisbon Agreement (n 15) art 11(1)(a)(ii).

175 Ibid art 12.

176 Caribbean Basin Economic Recovery Act 1983 (United States), ch 15.

177 Ibid.

178 Ibid.

179 EU Economic Partnership (n 115) art 163.

discussions, Jamaica was a prolific actor in reopening the debate on the protection of country names against unauthorised commercial uses. Jamaica made lengthy submissions, proposing that many foreign products were using the name 'Jamaica' on their products, without any credible affiliation or authorisation from the country's government.[180] The Caribbean country argued that use of its name on foreign entrepreneurs' products negatively affected nation branding[181] and that local industries were prevented from using the name on similar classed products, or did so at the risk of being sued. Initially, the proposal was centred on amending Article 6*ter* of the Paris Convention to add country names to the list of state emblems, official hallmarks and emblems of intergovernmental organisations that are prohibited from use as trademarks or elements of trademarks.[182] The proposal has gained significant support from several member countries of the WIPO Standing Committee on the Law of Trademarks, Industrial Designs and Geographical Indications (WIPO SCT).[183] Jamaica and other proposers have since amended submissions and now support the adoption of a soft law approach in WIPO member countries.[184] As such, the current proposal centres on the use of the recommendations as 'guidelines for the examination and treatment of applications for the registration of trademarks which consist of or contain country names'.[185] These guidelines are meant to prevent the unauthorised use of country names as business identifiers and top-level domain names in connection with goods and services that are not from the country of origin. The proposal has facilitated dialogue on a delicate area in trademark law, where jurisdictions have either prohibited country names

---

180 Jamaica, 'Report to the WIPO Standing Committee on the Law of Trademarks Industrial Designs and Geographical Indications (SCT)' <http://www.wipo.int/export/sites/www/sct/en/comments/pdf/sct27/jamaicareport.pdf>. WIPO, 'Standing Committee on the Law of Trademarks, Industrial Designs and Geographical Indications' (2014) Proposal by the Delegation of Jamaica.

181 WIPO, 'Standing Committee on the Law of Trademarks, Industrial Designs and Geographical Indications, Twenty-Seventh Session Geneva' (2012).

182 Paris Convention, art 6.

183 The WIPO SCT discusses and helps to promote norms on problematic aspects of trademarks, GIs and industrial designs.

184 See WIPO, 'Proposal by the Delegations of Bulgaria, the Czech Republic, France, Germany, Hungary, Iceland, Italy, Poland, Portugal, Republic of Moldova, Romania, Spain and Switzerland' (2014) SCT/31/8; WIPO, 'Protection of Country Names Against Registration and use as Trademarks: Practices, Approaches and Possible Areas of Convergence – Comments by Members' (2017) SCT/37/3.

185 WIPO, 'Revised Draft Joint Recommendation Concerning Provisions on the Protection of Country Names, Standing Committee on the Law of Trademarks, Industrial Design and Geographical Indications' (2014) SCT/32/2.

as trademarks for being geographically mis-descriptive, or have allowed country names, if used in conjunction with more distinctive signifiers. A body of data on the topic is being created at WIPO that may be valuable for comparative research or, policy review purposes.[186] Has this level of partnership in WIPO SCT built strong partnerships for Jamaica? That the country is not the only supporter of the initiative and that the issue has become one of the focal topics in WIPO SCT meetings indicate that the country is building partnerships in the network. However, it is more important to consider whether these relationships matter to Jamaica and the Caribbean as IP development builders. The forum works as a capacity builder if the region can use the proceedings to influence GI reciprocity among members, or greater protection of place-based goods. Apart from becoming influential actors in IP norm-setting, such epistemic shifts may be beneficial to Caribbean-based potential GI industries by establishing and securing foreign consumer markets.

V. CONCLUSION: STALLED PROGRESS OR RENEWED PROSPECTS?

Geographical indications are relevant in narrowing the IP and development divide in the Caribbean only if conceptualised through a lens of innovation and investment in development of that innovation. The region and its countries are not framers or influencers of GI rules and so, the perception that GIs lead to socio-economic development should be revisited. The global treatment of GIs is contested and the region will find that its strongest consumer markets, such as the United States and Canada, may not offer the most expansive protection for their products. Mixed attitudes towards GI registration, who should be involved in GI governance, and domestic economic constraints may affect product registration and the sustainability of industries. Sustainable development targets, such as reducing inequalities between and within countries and fostering innovation, become more realistic goals if an innovative and diversified approach is taken.

In terms of product innovation, Caribbean countries should consider creating synergies between GI products and their waste materials. Blue Mountain coffee and Demerara sugar, for example, could be tapped for

---

[186] WIPO, 'Proposal by the delegations of Georgia, Iceland, Indonesia, Italy, Jamaica, Malaysia, Mexico, Monaco, Peru, Switzerland and the United Arab Emirates' (2018) SCT/39/8.

their bio-fuel potential. In Trinidad and Tobago, the possibility of producing renewable energy from cocoa shells used in its GI industry may have positive spill-over effects on the regions' economies. This may contribute to job creation and increased income, two relevant goals of sustainable development. As yet, such approaches are not incorporated in Jamaica's or Trinidad and Tobago's national IP strategy but should not be ruled out. Against this background, the region has the potential to influence global GI norms and shift the scale towards local development outside of tourism initiatives.

4. New frameworks for the ownership and licensing of traditional knowledge associated with genetic resources in Africa*

Enyinna Nwauche**

I. INTRODUCTION

This chapter evaluates new national and regional frameworks for the protection of traditional knowledge associated with genetic resources (aTK) in Africa. The regional framework is the Swakopmund Protocol.[1] The national statutory frameworks are the Protection of Traditional Knowledge Act (Kenya),[2] the Protection of Traditional Knowledge Act (Zambia),[3] and the constitutional property jurisprudence of the Republic of South Africa 1996.[4] This jurisprudence provides interpretative context for the 2015 South African ABS Regulations[5] made pursuant to the National Environmental Management Biodiversity Act 2004, which recognise community ownership and management of traditional knowledge

* All online sources were last accessed on 27 December 2018.

** This is a revised version of an article intended for the 36th Congress of the International Association for the Advancement of Teaching and Research in Intellectual Property (ATRIP) Wellington New Zealand 2018. The author is grateful to the WIPO for sponsorship to prepare and attend the conference.

1 Swakopmund Protocol for the Protection of Traditional Knowledge and Expressions of Folklore within the Framework of the African Regional Intellectual Property Organisation (ARIPO) 2010.

2 Kenyan Protection of Traditional Knowledge and Cultural Expressions Act 2016.

3 Zambian Protection of Traditional Knowledge, Genetic Resources and Expressions of Folklore Act 2016.

4 Section 25 of the South African Constitution 1996 protects property as a constitutional right.

5 Regulations on Bio-prospecting, Access and Benefit-Sharing 2015, South Africa (SA ABS Regulations).

(TK). These new frameworks arguably deviate from other African states, such as Ethiopia, which, in domesticating the Nagoya Protocol on Access to Genetic Resources and the Fair and Equitable Sharing of Benefits Arising from their Utilisation to the Convention on Biological Diversity,[6] enacted legislation and adopted policies that recognise communal ownership but empower Competent National Authorities (CAN) to manage the licensing of a TK, with the participation of communities. The extent of the change which these new communal frameworks bring to the existing state-centric frameworks is still uncertain, at least in practice. This chapter contributes to our understanding of the communal frameworks.

The Nagoya Protocol was adopted to implement the third objective of the Convention for Biological Diversity (CBD) which is 'the fair and equitable sharing of benefits arising from the utilisation of genetic resources including by appropriate access to genetic resources and by appropriate transfer of relevant technologies, taking into account all rights over those resources and to technologies, and by appropriate funding'. Essentially the Nagoya Protocol establishes an access and benefit sharing (ABS) framework to enable third parties to access genetic resources and aTK.

An important point is that aTK is a subset of TK. There is much inclination to regard aTK as synonymous with TK. For example, Zambia[7] defines TK as meaning

> any knowledge, not limited to a specific subject area, technical or medical field associated with genetic resources, originating from a traditional community, individual or group that is the result of intellectual activity and insight in a traditional context and where the knowledge is embodied in the traditional lifestyle of a traditional community or is codified in knowledge systems and passed on from one generation to another.

Other national legislation, such as that of Kenya,[8] recognises that aTK is a subset of TK by providing that[9]

> 'traditional knowledge' means any knowledge (a) originating from an individual, local or traditional community that is the result of intellectual activity

---

[6] Nagoya Protocol on Access to Genetic Resources and the Fair and Equitable Sharing of Benefits Arising from their Utilisation to the Convention on Biological Diversity (opened for signature 2 February 2011, entered into force 12 October 2014) (Nagoya Protocol).

[7] Protection of Traditional Knowledge Act (Zambia), s 2.

[8] Protection of Traditional Knowledge Act (Kenya), s 2.

[9] See also the definition of traditional use or knowledge in the SA ABS Regulations.

> and insight in a traditional context, including know-how, skills, innovations, practices and learning, embodied in the traditional lifestyle of a community; or (b) contained in the codified knowledge systems passed on from one generation to another including agricultural, environmental or medical knowledge, knowledge associated with genetic resources or other components of biological diversity, and know-how of traditional architecture, construction technologies, designs, marks and indications.

The importance of this clarification lies in recognising that focusing on the nature of aTK will enable a better understanding of the significance of communal ownership of aTK.

This chapter is organised as follows. Section II overviews the licensing of aTK in South Africa and Ethiopia. Section III examines the new frameworks of communal ownership and management of TK and its implications for the licensing of aTK in Kenya, Zambia and South Africa.

II. AFRICAN STATES AND THE NAGOYA PROTOCOL: ACCESS AND BENEFIT-SHARING FRAMEWORKS AND THE LICENSING OF TRADITIONAL KNOWLEDGE

This part of the chapter reviews how African states have domesticated the Nagoya Protocol and examples of aTK licensing within national frameworks.[10]

---

[10] Treaty obligations of African state parties to the Nagoya Protocol have been fulfilled through domestic legislation such as South African National Environmental Management: Biodiversity Act (NEMBA) 2004; the 2008 Regulations on Bio-Prospecting, Access and Benefit Sharing; the Environmental Management and Co-ordination Act (Kenya) 1999 and Environmental Management and Co-ordination (Conservation on Biological Diversity and Resources, Access to Genetic Resources and Benefit Sharing) Regulations 2006; the Industrial Property Act 2009 (Burundi); the Ethiopian Proclamation No 482/2006 on Access to Genetic Resources and Community Knowledge and Community Right (Ethiopian ABS Legislation) and the Access to Genetic Resources and Community Knowledge and Community Rights Council of Ministers Regulation 109/2009 (Ethiopian Proclamation Regulations). Uganda has complied through the National Environment Act and the 2005 Regulations. Other African States have chosen to adopt policies and establish administrative structures to engage with ABS processes including Malawi (The Procedures and Guidelines for Access and Collection of Genetic Resources in Malawi). Some other States, such as Cameroon (The National Strategy on Access to Genetic Resources and the Fair and Equitable Sharing of Benefits arising from Their Utilisation 2012) who are not parties to the Nagoya Protocol (n 6) appear to have been inspired by the Protocol.

Article 13 of the Nagoya Protocol requires each state party to designate a national focal point and Competent National Authority (CNA), which is required to provide information on procedures for obtaining prior informed consent (PIC) of indigenous and local communities and establishing mutually agreed terms for access to TK. African States have chosen to use the CNA to license aTK with the involvement of traditional and indigenous communities.

For example, in South Africa, SA ABS Regulations require notifications,[11] discovery phase export permit,[12] a biotrade permit,[13] a bioprospecting permit[14] or an integrated biotrade and bioprospecting permit[15] and export permit for research other than bioprospecting[16] to access aTK. The Minister of Environmental Affairs issues permits, or a Member of the Executive Council of South Africa's provincial governments issue export permits for research, other than bioprospecting,[17] on some conditions.[18] For indigenous communities who are owners of aTK, the conditions require the approving authority to take into account relevant factors such as documentary proof that the relevant stakeholders have been identified by the applicant.[19] Another condition is documentary proof that there has been disclosure of relevant information to all identified stakeholders. The issuing authority must also take into account whether the applicant has obtained PIC of affected indigenous communities or individuals, and whether benefit-sharing agreements have been entered into with such communities or individuals. There must be documentary proof of this. Also relevant are any comments received from the stakeholders (including affected indigenous communities or individuals) during the consultation meetings,[20] and that there is a community resolution authorising a

---

[11] Notifications are required by para 13 of the SA ABS Regulations by any person involved in the discovery phase of bio-prospecting involving aTK.

[12] A discovery phase export permit is needed by any person who wishes to export from the Republic any indigenous genetic and biological resources for bio-prospecting for commercial research. See para 14 of the SA ABS Regulations.

[13] A biotrade permit enables a third party to engage in biotrade, which is further defined by the NEMBA Regulations, s 1, as 'the buying and selling of milled, powdered, dried, sliced or extract of indigenous genetic and biological resources for further commercial exploitation'. See further SA ABS Regulations, para 16.

[14] SA ABS Regulations, para 17.

[15] Ibid para 18.

[16] Ibid para 19.

[17] Ibid para 4(2).

[18] Ibid para 9.

[19] NEMBA 2004, s 82(1).

[20] This consultation is provided for in para 7 of the SA ABS Regulations.

representative to give PIC, give access to aTK and to enter into benefit-sharing (BS) and material transfer agreements (MTA). Ultimately the issuing authority decides to approve or refuse the application for a notification or permit. Even though, within the framework of the 2015 SA ABS Regulations, there are provisions for applicants to challenge a refusal to register a notification or refuse an application for a permit,[21] communities have no explicit recourse to a review or appeal of any decision. Apart from a provision for consultation with indigenous communities,[22] there appears to be no other way communities can intervene in the licensing of their aTK. Ethiopian law[23] recognises local communities as owners of community knowledge,[24] who have a right to regulate access to their knowledge[25] and share in any benefit from its utilisation.[26] The Ethiopian CNA is the Institute of Biodiversity Conservation (IBC), to which all applications for access to aTK are made.[27] Ethiopia recognises a procedure that enables communities to regulate access to their knowledge by giving them a right to grant consent; refuse consent; withdraw or place restriction on the consent if convinced that their consent will be detrimental to their socio-economic life, natural or cultural heritage and right.[28] Furthermore, community consent is given after an identification of the relevant community and compliance with the procedure for communicating their consent to the IBC.[29] The IBC on receipt of the application is obliged to send the application to the identified relevant community based on a 'survey it has undertaken on the distribution of genetic resources/community knowledge'.[30]

The approval of the BS agreement in South Africa is dependent on the satisfaction of the Minister that it is fair and equitable to all parties.[31] To arrive at this decision, the Minister may seek technical advice or invite public comment. Nothing appears to imperil the capacity of indigenous communities to challenge the terms and conditions of a BS agreement. In

---

21 NEMBA 2004, ss 94–96.

22 SA ABS Regulations, para 7.

23 Ethiopian ABS Legislation, s 5.

24 Ibid s 2 (community knowledge is defined as 'knowledge practices, innovations or technologies created or developed over generations by local communities on the conservation and use of genetic resources').

25 Ibid s 6(1).

26 Ibid s 6(3).

27 Ibid s 11(1).

28 Ibid s 7.

29 Ethiopian Proclamation Regulations, para 21.

30 Ibid para 21(2).

31 SA ABS Regulations, para 30.

fact, such capacity is crucial since indigenous communities are in a good position to monitor the efficacy of BS agreements.

Under South African law BS agreements should include monetary and non-monetary benefits.[32] The same is true of Ethiopia.[33] It is striking and perhaps not surprising that monetary benefits have pride of place. In South Africa all monies arising from BS agreements are to be paid into a Bioprospecting Trust Fund.[34] Indigenous communities are the beneficiaries of the Trust Fund and are informed of money received and amounts due them. The Director General of the Ministry of Environmental Affairs is the trustee and annually distributes the funds.[35] In Ethiopia, all money obtained from access to aTK is paid into an Access Fund.[36] Half of the money the state obtains for access to GR is shared with the community but no proportion is ascribed to the money from access to aTK.[37] These monies are to be devoted to financing development projects designed to benefit the community which is the custodian of the aTK.[38] These projects are determined by different government structures in the Ethiopian Federation.[39] Monetary benefit includes benefits from exploiting patents based on aTK.

The manner in which the consent of communities to the exploitation of their aTK in the form of third-party acquisition of patents based on the aTK is obtained is generally considered as an important aspect of a BS agreement.

---

32 Ibid para 39(3). This would include conservation of the indigenous genetic and biological resources; support for further research on indigenous genetic and biological resources and aTK; enhancement of the scientific knowledge and technical capacity to conserve, use and develop indigenous genetic and biological resources; any other activity that promotes the conservation, sustainable use and development of indigenous biological resources for the benefit of South Africa; or improve livelihoods of the communities and enhancement of technical capacity of the communities or individuals involved.

33 See Ethiopian ABS Legislation, art 19. These benefits would include licence fees; upfront payments; milestone payments; royalties; research funding; joint ownership of intellectual property; employment opportunities; participation of Ethiopian nationals who are employees of the IBC or the relevant institutions in the research based on the genetic resources or community knowledge accessed; priority to supply the raw material of genetic resource required for producing products therefrom; access to products and technologies developed from the use of genetic resource or community knowledge accessed; training, both at institutional and local communities levels, to enhance local skills in genetic resources conservation, evaluation, development, propagation and use; and any other appropriate benefit.

34 NEMBA 2004, s 87(5).

35 SA ABS Regulations, para 40.

36 Ethiopian Proclamation Regulations, para 26.

37 Ethiopian ABS Legislation, art 9.

38 Ethiopian Proclamation Regulations, para 28.

39 Ibid para 30.

In South Africa, the Patent Act[40] requires applicants to declare in the complete specification whether TK or use is involved in the invention for which a patent is sought. Such a declaration requires that a BS agreement and a bioprospecting permit be filed along with the application for a patent. While there is evidence of these disclosure requirements in protecting aTK, in South Africa[41] the possibility that some aTK-based patents have been registered without appropriate disclosure is likely because, as stated above, South Africa examines patents as to form.[42] Even if South Africa were to examine whether patent applications comply with substantive requirements,[43] disclosure requirements will be better enforced by the vigilance of communities.[44] Unlike the vague nature of the South African BS Agreement, Ethiopia specifically recognises 'joint ownership of intellectual property as a form of benefit to be given to communities'.[45] To strengthen this benefit, the access permit holders must negotiate a new agreement with the IBC if they intend to apply for intellectual property rights over genetic resources.[46] They also must obtain written and explicit consent of the IBC before applying for a patent and disclose the origin of the aTK in the application.[47]

In conclusion, it is important to consider whether Nagoya Protocol states are free to recognise that indigenous and local communities can license their aTK in addition to the significant role reserved for CNAs as representatives of the state.[48] National legislatures domesticating the

40 Patent Act 1998 (South Africa) as amended by the Patent Amendment Act 2005 (South Africa), ss 30(A)–30(B).

41 Examples abound. The San people successfully challenged a CSIR Patent on the P57 extract from *Hoodia Gordoni* leading to BS agreements in 2003, 2006 and 2007. Another example is the objection of Xhosa communities of the Eastern Cape of South Africa to the grant of European patents relating to *Pelargonium sidoides*. See Roger Chennells, 'Traditional Knowledge and Benefit Sharing After the Nagoya Protocol: Three Cases from South Africa' (2013) 9(2) LEAD 165; See AF Myburgh, 'Lessons from a Town like Alice' (2010) Without Prejudice <www.gleason.co.za> (subscription required); Emeka Amaechi, 'Using Patents to Protect Traditional Knowledge on Medicinal Uses of Plants in South Africa' (2015) 11(1) LEAD 53.

42 Patents Act, s 34.

43 Patents Act, s 25(1) requires that for applications for a patent to be successful they must be new, involve an inventive step and be capable of being used or applied in trade or industry or agriculture.

44 See Rachel Wynberg and Roger Chennells, 'Green Diamonds of South Africa: An Overview of the San-Hoodia Case' in Rachel Wynberg, Doris Schroeder and Roger Chennels (eds), *Indigenous Peoples, Consent and Benefit Sharing: Lessons from the San-Hoodia Case* (Springer 2009) 89.

45 Ethiopian ABS Legislation, art 19(6).

46 Ibid art 17.

47 Ibid.

48 The Nagoya Protocol (n 6), art 7 provides that in accordance with domestic

Nagoya Protocol have been faithful to their treaty obligations, with limited management roles reserved for communities. Many communities would argue that state control and management of the licensing of aTK is not the problem, but the design and implementation of the licensing process is problematic. In South Africa, for example, a number of shortcomings have been identified, such as the confusion in the identity of communities with whom PIC is to be obtained because of the concurrent and multiple ownership of aTK; and the consequence of a regulation-free period that enables third parties to decide whether available aTK and GR are commercially viable.[49] In the other African states it is doubtful if, in reality, there is a licensing process, even though many states brandish the enactment of national frameworks of the Nagoya Protocol as a worthy achievement. There is no doubt that reforms to the aTK licensing process would be good for many stakeholders, including owner communities. The aTK communities would welcome recognition of their ownership rights and a more enhanced role as the effective managers of their aTK, even if they are recognised as owners of the aTK, as in Ethiopia. The overwhelming state practice of mandating CNAs to grant licences is a result of the perceived incapacity and ignorance of traditional communities in managing their aTK. It is also evidence of paternalism and a belief that aTK is a national treasure.

It is not self-evident that CNAs have done a better job in managing aTK in the African states. For example, there are widespread reports of the inability of the IBC to ensure that the terms of access to Ethiopian GR are observed.[50] Summarising the Ethiopian ABS framework, Fikremarkos and Imiru argue that[51]

---

law aTK held by local and indigenous communities is accessed with their PIC or approval and involvement. It would appear plausible that this section does not entitle local and indigenous communities to license their aTK.

[49] See, for example, NR Couch, E Douwes, MM Wolfson, GF Smith and TJ Edwards, 'South Africa's Bioprospecting, Access and Benefit-Sharing Legislation: Current Realities, Future Complications, and a Proposed Alternative' (2008) 104 S Afr J Sci 55.

[50] See generally Fikremarkos Merso and Imeru Tamrat, 'Ethiopia's Experience in Access to Genetic Resources and Benefit Sharing: The Hope for Economic Benefits and the Risks for Research and Innovation' cited in Gizachew Girma, 'Protection of Traditional Knowledge under International and Ethiopian Law with a Particular Reference to Traditional Medical Knowledge: Current Trends, Prospects and Challenges' 85–86 <https://chilot.me/wp-content/uploads/2013/05/protection-of-traditional-knowledge-under-international-and-ethiopian-law.pdf>.

[51] Ibid.

> [E]nsuring benefit sharing to local communities with their informed and full participation is the main objective of the ABS Law, but whether this objective has been translated into its provisions is questionable. Although the law places a great deal of importance to communities and capitalizes on their participation and decision making, that has remained largely at the level of rhetoric, and in fact, the law accords all the decision making power to the government.

This should not be surprising because of serious governance lapses in the many African states. It would be strange if African CANs performed better than other government institutions. Where there is thin evidence of the impact of CNAs, their success could be assessed by their output of permits granted. Assessing CANs' effectiveness is difficult because of limited and inadequate information on their work. What evidence is available paints a picture of average success in the licensing of aTK.[52] On the other hand, if the number of approved licences is a yardstick, it may well be that the CNAs are doing well because they have been meticulous in the grant of permits and we have not determined an optimum number of permits that are suitable for a State.

III. FRAMEWORKS OF THE OWNERSHIP AND LICENSING OF ATK IN AFRICA

This section provides an evaluation of the frameworks for the ownership and licensing of aTK in Africa, which represent the affirmation and recognition of communal ownership and management of aTK in addition to the state management of national frameworks for the protection of aTK. Some frameworks are statutory frameworks, such as the Kenyan PTKCE and the Zambian PTKGREF. Other frameworks consist of plausible outcomes of a constitutional reading of statutory frameworks such as the 2015 SA ABS Regulations.

---

[52] See Rachel Wynberg, 'Making Sense of Access and Benefit Sharing in the Rooibos Industry: Towards a Holistic, Just and Sustainable Framing' (2017) 110 S Afr J Bot 39, 41 where the author states that by 2014, 15 bioprospecting permits had been issued. In Ethiopia, where there appears to be a distinction between access to GR and community knowledge, there is information of the grant of access to GR and not of aTK. Available evidence in Ethiopia indicates that ABS agreements have been concluded for *Teff* (*Eragrostis teff*) and *Vernonia* (*vernonia galamensis*). See Abeba Tadesse, 'Material Transfer Agreements on Teff and Vernonia-Ethiopian Plant Genetic Resources' (2009) 2(4) JPL 77.

A. Statutory Frameworks

Three crucial points need to be borne in mind as we examine The Kenyan PTKCE and the Zambian PTKGREF. The first is that they are domestications of the Swakopmund Protocol[53] adopted by the African Regional Intellectual Property Organisation (ARIPO).[54] The Swakopmund Protocol lays down minimum standards in broad norms for State Parties to follow; it does not grant rights. Zambia specifically recognises in its long title that the legislation gives effect to the ARIPO Swakopmund Protocol. The Kenyan PTKCE does not expressly refer to the Swakopmund Protocol, but its provisions draw inspiration from it. Articles 7 and 8 of the Protocol recognise the exclusive rights of local and traditional communities to control the exploitation of their TK, including to license and assign such knowledge. Article 8(2) requires all access authorisation assignments or licences to be in writing, which must be approved by a national competent authority, failing which the documents shall be void. Such exploitation, according to article 9 of the Protocol, shall include the fair and equitable sharing of benefits from the commercial and industrial use of such knowledge. This point is reinforced by Article 14 of the Protocol, which entrusts the ARIPO office and national competent authority with the tasks of awareness-raising, education, guidance, monitoring, registration, dispute resolution, and other activities in the protection of TK.

Second, these frameworks are constitutionally inspired, which is clearer for Kenya than Zambia. Section 11 of the 2010 Constitution of the Republic of Kenya recognises culture as the foundation of the nation and as the cumulative civilisation of the Kenyan people and nation, and requires the State to promote the intellectual property rights of the people of Kenya. The same section enjoins Parliament to enact legislation, first

---

[53] On 9 August 2010, ARIPO and its Member States held a Diplomatic Conference at the coastal town of Swakopmund in Namibia for the adoption of the Protocol on the Protection of Traditional Knowledge and Expressions of Folklore. The Protocol was adopted by the Member States and signed by nine States that presented their credentials at the Conference. The nine Member States are Botswana, Ghana, Kenya, Lesotho, Liberia, Mozambique, Namibia, Zambia and Zimbabwe. The Protocol entered into force on 11 May 2015.

[54] There are 19 member states: Botswana, The Gambia, Ghana, Kenya, Lesotho, Malawi, Mozambique, Sierra Leone, Somalia, Sudan, Swaziland, Uganda, Tanzania, Zambia, Zimbabwe, Liberia, Rwanda, Sao Tome and Principe, and Namibia. Countries like Angola, Egypt, Eritrea, Ethiopia, Mauritius, Nigeria, Seychelles and South Africa are regarded as potential member states and have observer status in the organs of the organization.

to ensure communities receive compensation or royalties for the use of their culture and cultural heritage and, second, to recognise and protect ownership of indigenous seeds and plant varieties, their genetic and diverse characteristics and their use by communities in Kenya. Article 40(5) further provides that the State shall support, promote and protect the intellectual property rights of the people of Kenya. In furtherance of this constitutional framework, the Kenyan PTKCE was promulgated by the Kenyan Parliament. This is recited in its long title. For Zambia, there appears to be an indirect constitutional inspiration because the Zambian Constitution 1991 (as amended)[55] obligates the Zambian State to protect genetic resources and biological diversity as well protect and enhance intellectual property in, and indigenous knowledge of, biodiversity and genetic resources of local communities. Third, these frameworks are also domestications of the Nagoya Protocol.

At the heart of these frameworks is a recognition of the ownership and management of aTK by communities. Thus the Kenyan PTKCE recognises owners[56] and holders[57] of TK,[58] and grants them exclusive rights to authorise the exploitation of their TK as well as prevent any person from exploiting their TK without their PIC.[59] To buttress this point, section 22 of the Kenyan PTKCE recognises the right of owners of TK to assign and

---

55 See Constitution of Zambia, s 257. The amendment is by the Constitution of Zambia (Amendment Act) 2016.

56 Section 2 of the Protection of Traditional Knowledge Act (Kenya) define 'owner' as 'local and traditional communities, and recognized individuals or organizations within such communities in whom the custody or protection of traditional knowledge and cultural expressions are entrusted in accordance with the customary law and practices of that community'; 'Community' is in turn defined by the same section as 'a homogeneous and consciously distinct group of the people who share any of the following attributes (a) common ancestry; (b) similar culture or unique mode of livelihood or language; (c) geographical space; (d) ecological space; or (e) community of interest'.

57 'Holder' is defined in s 2 as 'recognized individuals or organizations within communities in whom the custody or protection of traditional knowledge and cultural expressions are entrusted in accordance with the customary law and practices of that community'.

58 Ibid s 2 defines TK as 'any knowledge (a) originating from an individual, local or traditional community that is the result of intellectual activity and insight in a traditional context, including know-how, skills, innovations, practices and learning, embodied in the traditional lifestyle of a community; or (b) contained in the codified knowledge systems passed on from one generation to another including agricultural, environmental or medical knowledge, knowledge associated with genetic resources or other components of biological diversity, and know-how of traditional architecture, construction technologies, designs, marks and indications'.

59 Protection of Traditional Knowledge Act (Zambia), s 17.

conclude written[60] licensing agreements after appropriate and documented consultations with members of communities.[61] These consultations should be in accordance with 'community rules prescribing the procedures for the authorisation of the exploitation of their TK'.[62] The Zambian PTKGREF recognises the right of communities to license their TK but cannot assign same.[63]

The Kenyan PTKCE and the Zambian PTKGREF require third parties to obtain the prior and informed consent (PIC) of owners of TK.[64] PIC is tied to the conclusion of a BS agreement regarded as a user agreement, which must provide for the sharing of financial and other benefits.[65] A third party engaged in discussions with owners of TK is required to inform the Kenyan Cabinet Secretary that they have entered into negotiations and provide a copy of the proposed user agreement for advice and comment as well as provide a copy of the agreed user agreement.[66] Agreements not registered by the Kenyan Cabinet Secretary shall be null and void.[67] The same is true of agreements not registered by the Zambian Patents and Companies Registration Agency.[68] The Kenyan PTKCE highlights benefits from intellectual property rights dependent on TK which are characterised as 'derivative works'.[69] It declares that intellectual property rights in derivative works shall vest in the creator of the work who is obligated to enter into a BS agreement with the owners of the TK,

---

60 Protection of Traditional Knowledge Act (Kenya), s 22(4) declares oral licences null and void and of no effect.

61 Ibid s 25(3). See also Protection of Traditional Knowledge Act (Zambia), s 18(1).

62 Protection of Traditional Knowledge Act (Kenya), s 10(2)–10(3).

63 Protection of Traditional Knowledge Act (Zambia), s 19(1).

64 Protection of Traditional Knowledge Act (Kenya), s 24.

65 These benefits include compensation, fees, royalties or other payments for the use; whether the use will be exclusive or non-exclusive; duration of the use to be allowed and rights of renewal; disclosure requirements in relation to the use; possible sharing by the owners of any intellectual property rights arising from the use of the TK; access arrangements for the owners; applicable controls on publication; assignment of rights, where appropriate; dispute resolution mechanisms; confidentiality and disclosure in relation to secret TK and respect for moral rights of the traditional owners. See Protection of Traditional Knowledge Act (Kenya), s 34. The Protection of Traditional Knowledge Act (Zambia) is not as elaborate. Section 20(3) recognises that BS may include non-monetary benefits such as contributions to community development.

66 Protection of Traditional Knowledge Act (Kenya), s 36(2)–36(3).

67 Ibid s 35(2).

68 Established in accordance with the Patents and Companies Registration Agency Act 2010 (Zambia).

69 Protection of Traditional Knowledge Act (Kenya), s 4.

reflecting fair equitable monetary or non-monetary compensation to the right holders; identification and disclosure of the origin of the TK; and an obligation against derogatory treatment.[70] It would appear that owners and holders of TK are not entitled to oppose the grant of intellectual property rights. There are no specific references to intellectual property rights in the Zambian PTKGREF, indicating that communities cannot oppose the grant of intellectual property rights based on TK. In comparison, communities in Zambia may not only oppose the grant of intellectual property rights based on the TK, they may also seek to register IP rights for their benefit.[71]

In Kenya, assignments and licensing entitle third parties to engage in a number of activities, such as reproduction; performance or display; broadcast; translation, adaptation, arrangement, transformation or modification; fixation; electronic transmission; derivative works and the sale of TK.[72]

There is an implicit recognition that what qualifies as TK is subject to contention for a number of reasons. First, section 6 of the Kenyan PTKCE sets out a protective criterion for TK that is arguably vague. TK is defined as

> generated, preserved and transmitted from one generation to another, within a community, for economic, ritual, narrative, decorative or recreational purposes; (b) individually or collectively generated; (c) distinctively associated with or belongs to a community; and (d) integral to the cultural identity of community that is recognized as holding the knowledge through a form of custodianship, guardianship or collective and cultural ownership or responsibility, established formally or informally by customary practices, laws or protocols.[73]

Second, there are exceptions and limitations in the protection of TK provided for by section 19(1) of the Kenyan PTKCE, which excludes 'the needs of non-commercial use, including teaching and research for educational purposes, personal or private use, criticism or review, reporting of current events, use in the course of legal proceedings, the making of recordings and reproductions of TK or cultural expressions for inclusion in an archive or inventory exclusively for the purposes of safeguarding knowledge or cultural heritage, and incidental uses' from

---

70 Ibid s 20.

71 Protection of Traditional Knowledge Act (Zambia), s 4(1)(a), 4(2) and 4(4).

72 Protection of Traditional Knowledge Act (Kenya), s 18.

73 Protection of Traditional Knowledge Act (Zambia), s 14.

the protective framework.[74] Also excluded are the normal usage development exchange dissemination and transmission of TK by members of the owner communities,[75] which is also recognised by the Zambian PTKGREF.[76]

Kenyan communities are entitled in the exercise of their ownership rights to institute a civil action against any person who exploits TK without their permission.[77] In Zambia the Registrar of the Patents and Companies Registration Agency has original jurisdiction over infringement disputes.[78] Parties and the Registrar can appeal to the High Court.[79] The Kenyan PTKCE recognises the moral rights of communities, which are declared to be the right of attribution of ownership or paternity; the right against false attribution; the prohibition of material distortion mutilation or alteration of TK prejudicial to the honour or reputation of the owners or the integrity of the TK and protection against false and misleading claims to authenticity and origin.[80] While a panoply of remedies is available to owners of TK,[81] third parties are liable to criminal infringement if they are engaged in trade of goods and services utilising TK without authorisation.[82]

Kenya and Zambia are involved in the licensing of TK in many ways.

---

[74] Protection of Traditional Knowledge Act (Zambia), s 3(3) excludes educational research and experimental purposes from the protection of the legislation.

[75] Protection of Traditional Knowledge Act (Kenya), s 19(1)(a)–(b).

[76] Protection of Traditional Knowledge Act (Zambia), s 22.

[77] Protection of Traditional Knowledge Act (Kenya), s 10(2).

[78] Protection of Traditional Knowledge Act (Zambia), ss 56–62.

[79] Ibid s 64.

[80] Protection of Traditional Knowledge Act (Kenya), s 21. Only the right of acknowledgment and indication of source is protected by Protection of Traditional Knowledge Act (Zambia), s 21.

[81] Protection of Traditional Knowledge Act (Kenya), s 39. These remedies include injunction; damages for loss resulting from the unauthorized use; declaration that the cultural rights of the holders have been contravened; order for public apology for the contravention; order that any false attribution of ownership, or derogatory treatment, of the TK, cease or be reversed; order for the account for profits made by the infringer in exploiting the infringing articles; order for the forfeiture of profits made by the infringer in exploiting the infringing articles of the owner; order for the delivery up or forfeiture to the holders of articles made in contravention of their rights, as provided for under this Act; seizure of infringing goods; revocation or invalidation of intellectual property rights inappropriately acquired over TK or derivatives thereof; or such other orders as the Court considers appropriate.

[82] See Protection of Traditional Knowledge Act (Kenya), s 37. See also Protection of Traditional Knowledge Act (Zambia), s 71.

The first is as agents of owner communities if appropriately authorised.[83] Second, in the exercise of their eminent domain and in furtherance of the public interest both states are empowered to grant compulsory licences to enable third parties to exploit TK, where the TK is not sufficiently exploited or where the owners and holders refuse to grant licences for exploitation.[84] In both cases, the appropriate government is saddled with extensive public consultation obligations in addition to the prior and informed consent of the owners and holders of the TK.[85] Third, the two states are involved in resolving issues of multiple and concurrent ownership of TK which pose serious challenges to third parties who wish to license TK. To deal with these challenges, claimants to the ownership of TK are required to engage with each other in accordance with customary laws and practices or other means.[86] The Kenyan government is to be informed when the parties resolve and agree on the owners of the TK. If there is no agreement between the parties, ownership reverts to the Kenyan government.[87] Fourthly, both States are saddled with the responsibility of keeping a register of TK and of licences granted to third parties.[88] Fifthly, Kenyan and Zambian CNAs[89] would have to reimagine their role in the licensing of aTK within the framework of existing national frameworks for implementing the Nagoya Protocol. In Kenya[90] the National Environmental Management Authority permits based on satisfaction of requirements including a BS agreement is at the heart of community consent.[91] For Zambia, no CNA has been identified, which suggests that no serious framework exists for licensing aTK.

To sum up this section, some issues need further elaboration. First, the Kenyan and Zambian statutory frameworks are a communal ownership

---

[83] See Protection of Traditional Knowledge Act (Kenya), s 25(b) and Protection of Traditional Knowledge Act (Zambia), s 18(1).

[84] See Protection of Traditional Knowledge Act (Kenya), s 12 and Protection of Traditional Knowledge Act (Zambia), s 23.

[85] Protection of Traditional Knowledge Act (Kenya), ss 27, 28 and 29.

[86] Ibid s 30.

[87] Ibid s 31. Similar provisions are found in the Protection of Traditional Knowledge Act (Zambia), s 11.

[88] Protection of Traditional Knowledge Act (Kenya), s 8 and Protection of Traditional Knowledge Act (Zambia), s 11.

[89] The Kenyan CNA is the National Environment Management Authority.

[90] See the Environmental Management and Coordination (Conservation of Biological Diversity and Resources, Access to Genetic Resources and Benefit Sharing Regulations) 2006 (Kenya).

[91] See Martin Brink, 'Implementation of Access and Benefit Sharing Policies in Sub-Saharan Africa: Inventory Analysis and Proposals' <http://edepot.wur.nl/280508>.

and mixed state and community management model. In this way they differ from the Swakopmund Protocol. Opponents of this model could claim it violates the terms and spirit of the Nagoya Protocol. On closer examination, however, the Nagoya Protocol supports the Kenyan and Zambian framework. The statutory frameworks, as well as the involvement of the State in the management of the licensing framework as outlined above, satisfy the Nagoya Protocol's requirement for clarity and certainty in access and BS.[92] Second, the recognition of communal ownership and management affirms the inherent dignity of communities and equips them with the capacity to negotiate BS agreements that truly reflect their wishes. It is true that some communities are fractured and third parties may end up in endless negotiations because of the power dynamics of some communities. Where this occurs, it is important to remember the powers of the Kenyan and Zambian States to compulsorily license access to TK to ensure that this knowledge is available for innovation and the good of society. Be that as it may, there will be challenges that seemingly diminish communal ownership. Third, the statutory frameworks, discussed above, enable communities to decide what they want for their aTK. They may wish to license or apply for a patent for their aTK, which may thereafter become the subject of further licensing. This is important because it is not self-evident that state licensing of aTK is to the benefit of communities. For example, available evidence suggests that no licensing of aTK had taken place in Kenyan communities. The 2015 ABS Initiative Country Diagnostic for Kenya concluded that over 50 access permits have been granted by the National Environmental Management Authority, but none related to aTK. This has occurred even though 'many of the supply chains for natural ingredients sourced in Kenya – from henna (Lawsonia inermis), prickly pear (Opuntia ficus-indica), and Aloe vera to gum arabic (from Senegalia (Acacia) senegal and Vachellia (Acacia) seyal), essential oils and medicinal plants – involve local communities'.[93]

It would seem from this observation that third parties have freely accessed aTK of Kenyan communities who would certainly have licensed their aTK under the PTKCE. There is little evidence that the inadequacies of the Kenyan framework lead to the promulgation of the PTKCE. Yet, an inescapable conclusion is to point to some connection between the inefficiencies of the State and the need to protect Kenyan communities.

---

92 Nagoya Protocol (n 6), art 6(3).

93 See The ABS Capacity Development Initiative <www.abs-initiative.info/partner-countries/Kenya>.

B. Constitutional Framework of Communal Ownership and Management of aTK

This section considers how African constitutions support the communal ownership and management of aTK. These constitutional considerations are important where national statutory frameworks do not fully support such principles. An example is South Africa, where, in the main, there is no obstacle to an understanding that communities are contemplated by section 25(1) of the Constitution of the Republic of South Africa 1996, which provides that '[n]o one may be deprived of property except in terms of law of general application and no law may permit arbitrary deprivation of property'. The recent recognition by the South African government that 'the South African Constitution already protects intellectual property rights from arbitrary deprivation' affirm the provisions of section 25. While there is little doubt that national intellectual property laws ordinarily include copyright patents and trademarks, it is not a jurisprudential leap to include the right of communities to their TK in the purview of section 25. No one doubts that communities can own land and in the same measure they own intellectual property such as their TK. To argue otherwise is now trite.

South Africa's experience in access and BS illustrates the difference between recognition of community interest in aTK and the consequence of the ownership and management of aTK by communities. The analysis in Section II of this chapter suggests a modest aTK licensing regime where permits have been granted by the South African government based on BS agreements between third parties and communities. There is little evidence that permits have been granted, in disregard of a BS agreement, suggesting the significance of the recognition of the rights of communities. However, the South African framework does not recognise the rights of communities to license aTK. The difference between recognition and community ownership and management is evident in the claim by the Khoisan communities to ownership of aTK associated with rooibos tea, even though the South African government had, in 2014, declared that 'there is no evidence to dispute the claim by the San and Khoi people of South Africa that they are the rightful holders of aTK associated with rooibos and honeybush'[94] and recommended that 'any individual or organization involved in bioprospecting or biotrade using rooibos or honeybush

[94] See DEA, 'Traditional Knowledge Associated with Rooibos and Honeybush Species in South Africa' <https://naturaljustice.org/publication/traditional-knowledge-associated-rooibos-honeybush-species-south-africa/>.

species is urged to engage with the Khoi or San communities to negotiate a BS agreement in terms of NEMBA or the BABS Regulations'.[95] If the Khoi or San communities are constitutionally recognised owners of TK associated with Rooibos, they would not need government affirmation of their ownership. Also, they would be far more confident in their negotiations with third parties. It is true that ownership would not obliterate the controversies and doubt of the rights of the Khoi or San communities to the TK associated with rooibos and would likely end up in South African courts. This possibility of judicial action illustrates some of the consequences of ownership. Even though there is no certainty that the Khoi or San communities will win challenges to their rights, the threat or otherwise of such action becomes part of the matrix that these communities will take into consideration in their discussions with third parties. The fact that third parties have reached BS agreements with Khoi and San communities bodes well for third parties afraid that these communities could unnecessarily hold up their commercialisation initiatives. Even though there is evidence that civil society organisations[96] have facilitated South African communities in negotiating BS agreements, that illustrates the maturity of these communities in protecting their aTK.

In exercise of their constitutional rights, local and traditional communities would be able to seek patents based on their aTK. The contention that intellectual property rights are inappropriate for the protection of TK often ignores the realities of such rights acquired by third parties over aTK. It seems far more appropriate that the owners of the aTK should be able to patent inventive applications of their knowledge, where they are able to satisfy the requirements of patentability. If these communities require third parties to assist them, their constitutional rights will assist them greatly.

The constitutional recognition of the rights of communities will also not resolve the multiple and concurrent claims of ownership of aTK, which present difficult challenges to third parties who seek certainty in their bid to access aTK. If communities are unable to resolve their differences, governments can certainly assist in accordance with the provisions of the national frameworks that are considered above. If good-faith negotiations

---

95 See DEA, 'Statement on the Report of the Study Conducted on the Traditional Knowledge Associated with Rooibos and Honeybush Species in SA' <http://www.polity.org.za/article/dea-report-of-the-study-conducted-on-the-traditional-knowledge-associated-with-the-rooibos-and-honeybush-species-in-sa-2015-05-19>.

96 An example is the organisation known as Natural Justice, which works with the San and Khoi Communities, <www.naturaljustice.org>.

among owner communities fail, as in other cases of public interest, the government can compulsorily license access to aTK.

IV. CONCLUSION

The statutory and constitutional frameworks represent renewed determination to ensure that communities protect their aTK by applying for patents or by licensing access to them. Enormous challenges will arise in the exercise of the rights of these communities in Africa, which certainly suggests that the dominant state-centric national frameworks in Africa are preferable. With the assistance of States and civil society organisations, it would appear reasonable to suggest that communities are in a better position to protect their aTK, including licensing access to third parties.

PART II

Designs and packaging and the purpose of international and regional frameworks

5. Designing disclosure: disclosure of cultural and genetic resource utilisation in design protection regimes*

Margo A. Bagley**

Intellectual colonialism is the modern manifest destiny.

Casey Brown, Ho-Chunk Nation of Wisconsin[1]

I. INTRODUCTION

The idea of industrial design, making useful articles aesthetically pleasing, is ancient in its origins,[2] and has been recognised as a protectable category of industrial property since the signing of the Paris Convention

* All online sources were last accessed on 27 December 2018.

** This chapter is a derivative of, and incorporates large portions of, Margo A Bagley, Ctr For Int'l Governance Innovation, 'Illegal Designs? Enhancing Cultural and Genetic Resource Protection Through Design Law' (2017) and was prepared with generous support from the Centre for International Governance Innovation. It also borrows from Margo A Bagley, 'Ask Me No Questions: The Struggle for Disclosure of Cultural and Genetic Resource Utilization in Design Applications' (2018) 20 Vand J Ent & Tech L 975. Special thanks to Shawn Gannon, Kurt Zhao and Chen Wang for excellent research assistance. It also benefitted from input from participants at the International Intellectual Property Scholars Workshop at New York University School of Law and the ATRIP Conference at Victoria University of Wellington, New Zealand.

1 Quoted in D J Pangborn, 'A Navajo Artist Breaks Down His Tribe's Urban Outfitters Lawsuit' (August 2016) Vice: Creators <https://creators.vice.com/en_us/article/8qvjpb/navajo-artist-urban-outfitters-lawsuit>.

2 See for example Graeme B Dinwoodie and Mark D Janis, *Trade Dress and Design Law* (Aspen 2010) 3, 5; Jason J Du Mont and Mark D Janis, 'The Origins of American Design Patent Protection' (2013) 88 Ind L J 837, 839–40; Dan Hunter and Suzannah Wood, 'The Laws of Design in the Age of Mechanical Reproduction' (2016) 37 Adelaide L Rev 403, 407.

in the mid-1800s.[3] In fact, the first trade agreement between France and the UK, signed in 1860, provided protection for 'rights of property . . . in patterns of every description'.[4] However, for most of the twentieth century, design protection was something of a backwater compared to utility patents, trade marks, and copyrights,[5] with many companies perceiving little value in this form of intellectual property (IP) coverage.[6] That has changed significantly in recent years, with design application filings increasing year after year in many jurisdictions around the world.[7] Global filings of design applications numbered approximately 872,600 in 2015 as compared to 406,500 in 2005 and 187,200 in 1995.[8] Figure 5.1

---

[3] See Paris Convention for the Protection of Industrial Property (signed on 20 March 1883, revised on 14 July 1967, last amended 28 September 1979) 21 UST 1583, 828 UNTS 305. (Paris Convention).

[4] Treaty of Commerce between Great Britain and France (signed on 23 January 1860) art XII, British and Foreign State Papers Volume 50 (1860) 23, cited in Natalia Kapyrina, 'Design Rights in EU PTAs – Where Does Such Internationalization Lead?' (2019) 53 J World Trade 4.

[5] Some elements of a design, such as surface ornamentation, can be protected by copyright or, if the design serves as a source indicator, by trade mark. See WIPO Secretariat, 'Possible Areas of Convergence in Industrial Design Law and Practice' (2009) SCT/21/4, ss 101, 104 ('In the majority of jurisdictions, a given object can be protected at the same time by design law and by trademark law . . . . Industrial designs as ornamental and aesthetic creations can in theory be protected, not only by design *sui generis* law, but also by copyright').

[6] See Sarah Burstein, 'Costly Designs' (2015) 77 Ohio St L J 107, 109–10 (noting 'design patents were decidedly out of vogue for most of the twentieth century'); Peter Lee and Madhavi Sunder, 'Design Patents: Law Without Design' (2013) 17 Stan Tech L Rev 277, 278 ('While scholars, policymakers, and the bar have devoted substantial attention to copyrights, trademarks, and utility patents, design patents have largely languished on the periphery of intellectual property').

[7] See for example Robert J Walters, 'Is Design Patent Litigation Headed for a Turnaround?' (2013) BNA Pat Trademark & Copyright J, <https://www.bloomberglaw.com/product/law> (search by author and title) (discussing the impact of the *Apple v Samsung* litigation on increasing interest in design patent protection); Margaret M Welsh and Steve M Gruskin, 'Patent Enforcement Update – Design Patents' (2014) Intell Prop Today <http://www.oppedahl.com/images/sughrue.pdf> ('With these recent developments, design patents are becoming a more useful, and in some cases a more threatening, tool in companies' patent portfolios. Companies are recognizing the value of a design patent and filing more applications than in the past').

[8] World Intellectual Property Organisation (WIPO), 'World Intellectual Property Indicators' (2016) 115, 118, www.wipo.int/edocs/pubdocs/en/wipo_pub_941_2016.pdf ('In 2015, the classes that accounted for the largest shares of the world total were furnishings (9.4%), articles of clothing (8.3%) and packages and containers (7%)'); see WIPO, 'WIPO IP Statistics Data Center', https://www3.wipo.int/ipstats/editIpsSearchForm.htm?tab=industrial (select the 'Industrial design' tab

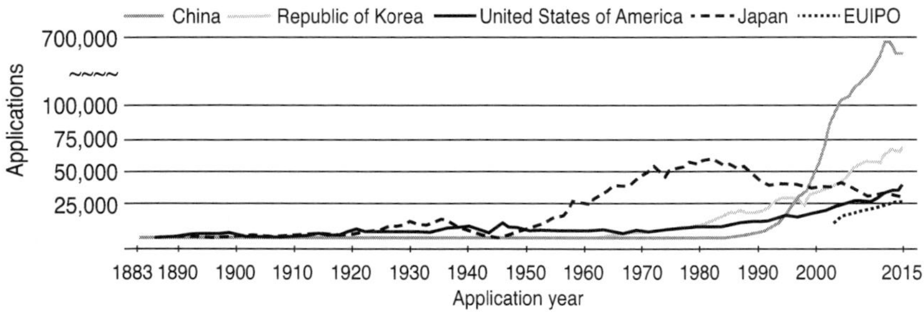

Source: World Intellectual Property Organisation (WIPO), 'World Intellectual Property Indicators' (2016) 115, 121.

Figure 5.1 Top five industrial design offices' application trends

depicts the generally steady growth in applications received by the top five industrial design offices.

The market importance of design protection is generating attention as well. A 2013 study by the European Union Intellectual Property Office (EUIPO) and the European Patent Office estimated that 12.2 per cent of EU employment and 12.8 per cent of EU gross domestic product was attributable to design-intensive industries.[9] The acquisition and enforcement of design rights by smartphone and tablet makers Apple and Samsung illustrate both the increasing interest in design protection and the value such protection can provide. In 2001 Apple obtained ten US design patents and Samsung obtained eight. However, by 2011, those numbers had increased to 123 and 333, respectively.[10] Moreover, Apple's 2012 jury award against Samsung of more than $1 billion (later reduced on appeal), most of which apparently resulted from design patents,[11] may have spurred

and further select '1 – Total design applications (direct and via the Hague system)' under indicator, 'Total count by filing office' under report type, 1995 to 2015 under year range, and 'World' under select office).

[9] European Commission, Industrial Design Protection <https://ec.europa.eu/growth/industry/intellectual-property/industrial-design/protection_en>. The euipo was formerly the Office for Harmonization in the Internal Market. See Council Regulation (EC) 2015/2424 [2015] OJ L 341/21, art 1(7).

[10] Jeffrey Stone and Brett Klein, 'Design Patent Flexes Muscles' (December 2012) DuetsBlog <www.duetsblog.com/2012/12/articles/idea-protection/design-patent-flexes-muscles/>.

[11] Ibid ('The verdict resulted in $1.05 billion owed to Apple by Samsung, primarily due to design patent infringement'); see also *Apple Inc v Samsung Elecs* (2012) 678 F3d 1314 (Fed Cir); Christopher Buccafusco and Jeanne Curtis, 'The Design Patent Bar: An Occupational Licensing Failure' (2018) <https://ssrn.com/

Samsung to file for an increased number of design patents. In 2015 Apple obtained 189 US design patents and Samsung obtained 1,428.[12] Apple's win was a wake-up call that resonated beyond Samsung, as it demonstrated to many observers and producers the potential value of design protection.

An area of increasing interest in the design space involves the exploitation of ethnically and culturally distinctive works. The use of Native American, Aboriginal, Pacific Islander, and pan-African imagery is not new, but its value and allure, including as sources of designer inspiration, appear timeless.[13] In addition, the use of natural materials such as those employed by Indigenous peoples in handicrafts or as sacred objects also remains high.[14] Figure 5.2 showing an early 20th-century Romanian coat

---

abstract=3245319> ('Design patents aren't only expanding in raw numbers. They also seem to be increasingly valuable to firms' IP portfolios. The recent smartphone litigation between Apple and Samsung resulted in enormous infringement verdicts that were largely based on Apple's design patents. Accordingly, we expect design patents' legal and economic significance to continue to grow').

[12] Larry Cady, 'IFI Has Not Forgotten About Design Patents: The US Design Top 50' IFI Claims Pat Servs (September 2016) <https://www.ificlaims.com/news/view/blog-posts/ifi-has-not-forgotten.htm>.

[13] See WIPO, 'Gnaritas Nullius (No Ones' Knowledge): The Public Domain and Colonization of Traditional Knowledge' (2010) WIPO/GRTKF/IC/17/INF/5(A), 3 ('Elaborate Indigenous artistic techniques and designs in sculpture, painting, music, drama, dance, continue to thrive in traditional and evolved forms, and have intrigued art historians and the art world for centuries'); Monica B Visionà, Robin Poynor and Herbert M Cole, *A History of Art in Africa* (2nd edn, Prentice Hall 2005) 16–23 (noting 'European modernism's universally acknowledged debt' to African art and describing its collection, improper appropriation, and mislabelling during colonisation); Tom Greaves (ed), *IPR: A Current Survey* (Society for Applied Anthropology 1994) 1, 3–4 ; Jennie D Woltz, 'The Economics of Cultural Misrepresentation: How Should the Indian Arts and Crafts Act of 1990 Be Marketed?'(2007) 17 Fordham Intell Prop Media & Ent L J 443, 445 ('The high demand for Indian goods, fueled in part by the New Age movement and increased travel and consumerism in America in the 1970s and 1980s, results in the diversion of millions of dollars a year from Indian communities [due to counterfeits])' (footnote omitted)). For additional examples see the Traditional Maasai Beaded Fringe, in Allison M Kotowicz, 'Maasai Identity in the 21st Century' (2013) University of Wisconsin Milwaukee Dissertation 100, as compared to the Beaded Fringe from the 2016 Valentino Spring / Summer Collection at Sarah Mower, 'Spring 2016 Ready-To-Wear Collection: Valentino' (October 2015) Vogue <https://www.vogue.com/fashion-shows/spring-2016-ready-to-wear/valentino>; and New Zealand Maori Carvings and Depictions on Shower Curtains, in 'Store Sells 'Profoundly Hurtful' Maori Shower Curtains Depicting Tribal Leaders' (June 2016) STUFF: BUS. DAY <http://www.stuff.co.nz/business/81277960/Store-sells-profoundly-hurtful-Maori-shower-curtains-depicting-tribal-leaders>.

[14] As Professor Paul Kuruk explains: 'Advanced technological processes have facilitated the commercial exploitation of works of art, craft, and knowledge of

Figure 5.2 Early 20th-centrury Romanian coat and Tory burch copy

and Tory Burch copy provides a striking example of this trend.[15] Sadly, the demand for endangered species-derived prestige items also shows no sign of waning.[16]

---

traditional societies on a scale that is unprecedented. . . . Associated with these forms of folklore commercialization is a serious concern that traditional societies may be short-changed or even harmed during the process. . . . These communities are also harmed by uses that degrade cultural items to the extent the items are displayed outside their traditional setting and for purposes different from those for which they were originally created. For instance, this occurs when religious artifacts are sold as mere decorative art. There is further harm where commercial copies of cultural works misrepresent communal values, are of inferior quality, or are made from different materials.' Paul Kuruk (n14) 770–73.

[15] Mary Anderson, 'The UN Wants to Make Cultural Appropriation Illegal' (June 2017) ('The issue is bigger than just copying a design – cultural appropriation is one brand profiting off of another culture's creations') <https://www.revelist.com/style-news/un-cultural-appropriation/8128/the-issue-is-bigger-than-just-copying-a-design--cultural-appropriation-is-one-brand-profiting-off-of-another-cultures-creations/2>. See also Adrija Sen, 'Dior Has (Again) Copied a Local Artist's Design. When Are We Going to Hold Brands Accountable?' (July 2018) Vagabomb <https://www.vagabomb.com/Dior-Has-Again-Copied-a-Local-Artists-Design/> ('Bihor, a small village in Romania. Bihor is taking on the international giant for blatantly copying a Romanian folk coat, and passing it off as their own design in their pre-fall 2017 collection'); See also Andželika, 'Romanian People Noticed that Dior Copied Their Traditional Clothing and Decided to Fight Back in a Genius Way' ('The issue is bigger than just copying a design – cultural appropriation is one brand profiting off of another culture's creations') <https://www.boredpanda.com/dior-copy-traditional-romanian-design-clothes/?utm_source=google&utm_medium=organic&utm_campaign=organic> (describing communities ad campaign).

[16] See also Rachel Nuwer, 'A Mausoleum for Endangered Species' New York

Another area of expanding design interest is in patterns and materials created through biotechnology. The do-it-yourself ethos common to synthetic biology[17] aficionados is helping to fuel a biodesign explosion that includes fashion and fabrics, such as leather 'grown' from mushrooms and scarves dyed with bacterial secretions.[18] We are living in a brave new biocreative world.

The increasing awareness of the value of design protection is also evident in efforts to facilitate the ability to gain such protection globally. The World Intellectual Property Organization (WIPO) Hague Agreement Concerning the International Registration of Industrial Designs (the 'Hague Agreement') allows applicants to file a single application that can contain up to 100 designs, which creates protection in all member countries that do not indicate rejection of the application within a specified period.[19] The United States fully joined the Geneva Act of the Hague Agreement[20] in 2015,[21] extending this benefit to US designers and paving the way

---

Times (July 2017) (describing a Colorado repository containing 1.3 million confiscated items).

[17] Synthetic biology involves the design and construction of novel artificial biological pathways, organisms or devices, or the redesign of existing natural biological systems and the creation of standardised biological parts that can be assembled into more complex modules to perform particular functions. For a discussion of synthetic biology issues relating to genetic resources and associated traditional knowledge research, see Nat'l Acads of Sci Eng'g & Med, 'A Proposed Framework For Identifying Potential Biodefense Vulnerabilities Posed by Synthetic Biology: Interim Reports' (2017); see also Margo A Bagley, 'Digital DNA: The Nagoya Protocol, Intellectual Property Treaties, and Synthetic Biology' (2015) <https://www.wilsoncenter.org/publication/digital-dna-the-nagoya-protocol-intellectual-property-treaties-and-synthetic-biology>

[18] See for example MyCoworks < http://www.mycoworks.com/#about> (leathers grown from mushrooms and agricultural byproducts). See also; Natsai Audrey <http://natsaiaudrey.co.uk/> (describing a design-led microbiology protocol that replaces harmful synthetic pigments with natural dyes excreted by bacteria used to produce scarves dyed with bacterial secretions) and Priscilla Frank, 'Incredible Bacteria-Laced Fabric Combines Art, Biology and Fashion' (December 2017) Huffington Post <http://www.huffingtonpost.com/2014/12/19/the-fold-studio-natasai-au_n_6340294.html>).

[19] See Geneva Act of the Hague Agreement Concerning the International Registration of Industrial Designs (July 1999) 2279 UNTS 3, ch 1.

[20] The Hague Agreement comprises three independent acts: the London Act of 1934, the Hague Act of 1960 and the Geneva Act of 1999. See WIPO, 'Summary of the Hague Agreement Concerning the International Registration of Industrial Designs' <https://www.wipo.int/treaties/en/registration/hague/summary_hague.html>.

[21] Press Release, US Patent & Trademark Office, 'United States Deposits Instrument of Ratification to Geneva Act of the Hague Agreement Concerning

for increased use of the Hague system. WIPO, which administers the agreement, received 5,562 applications containing a total of 18,716 designs via the Hague system in 2016, representing a 35 per cent increase over 2015 and the seventh consecutive year of growth in filings.[22]

While the Hague Agreement creates an international, centralised registration system, it does not directly affect the filing of design applications in national offices. Countries seeking the harmonisation and simplification of industrial design formalities at the national level thus have been working to achieve that end through negotiation of another international instrument – the draft Design Law Treaty (DLT) currently under discussion in the WIPO Standing Committee on the Law of Trademarks, Industrial Designs and Geographical Indications (SCT). The DLT, which is intended to be a formalities treaty but may have some substantive effects, is expected to facilitate obtaining design rights globally by limiting the requirements countries may impose on design protection applicants.[23]

These three areas of increasing interest – design protection, creative cultural motifs, and biotech-derived design elements – may appear disparate, yet they are converging in ways that raise concerns for some low- and middle-income countries (LMICs) that are rich in biological diversity, traditional knowledge, and creative cultural products and artefacts. This is because cultural and genetic resources, namely traditional cultural expressions (e.g., designs, artefacts, carvings and paintings),[24]

---

the International Registration of Industrial Designs' (February 2015) <https://www.uspto.gov/about-us/news-updates/united-states-deposits-instrument-ratification-geneva-act-hague-agreement>.

[22] WIPO (n 8) (select the 'Hague' tab and further select '7 – Designs in applications by office' under indicator, 'Yearly statistics' under report type, 2010 to 2016 under year range, and 'Total' under office of contracting party).

[23] See WIPO, 'Relationship Between the Hague System for the International Registration of Industrial Designs and the Draft Design Law Treaty' (2013) WIPO SCT/29/4 (Relationship Between the Hague System and the Draft Design Law Treaty) ss 1, 4, 5, 12.

[24] See for example 'Totem Bottle', Can Indus Design No 151,320 (registered 23 July 2014). For further examples see Priya Patel, 'My Culture Is Not Your Couture' Odyssey (2016) <https://www.theodysseyonline.com/my-culture-is-not-your-couture>; Alexandra J Roberts (@lexlanham) Twitter (October 2017) <https://twitter.com/lexlanham/status/916379949161959424?lang=en>; Aboriginal Industrial Designs <http://nationalaboriginaldesignagency.com.au/category/media/>; Can Des Reg 151320 'Totem bottle' (2014); Fr Des Reg 20125711-0003 'Parure africaine II'; Fr Des Reg 'African warrior decorative pattern' 962966-0007 (1996); Fr Des Reg 28023-0001 'African box' (1936); Fr Des Reg 932111-0016 'Bride mule'; Chinese Des Pat 201530476508.4 'Teacup pad' (2015); Chinese Des Pat 'African

Source: Aranda (2018), <https://www.aranda.co.za/>.

Figure 5.3 Traditional Basotho blanket designs

traditional knowledge (e.g., distinctive weaving or painting techniques),[25] and biological or genetic resources (e.g., DNA, enzymes, fibres and microorganisms),[26] can be used to create protectable designs.[27] A recent example concerns traditional Basotho blanket designs, some of which are shown in Figure 5.3. Louis Vuitton's production of a shirt with strikingly similar design raises clear issues of cultural appropriation.[28] A controversy in the WIPO SCT regarding policy space for design application disclosure of origin requirements[29] relating to such cultural and genetic resources

mask' 201430452690.5 (2014); Fr Des Reg 20123822 – 015; 'Navajo bracelet'; Fr Des Reg 20134945 - 001 'Yuma bracelet'; Fr Des Reg 20135496 – 001 'Carré de soie 80x80, collection Kwa Zulu'.

[25] See (n 15). For a Ghanaian Kente pattern on a Christian Louboutin bag, see Figure 5.4.

[26] See (n 17) and (n 18).

[27] See (nn 119–42) and accompanying text.

[28] See Mary Corrigall, 'Fab or Cultural Faux Pas? Louis Vuitton's Basotho Blanket-Inspired Collection' (July 2017) Sunday Times <https://www.timeslive.co.za/sunday-times/lifestyle/fashion-and-beauty/2017-07-13-the-evolution-of-the-basotho-blanket/>. See also Aranda (2018) <https://www.aranda.co.za/>. See also Mayeni Jones, 'When does cultural borrowing turn into cultural appropriation?' BBC Africa (2017) <https://www.bbc.com/news/world-africa-41430748> ('Blankets from Lesotho are at the centre of controversy in the fashion world, with some arguing that powerful people are appropriating them for their own benefit').

[29] This chapter does not address the normative question of whether disclosure of origin requirements are beneficial or negatively impact legal certainty. Various authors have explored such questions, and this author addresses them in Margo A Bagley, 'Of Disclosure "Straws" and IP System "Camels": Patents, Innovation,

is a manifestation of these concerns. Triggered by an African Group proposal,[30] the controversy has brought negotiations on the DLT to a virtual standstill.

At the time of writing, WIPO Members are engaged in protracted, text-based discussions in the WIPO Intergovernmental Committee on Intellectual Property and Genetic Resources, Traditional Knowledge, and Folklore (IGC), which may result in one or more legal instruments directed to genetic resources, traditional knowledge, and traditional cultural expressions.[31] However, it is very possible that a decision on the content of the draft DLT could constrain outcomes relating to disclosure provisions in the IGC texts, raising policy coherence concerns that may not be immediately apparent to negotiators in either committee.

This chapter focuses on the controversy in the WIPO SCT over the draft DLT cultural and genetic resource disclosure of origin provision, on possible justifications countries may have for desiring the flexibility to impose disclosure requirements on design protection applicants, and on the broader ramifications of the dispute for negotiations in the IGC. Section II provides an introduction to design protection regimes and the WIPO draft DLT. Section III describes the African Group's proposal for cultural and genetic resource disclosure of origin policy space in the draft DLT, arguments for and against the proposal, and developments in national and regional traditional knowledge, traditional cultural expression, and biological and genetic resource protection systems that ostensibly led to the proposal. Section IV focuses on advances in biotechnology that are fuelling the design creation and the biological and genetic resource misappropriation[32] concerns that, in part, underlie the desire for disclosure or origin policy space. Section V provides concluding thoughts on the controversy.

---

and the Disclosure of Origin Requirement' in Daniel F Robinson, Ahmed Abdel-Latif and Pedro Roffe (eds), *Protecting Traditional Knowledge: The WIPO Intergovernmental Committee on Intellectual Property and Genetic Resources, Traditional Knowledge and Folklore* (Routledge 2017) 85. Rather, the focus of this chapter is on whether countries should have the policy space to impose disclosure of origin requirements in industrial design applications.

[30] See (nn 76–84).

[31] See Bagley (n 29) 89–90.

[32] The term 'misappropriation' has many meanings and may include uses of resources that may have been properly acquired for one purpose, but are being used for a non-permitted purpose or by unauthorised parties: 'Misappropriate', New Oxford American Dictionary (3rd edn, Oxford 2016).

II. DESIGN LAW AND THE WIPO DRAFT DESIGN LAW TREATY

Design protection encompasses a wide swath of eligible subject matter. There are 219 international design classification categories and 5,167 entries, ranging from automobiles to salad bowls to zip fasteners.[33] The design right covers the ornamental appearance of a useful article. For example, design protection in the United States applies to 'an ornamental design' for 'an article of manufacture',[34] while the European Union applies design protection to the 'appearance' of an 'industrial or handicraft item'[35] and China limits such protection to new designs for the shape or pattern of products that 'are rich in an aesthetic appeal and are fit for industrial application'.[36] Regardless of jurisdiction, design protection generally is available for designs not solely dictated by the function of the product in which the design subsists or to which it is applied. Such protection does not, however, extend to the way the product works, which is the province of utility patents.[37]

Article 25 of the Agreement on Trade Related Aspects of Intellectual Property (TRIPS) specifies that '[m]embers shall provide for the protection of independently created industrial designs that are new or original';[38] however, TRIPS does not stipulate the means of protection that countries must adopt. As such, it is unsurprising that national design protection systems, while having some commonalities, retain a number of distinctive differences.

---

33 WIPO, 'International Classification for Industrial Designs' (10th edn 2013) 501E/10 119, 131, 155; WIPO, 'About the Locarno Classification' <http://www.wipo.int/classifications/locarno/en/preface.html>. See Locarno Agreement Establishing an International Classification for Industrial Designs (signed on 8 October 1968) 828 UNTS 435.

34 35 USC (2012), s 171(a).

35 Council Regulation (EC) 6/2002 of 12 December 2001 on Community Designs [2002] OJ L 3/1, art 3(a) (CDR).

36 Zhonghua Renmin Gongheguo Zhuanli Fa (中华人民共和国专利法) (Patent Law of the People's Republic of China) 2009, art 2.

37 See for example Industrial Design Act 1985 (Canada), s 5.

38 Agreement on Trade-Related Aspects of Intellectual Property Rights (opened for signature 15 April 1994, entered into force 1 January 1996) 1869 UNTS 299 (TRIPS).

A. Design Protection Regimes

Most countries, including the members of the European Union, Brazil, Canada, many African countries, Japan and South Korea, protect designs as a distinct IP right separate from patents.[39] For example, the EUIPO, the agency responsible for EU-wide design protection, grants a registered community design (RCD) that protects 'the appearance of the whole or a part of a product resulting from the features of, in particular, the lines, contours, colours, shape, texture and/or materials of the product itself and/or its ornamentation'.[40]

While the design covered by the RCD is required to be novel, the EUIPO – as with most other industrial design offices – does not engage in a substantive novelty examination during the registration process; instead, the application undergoes a purely formal, relatively speedy review.[41] Thus, design protection can often be obtained more quickly and less expensively than a utility patent. Yet a design right can be just as valuable as a utility patent if infringement is found and an injunction barring importation or sale of the article embodying the design is granted. Such an EU-wide injunction was granted, albeit temporarily, against Samsung in 2011 in its wide-ranging litigation with Apple over, inter alia, cellphone and tablet designs.[42] The injunction barred the sale of certain Samsung

---

[39] See Industrial Property Code 1996 (Brazil); CDR, art 3(a); Ishō-hō (Design Act) Law 1959 (Japan), art 9; Patents and Designs Act 1990 (Nigeria), s 12; San-eob Dijain Bohobeob (Industrial Design Protection Act) 1961, art 2(1).

[40] CDR, art 3 (a).

[41] Ibid s 18; see Gordon Humphreys, 'Legal Reform of the Community Design: A Precis of Two Reports' (2017) <http://fordhamipinstitute.com/wp-content/uploads/2017/04/Humphreys_Gordon_Article2017.pdf>. Canada is an exception as the Industrial Design Act specifies that '[t]he Minister shall examine each application for the registration of a design to ascertain whether the design meets the requirements of this Act for registration', Industrial Design Act (Canada), s 5. The United States is another exception as US law also requires design patent applications to be substantively examined for novelty and non-obviousness (See 37 CFR s 1.104 (2018)). However, according to Professor Crouch, the United States actually has a de facto registration system: '[T]he USPTO's examination of design patent novelty can best be described as a *farce*. In a 2010 study, I found that the vast majority of design patent applications do not receive even a single rejection during the examination process and only 1.2% are the subject of an obviousness or novelty rejection.' Dennis Crouch, 'UK Appellate Court Confirms Pan-European Win for Samsung on iPad Community Design Charges' (October 2010) Patentlyo <https://patentlyo.com/patent/2012/10/apple-samsung-european-community-design.html>.

[42] Hyunjoo Jin and Poornima Gupta, 'Apple Blocks Samsung from Selling Galaxy Tablet in EU' (August 2011) Reuters <https://www.reuters.com/article/

tablets in the European Union based on Apple's RCD despite the fact that the RCD did not extend protection to the way the Apple tablet worked or how it was made.[43]

While most countries protect designs with *sui generis* design regimes, a few countries – including the United States and China – protect designs through the grant of patents. A design patent is simply a type of patent granted on the ornamental design of a functional item. While a standard utility or invention patent protects the way an article is used or works, a design patent protects the way it looks.[44] However, as noted above, the design cannot be dictated solely by the function of the article. In other words, if the article needs that particular design in order to work properly or more effectively, the design is not protectable.

Design protection can be very beneficial. Its advantages include speedy, often purely formal examination, the establishment of an alternative basis to utility patents for alleging infringement, and the possible remedies of injunctive relief and damages.[45] The term of design protection varies across jurisdictions from a short three years for unregistered community designs in the European Union to 25 years for EU-registered community designs, 15 years for US design patents, and 10 years for design rights in China and Canada.[46] The exclusivity afforded by design protection may

---

us-apple-samsung-injunction/apple-blocks-samsung-from-selling-galaxy-tablet-in-eu-idUSTRE7786RY20110810>.

43 See Cyrus Farivar, 'German Court Suspends EU-Wide Injunction Against Samsung' (August 2011) Deutsche Welle <http://www.dw.com/en/german-court-suspends-eu-wide-injunction-against-samsung/a-15323043>; Chris Foresman, 'Apple's Worldwide Court Battles v Samsung: Where They Stand' (September 2011) Wired <https://www.wired.com/2011/09/apple-court-battles-samsung/>.

44 See US Patent & Trademark Office, 'Manual of Patent Examining Procedure' (9th edn 2018) s 1502.01 (USPTO Manual). 'In general terms, a "utility patent" protects the way an article is used and works, while a "design patent" protects the way an article looks. The ornamental appearance for an article includes its shape/configuration or surface ornamentation applied to the article, or both. Both design and utility patents may be obtained on an article if invention resides both in its utility and ornamental appearance.'

45 See Andrew Beckerman-Rodau, 'Design Patent Evolution: From Obscurity to Center Stage' (2015) 32 Santa Clara High Tech LJ 53, 57 ('In most countries an industrial design registration system is used under which a design is registered without any examination of the design by a governmental agency'); David Orozco, 'Rational Design Rights Ignorance' (2009) 46 Am Bus LJ 573, 585 ('Design patent infringement can lead to significant monetary damages, and . . . it offers the owner the right to request a preliminary injunction').

46 See for example 35 USC (2012), s 173; Industrial Design Act 1985 (Canada), s 10(1); Zhonghua Renmin Gongheguo Zhuanli Fa (中华人民共和国专利法) (Patent Law of the People's Republic of China) 2009, s 42; CDR, arts 11–12.

also allow a registrant to segue into perpetual trade dress protection if the design comes to serve as a non-functional indicator of source or origin, which happened with the distinctive shape of the Coca-Cola soft drink bottle.[47]

How one determines infringement of a design right also varies by jurisdiction. In the United States, courts consider whether two designs are substantially similar from the perspective of an ordinary observer familiar with prior art designs.[48] For EU RCDs, an infringing design comprises 'any design which does not produce on the informed user a different overall impression',[49] where the informed user is deemed to be aware of existing designs. Importantly, even though the registration may indicate the type of item to which the design is applied, protection extends to incorporation of the design in any product.[50]

The subject matter of design often can be protected by copyright or trade mark law, raising cumulation and pre-emption concerns.[51] Design protection is also available for surface ornamentation or patterns, which generally qualify for copyright protection as artistic works as well.[52] From one perspective, the protection of distinct patterns makes sense as many design patents for the appearance of articles do not include the pattern that actually appears on the article as it is produced and sold.[53] A US

---

47 For the original design of Coca-Cola's signature contour bottle, see US Patent No 48,160 (filed 16 November 1915). See Phil Mooney, 'The Contour Bottle Is Born' (2009) Coca-Cola <http://www.coca-colacompany.com/stories/the-contour-bottle-is-born>; see also Burstein (n 6) 131–32 (describing how a design patent can help its owner obtain trade dress protection); Tiffany Mahmood, 'Design Law in the United States as Compared to the European Community Design System: What Do We Need to Fix?' (2014) 24 Fordham Intell Prop Media & Ent LJ 555, 581 ('Trade dress provides protection for packaging and products that have essentially become part of the designer's brand').

48 See *Egyptian Goddess Inc v Swisa Inc* (2008) 543 F3d 665, 670 (Fed Cir).

49 CDR, art 10(1).

50 See *Procter & Gamble Co v Reckitt Benckiser (UK) Ltd* [2006] EWHC 3154 [21]–[22].

51 See Dinwoodie and Janis (n 2) 24 (identifying a 'cumulation/preemption' problem illustrated by the design protection laws of the United States and certain foreign jurisdictions: 'should a designer be able to claim rights in the same design under multiple regimes ("cumulation"), or should protection under one regime preclude protection under another ("preemption")?').

52 Richard Stim, 'Design Patents: Ornamental Design?' (2018) Intell Prop L Firms <http://www.intellectualpropertylawfirms.com/resources/intellectual-property/patents/design-patents-w>; see also US Pat & Trademark Office, USPTO Patent Full-Text Databases <http://patft.uspto.gov> (listing more than 300 fabric designs).

53 See (n 53) and (n 54); see also US Pat & Trademark Office, 'Design

design patent for the 'Paloma' handbag as shown in Figure 5.4,[54] obtained by Christian Louboutin, and correlating product advertisement in Figure 5.5, illustrate this practice.

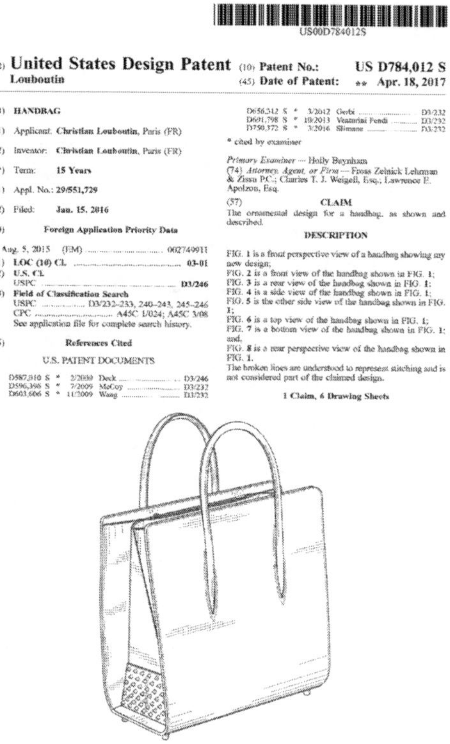

US00D784012S

(12) **United States Design Patent** (10) **Patent No.: US D784,012 S**
Louboutin (45) **Date of Patent: ** Apr. 18, 2017**

(54) **HANDBAG**

(71) Applicant: **Christian Louboutin**, Paris (FR)

(72) Inventor: **Christian Louboutin**, Paris (FR)

(**) Term: **15 Years**

(21) Appl. No.: **29/551,729**

(22) Filed: **Jan. 15, 2016**

(30) **Foreign Application Priority Data**

Aug. 5, 2015 (EM) 002749911

(51) **LOC (10) Cl.** **03-01**

(52) **U.S. Cl.**
USPC **D3/246**

(58) **Field of Classification Search**
USPC D3/232-233, 240-243, 245-246
CPC A45C 1/024; A45C 3/08
See application file for complete search history.

(56) **References Cited**

U.S. PATENT DOCUMENTS

D587,910 S * 2/2009 Deck D3/246
D596,396 S * 7/2009 McCoy D3/232
D603,606 S * 11/2009 Wang D3/232
D656,312 S * 3/2012 Gerbi D3/232
D691,798 S * 10/2013 Venturini Fendi D3/232
D750,372 S * 3/2016 Slimane D3/232

* cited by examiner

Primary Examiner — Holly Baynham
(74) *Attorney, Agent, or Firm* — Fross Zelnick Lehrman & Zissu P.C.; Charles T. J. Weigell, Esq.; Lawrence E. Apolzon, Esq.

(57) **CLAIM**

The ornamental design for a handbag, as shown and described.

DESCRIPTION

FIG. **1** is a front perspective view of a handbag showing my new design;
FIG. **2** is a front view of the handbag shown in FIG. **1**;
FIG. **3** is a rear view of the handbag shown in FIG. **1**;
FIG. **4** is a side view of the handbag shown in FIG. **1**;
FIG. **5** is the other side view of the handbag shown in FIG. **1**;
FIG. **6** is a top view of the handbag shown in FIG. **1**;
FIG. **7** is a bottom view of the handbag shown in FIG. **1**; and,
FIG. **8** is a rear perspective view of the handbag shown in FIG. **1**.
The broken lines are understood to represent stitching and is not considered part of the claimed design.

1 Claim, 6 Drawing Sheets

Source: www.uspto.gov.

Figure 5.4 Louboutin handbag design patent

Patent Application Guide' (2018) <https://www.uspto.gov/patents-getting-started/patent-basics/types-patent-applications/design-patent-application-guide> ('Since a design is manifested in appearance, the subject matter of a design patent application may relate to the configuration or shape of an article, to the surface ornamentation applied to an article, or to the combination of configuration and surface ornamentation'). For additional examples, see Andrew Rapacke, 'Design Patent Law: 2017 Year in Review' (2018) <https://arapackelaw.com/wp-content/uploads/2018/01/2017_designpatent_YER.pdf>.

[54] US Patent No D784,012 S (filed 15 January 2016) as well as US Patent Nos D679,099 (sheet material with camouflage pattern) and D766,598 (plaid fabric).

Source: Net-A-Porter, 'Christian Louboutin: Paloma Medium Studded Embroidered Leather Tote' <https://www.net-a-porter.com/ca/en/product/838670/christian_louboutin/paloma-medium-studded-embroidered-leather-tote>.

Figure 5.5 Advertisement for Louboutin 'Paloma' handbag with Kente pattern

This approach allows a manufacturer broader protection, as the design patent covers the appearance of the article even if a variety of different pattern designs are used on it in practice. Thus, if a manufacturer desires protection for a particular pattern, it would be logical to register it separately so that it would be infringed when placed on *any* article.

Concerns may arise, however, where patterns cover traditional cultural expressions or designs made using traditional knowledge. Whether Louboutin has permission from the Ghanaian government to use the Kente pattern is unknown.[55] Even if not, as Professor Osei-Tutu rightly

[55] Ghana Copyright Act 2005, s 76 provides explicit protection for Kente designs and vests rights in the president of Ghana in trust for the Republic of Ghana's citizens. See Begona Venero Aguirre and Hai-Yuean Tualima, 'WIPO

explains, uses of traditional knowledge or traditional cultural expressions in countries where they are not protected under domestic law is not illegal, and there is no international treaty requiring countries to provide such protection.[56] It is also unclear whether Louboutin has sought design protection for the Kente-based pattern appearing on the 'Paloma' handbag in Figure 5.5. Such a pattern, if original, is eligible for design protection that is covered by design rights.

Likewise, the cited examples above are the type of subject matter that is eligible for design protection, but they are not known to be the subject of design protection. At least two factors contribute to the difficulty in ascertaining whether a design is, in fact, protected by a design right. First, searching for designs is challenging as one is effectively searching for pictures using words. Moreover, the IP offices granting such rights do not require detailed word descriptions for the designs, as what the design covers is expected to, in effect, speak for itself. Thus a vast array of visually distinct and diverse images may be protected by registrations that simply describe them as 'surface ornamentation for fabric', 'tartan', or the like, and giving no indication by appellation of the specific features or origin of the protected design.[57]

Second, many countries allow registrants to delay publication of a design registration for a specified time period, a practice that will be mandatory (minimum six-month publication delay) under the provisions of the draft DLT.[58] Thus, a design application may have been filed and a design registered, yet third parties would be unaware of the grant of protection until at least six months after the right had been granted.

Design protection has long been one of the least harmonised areas of IP law. TRIPS devotes a mere two articles to industrial design protection, compared to six for copyright (which explicitly incorporates provisions from the Berne Convention for the Protection of Literary and Artistic

---

Protect and Promote Your Culture: A Practical Guide to Intellectual Property for Indigenous Peoples and Local Communities' (2017) 27 <http://www.wipo.int/edocs/pubdocs/en/wipo_pub_1048.pdf>.

[56] J Janewa Osei-Tutu, 'Harmonizing Cultural IP Across Borders: Fashionable Bags & Ghanaian Adinkra Symbols' (2017) 51 Akron L Rev 1197.

[57] See Communication from the United States, 'Traditional Cultural Expressions: A Discussion Paper' (2017) WIPO/GRTKF/IC/33/; see also Scottish Reg Tartans, 'About Us' (2018) <https://www.tartanregister.gov.uk/aboutUs>.

[58] See Draft Design Law Treaty, art 9 ('A Contracting Party shall allow the industrial design to be maintained unpublished for a period fixed by its applicable law, subject to the minimum period prescribed in the Regulations'); Draft Regulations Rule 6 ('The minimum period referred to in Article 9(1) shall be six months from the filing date or, where priority is claimed, from the priority date').

Works), seven for trade marks (10 including provisions on geographical indications, which some countries address under trade mark law), and eight for patents.[59] According to Jerome Reichman, 'industrial design has posed the intellectual property world's single most complicated puzzle'.[60] Jason Du Mont and Mark Janis likewise note that '[t]he design protection debate is one of intellectual property law's most intractable, engrossing decades of legislative effort in the United States alone'.[61]

Despite this lack of harmony, or perhaps because of it, the draft DLT requirements putatively reflect areas of convergence and common trends among member states.[62] As discussed below, this push for convergence in relation to a newly popular and controversial right is creating an existential challenge to the WIPO draft DLT negotiations and raising fundamental questions regarding cultural values, legal experimentation, and policy coherence.

B. The WIPO Draft DLT: Substantive Formality

The draft DLT is principally directed toward making the cross-border acquisition and protection of industrial design rights more efficient and effective.[63] Like the WIPO Patent Law Treaty (PLT), the DLT is styled as a formalities treaty.[64] As such, it ostensibly focuses on minimising administrative requirements that countries can impose on applicants who apply for protection in a member state. The DLT does not purport to change the substantive scope of a country's domestic design law. For example, the DLT (like the Berne Convention, Paris Convention and TRIPS) does not provide a definition of a protectable design.

This is not to say, however, that characterising the DLT as a formalities treaty means it, in fact, has no effect on substantive aspects of domestic design law. The draft DLT contains several nominally formal provisions with arguably substantive effects. For example, Article 17 prevents any

---

59 See generally TRIPS (n 38).

60 Jerome H Reichman, 'Past and Current Trends in the Evolution of Design Protection Law – A Comment' (1993) 4 Fordham Intell Prop Media & Ent LJ 387, 387.

61 Du Mont and Janis (n 2) 839–40.

62 Relationship Between the Hague System and the Draft Design Law Treaty, s 13 (noting the DLT provisions 'were established as a result of a process that identified areas of convergence and common trends among members of the SCT').

63 Ibid ss 3–5.

64 Ibid s 4 ('The aim of the draft DLT is to establish a dynamic and predictable legal framework for the simplification and harmonization of industrial design formalities and procedures set by national/regional offices').

country that requires recorded licences of design rights from invalidating a registration for non-compliance with that requirement.[65] Moreover, the draft DLT regulations would require countries to allow use of dotted lines to indicate unclaimed subject matter, a tool that effectively expands the scope of the design right.[66]

Article 3 of the proposed DLT is the heart of the treaty and prescribes a 'closed' list of elements or information that countries can require of applicants seeking to protect designs in DLT member states.[67] Put differently, it sets out the *maximum* content that can be required in a design application by a contracting party to the DLT.[68] For example, it allows countries to require applicants to provide their name and address, a registration request, correspondence information, representation of the design, and an indication of the product(s) incorporating the design.[69]

However, by delineating a closed list of application requirements that countries can impose on applicants, the DLT in effect moves beyond formalities to placing substantive limits on countries in relation to design registration. In response, a group of countries has been seeking to create space in the agreement for both substantive and formal policy flexibility.

---

65 WIPO, 'Industrial Design Law and Practice – Draft Articles' (2015) SCT/33/2.

66 See also Dinwoodie and Janis (n 2) 2014–2015. Waltmire describes an excellent illustration from the *Apple v Samsung* litigation: 'The Samsung Galaxy S 4G smartphone on the right has a different back shape and lacks a circular home button on the front as compared to the [iPhone patent,] . . . [b]ut a jury determined that the Galaxy infringed the [iPhone patent] in the case of *Apple v Samsung*. . . . Did the jury ignore those different elements of the Galaxy phone? Yes. And they were right to ignore them. Apple drafted the [iPhone patent] in a way that requires that the differences in the back shape and the home button be ignored. Apple did that by providing those features in broken lines. . . . If Apple would have shown all sides and all features of the iPhone in solid lines in [its patent], then it is possible that the jury would have determined that the Galaxy did not infringe the [iPhone patent].' Eric Waltmire, 'How to Broaden Design Patent Protection with Broken Lines: Apple v Samsung' (May 2015) Eric Waltmire's Blog <http://www.waltmire.com/2015/05/07/broaden-design-patent-protection-broken-lines-apple-v-samsung/>.

67 WIPO (n 65) 6–8.

68 See Relationship Between the Hague System and the Draft Design Law Treaty, s 4 ('The draft DLT does not create a single set of standard requirements, but rather a maximum set of requirements to be applied by the Offices of Contracting Parties').

69 See WIPO, 'Industrial Design Law and Practice – Draft Articles' (2016) SCT/35/2.

III. THE AFRICAN GROUP DISCLOSURE OF ORIGIN PROPOSAL

Just a decade ago, a requirement that a designer disclose the origin of traditional cultural expressions, traditional knowledge, or biological or genetic resources used in creating a design in an application to register the design was virtually unheard of in national or regional protection systems for any type of IP right.[70] Yet, as a recent WIPO study confirms, disclosure of origin requirements are proliferating – particularly in relation to utility patents and genetic resources.[71]

While there are no definitive definitions for the terms, another recent WIPO publication describes traditional knowledge as being generally understood to encompass 'the know-how, skills, innovations and practices developed by indigenous peoples and local communities' and traditional cultural expressions as generally referring to 'the tangible and intangible forms in which traditional knowledge and cultures are expressed'.[72] Genetic

---

[70] See for example Alison L Hoare and Richard G Tarasofsky, 'Asking and Telling: Can "Disclosure of Origin" Requirements in Patent Applications Make a Difference?' (2007) 19 JWIP 149, 156 ('To date, [disclosure or origin requirements] have had limited impact . . . because they have not been in place very long [and] . . . they only refer to national patent applications . . . Consequently, there have been very few patent applications in which disclosure has been made'). Since that time, the international community has seen the enactment of the Nagoya Protocol and Swakopmund Protocol, as well as domestic laws requiring disclosure. See Nagoya Protocol on Access to Genetic Resources and the Fair and Equitable Sharing of Benefits Arising from their Utilisation to the Convention on Biological Diversity (opened for signature 2 February 2011, entered into force 12 October 2014) (Nagoya Protocol); Swakopmund Protocol on the Protection of Traditional Knowledge and Expressions of Folklore (9 August 2010) (Swakopmund Protocol).

[71] See WIPO, 'Key Questions on Patent Disclosure Requirements for Genetic Resources and Traditional Knowledge' (2017) <http://www.wipo.int/edocs/pubdocs/en/wipo_pub_1047.pdf> ('At the time this study was published, more than 30 countries – including both developed and developing countries – had implemented such requirements through national or regional laws').

[72] See Aguirre and Tualima (n 55) 9. The term 'traditional' in both phrases relates not to the age of the subject matter – new traditional knowledge and new traditional cultural expressions are constantly being created – rather, it refers to the manner and communal context in which the cultural resources are created. See Matthias Leistner, 'Analysis of Different Areas of Indigenous Resources: Traditional Knowledge' in Silke von Lewinski (ed), *Indigenous Heritage and Intellectual Property* (Kluwer Law International 2004) 49, 56. Exact definitions for traditional or indigenous knowledge and new traditional cultural expressions differ and are the subject of heated discussion in the WIPO IGC, but these phrasings will be used for the purposes of this chapter. See for example ibid 55–56.

resources are defined in the Convention on Biological Diversity (CBD) as 'genetic material [defined as 'material of plant, animal, microbial or other origin containing functional units of heredity'] of actual or potential value' (tangible and intangible).[73] The CBD also defines biological resources to include 'genetic resources, organisms or parts thereof, populations, or any other biotic component of ecosystems with actual or potential use or value for humanity'.[74]

As awareness concerning different ways in which cultural and genetic resources can be misappropriated is evolving, some developing countries have begun exploring whether disclosure of origin requirements are appropriate in the design context and, in some cases, are already instituting them.[75] Thus, it is not completely surprising that in November 2014 the African Group inserted an additional item into Article 3's closed list that ultimately brought negotiations on the DLT to an impasse. The provision would allow, but not compel, countries to require the disclosure of the origin of traditional cultural expressions, traditional knowledge, or biological or genetic resources used in creating a design.[76] The proponents deemed this amendment necessary because, as noted above, protectable designs can be based on and use all three types of subject matter.

The African Group offered an improved version of the amendment during the 34th session of the WIPO SCT in November 2015, which is now reflected in the current draft articles:[77]

> (1) [Contents of Application; Fee] (a) A Contracting Party may require that an application contain some, or all, of the following indications or elements:
>
> > (i) a request for registration;
> >
> > . . .

---

[73] Convention on Biological Diversity (opened for signature 5 June 1992, entered into force 29 December 1993) 1760 UNTS 79; 31 ILM 818 (CBD), art 2.

[74] Ibid.

[75] See generally WIPO, Disclosure Requirements Table (2017) <http://www.wipo.int/export/sites/www/tk/en/documents/pdf/genetic_resources_disclosure.pdf>.

[76] Catherine Saez, 'WIPO New Proposal on Disclosure Requirement in Design Applications' (November 2014) Intell Prop Watch <http://www.ip-watch.org/2014/11/25/wipo-new-proposal-on-disclosure-requirement-in-design-applications/>.

[77] WIPO, 'Industrial Design Law and Practice II; see also WIPO, 'Standing Comm on the Law of Trademarks, Indus. Designs & Geographic Indications' (2016) SCT/34/8 (SCT Report I).

> [(ix) a disclosure of the origin or source of traditional cultural expressions, traditional knowledge or biological/genetic resources utilized or incorporated in the industrial design;]
> (x) any further indication or element prescribed in the Regulations.

To be clear, the African Group proposal was and is intended to be permissive, giving countries the right, but not the obligation, to require disclosure of origin – unlike the mandatory disclosure of origin provision many countries are seeking in the IGC negotiations.[78] The African Group proposal is justifiably important for several reasons:

- It strengthens complementarity and mutual supportiveness of the traditional cultural expressions, traditional knowledge, and biological or genetic resources international regime complex[79] that involves scientific, cultural, and natural resources.
- It enables policy coherence across IP, biodiversity, cultural resources, human rights, and trade regimes.
- It can facilitate member state compliance with access and benefit-sharing (ABS) obligations under national, regional and international laws and agreements by increasing transparency in domestic design protection systems.
- It provides domestic policy space for beneficial legal experimentation.[80]

To call the African Group proposal controversial would be an extreme understatement. Countries opposed to the African Group amendment to Article 3 launched a vigorous and sustained objection to the proposal based on four primary concerns:

---

[78] For a discussion of the WIPO IGC disclosures of origin issue, see Bagley (n 29) 98; Georges Bauer, Cyrill Michael Berger and Martin Girsberger, 'Disclosure Requirements: Switzerland's Perspective' in Robinson, Abdel-Latif and Roffe (n 29) 244; Dominic Keating, 'The WIPO IGC: A US Perspective' in ibid 265; Dominic Muyldermans, 'Genetic Resources, Traditional Knowledge and Disclosure Obligations: Some Observations from the Life Science Industry' in ibid 230.

[79] See Kal Raustiala and David G Victor, 'The Regime Complex for Plant Genetic Resources' (2004) 58 Int'L Org 277, 279 (introducing the concept of regime complexes).

[80] See WIPO, 'Standing Comm on the Law of Trademarks, Indus Designs & Geographical Indications' (2016) SCT/35/8 (SCT Report II); SCT Report ss 21, 29, 56, 57; Saez (n 76).

- The African Group proposal was introduced very late in the DLT negotiation process when the agreement was largely finalised in anticipation of a diplomatic conference, and the only outstanding issue was believed to be technical assistance.
- Disclosure of origin requirements are not common core features of industrial design systems and do not belong in a formalities treaty, or at most could be accommodated by interpretation of the draft regulations to the DLT.[81]
- A disclosure of origin requirement would introduce untenable uncertainty for designers and create a chilling effect on filings by serving as a basis for rejection or invalidation involving the application of vague criteria.
- The origin of genetic resources, in particular, is widely considered irrelevant to the registrability of a design.[82]

Resistance to the provision's inclusion has been exceptionally strong and, to date, no agreement has been reached on various proposals to address member state concerns.

Despite the objections, the African Group – supported to varying degrees by the delegations of Iran, India, Saudi Arabia and several members of the Asia-Pacific group of countries[83] – has remained steadfast in its demand for disclosure of origin policy space in the draft DLT. The

---

[81] Catherine Saez, 'Another Setback for Design Law Treaty at WIPO; GIs in Contention' (November 2014) Intell Prop Watch <http://www.ip-watch.org/2014/11/27/another-setback-for-design-law-treaty-at-wipo-gis-in-contention/>; see also WIPO, 'Industrial Design Law and Practice – Draft Regulations' (2014) SCT/31/3 (listing draft Rule 2's requirements under Article 3 of the draft DLT). Draft Rule 2(1)(x) states that parties can also require applicants to provide 'an indication of any prior application or registration, or other information, of which the applicant is aware, that could have an effect on the eligibility for registration of the industrial design', ibid. This language seems to open up the closed list of Article 3. However, member states disagree on whether it is broad enough to include a formal or substantive disclosure of origin requirement. See SCT Report I (n 77) ss 29, 31. Moreover, Article 23(4) of the draft DLT states '[i]n the case of conflict between the provisions of this Treaty and those of the Regulations, the former shall prevail'; Industrial Design Law and Practice II, annex at 37. Consequently, the African Group expressed its discomfort with relying for disclosure of origin policy space on a regulation that appears to be in facial non-compliance with an article of the agreement. See for example SCT Report I, s 52.

[82] See SCT Report II (n 80), ss 13–14, 23, 28, 32, 34, 36. SCT Report I, annex at 2.

[83] SCT Report II (n 80), ss 16, 19, 20, 30, 40; SCT Report I, ss 42, 46.

timing of the introduction of the amendment is a reflection of the new and unprecedented nature of the issue in the design context. One of the challenges to legal harmonisation is that the harmonising process is slow and advances in law, science and digital technologies are creating evolving scenarios that may have been unimaginable at the time efforts to harmonise an area began.[84] Thus, it is difficult to pin down with precision whether and to what extent an area is likely to be affected by later developments. This is such an area.

For example, as work on the DLT was beginning in 2008, the objectives were to 'identify possible areas of convergence on industrial design law and practice in WIPO SCT Members, highlighting particular issues to be addressed in that context and taking into account existing international instruments'.[85] The international instruments considered at that time included the Paris Convention, the PLT, the Singapore Treaty on the Law of Trademarks, and TRIPS.[86] However, since that time, the Nagoya Protocol on Access to Genetic Resources and the Fair and Equitable Sharing of Benefits Arising from Their Utilization to the Convention on Biological Diversity (the 'Nagoya Protocol') was adopted in 2010 and came into force in 2014, requiring compliance with ABS obligations in relation to genetic resources and associated traditional knowledge.[87] Also, the regional Swakopmund Protocol on the Protection of Traditional Knowledge and Expressions of Folklore (the 'Swakopmund Protocol') came into effect in 2015 and, as discussed below, requires several African countries to provide a variety of protections for traditional knowledge and traditional cultural expressions.[88] As the DLT is still in the negotiating phase, consideration of the interplay between the DLT and the obligations contained in these agreements seems quite ripe for consideration by the WIPO SCT.

A. Motivating Factor: Policy Space

As noted above, design protection is becoming more attractive, with increasing numbers of design applications filed each year and increasing opportunities for misappropriation of a country's cultural and genetic resources through the design system. Thus, for many developing countries

---

[84] Peter K Yu, 'Currents and Crosscurrents in the International Intellectual Property Regime' (2004) 38 Loy LAL Rev 323, 434–35.

[85] WIPO (n 5) s 1.

[86] Ibid s 3.

[87] See Nagoya Protocol (n 70) art 15(1).

[88] See Swakopmund Protocol, s 1.1; (n 91–94) and accompanying text.

grappling with the challenges arising from more traditional forms of IP such as patents and copyrights,[89] the nuances of possible issues pertaining to design protection simply may not have been apparent earlier in the DLT negotiations.

For this same reason, few countries are currently requiring disclosure of origin in relation to design protection, but it is an emerging practice. At least 20 African countries, including South Africa and the 19 countries that comprise the African Regional Intellectual Property Organization (ARIPO),[90] are all likely to need the policy space to require disclosure of origin – at least for traditional knowledge and traditional cultural expressions incorporated into designs.

On 11 May 2015, the ARIPO Swakopmund Protocol entered into force.[91] It provides holders of traditional knowledge and expressions of folklore, also known as traditional cultural expressions, with certain rights and protections in relation to their cultural resources. In particular, section 10, relating to traditional knowledge, specifies that '[a]ny person using traditional knowledge beyond its traditional context shall acknowledge its holders, *indicate its source* and, where possible, *its origin*, and use such knowledge in a manner that respects the cultural values of its holders'.[92]

Likewise, Section 19, relating to expressions of folklore (another name for traditional cultural expressions) mandates the following:

> 19.2. In respect of expressions of folklore of particular cultural or spiritual value or significance to a community, the Contracting States *shall provide adequate and effective legal and practical measures to ensure that the rel-*

---

[89] See Boatema Boateng, *The Copyright Thing Doesn't Work Here* (University of Minnesota Press 2011) 168.

[90] African Regional Intellectual Property Organisation (ARIPO) <http://aripo.org/about-aripo/membership-member-states>. ARIPO is a regional IP organization for a number of English-speaking African countries. See ARIPO, 'About Us' <http://aripo.org/about-aripo/>.

[91] ARIPO, 'Entry into Force of the ARIPO Swakopmund Protocol on the Protection of Traditional Knowledge and Expressions of Folklore' <http://www.aripo.org/news-events-publications/news/item/54-entry-into-force-of-the-aripo-swakopmund-protocol-on-the-protection-of-traditional-knowledge-and-expressions-of-folklore>. To date, Botswana, Zimbabwe, the Gambia, Rwanda, Liberia, Malawi, Zambia, and Namibia have deposited instruments of ratification, but implementing legislation is in varying stages of completion in each country. SCT Report I, s 29; ARIPO, 'Zambia Ratifies the Swakopmund Protocol' <http://www.aripo.org/news-events-publications/news/item/79-zambia-ratifies-the-swakopmund-protocol>.

[92] Swakopmund Protocol, s 10 (emphasis added).

> *evant community can prevent the following acts* from taking place without its free and Prior Informed Consent:
>
> > [(a)]
> >
> > . . .
> >
> > iv). *the acquisition or exercise of intellectual property rights over the expressions of folklore* or adaptations thereof;
>
> 19.3. In respect of the use and exploitation of other expressions of folklore, the Contracting States *shall provide adequate and effective legal and practical measures to ensure that*:
>
> > (a) *the relevant community is identified as the source* of any work or other production adapted from the expressions of folklore[.][93]

These provisions require ARIPO Members to, among other things, ensure proper acknowledgement and source identification of cultural resource holders and enable such holders to prevent the acquisition of IP rights over those resources and adaptations thereof.[94] A disclosure of origin requirement for industrial design applications appears to be a necessary element for complying with these provisions of the protocol, and the draft DLT without the African Group amendment would prevent parties to the protocol from employing such a requirement. Thus, while a disclosure of origin requirement is not a common core feature of design regimes, that seems to be an insufficient reason for denying countries the right to employ these requirements to meet treaty and domestic policy objectives and obligations.

According to the WIPO Secretariat, 'the draft DLT aims at simplifying and harmonizing industrial design formalities and procedures set by national/regional offices, so as to reduce discrepancies among future Contracting Parties'.[95] Harmonisation historically was seen as an unexceptional goal because territoriality is inefficient and imposes numerous

---

93 Ibid ss 19.2, 19.3.

94 The pending South African Protection, Promotion, Development and Management of Indigenous Knowledge Systems Bill 2016, in conjunction with the Intellectual Property Laws Amendment Act 2013, provides for disclosure of indigenous knowledge, indigenous cultural expressions, and indigenous knowledge associated with natural resources. See Intellectual Property Laws Amendment Act 2013 (South Africa), ss 28B(4)(b), 43B(6)(b), 53B(3)(b); Protection, Promotion, Development and Management of Indigenous Knowledge Bill B 6B 2016 (South Africa), s 13(2)(b)(iii).

95 Relationship Between the Hague System and the Draft Design Law Treaty, s 19.

costs on inventors and creators.[96] For this reason, certain countries and other parties with multinational interests have sought for more than a century to increase the level of harmonisation in the various global IP systems.[97] However, harmonisation also has its downside and there is growing criticism of its negative impacts, including the way it constrains the policy choices of sovereign nations facing diverse societal needs. Moreover, harmonisation in international IP agreements does not equate to harmonisation in domestic implementing legislation and LMICs may lack the sophisticated interpretive tools high-income countries use to creatively and favourably implement treaties in national law. This, paradoxically, can result in more stringent IP protection standards in the very countries most in need of flexibility.[98]

Another drawback of harmonisation is its negative impact on legal experimentation and domestic policy preferences. As Lisa Ouellette notes, 'optimal innovation policy likely varies across heterogeneous jurisdictions' and '[l]ocking the world into uniform[ity]' makes it difficult to assess the true impact and role of IP protection because 'empirical progress depends on policy variation'.[99] It is just such space for policy variation that the African Group proposal seeks to inject into the DLT. There are many aspects of calibrating cultural and genetic resource protection that would benefit from legal experimentation across jurisdictions, including whether a disclosure of origin requirement should be employed at all and, if so, in what form and to what ends. Countries should not be prevented from engaging in such experimentation or from adopting justifiably distinctive approaches in their domestic design regimes – especially in light of the historical lack of comparative design law harmonisation.

---

96 See Edward Lee, 'The Global Trade Mark' (2014) 35 U Pa J Int'l L 917, 933; Peter K Yu, 'The International Enclosure Movement' (2002) 82 Ind LJ 827, 901.

97 See Yu (n 84) 901–02.

98 Ibid. An example of this phenomenon is the revised Bangui Agreement, which prevents Organisation Africaine de la Propriété Intellectuelle Members from utilising flexibilities in the Doha Declaration without first going through a judicial procedure in national civil courts. See Carolyn Deere, *The Implementation Game: The TRIPS Agreement and the Global Politics of Intellectual Property Reform in Developing Countries* (Oxford 2009) 276; see also Ruth L Okediji, 'Reframing International Copyright Limitations and Exceptions as Development Policy' in Ruth L Okediji, *Copyright Law in an Age of Limitations and Exceptions* (Cambridge University Press 2017) 448–50.

99 Lisa Larrimore Ouellette, 'Patent Experimentalism' (2015) 101 Va L Rev 65, 67–68; see also Yu (n 84) 832 ('[T]he one-size-fits-all templates [in TRIPS and other] agreements have drastically reduced the policy space available to less developed countries').

B. Motivating Factor: Policy Coherence

The African Group proposal appears to be a reasonable tool to facilitate policy coherence.[100] African Group members and many other biodiverse countries in the global South are party to the CBD and one or more other treaties, such as the Nagoya Protocol, the Food and Agriculture Organization's International Treaty on Plant Genetic Resources for Food and Agriculture, and, in some cases, regional agreements such as the Swakopmund Protocol or the Andean Decision. These countries are also in the process of modifying their domestic laws to better protect biodiversity and valuable cultural and natural resources from misappropriation. It would be illogical, and would create incoherent internal policy positions, for these countries to agree not to require disclosure of origin in design applications just when they are modifying their laws to facilitate transparency, acknowledgment of rights, and improved stewardship of cultural resources. As such, the African Group proposal could benefit *all* CBD members, particularly those rich in cultural and genetic resources, as it could help them comply with their ABS goals and obligations.

The issue of inserting disclosure of origin provisions into formalities treaties is not new to WIPO. Such concerns were first raised in the WIPO Standing Committee on Patents (SCP) in 1999, when a group of Latin American member states proposed inserting a disclosure of origin requirement into the draft PLT.[101] This turn of events precipitated a political compromise in which matters relating to genetic resources and traditional knowledge would be addressed in WIPO – but in a new forum, the IGC, and not in the SCP.[102] This allowed a diplomatic conference on the PLT to proceed to a successful conclusion, producing a treaty devoid of any mention of genetic resources or traditional knowledge. In light of this history, the myriad developments relating to genetic resources and traditional knowledge outside of WIPO such as the Nagoya Protocol, and the painfully slow progress of the IGC, it is unsurprising that the African

---

[100] See for example Jean-Frederic Morin and Mathilde Gauquelin, 'Trade Agreements as Vectors for the Nagoya Protocol's Implementation' (2016) CIGI Papers No 115, 1. See also Nuno Pires de Carvalho, 'Sisyphus Redivivus? The Work of WIPO on Genetic Resources and Traditional Knowledge' in Charles R McManis and Burton Ong (eds), *Routledge Handbook of Biodiversity and the Law* (Routledge 2018) 337, 339–40.

[101] See Florian Rabitz, *The Global Governance of Genetic Resources: Institutional Change and Structural Constraints* (Routledge 2017) 96.

[102] See Ruth L Okediji, 'Legal Innovation in International Intellectual Property Relations: Revisiting Twenty-One Years of the TRIPS Agreement' (2014) 36 U Pa J Int'l L 191, 217–18.

Group has remained adamant in its demand for disclosure of origin policy space to be explicitly retained in the draft DLT.[103]

The WIPO IGC's first meeting was in 2001, and while there has been much talk in successive meetings, real progress largely began with the start of text-based negotiations in 2009.[104] The current mandate of the WIPO IGC is to continue to engage in text-based negotiations leading to one or more international legal instruments.[105] Recent negotiations have yielded three draft texts: a genetic resources text that would include provisions such as a requirement that inventors seeking patent protection disclose the origin of genetic resources and associated traditional knowledge used in developing a claimed invention, as well as two texts – for traditional knowledge and traditional cultural expressions texts – that would include, among other things, a suite of moral and economic rights for certain categories of traditional knowledge and traditional cultural expressions.[106]

As currently written, the disclosure of origin requirement in the draft genetic resources text has the possibility of being applied to all IP applications, or only to utility patent applications, as both terms are bracketed.[107] Member States almost agreed to a compromise approach that would have applied the DOO requirement only to utility patent applications, while requiring consideration of the applicability of DOO to other kinds of IP applications at a future date during IGC 36 in June 2018.[108] However, two countries blocked the revised text, and substantive discussions on genetic resources are not scheduled to resume until sometime in 2019.[109]

---

[103] Ahmed Abdel-Latif, 'Genetic Resources, Patents and Benefit Sharing: State of Play and Challenges Facing Multilateral Discussions' in Jacque de Werra (ed), *Intellectual Property in the Pharmaceutical Industry* (Routledge 2012) 59, 63.

[104] International Centre for Trade and Sustainable Development, 'WIPO Traditional Knowledge Committee Pushes Toward Text-Based Talks' (December 2009) <http://www.ictsd.org/bridges-news/bridges/news/wipo-traditional-knowledge-committee-pushes-toward-text-based-talks>.

[105] WIPO, 'Matters Concerning the Intergovernmental Committee on Intellectual Property and Genetic Resources, Traditional Knowledge and Folklore' (2015) <http://www.wipo.int/export/sites/www/tk/en/igc/pdf/igc_mandate_1617.pdf>.

[106] See WIPO, The Protection of Traditional Cultural Expressions: Draft Articles (2014) WIPO/GRTKF/IC/28/6; WIPO, The Protection of Traditional Knowledge: Draft Articles (June 2014) WIPO/GRTKF/IC/28/5; Communication from Canada et al, 'Joint Recommendation on Genetic Resources and Associated Traditional Knowledge' (May 2014) WIPO/GRTKF/IC/28/7.

[107] The Protection of Traditional Cultural Expressions (n 106); The Protection of Traditional Knowledge (n 106).

[108] WIPO, 'IGC 36 Draft Report' (2018) WIPO/GRTKF/IC/38/REF/36/11.

[109] Ibid.

Moreover, the text only relates, at most, to traditional knowledge associated with genetic resources and not freestanding traditional knowledge.[110]

The draft traditional knowledge text also contains a disclosure of origin requirement that cuts across all IP areas as it requires disclosure of origin in 'intellectual property applications'.[111] As such, if the DLT is allowed to move forward without policy space for countries to require disclosure of origin in design applications, countries would be foreclosed from maintaining the current mandatory disclosure of origin provision in the traditional knowledge text as it would have to be reframed to exclude design applications.

It is possible that some countries are mistakenly viewing the African Group proposal provision as a forum-shifting tool – a strategy for the African Group to achieve via the DLT what it has been unable to obtain thus far in the IGC.[112] Such a view is erroneous. In the WIPO IGC, the African Group and many other countries are seeking new economic and moral rights in relation to traditional cultural expressions and traditional knowledge, and in the genetic resources context only, a mandatory disclosure of origin requirement for genetic resources in utility patent applications.[113] These are fundamentally different objectives to those being sought for the draft DLT, where the African Group seeks only permission for countries to be able to require disclosure of origin, and even then, only for design applications – not utility patent, trade mark, or other kinds of IP applications.

Even though the disclosure requirement could relate to biological or genetic resources, traditional knowledge, or traditional cultural expressions, this is a much narrower, much less economically significant concern

---

[110] Whether or not the disclosure requirement would apply to traditional knowledge associated with genetic resources is another contested issue and the phrase is bracketed in the draft text. WIPO, 'IGC 36 Draft Report' (2018) WIPO/GRTKF/IC/38/REF/36/11.

[111] The traditional cultural expressions text does not contain a disclosure of origin requirement currently. See The Protection of Traditional Knowledge (n 106) 9.

[112] See Laurence R Helfer, 'Toward a Human Rights Framework for Intellectual Property' (2007) 40 UC Davis L Rev 971, 981 (describing the international intellectual property system as 'a "regime complex" – a multi-issue, multi-venue, mega-regime in which governments and NGOs shift norm creating initiatives from one venue to another within the conglomerate, selecting the forum in which they are most likely to achieve their objectives').

[113] See SCT Report I, ss 29, 56, 57. The traditional knowledge draft text also currently includes a mandatory disclosure of origin requirement for traditional knowledge in IP applications more broadly.

in the design context than the provisions sought in the WIPO IGC. It thus may be unwise for the African Group to exchange agreement on its draft DLT proposal for anything in relation to the WIPO IGC. The two issues – while emanating from similar cultural and genetic resource policy concerns – are separate but related, and one cannot substitute one for the other. This is because, without the policy space to require disclosure of origin for cultural and genetic resource utilisation in industrial design applications, WIPO Members in the IGC would be pre-emptively foreclosed from requiring disclosure of origin for traditional knowledge or genetic resources in design applications before those issues have been fully resolved in that forum.

While policy space for a disclosure of origin requirement for cultural resources might be acceptable for some current opponents of the African Group proposal, many draw the line at allowing policy space for a biological or genetic resource disclosure of origin requirement for designs.[114] This is because the design right generally only protects appearance, not the underlying material from which an article is made.[115] In other words, design protection normally would not prevent a third party from making an article out of any particular material, as long as the protected design is not substantially identically reproduced. For example, an EU RCD covering the appearance of denim jeans designed to appear acid-washed via treatment with the enzyme cellulase does not prevent the enzyme treatment from being used to develop jeans with an appearance different from that shown in the RCD registration.[116] However, as noted above in Section II.A, the EU RCD protects 'the appearance of the whole or a part of a product resulting from the features of, in particular, the . . . texture and/or materials of the product itself and/or its ornamentation'.[117] This language suggests that in some cases the material of construction may be relevant to the scope of protection of the RCD.

In addition, there are valid policy reasons for countries wanting to know

---

[114] See Catherine Saez, 'WIPO Members Urged to Overcome Differences on Disclosure of Origin of Designs' (April 2016) Intell Prop Watch <http://www.ip-watch.org/2016/04/26/disclosure-of-origin-of-designs-at-issue-in-potential-wipo-treaty/>.

[115] However, as noted above, the EU RCD protects 'the appearance of the whole or a part of a product resulting from the features of, in particular, the . . . texture and/or materials of the product itself and/or its ornamentation'; CDR art 3(a). This language suggests that in some cases, the material of construction may be relevant to the scope of protection of the RCD.

[116] See WIPO, 'A Stitch in Time: Smart Use of Intellectual Property by Textile Companies' (2005) 8.

[117] CDR, art 3(a).

about the origin of materials used to create protectable designs.[118] The following scenario involving illegal uses of biological or genetic resources in design creation provides an apt illustration.

IV. BIOLOGICAL AND GENETIC RESOURCES, ILLEGAL DESIGN CREATION, AND DISCLOSURE REQUIREMENTS

As noted above, the argument against a disclosure of origin requirement for biological or genetic resources in the DLT seems logical in light of the limits of design protection. However, such resources *can* matter in design creation, especially if their use involves illegal activity. Consider the following illustration from the utility patent context:[119]

> Set in eighteenth-century France, author Patrick Suskind's novel Perfume tells the story of Jean-Baptiste Grenouille, a man who, from birth, had no personal body odor, which had the effect of alienating him from others. Lacking a personal scent but having an unusually refined sense of smell, Grenouille, an inventor, became obsessed with developing the perfect perfume that would cause people to adore him. He succeeded in his quest. Unfortunately, his method of creating this compound was to murder young women and extract fragrance compounds from their bodies.
>
> Fast forward to the twenty-first century and imagine that Grenouille seeks a patent on his useful, novel, and nonobvious composition of matter. Should the fact that he murdered people in order to create the invention have any impact on his ability to obtain a patent, or on the enforceability of any patent he does obtain?[120]

Although this is a hypothetical question, a number of countries consider whether illegal or immoral activities contributed to creating inventive subject matter when making utility patent grant decisions. Examples include the *Brüstle v Greenpeace* decision of the Court of Justice of the

---

[118] See for example Paul Kuruk, 'Regulating Access to Traditional Knowledge and Genetic Resources: The Disclosure Requirement as a Strategy to Combat Biopiracy' (2015) 17 San Diego Int'l L J 1, 43 ('Switzerland identified transparency, traceability, technical prior art, and mutual trust as policy specific objectives underlying the disclosure requirement').

[119] This scenario was first used in Margo A Bagley, 'The New Invention Creation Boundary in Patent Law' (2009) 51 WM & Mary L Rev 577. Additional material and concepts from that piece also have been borrowed for this section.

[120] Ibid 578 (citing Patrick Suskind, *Perfume: The Story of a Murderer* (Penguin 2015)). Special thanks to Doris Walter of the German Patent & Trademark Office for inspiring this hypothetical.

European Union (CJEU), where the destruction of human embryos to create embryonic cell cultures was deemed immoral as violative of the EU Biotechnology Directive, and the invention – the claimed cell culture – was deemed unpatentable despite the fact that it was considered novel and displayed an inventive step.[121] Similarly, the Third Amendment to the Chinese Patent Act denies patentability to utility patent inventions made with genetic resources acquired in violation of Chinese laws.[122] As with *Brüstle*, the invention may be otherwise patentable, but for policy reasons the legislature concluded patent rights were inappropriate.

These same kinds of concerns are relevant for illegal activity in the creation of protectable designs. Consequently, countries should have the policy flexibility to require disclosure of origin for biological or genetic resources. Countries such as China and India choose not to extend patent protection to an invention made using illegally acquired genetic resources even if the invention does not claim the genetic resources per se.[123] Similarly, because industrial design rights allow owners to exclude from the marketplace the *actual products* whose appearance infringes (i.e., appears substantially similar to) the registered design, countries may refuse to extend a right to exclude – under the doctrine of unclean hands or similar reasoning[124] – to owners of designs made using illegally acquired or used biological or genetic resource. The imposition of a formal disclosure of origin requirement for design applications could facilitate the identification of relevant 'illegal' designs for such countries.

The design world is bursting with uses of biological or genetic resources to create original designs, from headphones containing 'African padauk wood' panels[125] to original glassware and other items made from a bioplastic derived from shrimp shells (see Figure 5.6).[126] Focusing on the

---

121 Case C-34/10 *Brüstle v Greenpeace eV* (2011) ECR I-9849 (ECJ) I-9871.

122 Zhonghua Renmin Gongheguo Zhuanli Fa (中华人民共和国专利法) (Patent Law of the People's Republic of China) 2009, art 5.

123 Ibid; see Bagley (n 119) 586 (remarking that countries including China and India 'are changing their laws to deny patentability to inventions created with illegally acquired genetic resources').

124 See for example *Precision Instrument Mfg Co v Auto Maint Mach Co* (1945) 324 US 806 (SCOTUS) 814–16 (noting the maxim: 'he who comes into equity must come with clean hands').

125 See 'Headphone', Can Indus Design No 124,087 (registered 23 April 2009). The description states: 'The design consists of the features of shape, configuration, pattern and ornamentation of the HEADPHONE shown in the drawings . . . A housing of each headphone unit has [a] solid African padauk wood pattern.'

126 See (nn 52–54); see also Biodesign Challenge, 'Materials' <http://biodesignchallenge.org/themes/materials/>.

Source: Biodesign Challenge, 'Materials', <http://biodesignchallenge.org/themes/materials/>.

Figure 5.6 Bioplastic cups derived from shrimp shells

fashion space, innovative examples abound, including versatile leather substitutes crafted from the yeast and bacteria that produce kombucha,[127] or mushroom 'skin' grown under various conditions to create 'leathers' that mimic, and in some cases improve upon, cow, alligator, snakeskin, and other kinds of animal pelts.[128] Other examples include genetically engineered silkworms that produce coloured fluorescent silks,[129] synthetic biology-based spider silk made without spiders,[130] and lab-grown cotton.[131] Moreover, some creators in the vibrant do-it-yourself synthetic

[127] Ibid; see Frank (n 18).

[128] See n 17; see also MyCoworks (n 18). MyCoworks uses a ubiquitous type of mushroom that grows around the world.

[129] See US Patent (n 54); see also Tetsuya Iizuka et al, 'Colored Fluorescent Silk Made by Transgenic Silkworms' (2013) 23 Advanced Functional Materials 5232, 5237.

[130] Sarah Buhr, 'Bolt Threads Debuts Its First Product, a $314 Tie Made from Spiderwebs' (March 2017) TechCrunch <https://techcrunch.com/2017/03/10/bolt-threads-debuts-its-first-product-a-314-tie-made-from-spiderwebs/>.

[131] See for example Abrahim El Gamal, 'Lab-Grown Leather and Spider

biology community are even offering classes that teach enrollees how to create their own biodesigned materials, including edible wearables.[132] For examples, see the Kimono Grown from Kambucha[133] and the fluorescent silk dress from genetically engineered silkworms.[134]

However, some of the new uses are somewhat disturbing. In June 2016, art school graduate and designer Tina Gorjanc unveiled her critical design show entitled 'Pure Human', featuring a collection of fashion items that theoretically could be made from leather (patent pending) grown from DNA extracted from a hair sample from the deceased designer Alexander McQueen.[135] As reported by the *New York Times*, the flesh-toned biker jackets, totes, and other items comprising the collection bore freckles, tattoos, and other markings strikingly similar to those on McQueen's body.[136] The article asserts that Gorjanc did not obtain permission from anyone associated with McQueen's estate to use his DNA in any way.[137]

The CBD and many national laws do not cover human genetic resources per se; however, the laws of some countries such as China do.[138] Even for

---

Silk Are the Future of Your Wardrobe' (November 2017) <https://massivesci.com/articles/biofabrication-grow-organic-leather-smart-clothing/>; Abrahim El Gamal, 'Lab-Grown Leather and Spider Silk Are the Future of Your Wardrobe>; NatureWorks, 'How Ingeo Is Made' (2018) <www.natureworksllc.com/What-is-Ingeo/How-Ingeo-is-Made>. NatureWorks is a manufacturer of bioplastics sourced from the long-chain sugar molecules found in corn, cassava, sugar cane, and beets.

132 Genspace NYC, 'Biotextiles: Grow Your Own Materials for Fashion Design' (March 2017) EventBrite <https://www.eventbrite.com/e/biotextiles-grow-your-own-materials-for-fashion-design-tickets-32474114952?utm-medium=discovery&utm-campaign=social&utm-content=attendeeshare&utm-source=strongmail&utm-term=listing#> (select 'view details').

133 Suzanne Lee, 'Biocouture Growing Textiles' Design Boom <https://www.designboom.com/design/suzanne-lee-biocouture-growing-textiles/>.

134 Iizuka et al (n 129) 5237.

135 Elizabeth Paton, 'Fashion That Gets Under the Skin' (July 2016) New York Times <www.nytimes.com/2016/07/19/fashion/leather-dna-alexander-mcqueen.html>.

136 Ibid. Gorjanc added the tattoos and freckles herself, as the 'grown skin' would not include such markings. Linda Yang, 'The Designer Who Plans to Make Handbags Out of Alexander McQueen's Skin' (July 2016) <https://broadly.vice.com/en_us/article/wnww7b/alexander-mcqueen-skin-jacket-handbag?>.

137 Paton (n 135).

138 See Zhonghua Renmin Gongheguo Zhuanli Fa (中华人民共和国专利法) (Patent Law of the People's Republic of China) 2009, art 5 ('Patent rights shall not be granted for inventions that are accomplished by relying on genetic resources which are obtained or used in violation of the provisions of laws and administrative regulations'); see also Zhonghua Renmin Gongheguo Zhuanli Fa Shishi Xize (中国人民共和国专利法实施细则) (Implementing Regulations of the Patent Law

those that do not, a use such as the one theorised by Gorjanc may still be problematic if, for example, informed consent from the relevant human being was not obtained. Even though Gorjanc apparently was attempting to highlight moral and ethical issues at the intersection of biotechnology, IP, and fashion with her work, the use of McQueen's DNA without consent would raise ethical concerns that a country could begin to address in national law with a disclosure of origin requirement as a compliance-facilitating mechanism.[139]

The global market for plant-based innovation and associated products is growing rapidly and includes plant-derived pharmaceuticals, fibres, textiles, cosmetics and, as noted above, fashionable clothing and accessories.[140] As such, the use of biological or genetic resources in the design and manufacture of goods is indisputably an important element of global trade. Companies engaged in innovative product development are increasingly looking for environmentally friendly product components and alluring product designs.[141] This trend emphasises the use of plant-based material and thus increases the likelihood of biological or genetic resources being used in products that may ultimately be the subject of design protection.[142]

To be clear, many of these inventions are significant technological

---

of the People's Republic of China) 2003, art 26 ('The genetic resources referred to in the Patent Law means any material taken from *human*, animal, plant or micro-organism, containing genetically functioning units with actual or potential value').

139 Paton (n 135).

140 See for example Jian Yao, Yunqi Weng, Alexia Dickey, Kevin Yueju Wang, 'Plants as Factories for Human Pharmaceuticals: Applications and Challenges' (2015) 16 Int'L J Molecular Sci 28549, 28550; Paton (n 135).

141 See Michael Hozik, 'Making the Green by Going Green: Increased Demand for Green Products and the FTC's Role in a Greener Future' (2016) Geo Envt L Rev <https://geir.org/2016/02/01/> ('[A] rapid expansion in green-conscious customers has spurred a surge of companies making green claims, sparking gridlock at the United States Patent and Trademark Office. Between 2006 and 2007, filings for eco-friendly labels doubled and stores offered 73% more green products in 2010 compared to 2009').

142 See for example American Chemical Society, 'Going Green with Plant-Based Resins' (August 2017) <https://www.acs.org/content/acs/en/pressroom/presspacs/2017/acs-presspac-august-16-2017/going-green-with-plant-based-resins.html>. As Boateng notes: 'The marginalization and appropriation of indigenous cultural products, be they medicinal plants or fabric designs, relegates them to the status of raw materials, rather than artistic and scientific goods in their own right. This leaves them open to appropriation – often by groups and individuals who then claim ownership of their appropriations by recourse to intellectual property law.' University of Minnesota Press, 'Examining Ghana's Use of Intellectual Property Law to Protect Adinkra and Kente Fabrics' (April 2017) <http://www.uminnpressblog.com/2011/04/examining-ghanas-use-of-intellectual.html>.

advances, far removed from the raw starting materials used in their development. However, that does not necessarily remove them from the purview of national laws relating to biological and genetic resources or from ABS obligations. Rather, such changes in the raw materials may simply affect the *amount* of benefits to be shared, not the fact that benefits *are* to be shared.[143] Moreover, it would be erroneous to assume that just because one is using a plant – and not traditional knowledge – there is no relevant indigenous contribution in relation to the plant. Many indigenous groups have been modifying and interacting with the natural environment for millennia in ways that protect, conserve and possibly improve the quality of medicinal and other plants. Such efforts include developing and imposing strict harvesting protocols for medicinal plants, imposing boundaries to protect herb growth areas, and more.[144]

To the extent misappropriation of cultural and genetic resources is viewed as a form of theft, it implicates notions of morality, as theft is widely considered morally wrong.[145] Interestingly, morality-tinged concerns are not foreign to design applications. For example, section 1504.01(e) of the US Patent and Trademark Office's *Manual of Patent Examining Procedure* states: 'Design applications which disclose subject matter which could be deemed offensive to any race, religion, sex, ethnic group, or nationality, such as those which include caricatures or depictions, should be rejected as nonstatutory subject matter under 35 U.S.C. 171.'[146] This provision does not implicate a disclosure of origin requirement but it does evidence a governmental concern in relation to design rights that is distinct from whether the design is sufficiently ornamental, novel or inventive to be

---

143 This is not a new concept to IP, as copyright vests the right to make derivative works, be they songs or other writings, in the creator of the original work, a work that itself may evidence only a modicum of creativity and originality. See 17 USC (2012), ss 102–03; *Feist Publ'ns Inc v Rural Tel Serv Co* (1991) 499 US 340 (SCOTUS) 345.

144 See Mohamed Khalil, 'Biodiversity and the Conservation of Medicinal Plants: Issues from the Perspective of the Developing World' in Timothy M Swanson (ed), *Intellectual Property Rights and Biodiversity Conservation: An Interdisciplinary Analysis of the Values of Medicinal Plants* (Cambridge 1995) 232, 242–43. Chidi Oguamanam, 'Between Reality and Rhetoric: The Epistemic Schism in the Recognition of Traditional Medicine in International Law' (2003) 16 St Thomas L Rev 59, 74–75.

145 See Margo A. Bagley, The Morality of Compulsory Licensing as an Access to Medicines Tool (2018) 102 Minn L Rev 2463 (describing the use of theft rhetoric as a proxy for morality in US intellectual property cases).

146 USPTO Manual, s 1504.01(e); Cf *Matal v Tam* (2017) 137 S Ct 1744 (SCOTUS) 1751 (striking down a law denying trade mark protection to disparaging marks).

eligible to receive protection. However, morality can be subjective, and views of what is moral can change – often fluidly – over time, complicating legal certainty if design protection is forfeited by immoral activity. If, instead of employing a possibly vague morality provision, a country chooses to deny design protection to subject matter made through activity declared illegal under national law, applicants seeking design protection should have sufficient legal certainty to be able to govern their actions accordingly.[147]

In *Brüstle v Greenpeace*, the CJEU clarified that the EU Biotechnology Directive barred the patenting of inventions involving the destruction of human embryos at any point in the making of the invention.[148] In other words, even if an immoral activity took place early in the invention-creation process and did not explicitly appear in the claims, that still could be a basis for invalidating the patent. One commentator, recognising the logical implications of the decision, noted that it 'could be relied on . . . to oppose the issuance, or challenge the validity, of patents covering any inventions *obtained through illegal activities*, including *biotech inventions reached through the misappropriation of genetic resources*'.[149]

Thus, there is precedent in the utility patent context for assessing whether and to what extent patent protection should be available for subject matter deriving from illegal activity. The underlying concern is that there are activities that a government deems illegal that are rewarded downstream by an IP right. Industrial design rights are different from utility patent rights but these same concerns about rewarding illegal activity are quite applicable to this form of protection.

A. Formality Versus Substance

During the 34th session of the WIPO SCT, the African Group noted that the draft DLT had been compared to the PLT as a 'formalities' treaty[150] but that the comparison has important limits. For example, unlike the draft DLT, the PLT does not prevent contracting states from requiring disclosure of information in applications. In this way, the DLT ventures much further into substantive territory than the PLT. The PLT, however, does 'limit the form and content of applications to be no more [than] as

---

147 See also discussion below regard *ordre public*.

148 See Case C-34/10 *Brüstle v Greenpeace eV* (2011) ECR I-9849 (ECJ) I-98719875.

149 Enrico Bonadio, 'Stem Cells Industry and Beyond: What Is the Aftermath of Brüstle?' (2012) 1 Eur J Risk Reg 93, 97 (emphasis added).

150 SCT Report I, s 29.

required under the [Patent Cooperation Treaty] PCT'.[151] But the PLT states explicitly in Article 2 that '[n]othing in this Treaty or the Regulations is intended to be construed as prescribing anything that would limit the freedom of a Contracting Party to prescribe such requirements of the applicable substantive law relating to patents as it desires'.[152]

The African Group noted that the draft DLT contained no such explicit recognition of its formal limitations, which compounds the concerns regarding the closed list in Article 3. In response to this concern, and in an effort to find a compromise solution, the WIPO SCT Chairman introduced an amendment during the 34th session of the WIPO SCT consisting of a new Article 1*bis* based on language from the PCT and PLT, which specified that nothing in the DLT was intended to prevent a country from prescribing substantive law requirements relating to industrial designs.[153] Thus, proponents could only require disclosure of origin in national law as a substantive condition of design protection and registrability.

On the surface, this appears appealing to both sides: the DLT could move forward and countries would have the ability to require disclosure of origin as a substantive condition of design protection. In isolation, however, this approach is problematic.[154] As a substantive requirement, failure to comply with the disclosure of origin could result in imposition of some of the harshest penalties in IP, such as revocation of the design right. The availability of revocation as a penalty for non-disclosure is one of the key controversial issues in WIPO IGC discussions regarding a mandatory disclosure of origin provision for genetic resources and associated traditional knowledge, and many countries currently opposing the African Group proposal are the same countries opposing revocation as a penalty for disclosure of origin violations in the WIPO IGC discussions.[155]

---

151 Ibid.

152 Patent Law Treaty (adopted 1 June 2000) 2340 UNTS 3, art 2 (Patent Law Treaty).

153 SCT Report I, s 82.

154 Such a provision is an important addition to the DLT and is consistent with similar provisions in the Patent Law Treaty (n 152) and Patent Cooperation Treaty (adopted 19 June 1970) 28 UST 7645 (Patent Cooperation Treaty), for example. See Patent Law Treaty (n 152), art 6; Patent Cooperation Treaty, art 27. However, it is not sufficient to allow policy space for formal disclosure of origin requirements. See Nuno Pires de Carvalho, 'Requiring Disclosure of the Origin of Genetic Resources and Prior Informed Consent in Patent Applications Without Infringing the TRIPS Agreement: The Problem and the Solution' (2000) 2 Wash U JL & Pol'y 371, 389.

155 See WIPO, 'Summary of Replies to the Questionnaires (Parts I and II) on Industrial Design Law and Practice (2008) SCT/18/7 and SCT/18/8 REV (2008) WIPO/STrad/INF/2 Rev1 59–60.

Thus, it seems contrary to the stated interests of such countries to support disclosure of origin as a substantive requirement for design protection.

However, as a formality, facial non-compliance with a disclosure of origin requirement should only result in a cessation of further processing of the design application. If the requirement was facially met and after the design was registered it was shown that the applicant had lied about the origin of the design, the design right need not be revoked. Instead, the applicant or rights holder could be punished outside of the design system, such as in an action for perjury (which could be a fine or another penalty).[156]

If the goal of a disclosure of origin requirement is to facilitate transparency regarding improper or unauthorised uses of cultural or genetic resources, its categorisation as a formal requirement seems appropriate. It makes sense that the harsher remedy of revocation should be available, if at all, only for violation of the underlying law regarding use of the resources without consent or benefit sharing. Thus, if the parties to the DLT rely solely on proposed Article 1*bis* for policy space for disclosure of origin requirements, they would be – albeit unintentionally – channelling such requirements to substantive provisions in national laws.

A formal disclosure of origin requirement may seem pointless for the many design protection regimes employing a formalities-only examination before a design is registered. With no substantive examination for novelty, the disclosed information would not be used by an examiner to assess whether protection should be granted. Nevertheless, a disclosure of origin requirement could still be beneficial in several ways. Importantly, it could have a deterrent effect on would-be applicants who know they have misappropriated a design. In addition, if an applicant truthfully discloses origin, that could make it easier for the IP office or court to assess the validity of any post-grant challenge to the registration. Moreover, if an applicant misrepresents the origin and obtains a registration, he or she could be subject to various penalties under domestic law if the falsehood is later uncovered.

Concern regarding how a disclosure of origin regime might be implemented in a domestic design system has fuelled some countries' resistance

---

[156] Imposing fines is the approach taken by Switzerland with regard to violations of the disclosure of origin requirement for utility patent applications. See Delegation of Switzerland, 'The Declaration of the Source of Genetic Resources and Traditional Knowledge in the Swiss Patent Act and Related Swiss Regulations on Genetic Resources – Submission by Switzerland in Response to Document WIPO/GRTKF/IC/30/9' (2016) WIPO/GRTKF/IC/31/8.

to the African Group proposal.[157] While a discussion of the optimal structure of a domestic design disclosure of origin regime for countries choosing to employ such a requirement is beyond the scope of this chapter, there are elements that, if adopted, might alleviate some of the concerns of opponents of the African Group proposal.

One such element could be linking domestic traditional knowledge or traditional cultural expression registries, such as those provided for by the Swakopmund Protocol, and domestic disclosure of origin design application requirements. Such registries, to the extent they provide domestic protection for registered subject matter (somewhat akin to a geographical indications registry), could enhance certainty by enabling challenges to be based on registered, publicly available works. However, such registries may be detrimental to the extent they deny protection to those who need it most: indigenous peoples and local communities who may be unaware of or have easy access to the registries, or may lack the financial wherewithal to register their cultural information. Such registries also would be problematic for holders or owners of cultural resources that are not suitable for inclusion in a registry due to secrecy or other reasons. In addition, imposing a requirement of registration prior to bringing a challenge might help to some extent, but many issues still would need to be addressed to develop a system that effectively balances legal certainty with justice and fairness for owners and creators of cultural and genetic resources.

B. The Cost of Protection

As noted above, design protection in many countries is relatively inexpensive to obtain, certainly relative to utility patent protection. Yet the low cost for the design rights holder can impose a very high cost on the public. This is because it may be easy to obtain a design right that should never have been granted, and that will be expensive to invalidate in court or even in an administrative action.[158]

The WIPO statistics on the increasing numbers of design filings indicate we can expect a concomitant rise, over time, in litigation involving enforcement of design rights.[159] As Jason DuMont and Mark Janis note,

---

157 See for example SCT Report I (n 77), s 21.

158 See Burstein (n 6) 109, 125, 128 (describing the costs of bad design patents).

159 United States Patent and Trademark Office, 'The Drastic Rise in Patent Litigation (2000–2015) <https://www.uspto.gov/learning-and-resources/ip-policy/economic-research/drastic-rise-patent-litigation-2000-2015>.

'application-filing trends suggest that intellectual property litigation over designs will become increasingly common worldwide'.[160]

The impact on competition can be especially devastating to indigenous peoples and local communities seeking access to foreign markets (such as the European Union and the United States) for their wares, who may find such access blocked by design rights. It is important to note that 'traditional' knowledge is not necessarily 'old' knowledge. The word 'traditional' in this context refers to the fact that the knowledge was created or evolved in a communal context, in other words, the *way* it was created, not its age.[161]

The costs to competition of design protection can be quite significant. In fact, legislators in Turkey recently approved exceptions to design protection rights for automobile spare parts replaced by insurers.[162] Moreover, members of the US Congress recently reintroduced the Promoting Automotive Repair, Trade, and Sales Act of 2017 (PARTS Act) over similar concerns.[163] The PARTS Act targets the use by original equipment manufacturers of design patents to prevent competitors from offering fairly standard replacement parts (i.e., bumpers, side mirrors, and light fixtures) for sale during the full term of the design patent, which often exceeds the time period the automobile owner retains the vehicle.[164] The PARTS Act would limit the enforcement period (only as against alternative replacement parts suppliers) for design patents on external automobile replacement parts from the normal 15-year term to 30 months from the first day the part is offered for public sale.[165] Whether the PARTS Act will become law and, if so, in what final form is unknown, but the

---

160 Du Mont and Janis (n 2) 839.

161 See Ulia Popova-Gosart (ed), *Traditional Knowledge & Indigenous Peoples* (Information & Education Network of Indigenous Peoples 2009).

162 See Işik Özdoğan and Ezgi Baklaci, 'Spare Parts: Exceptions to Design Rights Protection' (June 2017) WIPR <https://www.worldipreview.com/contributed-article/spare-parts-exceptions-to-design-rights-protection>; Asia Insurance Review, 'Turkey: Use of Equivalent Auto Parts to Help Cost Control' (March 2017) <http://www3.asiainsurancereview.com/News/View-NewsLetter-Article?id=38556&Type=MiddleEast>.

163 Promoting Automative Repair, Trade, and Sales Act 2017 (United States); John Huetter, 'Aftermarket-Centered PARTS Act Back for New Congress' (April 2017) Repairer Driven News <http://www.repairerdrivennews.com/2017/04/05/aftermarket-centered-parts-act-back-for-new-congress/>.

164 Huetter (n 163).

165 David Rood, 'Is Congress Finally Getting Serious About Curtailing Design Patents in the Auto Industry?' (June 2017) Foley & Lardner <https://www.autoindustrylawblog.com/2017/06/22/is-congress-finally-getting-serious-about-curtailing-design-patents-in-the-auto-industry/>.

bipartisan support for the bill and its reintroduction suggests the issue is one that is worthy of attention.

Disclosure requirements already play various roles in the IP system. For example, Article 29 of TRIPS mandates that members require applicants to disclose an invention in a patent application in a particular manner that would justify, on a quid pro quo basis, the grant of an exclusive right as being in the best interests of society.[166] Similarly, allowing countries to require disclosure of origin in the proposed DLT enables countries to ensure that the grant of a design right is consistent with a range of policy objectives, including protecting and promoting indigenous innovation and conservation. As such, a disclosure requirement is similar to other policy-based limitations on design rights. For example, Article 6(2) of the Canadian Industrial Design Act mandates the rejection of designs that are 'contrary to public morality or order'.[167] Similarly, Article 9 of the EC Design Regulation states that '[a] Community design shall not subsist in a design which is contrary to public policy or to accepted principles of morality'.[168]

It is also worth noting the DLT is being negotiated in the WIPO SCT. 'Origin' is a fundamental concept and requirement in relation to both trade marks and geographical indications. Trade marks receive protection only if they serve as accurate indicators of source or origin.[169] Likewise, the whole basis of protection for geographical indications is that the origin of the product, as well as the techniques and practices employed by the artisans in that locale, renders it sufficiently distinctive to be accorded protection.[170] It thus makes sense that origin should be recognised as a factor worthy of consideration in relation to the remaining subject matter area of the WIPO SCT – industrial designs.

Finally, what a country does with information gleaned from a disclosure of origin requirement, whether formal or substantive, is a matter of national law in the same way that Article 3 of the draft DLT allows individual nations to determine how other information they gather should be used. Disclosure reveals information that can be used for multiple purposes, and the particular use may not be specified *ex ante*. Thus, the uses to which a country puts information gleaned from a design application disclosure of origin requirement should be irrelevant to the question

---

166 TRIPS (n 38) art 29.

167 Industrial Design Act 1985 (Canada), s 7(e).

168 CDR, art 9.

169 See for example The Lanham Act (United States), s 1127.

170 See WIPO, 'Geographical Indications' <http://www.wipo.int/geo_indications/en/>.

of whether a formalities treaty like the DLT should prevent the imposition of such a requirement in the first instance.

V. CONCLUSION

The African Group proposal reflects concerns about justice, fairness and governments' commitments to protect certain resources and values. This creates tension as the IP system often has been isolated from these kinds of concerns. The issue of misappropriation has moral overtones as it relates to theft, and the public policy goals of national laws in this area may be undermined by a government's inability to track the unlawful dispersion of its resources. A properly constructed disclosure of origin requirement can enhance transparency and facilitate information gathering without overly burdening applicants or IP offices.

Given the importance of this issue to several WIPO Members, it seems necessary for any final DLT to contain clear policy space for countries to require disclosure of origin for cultural and genetic resources.[171] If the references to disclosure of source or origin for traditional knowledge, traditional cultural expression, and genetic resources are removed and replaced with more nebulous language, that could indicate to legislators, judges, scholars and others who will interpret the treaty in the future that such a disclosure requirement is not allowed. Such policymakers may look to the 'travaux préparatoires', the official record of the DLT negotiation, to determine how its provisions should be interpreted.[172] The fact that specific language allowing countries to require DOO in design applications appeared in the draft document for several years and then was removed could suggest that the requirement was considered and rejected.

---

[171] An 'agreed statement' in conjunction with the DLT is another possible compromise tool for allowing countries to employ a disclosure of origin requirement. See for example WIPO, 'Agreed Statements Concerning WIPO Performances and Phonograms Treaty' <http://www.wipo.int/treaties/en/text.jsp?file_id=295690>.

[172] The traveaux préparatoires and negotiating history is, in accordance with art 32 of the Vienna Convention, only relevant once a full interpretation of ordinary meaning, in context and in light of object and purpose, has been completed under art 31, and then the role of this 'supplementary' material is to confirm that meaning or resolve and ambiguity (Vienna Convention on the Law of Treaties (opened for signature 23 May 1969, entered into force 27 January 1980) 1155 UNTS 331 (VCLT) arts 31–32). For a review of treaty interpretation in the context of international IP, see Susy Frankel, 'The WTO's Application of "the Customary Rules of Interpretation of Public International Law" to Intellectual Property' (2006) 46 Va J Int'l L 365.

This is especially likely in view of the statements on the record by some delegations that a disclosure of origin requirement should not be allowed in design applications.[173]

As the examples described above illustrate, valid concerns attest to the reasonableness of countries desiring transparency regarding the use of such resources in the development of articles protected by industrial design rights. As technology continues to evolve and policy implications crystallise, countries will continue to need space to frame their laws in ways that will appropriately reward the innovation process, while adequately respecting cultural and genetic resource appropriation concerns.

---

173 SCT Report I (n 77).

6. Lost in communication: a few thoughts on the object and purpose of the EU design protection

Anna Tischner*

I. INTRODUCTION

For a long time designs were the most defamed objects of intellectual property (IP), named by the eminent representatives of academia a poor cousin,[1] a poor relative,[2] a neglected child, a younger and less considered brother,[3] Cinderella[4] or the least important of the four pillars of IP protection.[5] To change this insulting position of design in the family of IP, but above all to address industry and market needs, 20 years ago a new *sui generis* design regime was introduced in Europe with the ambition to create a modern and autonomous form of protection which stands *ex aequo* alongside other IP rights.[6] The EU design regime is commonly

* All online sources were last accessed on 29 December 2018.

1 Sam Ricketson, *The Paris Convention for the Protection of Industrial Property: A Commentary* (Oxford Univeristy Press 2015) 474.

2 Stephen P Ladas, *Patents, Trademarks, and Related Rights: National and International Protection* (Harvard University Press 1975) 828.

3 William Wallace, 'Protection for Designs in the United Kingdom' (1974) 4 IIC 421.

4 Charles-Henry Massa and Alain Strowel, 'Community Design: Cinderella Revamped' (2003) 2 EIPR 68.

5 Ewan Grist, 'Demystifying design protection' (June 2013) DesignWrites <http://f.datasrvr.com/fr1/313/94186/DesignWritespdf.pdf>.

6 See Annette Kur, 'The Green Paper's "Design Approach" – What's Wrong With It?' (1993) 10 EIPR 374, 376 ('[T]he unfortunate but common view that designs must belong either to the patent or the copyright side, *tertium non datur*, . . . has plagued designs ever since they entered the sphere of law, to the effect that they always have been denied a proper place of their own within the legal system. It was exactly this fruitless "patent versus copyright" dilemma which the authors of the Green Paper have tried to escape in choosing a genuine approach.') See Annette Kur, Marianne Levin and Jens Schovsbo (eds), *The EU Design Approach: A Global Appraisal* (Edward Elgar Publishing 2018), 1–27.

assessed as a highly successful one.[7] However, recent decisions in design cases in Europe have caused some disappointment among designers and design industries and have undermined trust in *sui generis* design protection.[8]

At a time of enormous expansion and hypertrophy of IP protection it seems advisable to turn back to universal and rudimentary issues.[9] An extremely refreshing circle of three interrelated questions – What? How? and Why? – may help to address the initial problem of the object and purpose of the European design protection and to verify its adequacy. The first question: 'What do we protect in the design regime?' influences the scope and content of the design right encompassed in the query 'How do we protect it?'[10] which is connected to the teleological problem 'Why

[7] At least taking into account the increasing number of the RCD filings and renewals; Conf EUIPO Annual Report, 22–25 <https://euipo.europa.eu/ohimportal/en/annual-report>.

[8] See for example *Magmatic Ltd v PMS International Ltd* [2016] UKSC 12; *Samsung Electronics (UK) Ltd v Apple Inc* [2012] EWCA Civ 1339; Case T-90/16 *Thomas Murphy v European Union Intellectual Property Office* (GC, 4 July 2017); Joined Cases C-24/16 and C-25/16 *Nintendo Co Ltd v BigBen Interactive GmbH and BigBen Interactive SA* (CJEU, 27 September 2017). See also a report published by the United Kingdom Intellectual Property Office, authored by Alexander Carter-Silk and Michelle Lewiston, 'The Development of Design Law: Past and Future' (2012), pointing out that case law has contributed to the confusion and unpredictability of outcome that is perceived by industry. For an alternative view, see Robin Jacob, 'Woolly Lines in Intellectual Property Law', in Robin Jacob, *IP and Other Things: A Collection of Essays and Speeches*, (Hart Publishing 2015) 98 ('For in my experience in the end in design cases the courts tend to go by gut reaction rather that the precise legal language of the law').

[9] This text was inspired by the articles of Jeanne C Fromer, 'Claiming Intellectual Property' (2009) 76 UCLR 719; Jeanne C Fromer and Mark P McKenna, 'Claiming Design' (2018) 167 Univ Pa Law Rev and a lecture by Lionel Bently, 'Interpreting the Intangible Object', given at Krakow Intellectual Property Law Summer School on 11 September 2017. See also in Polish, Anna Tischner, 'Graficzne Przedstawienie Wzoru Przemysłowego a Przedmiot i Zakres Ochrony Wzorniczej', in Piotr Kostański, Tomasz Targosz and Pawel Podrecki (eds), *Experientia Docet Księga Jubileuszowa Ofiarowana Pani Profesor Elżbiecie Traple* (Warsaw 2017) 699–712.

[10] There are two principles of the EU regime that make the question 'How?' extremely urgent in Europe. First, the design is protected in abstract and is thus not limited by the product indicated in the registration (discussed in Joined Cases C-361/15 P and C-405/15 P *Easy Sanitary Solutions BV and European Union Intellectual Property Office v Group Nivelles* (CJEU, 21 September 2017) [94]–[96]). Secondly, the scope of design right covers any use of design in product or in abstract (there is no concept of use of design as a design). The latter principle led the CJEU to a broad interpretation of citation limitation in design regime in

do we protect it'? And again the problem 'Why?' should inform the object of protection ('What?') whose proper individuation and identification appears to be one of the most acute problems of the EU design protection and will be a focus of critical review below.

II. DESIGN AS CREATED, AS EMBODIED, AS REGISTERED, AS USED, AS PERCEIVED, AS INTERPRETED . . . AS COMMUNICATED

Although we use the notion 'design' in different ways and contexts, little agreement exists as to its meaning. The slightly nonsensical saying of John Haskett,[11] famous British design writer and educator, illustrates perfectly how confusing the use of the term 'design' can be: 'Design[12] is to design[13] a design[14] to produce a design'.[15] Protection of the entire scope and value of this phenomenon through mechanisms such as the EU *sui generis* design regime offers is an illusion. Legal protection of design in Europe in the form of the special right is focused only on the design outcomes, which can, however, take a wide range of forms. They may relate to things, places and environments; they may also convey messages and enable communication and interaction.[16]

The EU *sui generis* design protection developed around the central concept of the external aspect of a product and the economic value which is attached to the appearance as a product's differentiator on the market.[17] The concept of the object of special design protection corresponds to the marketing role of the appearance of a product

Joined Cases C-24/16 and C-25/16 *Nintendo Co Ltd v BigBen Interactive GmbH and BigBen Interactive SA* (CJEU, 27 September 2017) [68]–[86] in which the court, like an equilibrist, tried to cope with a broad scope of design right and lack of adequate limitation covering the use in order to provide commercial information about goods legitimately commercialised on the market.

[11] John Haskett, *Design: A Very Short Introduction* (Oxford University Press 2005) 3.

[12] Design may be understood as a field or a discipline of human creativity.

[13] Design may indicate an action or a process.

[14] Design may also mean a concept, a proposal or a plan.

[15] But also an outcome of a design process, namely a finished product (which is not necessarily physical or tangible).

[16] Haskett (n 11) 6.

[17] EU Commission, 'Green Paper on Legal Protection of Industrial Design' (1991) Working Document of the Services of the Commission III/F/5131/91-EN, para 2.1.2. See the definition of 'design' in Directive 98/71/EC of 13 October 1998 on the Legal Protection of Designs [1998] OJ L289/28, art 1 (DD) and Council

recognised 'as an opportunity for differential advantage in the market place' that influences consumer product choice.[18] Design right may cover the appearance of material objects and the appearance of symbolic and visual communications (which are not physical or tangible).[19] Design outcomes in the form of a product's appearance may be created by one design feature or a combination of several features (shape, colour, surface, texture). The shape constituted by lines and contours seems to be the only design characteristic that can alone be sufficient to create the appearance of the product. Other features co-create the design and exist cumulatively; they are not self-sufficient.

A design as an outcome of the design process appears as a specific intentional object[20] in the moment when the designer's creative idea is embodied in a project (usually graphic, reduced to a drawing or 3D graphic model) or in a tangible object (a prototype or a real product).[21] The design individuated in this way may constitute the object of the viewer's operation of apprehending it (cognition, perception).[22] It is worthwhile looking at the problem of individuation of the object of IP law protection in the context of the act of communication between the moment of embodiment and cognition. In a model communication scenario, the sender communicates with the recipient by a message which is formulated in a common language and refers to a common context (circumstances, time and place).[23] Any code used to this end should be common to the

---

Regulation (EC) 6/2002 of 12 December 2001 on Community Designs [2002] OJ L3/1, art 3 (CDR).

18 Marielle Creusen and Jan P L Schoormans, 'The Different Roles of Product Appearance in Consumer Choice' (2005) 22(1) J Prod Innovat Manag 63.

19 See the broad definition of 'product' in DD, art 1 and CDR, art 3.

20 A notion introduced by Polish phenomenologist, ontologist and aesthetician Roman Ingarden, who distinguished between different modes of being such as 'expressing oneself' in an ontological sense (understood as embodiment) and in an epistemological sense (occurring during cognition). See Roman Ingarden, *Controversy over the Existence of the World* (vol 1, Frankfurt am Main 2013).

21 Justine Pila names this moment 'a "metaphysical individuation", according to which an object is individuated by "whatever it is that makes it the single object that it is"'; Justine Pila, *The Subject Matter of Intellectual Property* (Oxford University Press 2017) 18; E J Lowe, 'Individuation' in Michael J Loux and Dean W Zimmerman (eds), *The Oxford Handbook of Metaphysics* (Oxford University Press 2005) 75.

22 This moment can be named an 'epistemic individuation, according to which an object is individuated by the ability of a certain intelligent individual to single it out as a distinct object of perception' Pila (n 21) 18.

23 Based on the model of verbal communication process developed by Karl L Bühler and Roman Jakobson, the six factors of an effective verbal communication

sender and recipient as a precondition of undistorted communication. The system of coding, constructing and creating meaning is important but perception, reception, understanding, reconstruction and interpretation of the coded message is no less important. Context also matters. Nowadays cognitive science provides more advanced tools to analyse how people communicate.

Communication related to the subject matter of IP protection is of fundamental importance and constitutes a point of reference at different stages of emergence, existence and enforcement of IP protection (e.g. registration, validity, infringement and defences).[24] The message communicated at the very moment of emergence of the IP protection concerns a delineated object of protection and takes the form of claims.[25] The recipients of such a message are unspecified third parties, often competitors and users.[26] As captured concisely by Fromer, 'intellectual property claims exist almost entirely to provide notice'.[27] The mechanism of providing notice to the public does not work properly and is inadequate if codes of

---

are context, addresser (sender), addressee (receiver), contact (channel), common code and message.

[24] As a result, the individuation of an object of protection at different moments resembles turning and twisting of 'a nose of wax' in any direction – an accurate metaphor introduced by Mark A Lemley and Mark P McKenna, 'Scope' (2016) 57 William & Mary L Rev 2197, 2225.

[25] See *Magmatic Ltd v PMS International Ltd* [2014] EWCA Civ 181 [31] ('the scope of protection must be discerned from the graphical representation and the information it conveys').

[26] So explicitly, *Sealed Air Limited v Sharp Interpack Limited, Sharpak Aylesham Limited* [2013] EWPCC 23 [21] ('The design register fulfils an important function of giving notice to the public what designs have been registered. That function does not require the law to say that the representations must be interpreted by the informed user either. After all one of the most important groups of people interested in scrutinising the register will be rival manufacturers and designers of the products in question. They are not users. They will know how to interpret technical drawings. In practice users are much less likely to consult the register than manufacturers and designers.')

[27] Fromer (n 9) 719 and Fromer and McKenna (n 9) 47. See case T-16/16 *Mast-Jägermeister SE v EUIPO* (GC, 9 February 2017) [44]–[47], underlining the need for clarification 'for the purposes of ensuring legal certainty for third parties, who need to know precisely what the subject of the protection conferred on the design'. However, CDR, art 36(1) specifies that the representation must permit all the details of 'the matter for which protection is sought' to be clearly distinguished. That phrase refers to the requirement inherent in any registration, that is, to enable third parties to determine with clarity and precision all the details of the design for which protection is sought. Thus, imprecise representations would not enable third parties to determine unequivocally the matter to be protected by the design under consideration.

IP claiming, as well as the process of their cognition and interpretation, are unclear and blurred. The system of claiming under the European *sui generis* design regime adds further complications as it is not homogeneous, mostly because both formal and informal protection is offered. Consequently, there are two possible moments and forms of communicating the message about the object of design protection. The EU design regime is based then on a manifold claim format, which, in practice, may result in the permeation of rules specific to each of the claiming sub-regimes.[28]

III. VISUAL CODE

From the perspective of the European *sui generis* regime, design is not an idea for solving a design problem (a thought construction)[29] but a specific form of a product's appearance (an incorporation of an idea for solving a design problem which takes form of appearance). In that context, a very interesting question of the medium and language suitable for embodying and communicating designs arises.[30] This question should be addressed by means of the definition of the protected design, i.e. an embodiment of a design concept in the form of the specific appearance of a product. Visual information seems to be a natural tool to encapsulate and communicate design, which, by definition, is constituted of characteristics predominantly affecting the sense of sight (i.e. features such as shape, lines, contours, colours, texture, materials etc.).[31]

Nevertheless, design claims take visual form mostly because this form allows holistic encapsulation and perception of a design as a gestalt and

---

[28] See Fromer and McKenna (n 9) 42–47 for a discussion of the consequences of the elastic and manifold claim formats within one regime for the adequacy of notice and claim scope.

[29] Which in case of inventions is verbalised in patent claims.

[30] Cf Bruce Archer, 'Whatever Became of Design Methodology?' (1979) 1(1) Design Studies 17, which describes the process of solving design problems as 'the way designers (and everybody else, for that matter) form images in their mind's eye, manipulating and evaluating ideas before, during and after externalising them, [constituting] a cognitive system comparable with but different from the verbal language system. Indeed we believe that human beings have an innate capacity for cognitive modelling, and its expression through sketching, drawing, construction, acting out and so on, that is fundamental to human thought.'

[31] Opinion of Advocate General Bot in Joined Cases C-361/15 P and C-405/15 P *Easy Sanitary Solutions BV v EUIPO* (CJEU, 1 February 2017) [141] ('specific characteristics referred to in CDR, art 3 are therefore features which are visible to the eye'). See also David Stone, *European Union Design Law* (2nd edn, Oxford University Press 2016) 49.

best corresponds to the capabilities of the human brain.[32] In the case of design, pictures have stronger communicative power than words.[33] Although verbal description of the design outcomes is conceivable (e.g. in form of a verbal instruction for the production team), it does not allow for direct contact with the object of protection defined as a product's appearance.[34] Adequate verbal expression of design would require the translation of design features into appropriate language categories. It seems to prevent a holistic perception and is exposed to ambiguities in reception and interpretation.[35] Design so expressed would be a collection of unrelated verbalised elements like lines, colours, curves; consequently the design object as a whole would be lost. Cognitive studies confirm

---

[32] In line with the observation of Kurt Koffka, *Principles of Gestalt Psychology* (London 1935) 176 ('the whole is something else than the sum of its parts'). An interesting issue arises in the case of a set of tailoring patterns which are a visual presentation of elements indispensable to design creation and embodiment, which, however, as such are not perceived as a finished product's appearance. The practical consequences of this problem are well illustrated in Case No XXII GWwp 17/15 (Polish Community Design Court, 6 July 2015), in which the claimant tried to prove his right to Unregistered Community Design (UCD) providing the court with the contract on transfer of copyright to tailoring patterns only. The Polish court accepted this form of UCD ownership substantiation even though it was difficult to confirm *prima facie* that the pattern in form of sketches as attached to the copyright transfer agreement corresponded to the design of garment as later disclosed.

[33] Perfectly captured by the saying 'a picture is worth a thousand words' and in line with achievements of gestalt psychology concerning sensory (visual) perception according to which the human forms a percept (gestalt) independent of the parts.

[34] Cf the copyright discussion in *Abraham Moon & Sons Limited v Thornber & Others* [2012] EWPCC 37 [107], [109] relating to the ticket stamp being an instruction to the production team as to how to set up the machines in order to produce the required design in which the court taken that it is not doing 'violence to the language to regard the ticket as a graphic work. It may be of an unusual sort but it is a record of a visual image' and that 'the ticket is not simply a set of instructions which can be performed on a loom, it is also a record of an image and the image has been reproduced'.

[35] Cf Rudolf Arnheim, *Art and Visual Perception* (London 1974) 5 ('a whole cannot be attained by the accretion of isolated parts') and *Easy Sanitary Solutions* (n 10) [148]–[149] ('image . . . reflects the very nature of the object protected by Regulation No 6/2002 and the reason for which that protection is given to it. That image must show the appearance of the product in which the design is incorporated as a definitive whole which is recognisable by its lines, contours, colours, shape, texture or even its ornamentation or its materials, as provided for in art 3 of that regulation').

the existence of different modes of understanding visual and verbal information.[36]

Verbal language, however, can help to explain what has been visualised, if the image qualifies for ambiguous perception. On the one hand, it seems impossible to capture the essence of design protection verbally. On the other hand, certain design images may be unintelligible without some accompanied description. Although a picture is the best possible portrayal of the object of design protection and sight (vision) is one of the most objective (impartial) senses, it may be a source of varying percepts. This may even be 'not a matter of two different interpretations applying to one percepts, but of two percepts'.[37] It is possible that one image can be perceived as two totally different objects and create multiple meanings.[38] Verbal guidance used then as an adjunct to visual communication has the potential to influence, enhance or even change, the perception of the image.[39]

The EU design regime relies solely on visual information.[40] In the case of registered designs, communication of the object of protection is exclusively visual.[41] Designs are communicated through pictures. Visual claims constitute the content notice in the registered design regime (informing what protection is claimed for). The abstract components that structure a visual language are colour, form, line, shape, volume, value, texture, pattern, space and proportion, and they respond to the appearance characteristics. In visual design claims, those units are constructed into meaningful structures and shapes. In the EU design regime there is

---

36 See, for example, Benjamin K Bergen, *Louder than Words: The New Science of How the Mind Makes Meaning* (New York 2012).

37 Arnheim (n 35) 95.

38 With a perfect example of Wittgenstein's duck-rabbit illusion, first published in the German magazine, *The Fliegende Blätter*, 'Rabbit and Duck' (23 October 1892), a drawing which allows for two contradictory percepts.

39 Arnheim (n 35) 61 ('the perception of ambiguous shapes is influenced by verbal indications').

40 CDR, art 36(1) and (6). The visualisation of design features is in practice commonly confused in EU with the requirement of visibility of design features (see for example case T-494/12 *Biscuits Poult SAS v OHIM* (GC, 9 September 2014) [20]. Discrepancies in that regard which have arisen in the case law of Member States are reported in *Legal Review on Industrial Design Protection in Europe* (Brussels 2016) 54–63, recommending necessary amendments in the legal definition of design.

41 Case T-9/15 *Ball Beverage Packaging Europe Europe Ltd v EUIPO* (GC, 13 June 2017) [66]–[68] confirming the explanatory role of description, which may not have an influence on the question of what is the subject matter of the protection afforded by the design at issue.

no place for verbal (written) explanation which might influence the scope of protection, probably due to translation burdens and costs.[42] Under the EU design regime the language of words may be used only at the phase of verbalisation of sensations resulting from the contact with the appearance of a product, which takes place at later stages of the design right enforcement (i.e. within invalidation or infringement proceedings).[43]

IV. IN THE TRAP OF REGISTRATION

Registered designs are claimed in the application 'prior to and independent of any disputes with a potential infringer'.[44] The protected subject matter is delineated visually *ex ante*; for this reason claiming registered designs requires some prophetic skills in order to anticipate the situation the design will face on the market and predict what will be commercially preferable in future. It is necessary to think then through the scope of rights to be claimed.[45] However, the context in which the message about the object of protection is created, received and interpreted, which is one of the factors of effective communication, is variable over time. This creates additional difficulty in determining the content of that message.

---

42 This practical problem is mentioned only in EU Commission, 'Green Paper on Legal Protection of Industrial Design' (1991) Working Document of the Services of the Commission III/F/5131/91-EN, para 8.6.7. The role of description has evolved in the lawmaking process of the EU design law. The provision enabling explanation of the picture by a description was originally included in Max Planck Institute, 'Max Planck Institute Proposal: On the Way to a European Law of Designs' (1991) IIC 4, art 39(3) ('a description explaining the representation may be included'). Only with regard to the class indication did the Proposal explicitly state that 'the classification does not affect the scope of protection'. Almost the same regulation was included in the 'Proposal for a European Parliament and Council Regulation on the Community Design presented by the Commission' (1993) COM (93) 342 final, COD 463, 39 regarding the description as an optional element of the application. The official commentary of the Proposal of Regulation of 1993 provided 'that such texts may be helpful in order to identify the specific features of the appearance of the product which constitute the essence of the design and which might not show up very well in a picture or drawing'. However, in the 'Regulation Proposal' (1999) COM (99) 310 final, the description as an optional element explaining the representation was subjected to the principle that it does not affect the scope of protection of the design. This principle is maintained under CDR, art 36(3) and (6).

43 Fromer (n 9) 761, citing D Lichtman that 'mechanisms that reduce the costs of drafting [a claim] often increase the costs of reading and interpreting it'.

44 Fromer and McKenna (n 9) 19.

45 Ibid 8.

According to the IP claims taxonomy proposed by Fromer, claiming design is central as it consists of one central prototypical model which communicates categorical information and in practice covers a broader set of items.[46] The claimant identifies a model member of the set of designs protected by the right which is then used 'to determine whether other items are similar enough . . . to fall also within the same right'.[47]

Designers apply different tools to encode the outcomes of the design process. Pictorial representations may be used to notate visual information about the object of protection. In order to create the visual image of the object of protection, it is necessary to select appropriate agents, which will unambiguously convey to the eye and mind of the recipient the essence of the design. The encapsulation of the essence of design consists of translating the created appearance of an object that exists already in reality or is still in the designer's imagination, into a form suitable for the chosen medium so that the structural equivalent of this form in a given medium is created. Often the medium chosen forces a simplification or a certain degree of abstraction.

The features that form the product's appearance can be captured with the means of drawing, model, prototype, as well as the product (a real object), in line with the principle that 'each medium prescribes the way in which the features of a model are best rendered'.[48] All these possible 'embodiments' of the design (*corpora mechanica*)[49] provide an opportunity to get to know it and constitute a source of information about the subject of protection. Each of the above-mentioned forms of fixation of the essence of the object of design protection results in different percepts, creates different meanings and requires different rules of understanding and interpretation.

As regards the technique of the individuation of the object of protection,

---

46 Ibid 43, claiming by exemplar identifies 'a particular member or members of the set of protected designs rather that describing characteristics shared by these members' and Fromer (n 9) 724–730 and 764.

47 According to this taxonomy peripheral claiming requires identification of all members of the set of designs protected. Fromer (n 9) 727 and Fromer and McKenna (n 9) 42.

48 Arnheim (n 35) 140.

49 A Kopff, *Dzieło Sztuk Plastycznych i Jego Twórca w Świetle Przepisów Prawa Autorskiego* (A Work of Fine Art and its Creator in the Light of Copyright Regulations) (Kraków 1961) 25. A part of them may be qualified as *corpora communicativa* of design (as a drawing), and another part as *corpora vegetativa* – physical embodiments (as a product or a prototype). See A Wojciechowska, 'Wzornictwo Przemysłowe – Zagadnienie Przedmiotu Ochrony Prawnej' (Industrial Design – The Issue of the Subject of Legal Protection) (1990) 57 ZNUJ 47.

IP claiming may be done either (1) by characteristics or (2) by exemplar.[50] The first method requires a description of 'the necessary and sufficient characteristics common to all members of the set of protected embodiments' and is typical to patent regime.[51] The second is based on the 'actual work'[52] which reveals its copyright provenience. Relating the latter method to designs, the protected object shall be communicated by the 'actual design'. The question arises, what are the features sufficient for creating a design exemplar and where is a boundary between an exemplar and a selection of appearance characteristics? Does the 'actual design' mean a finished designed product or a finished design?

Fromer and McKenna assume that 'visual claims are difficult to conceive of as claims by characteristics'[53] and take claiming by exemplar 'as a given in design protection regimes'. It seems, however, that this approach does not take into account the possibility of visual description of the claimed characteristics and relies on verbal identification of those features only. Fromer and McKenna acknowledge, however, the need to optimise the notice function by the precise form of visual exemplar claiming, which may be supplemented by claiming by characteristic, in order to focus on the more relevant characteristics in an exemplar.[54] Nonetheless, claiming design by characteristics does not preclude use of the visual language, as it is conceivable that distilled essential design features for which protection is sought are shown and highlighted with an image (a drawing, a picture).[55]

European practice shows that designs are claimed either by a graphical representation of an exemplar (usually a photo of an actual product or a finished product in case of intangible design outcomes) or by a graphical description of the essential properties common to the set of protected embodiments, which usually takes the form of visual claims presenting selected features that are sufficient to constitute a design (in the form of a drawing or a model). The first method is focused on the photographic and most faithful representation of a finished object, the second is a true

---

50 Fromer (n 9) 727.

51 Ibid 727.

52 Ibid 729.

53 Fromer and McKenna (n 9) 50.

54 According to Fromer and McKenna (n 9), in case of designs two claiming regimes are combined: central and by exemplar, applied before litigation and by characteristics once litigated.

55 See M Schlötelburg, 'The Community Design: First Experience with Registrations' (2003) 383 EIPR 385 ('the selection of the means for representing a design is equivalent to the drafting of the claims in a patent: including features means claiming them').

representation in line with the reasoning that 'representing an object means showing some of its particular properties; one can often achieve the purpose best by deviating markedly from 'photographic' appearance'.[56] The level of generalisation in presenting the design is the result of an applicant's choice.[57] For both techniques disclaimers are acceptable.[58] Both methods of representing and communicating the design coexist which leads to problems with their interpretation. Case law suggests that visual claims by characteristics are perceived and interpreted the same way as visual exemplars.[59] This results in inadequately informed third parties, and disappointed right holders and designers. For the image to be 'a shortcut from mind to mind', it has to be encoded in a language understood the same way by both the sender and recipient.[60]

A drawing usually conveys selected properties of the product's appearance (shape, line, contour) as it constitutes a reduced representation of the design. Its choice as a medium communicating the essence of design protection expresses the decision that only certain features of the product's appearance constitute its essence, the protection of which is sought by the applicant. Line drawing is commonly interpreted as giving protection of the product contour regardless of other properties (colours, surface characteristics). Consistent with a better image being one that omits unnecessary details and selects essential features, a drawing alone is a visual interpretation of design.

A photograph is the most faithful optical recording of a product's appearance as it is not only able to communicate features like shape, lines, contours, but also colours, texture and materials. It is a perfect visual mode of claiming by exemplar. For a colour photograph, the specific colour scheme, along with other features (e.g. line, shape, texture) of a product's appearance creates the protected design. A black-and-white photograph raises more doubts about the features of the subject of

---

56 Arnheim (n 35) 159.

57 Explicitly on that problem, in *Procter & Gamble Co v Reckitt Benckiser (UK) Ltd* [2007] EWCA Civ 936 (Lewison J) [48] ('the registration holder is entitled to choose the level of generality at which his design is to be considered. If he chooses too general a level, his design may be invalidated by prior art. If he chooses too specific a level he may not be protected against similar designs').

58 European Union Intellectual Property Office (EUIPO), 'Guidelines for Examination of Registered Community Designs' (EUIPO Guidelines) (2018) para 5.3.

59 See the discussion of the Trunki case below in Section V.

60 Rebecca Tushnet, 'Worth a Thousand Words: The Images of Copyright Law' (2012) 125 Harv L Rev 683, 697 and 717 used after the case *W Va State Bd of Educ v Barnette* (1943) US319 (SCOTUS) [624], [632].

protection. Greyscale shades, which are reflected in the photograph, may only show contrast (difference in intensity of colours), which is a feature of the product's appearance. Depending on whether the photograph is coloured or greyscale, other design features are protected. Consequently that format may be used also in claiming by characteristics. Black-and-white photography is usually interpreted as a way of informing the public that the scope of exclusivity covers each colour scheme used.[61]

Technological progress has supported the process of design creation which has 'moved away from the drawing board and into the computer screens'.[62] Software allows higher precision, comprehensive documentation and project management, adding efficiency in the manufacturing process and reducing costs of product development. Designers use computer-aided design (CAD) technology to create and communicate the essence of the design without the need to create prototypes (real models). CAD is usually used to create a digital model (structural form) of the product based on curves and surfaces. The outputs of CAD may show the overall appearance of designed objects and convey information about shape but also about materials, processes, dimensions and tolerances. The widespread use of CAD is reflected in the increasing number of registrations in the EUIPO based on the graphical representations in the form of CAD pictures.[63] As the case law shows, however, the essence of this tool and the outputs of CAD seem to be incomprehensible to offices and courts identifying the object of design protection in individual cases.[64] Computer-made representations are assigned either to the logic of the drawing or to the logic of the photo. In many cases they seem to be closer to the former because they represent a reduced representation of certain features of the

---

[61] However, a black-and-white representation may provide information about the features of the design which is kept in these colours. In this case, the applicant should take care to specify the colour characteristics in shades of grey, for example by placing the pattern on a uniform but coloured (in colours other than shades of grey) background. See *Magmatic Ltd v PMS International Ltd* [2013] EWHC 1925 (LJ Kitchin) [32].

[62] Gerald Farin, Josef Hoschek and Myung-Soo Kim, *Handbook of Computer Aided Geometric Design* (Amsterdam 2002) 13.

[63] EUIPO informs that RCD e-filing accepts a new representation type for views as a tool for obtaining views in the application: 3D dynamic views. An uploaded 3D dynamic view in OBJ, STL or X3D format is transformed to static views of protected or unprotected design images. 3D dynamic views simulate 3D perspectives in 2D. Designs consisting in or containing a surface ornamentation should be submitted without using 3D dynamic views <https://euipo.europa.eu/ohimportal/en/the-advanced-form>.

[64] See below discussions at Section V.

pattern, but the courts often recognise the features of the photographic representation in them, which leads to their misinterpretation.

V. TO IMPROVE THE COMMUNICATION

Prior to the adoption of uniform design protection rules in Europe, the identification of the object of design protection was a national matter which was dealt with in different ways. Europeanisation and internationalisation of design protection has necessitated some structuring initiatives at the national, EU and international levels, aimed at improving legal certainty with regard to object delineation. Parallel to EUIPO guidance about the uniform EU design protection,[65] IP offices joined the European Trademark and Design Network Convergence programme in the field of graphic representation of designs (CP6).[66] Almost simultaneously with the publication of that Convergence, the problem of the lack of uniform rules for the graphic representation of industrial designs was raised at international level.[67] With regard to designs registered under the Hague Agreement,[68] Guidance on Preparing and Providing Reproductions in Order to Forestall Possible Refusals on the Ground of Insufficient Disclosure of an Industrial Design by Examining Offices was published in 2016.[69] National authorities have also reacted to the problems on an ad hoc basis.[70]

Foremost, the problem of design inconsistency resulting from different formats of representation was explicitly addressed in the CP6 recommending the selection of one format of graphic representation of the design (i.e.

---

65 EUIPO Guidelines (n 58).

66 EUIPO, 'The Common Communication for the CP6 Convergence Project on Graphic Representation of Designs' (2016) European Trade Mark and Design Network <https://euipo.europa.eu/ohimportal/en/news>.

67 Natalia Kapyrina, 'Le Dessin *du* Modèle: Vecteur de l'Harmonisation Internationale du Droit des Dessins et Modèles?' (2016) 19 JWIP 131.

68 Hague Agreement Concerning the International Registration of Industrial Designs (adopted 6 November 1925, entered into force 1 June 1928).

69 Rule 9(4) of the Common Regulations under the 1999 Act and the 1960 Act of the Hague Agreement <http://www.wipo.int/export/sites/www/hague/en/how_to/pdf/guidance.pdf>.

70 See for example DPN 1/16 'Guidance on use of representations when filing Registered Design applications' (hereinafter UK IPO Guidelines) <https://www.gov.uk/government/publications/designs-practice-notice-dpn-116/dpn-116-guidance-on-use-of-representations-when-filing-registered-design-applications#introduction>.

either a drawing or a photograph), as the scope of protection may vary with each format.[71] So far, the use of different formats (e.g. drawing and photograph) mixed in one application had been accepted by the office registering Community designs (now the EUIPO), which in practice had raised many doubts when identifying the object of protection.[72] In the light of this unambiguous recommendation, the position of the EUIPO and the Court (EU) presented recently in Case T-90/16 *Thomas Murphy v EUIPO*[73] is astounding as it equalises the contents of messages conveyed by both formats. It was assumed there that the outline of the design in the form of a drawing in the patent application with the United States Patent and Trade Mark Office (USPTO) is equivalent to a photograph of the contested design as its graphic representation for the EU registration.[74]

CP6 addresses the negative indication of the features of the product's appearance that are excluded from protection according to the applicant's intention, i.e. the disclaimer.[75] CP6 made it easier to distinguish between the design aspects which are claimed and unclaimed. Beforehand, clear recommendations were in the EUIPO Guidelines, only applicable to Community design applications.[76] The Guidelines present techniques for the representation of visual disclaimers with the help of broken lines when the design is presented in the form of a drawing, as well as colour shading, blurring, line restrictions (boundaries) which apply respectively to other formats of design representation.[77] Importantly, as different formats of the graphic representation of the design should not be combined, disclaimer techniques should not be mixed as well. Moreover, disclaimers may only be visual (verbal are inadmissible). Although all these documents are milestones to improving communication, with regard to object identification, case law shows that there are still grey areas about what is claimed, disclaimed, unclaimed.[78]

---

[71] The problem of design consistency is discussed in EUIPO Guidelines (n 58), para 5.2.

[72] Case T-525/13 *H&M Hennes & Mauritz BV & Co KG v OHIM* (GC, 10 September 2015).

[73] Case T-90/16 *Thomas Murphy v European Union Intellectual Property Office* (GC, 4 July 2017) [73]–[74].

[74] As a consequence the design representation in the earlier patent application with the USPTO has been accepted by the EUIPO as the basis for the date of priority of the EU design presented in the application form by means of a black-and-white photograph.

[75] CP6 (n 66), para 3.1.4.

[76] EUIPO Guidelines (n 58), para 5.3.

[77] Case T-68/10 *Sphere Time v OHIM* (GC, 14 June 2011).

[78] Dotted lines used in the design representation are interpreted also as a

Notwithstanding the attempts to improve the situation, deficiencies of communication concerning the object of design protection cast a shadow over the infringement dispute of the popular design of a children's ride-on suitcase (Trunki), which turned out to be an award-winning design and a market success. The design was graphically represented, for registration, by greyscale CAD drawings. The interpretation of this design became a point of contention, between the parties to the dispute and the courts. Only when it came to colour as a design feature did the courts agree that the design was not limited to particular colours as it was presented in grey (monochrome) shades.[79] As regards other design features, read on the basis of the computer-generated three-dimensional images, the findings were divergent. For the High Court the design was for the shape of the suitcase only,[80] while the Court of Appeal[81] and the Supreme Court[82] concluded that the applicant had claimed, in addition to the shape of the product, an unadorned surface resulting in the image of uncluttered (minimalistic) design. In the absence of any graphic elements on the surface of the product, it was interpreted that the lack of decoration (ornamentation) was a claimed design feature.[83]

This seems, however, an implied or even imposed design feature ('uncluttered design which conveys a distinct visual message'), which is not the result of a process of visual perception but rather verbal (over-) interpretation.[84] The graphic representation of the design, by computer modelling, was interpreted as if it were a photograph, without taking into account the fact that CAD is mainly used to record the structural features of a design. The language of design had been misunderstood or over-interpreted in that case. The lack of any graphic elements on the surface

---

positive information about transparency of certain design elements. Compare: *Procter & Gamble Co v Reckitt Benckiser (UK) Ltd* [2007] EWCA Civ 936; *Samsung Electronics (UK) Ltd v Apple Inc* [2012] EWHC 1882 (Pat); *Gimex International Groupe Import Export v The Chillbag Company Limited & Others* [2012] EWPCC 34; *Kohler Mira Ltd v Bristan Group Ltd* [2013] EWPPC Civ 2. See David Stone, 'Transparency Over the Use of Dotted Lines?' (2013) 8 JIPLP 437.

[79] *Magmatic Ltd v PMS International Group Plc* [2014] EWCA 181 [42]. The Supreme Court took the two-tone colouring of the CRD as guidance about claiming three-dimensional shape in two contrasting colours in *Magmatic Ltd v PMS International Ltd* [2016] UKSC 12 [53].

[80] *Magmatic Ltd v PMS International Ltd* [2013] EWHC 1925 [69].

[81] *Magmatic Ltd v PMS International Group Plc* [2014] EWCA 181 [41].

[82] *Magmatic Ltd v PMS International Ltd* [2016] UKSC 12 [44]–[47].

[83] Consequently, the presence of such elements on another product changed the overall impression created by the design.

[84] *Magmatic Ltd* (n 81) [41]; *Magmatic Ltd* (n 82) [44]–[45].

of the design representation was construed as a positive design feature of simplicity, minimalism, rather than as an undefined, open space, which can be exploited in a variety of ways in practice.[85] The design feature named as 'absence of ornamentation' has become a bargaining chip for design disputes.[86] This implied feature seems to be the result of assessment of the overall impression of a design and certainly not a feature which constitutes a design as defined in the CDR.[87]

Criticism should be also given to the observation made in the Court of Appeal when interpreting the graphical representation of the Trunki suitcase design, namely that it 'looks like a horned animal'.[88] The effects of verbal remarks will be discussed below, but this example already demonstrates that the process of objective identification of the protected subject matter, based solely on visual percepts, is confused with the more subjective interpretation of aesthetic impressions. A proper place and moment for that is rather the normative assessment of the overall impression created by the design.

The Trunki case reveals the malfunctions in communication relating to the object of design protection, i.e. discrepancies between the message as encoded with the help of computer-made representations and as decoded in the infringement dispute. The medium chosen to determine the creative idea was most probably treated by the designer as a tool for the recording of features other than those which were then perceived by the court as constituting the design. The CAD model was interpreted as a greyscale photo with a lack of regard for the specificity of the medium chosen to fix the essence of the design.[89] The court interpreted CAD output as an exemplar rather than visual information about claimed characteristics. As a result, the design has been lost in communication.

It is likely that in the Trunki case CAD images had not been used consistently at the moment of design registration (e.g. the controversial issue of the importance of information about colour contrasts between

---

85 *Magmatic Ltd* (n 82) [44].

86 As scrupulously reported in ibid [47]–[48]; *Samsung Electronics (UK) Ltd v Apple Inc* [2013] ECDR 1 [15]–[20]; Case 200.094.132/01 *Apple Inc v Samsung Electronics Co Ltd* (Düsseldorf Court of Appeal, 24 July 2012) 2, 22, 26; Cases T-525/13 and T-526/13 (Hague Court of Appeal, 24 January 2012) [5.1B, 5.3B1, 6.4]; *H & M Hennes & Mauritz BV & Co KG v OHIM* (GC, 10 September 2015) [37].

87 CDR, art 3. See Kapyrina (n 67) 138 for an interesting question posed regarding whether it is conceivable to protect the lack of a feature.

88 *Magmatic Ltd* (n 81) [41].

89 *Magmatic Ltd* (n 82) [46].

individual components of the product).[90] But a hindsight interpretation based on outdated language should not be the answer to technological changes in the process of creating and expressing designs. In this case a representation of the design was confused with its real appearance, which confirms that pictures are often interpreted too realistically.[91] Meanwhile, the visual representation of design may also make ideas visible,[92] even if ideas as such are unprotected. The observation of Rudolf Arnheim, art theorist and perceptual psychologist, seems to be the most accurate comment on the courts' attempts to identify the design in the Trunki case: 'What puzzles one must face if one assumes that the actual outlines on paper contain everything there is to the percept.'[93]

This case demonstrates the urgent need to navigate understanding of images in the EU design regime. Perhaps the introduction of the categories of designs as an option in the registration process, similar to trade mark categories, i.e. 'shape alone' design, 'shape plus other features' design, or additional explicit information as to whether the graphical representation constitutes claiming 'by exemplar' or 'by characteristics' would improve the quality of notice in claiming designs in Europe.[94]

In sum, the Trunki case is 'a missed opportunity' for CJEU guidance,[95] which would be welcomed given the modern language of designers. The consequences of this decision are worrying. As a remedy for the uncertainty caused by the Supreme Court's judgment, the UK IP Office issued

---

90 *Magmatic Ltd* (n 82) [42]; (n 84) [51]–[54].

91 The tendency to treat pictures as reality is discussed in Fromer and McKenna (n 9) 46 and Tushnet (n 60) 695.

92 Christina Spiesel, 'More than a Thousand Words in Response to Rebecca Tushnet' (2012) 125 Harv L Rev 40. The differences between perceiving pictures and perceiving reality in legal context are discussed by Neal Feigenson and Christina Spiesel in *Law on Display: The Digital Transformation of Legal Persuasion and Judgment* (New York 2009).

93 Arnheim (n 35) 95.

94 Although not discussed by the Court, the same problems may relate to design representations like the one in *Ball Beverage Packaging* (n 41). In the light of recent developments in case law it is not clear whether the graphic CAD representation of the design shows cans with no imprint, or rather cans of a certain shape (either imprinted or not), i.e. unornamented shape, shape with no imprint or just shape.

95 Sara Ashby, 'The UK Supreme Court and the Trunki Case: Missed Opportunities, Mysteries and Misunderstood' (2016) 38(9) EIPR 527, 530; David Stone, '*Trunki*—How did things go so wrong?' (2016) 11(9) JIPLP 662, 675. The reference to the CJEU was suggested not only by the claimant in that case but also by the Comptroller General of Patents, Designs and Trade Marks, in his capacity as Registrar of Designs. *Magmatic Ltd* (n 84) [27]–[29].

guidelines on the use of design representations for the purpose of design applications[96] in order to make applicants aware of the consequences of choosing a specific format of design representation. A simple line drawing is suggested there as a means to claim the protection of shape as a selected design feature ('shape only' design),[97] although for designers it is an old-fashioned visual language and technique.[98] This seems to ignore the widespread practice of computer modelling of designs. Unfortunately, the UK IPO Guidelines do not improve the state of legal certainty with statements, including 'basic line drawings may well be interpreted as an attempt to protect shape only' or 'as an attempt to register both shape and "minimalist" ornamentation (i.e. where plain undecorated surfaces are positively intended to be a feature of the design)'[99] which are the offspring of the Trunki and Samsung Apple design disputes.

The likely outcome of the Trunki case will be an increase in design applications that capture the same design in different formats (line drawings, photographs, CAD images) in order to safeguard the desired subject matter of the protection. It is doubtful whether this will improve the state of certainty in addition to the clogging of the register. Unfortunately, the interpretation of computer generated visual representations is neither addressed in CP6 nor in any other guidance. This suggests lawyers are ignorant of the specificity of the modern language of designers, which causes disturbed communication of the object of protection.[100]

Images should speak for themselves but if they do not, verbal language may be of some help. Sensitivity to this problem was visible already in the Green Paper, which pointed out that '[s]ometimes there might be a need

---

[96] UK IPO Guidelines (n 70).

[97] UK IPO Guidelines (n 70) ss 6 and 12. A similar recommendation is included in EUIPO, 'Legal review on industrial design protection in Europe' (June 2016) para 4.1, 101 <https://ec.europa.eu/growth/content/legal-review-industrial-design-protection-europe-0_en>.

[98] Nowadays ink, line and CAD drawings are in practice equal languages applied by designers to present the shape. I carried out a survey among a group of 40 design students and 75% of them answered that the core value of Trunki design (as represented graphically in CDR application) is constituted by the visually attractive and functional shape, which is intended for use in different colours and with different surface decoration. Moreover, 78% of them indicated that the visually attractive and functional shape is the design feature which the creator wanted to show as a feature worthy of protection, using CAD presentations.

[99] UK IPO Guidelines (n 70) s 9.

[100] See the comments of the design community on the consequences of the decision, published on ACID website after the Supreme Court Decision <https://www.acid.uk.com/supreme-court-rules-trunki/>.

to explain the features which constitute the design and which might not easily be perceived simply by looking at the reproduction. This should be made possible by joining a description to the application'.[101] However, the European legislator did not follow this path and excluded a verbal description from the catalogue of sources of information on the scope of design protection.[102] Can we cope without any verbal information in the case of ambiguous graphical design representations? Are we able to elaborate an unambiguous visual language, which designers use to encode the design value and which audiences (courts, IP offices, third parties) decode properly? Despite many documents and guidance on the graphical representation of design issued at EU and national level, there are still gaps which require a systemic solution, taking into account the specifics of the communication process. Guiding understanding of images on both sides of the communication channel seems to be the simplest solution. Otherwise, as the Trunki case shows, design registration may work only as a trap for diligent designers who place their trust in the registration system.

VI. WHOSE EYES TO BELIEVE? TO UNDERSTAND THE PICTURES

In the process of communication of the object of protection, the visual material is grasped by the human mind. According to the theory of visual perception 'all perceiving is also thinking'[103] and 'vision is a creative activity of the human mind'[104] which may be compared to reading and understanding. Both the drawing as a synthesis of design features, the model of the designed object and the photograph of the actual product are subject to interpretation, taking into account that 'seeing is not the mechanical registration of elements, but the grasping and understanding of the essential features of the structure'.[105] Pictures as an encoded message 'acquire meaning from our associations to them, drawn from our perceptual knowledge, experience, cultural setting'.[106]

In the case of a design claim it is the role of the office or the tribunal to objectively decode (in the invalidation or in the infringement proceedings)

---

[101] Green Paper on Legal Protection of Industrial Design (n 17) para 8.6.7.
[102] CDR, art 36(6).
[103] Arnheim (n 35) 5.
[104] Ibid 46.
[105] Ibid 6.
[106] Spiesel (n 92) 41.

the message communicated at the moment of emergence of design protection, taking into account all factors, i.e. the code used and the context and understanding of the hypothetical recipient of the message (the general public).

As pictures are open to interpretation and responses may be varied, some guidance as to how to read pictures is therefore indispensable. Problems in understanding the message about the subject of protection can be solved with the help of an expert who knows and understands the complexities of visual language. Understanding of the language used to encode a message and the context is a matter of fact not law, and consequently may be answered by reference to evidence.[107] Objectivity of interpretation results from not focusing on what was the essence and value of an intangible asset (design) for the creator or for the applicant at the moment of registration, but on what the recipient (the reader)[108] will perceive in design claims.[109] The intentions of the person asserting design protection are only relevant if they are expressed in the graphic representation by appropriate and accepted measures.[110]

The perception of the design by its market audience plays a key role in the assessment of the criteria for design protection (individual character) and consequently in delineating the scope of protection.[111] This gives rise to looking wrongly at the design through the lens of an informed user when identifying the object of protection.[112] The informed user will assess the overall impression of the design by comparing it with an earlier or later design. The role of the informed user is not to identify the object of protection. In practice, however, the three stages constitutive for the object and scope of design protection, i.e. design encoding (encapsulation), design

---

[107] In the Trunki case the Supreme Court considered the interpretation of a drawing to be a question of law (n 82) [52]. The court does not seem to separate the stages of identification of the subject matter of protection, which is based on facts, and the interpretation of the overall impression, which is a matter of law.

[108] *Magmatic Ltd* (n 82) [59] ('we should interpret the images on a Community Registered Design by reference to how it would appear to a reader in the light of the terms of the Principal Regulation, the Implementation Regulation and the practice of OHIM').

[109] Case C-488/10 *Celaya Emparanza y Galdos Internacional SA v Proyectos Integrales de Balizamientos SL* (First Chamber, 16 February 2012) [55] ('the scope of the rights conferred . . . must be determined objectively and cannot vary according to the circumstances pertaining to the conduct of the person applying for registration of a Community design').

[110] Otherwise however *Apple Inc* (n 86) [200].

[111] CDR, art 10.

[112] Stone (n 31) 152.

decoding (understanding) and the perception of design by the informed user (decisive for the assessment of individual character, the scope of protection and infringement) are blurred.

Only after the design is identified (decoded) can the next step in infringement proceedings be taken, i.e. to consider the overall impression it creates through the eyes of the informed user. 'The eye alone' should be the judge of the same or different overall impression created by two designs but 'judges and lawyers in general are highly uncomfortable with images'.[113] At this stage, the judge usually creates a verbal portrayal of the design – the vision experience is expressed in words for the purpose of normative evaluation and recording of legal reasoning. The judges engage in verbal description of the overall impression, which may consequently influence not only the scope, but also the object of design protection. This may lead to a phenomenon known as 'verbal overshadowing'.[114] The effects of 'overshadowing' are visible in the Trunki case, in which the verbal remark 'an animal with horns' influences the attention and changes the way the image is perceived.[115] Something may be lost or added as a consequence of this verbal intervention. The words used in reporting the design (i.e. 'design claimed for a wheeled suitcase in the shape of a horned animal') affect the perception of the design itself.[116]

Another factor that may affect the identification of the protected subject matter is the reception of a design on the market. As market communication was a function of design, mentioned when creating the European design regime,[117] it might be tempting to focus on how buyers understand a design when delineating the object of design protection. Moreover, the buyers' perception may change over time. Although there are no explicit grounds for considering this dynamic factor, it cannot be excluded that it will be taken into account indirectly when analysing the context in which the subject matter of protection is interpreted. In this respect, the

---

113 Rebecca Tushnet, 'The Eye Alone Is the Judge: Images and Design Patents' (2012) 19 J Intell Prop L 409.

114 Tushnet (n 60) 733–38 ('The phenomenon in which producing verbal descriptions decreases the accuracy of a memory of a nonverbal stimulus is known as verbal overshadowing'). Also discussed in Fromer and McKenna (n 9) 46.

115 *Magmatic Ltd* (n 81) [47].

116 The comment of Tushnet (n 60) 738 to a different case ('[g]iven the role of language in shaping perception, it might be more accurate to say that the appellate court and the trial court saw different works') fits perfectly with the divergences in design perception between the High Court and Court of Appeal in the Trunki case.

117 Kur (n 6) 377.

design regime comes closer to trade marks,[118] which may undermine the independence of the design regime.

An additional question arises regarding how to take context into account as there is no explicit mechanism to do so when claiming designs.[119] Even though the visual representation identifies the object of protection (visual claims), case law suggests that the scope of protection may take into account actually marketed designs (products). As 'designs do not exist in a vacuum'[120] the products are considered, at least for illustrative purposes, in order to confirm the conclusions already drawn from the assessment of the designs as represented in the applications for registration.[121] The question is, however, whether it is acceptable to take into account the real marketed products to deny the conclusions drawn from the assessment of graphical representation. The context in which the message about the protected registered design is encoded and interpreted may substantially influence the limits of the object of design protection and needs to be managed in a more predictable way.

VII. TERRA INCOGNITA: CLAIMING UNREGISTERED DESIGN

To respond to the needs of designs with limited commercial life, which are usually not worth registering, the EU unregistered design right (UCD) was created as an alternative and supplementary form of design protection.[122] The object identification of this experimental form of protection remains a conundrum.[123] Taking into account the lessons taken from other informal regimes and using Fromer's taxonomy, in the case of unregistered designs the protected subject matter is delineated *ex post* by exemplar as unregistered designs are not formally claimed and they are almost never claimed

---

118 Case C-252/12 *Specsavers International Healthcare Ltd and Others v Asda Stores Ltd* (CJEU, 18 July 2013) [32]–[41].

119 According to CDR, art 36(6) neither the indication of the products in which the design is intended to be incorporated or to which it is intended to be applied, nor a description explaining the representation, affect the scope of protection of the design as such. Cf Ashby (n 95) 530.

120 Ashby (n 95) 531, discussing examples of court decisions incorporating context consideration.

121 Case 2011 I-10153 *PepsiCo Inc v Grupo Promer Mon Graphic SA* (CJEU, 20 October 2011) [73]–[74].

122 Recitals 15, 16, 17 to CDR.

123 Discussed in Anna Tischner, 'The Role of Unregistered Rights – A European Perspective on Design Protection' (2018) 13(4) JIPLP 308, 309.

before a dispute.[124] Identifying the protected characteristics of the design during litigation can mean targeting or even manipulating it strategically for the particular dispute.[125] This form of object identification introduces substantial flexibilities which correspond to the primary aim of the protection and in practice may increase its value in comparison with inflexible and static formal design protection.

Since disclosure forms the UCD[126] it seems to be decisive also for delineating the object of the right. The design as disclosed (in the form of a product's appearance presented visually or physically) serves as a central claim by exemplar against which other designs are compared to determine copying and to assess their overall impression. The right holder, however, does not have the opportunity to make any positive statement about the scope of the protection sought when the protection is automatically created. The key question then is: what are the limits of the UCD holder's freedom in the object individuation (i.e. in tailoring claims)? Is it possible to abstract *ex post* one distilled design feature (e.g. shape only) from a more complex product's appearance (retrospectively in the infringement proceedings as a form for claim refinement) and claim its protection under the Unregistered Community Design Right (UCDR)? This issue is not explicitly addressed under the informal EU design regime.[127]

The only guidance at the EU level on the method of claiming unregistered Community design rights may be found in the *Karen Millen* case, in which the CJEU clarifies that 'given the lack of registration formalities for this category of design it is necessary for the holder of the design at issue

---

124 CDR, art 19(2).

125 Cf Fromer and McKenna (n 9) 32, discussing strategic behaviour in copyright claiming.

126 CDR, art 11.

127 The problem has already been faced in the UK where the speculative reasoning of claimants was commonly applied to prove copying of the unregistered design feature. The problem was partially solved in 2014 by amendments to the UK unregistered design definition. Section 213 of the Copyright, Designs and Patents Act 1988 defined 'design' as the design of any aspect of the shape or configuration, whether internal or external, of the whole or part of an article. Section 1(1) of the Intellectual Property Act 2014 amended section 213(2) by deleting the words 'any aspect of' with effect from 1 October 2014. The effect of this amendment is discussed in *Neptune (Europe) Ltd v Devol Kitchens Ltd* [2017] EWHC 2172 (Pat). However, this amendment has not changed the general rule applied under the UK unregistered design regime that the legal burden to identify the relevant aspects of the shape and configuration is on the claimant. *Farmers Build Ltd v Carrier Bulk Materials* [1999] RPC 461, 484 (CA).

to specify what he wants to have protected under that regulation'.[128] This statement, formulated incidentally in the context of the interpretation of Article 85(2) CDR, suggests almost unlimited strategic behaviour of the right holder which may be detached from the moment constitutive for the creation of this right, which, after all, provides some objective basis for determining what is to be protected. The CJEU discusses neither the code of claiming unregistered designs nor the limits of strategic claiming. It combines the determination of the object of protection with the presumption of validity as set out in Article 85(2) CDR stipulating that the UCDR holder needs to indicate only what constitutes the individual character of the design at issue, i.e. to point out 'the elements of the design concerned which give it its individual character'. The object identification rarely constitutes an independent step in the court's reasoning in the case of unregistered design rights.[129] It is usually implied in the discussion of infringement (or invalidity) factors, mostly in the context of determination of copying the design[130] and assessment of the overall impression created by the designs at issue.

The laconic statement of the CJEU in the *Karen Millen* case leaves doubts as to what should be the basis for determining the subject matter of protection: a visualised design in a form made available to the public or a design as verbalised by the right holder. The basic issue of the language used to encode the object of informal design protection is then controversial. The CJEU hint suggests that verbal language prevails, which is at odds with the principles of the EU design protection based on visuals. It seems that structurally the most correct is the reference to the product's appearance at the very moment of disclosure, taking into account the medium that reflects the whole design (i.e. a graphic representation – a photograph of the product, a drawing or a product as such). Immediately, however, the next question arises: how to identify the UCDR constituted by selected feature(s) of a more composite product's appearance. This question is usually combined with the problem of strategic behaviour of trimming or narrowing the right best to match what the alleged infringer has copied. Might the practice of indicating, abstracting or separating design features worthy of protection serve as a substitute for claiming registered designs by characteristics? Another crucial question is: to what extent should the modes of the later use of the design in the marketplace

---

[128] Case C-345/13 *Karen Millen Fashions Ltd v Dunnes Stores, Dunnes Stores (Limerick) Ltd* (CJEU, 19 June 2014) [46].

[129] Bently (n 9).

[130] CDR, art 19(2).

and the reaction of the competitors (the context) be taken into account in individuation of the object of protection?

Parallel availability of formal and informal design protection raises further concerns. The requirement of a graphic representation of a design protected by a registered right significantly limits the possibility of design protection to other features that constitute the appearance of the product (e.g. properties that can be perceived by touch); they are protectable only if they can be visualised, i.e. presented graphically in a clear, precise and objective manner.[131] The question is whether different formats of claiming unregistered designs change this situation and broaden the scope of design features protected by informal right.

Recalling the initial model of communication act, the design as disclosed (encoded at that moment) constitutes the object of unregistered Community design right and serves as the design claim under the unregistered design regime in Europe. The informal design regime leaves, however, more flexibilities and freedom as to the reconstruction and interpretation of the message so conveyed. The problems identified within the registered design regime, glaringly obvious after the Trunki case,[132] may increase the reliance on unregistered regimes providing a more flexible claim format. The flexibility inherent in this informal regime should not, however, encourage practices that run counter to the essence of protection under the *sui generis* design regime, e.g. prioritising verbal over visual language.

VIII. CONCLUSIONS: TO COMMUNICATE THE CRUX OF DESIGN WORTHY OF PROTECTION

The metaphor of communication makes it easier to locate and name the deficiencies of the relatively young EU design regime, which since its beginning has had the ambition to gain independence. The problem of identification of the object of protection shows, however, that its autonomy is questionable. Design claims oscillate between patent, copyright and, to some extent, even trade marks regimes, drawing a little from each regime, which results in misunderstandings and misinterpretations. The deficits in this area undermine the justification for this form of protection addressed in the question 'Why?' The initial problem of identification

131 See *Legal Review on Industrial Design Protection in Europe* (n 40).

132 *Magmatic Ltd* (n 82).

of the object of the *sui generis* design regime may be summarised by the question: 'Where are the designs worthy of protection?' That query gives rise to the supplementary question 'Why do we want to protect designs in the form of special design right?'

Some hints in that regard may be found in recital 7 to the Community Design Regulation, which declares that '[e]nhanced protection for industrial design not only promotes the contribution of individual designers to the sum of Community excellence in the field, but also encourages innovation and development of new products and investment in their production'. The fundamental justification for the EU design regime is 'that protection of designs must ultimately lead to the economic well-being of the EU region'.[133] The question is, however, what we perceive as welfare of the EU region nowadays. Certainly the special design regime in Europe was introduced to address the needs generated by 20th-century consumerism. When reforming design protection in Europe it is worth considering to what extent this regime may address the acute social and environmental challenges of the 21st century – namely sustainability,[134] global ecological crisis,[135] and migration movements and human mobility.[136] The EU design regime should not ignore the change in the role of design in the 21st century, which predicts itself to be very different from the previous one and, aside from dealing with the effects of consumerism, seems to have enough trouble of its own.

In the light of recital 7 CDR it is not clear what it means today to stimulate new product development and what types of products are concerned – innovative ones providing competitive advantage or competitive substitutes which are near-copies. If the design regime is to stimulate creativity in designs, then it should provide protection against copying

---

133 *Legal Review on Industrial Design Protection in Europe* (n 40); Uma Suthersanen, *Design Law: European Union and United States of America* (2nd Edn, Sweet & Maxwell 2010) 88; 'Explanatory Memorandum to Proposed Design Directive' COM(93) 344 [1993] OJ C345/1; 'Explanatory Memorandum to Proposed Design Regulation' COM(93) 342 [1994] OJ C29, para 3.1.

134 Anne Chick and Paul Micklethwaite, *Design for Sustainable Change. How Design and Designers Can Drive the Sustainability Agenda* (Fairchild Books 2011).

135 Visible in the right to repair movement aimed at introducing legislation that would legalise a customer's 'right to repair' and would force vendors to design products for longer life and easier maintenance. See the European Union, 'Parliament Press Release' (July 2017) <http://www.europarl.europa.eu/news/en/press-room/20170629IPR78633/making-consumer-products-more-durable-and-easier-to-repair>.

136 Taken into account in the *Design Thinking* creative process based on deeper understanding of a social context.

of the protected immaterial good and deter replication which does not advance the field. In the light of the case law discussed above it remains unclear, however, what kind of creativity the EU design regime is to stimulate and whether it is able to encourage valuable contributions to the human environment. The decisions discussed above may even suggest that the special design regime is aimed at promoting proliferation of new products which differ visually to a small extent and are cheaper market substitutes. Apart from difficulties in graphic representation of the object of protection and its interpretation, the above-discussed examples show that actually the greatest value of good design (expressed in its functions or other utility purposes – e.g. ergonomics, environmental friendliness) cannot be protected in this form.[137]

Last but not least, the design regime is designed to reward the investment in design. If encouraging creations by giving some market control is the aim of the design regime, then more clarity as to the object of the design protection is necessary, based on the clear content notice and predictable interpretation of it, otherwise designers and design industries will find this form of protection delusive and inadequate to their needs.[138]

---

137 Perfectly captured by the UK Supreme Court remark that 'unfortunately for Magmatic, however, this appeal is not concerned with an idea or an invention, but with a design' (n 82) [57].

138 Cf Carter-Silk and Lewiston (n 8) 6 ('The judicial approach to interpretation of legislation has often appeared disconnected from the object behind its enactment. Judgements frequently seem subjugated to a judicial desire not to extend design protection any further than is absolutely necessary, being more concerned with the limitations than with the object of the rights granted.')

7. Tobacco plain packaging, human rights and the object and purpose of international trade mark protection*

Genevieve Wilkinson**

I. INTRODUCTION

Intellectual property and human rights developed separately and they remain separate from each other, despite increasing interactions between them that can sometimes result in conflict. However, interpretive tools in public international law, such as reference to the object and purpose of an agreement, can increase the likelihood of harmonious interpretation between separate fields of law.[1] The visibility of intersections between intellectual property and human rights increased following the introduction of the World Trade Organization (WTO) Agreement on Trade-Related Aspects of Intellectual Property (TRIPS).[2] Human rights concerns were used persuasively to address concerns about the impact of the patent provisions of TRIPS on access to medicine[3] and remain relevant to that debate as well as others such as the protection of traditional knowledge for Indigenous peoples.[4] More recently, human rights arguments focusing on the impact of more expansive protection of copyright

* All online sources were last accessed on 27 December 2018.

** This research was undertaken with the research support of the Quentin Bryce Doctoral Scholarship. The author would like to thank Natalie Stoianoff and Beth Goldblatt for their generous feedback and encouragement and acknowledge comments from the participants at the ATRIP Annual Congress of 2017, particularly the insightful comments of Professor Susy Frankel on earlier drafts of this chapter.

1 Henning Grosse Ruse-Khan, *The Protection of Intellectual Property in International Law* (Oxford University Press 2016) 34.

2 Agreement on Trade-Related Aspects of Intellectual Property Rights (opened for signature 15 April 1994, entered into force 1 January 1996) 1869 UNTS 299 (TRIPS).

3 Noah Novogrodsky, 'After AIDS' (2013) 14 Melb U L Rev 643, 650.

4 Susy Frankel, 'Using Intellectual Property Rules to Support the Self-Determination Goals of Indigenous People' in Christophe Geiger (ed), *Research*

on privacy, freedom of expression and the right to a fair trial featured in debate surrounding the ratification of the Anti-Counterfeiting Trade Agreement (ACTA) in a number of countries.[5] Concerns about the human right to education remain relevant to the protection of copyright in educational materials.[6] The potential role of human rights in the context of trade marks has become increasingly apparent as owners of tobacco-related trade marks assert their rights against governments, attempting to limit their programmes to reduce tobacco consumption and improve health outcomes.[7]

This chapter considers the object and purpose of key international treaties regulating trade mark law from a human rights perspective. It uses the example of tobacco plain packaging legislation to argue that trade mark law can engage important human rights issues and a human rights approach is relevant to an analysis of the object and purpose of TRIPS and the Paris Convention. Different interpretations of the object and purpose of TRIPS permit or exclude a human rights perspective. This can be contrasted to an interpretation of the object and purpose of the Paris Convention. Disputes regarding tobacco plain packaging provide a valuable case study to consider the relationship between human rights and trade marks, engaging questions about human rights to health, freedom of expression, development and protection of moral and material interests in intellectual property itself. The important public health arguments raised by disputes regarding tobacco plain packaging legislation in the WTO (the WTO Disputes) can be viewed from the perspective of the human right to the highest attainable standard of health.[8] Despite this, a human rights perspective has not been the emphasis of the arguments made by Australia and was not considered by the Panel that determined the WTO

Handbook on Human Rights and Intellectual Property (Edward Elgar Publishing 2015) 645–648.

[5] Peter K Yu, 'Six Secret (and Now Open) Fears of ACTA' (2011) 64 SMU Law Review 975, 1033–1035, 1050–1059.

[6] Laurence R Helfer and Graeme W Austin, *Human Rights and Intellectual Property: Mapping the Global Interfaces* (Cambridge University Press 2011) 316–363; Lawrence Liang, 'Paternal and Defiant Access: Copyright and the Politics of Access to Knowledge in the Delhi University Photocopy Case' (2017) 1(1) Indian L Rev 36, 43.

[7] Samuel Murumba, 'Foxes and Hedgehogs at the Intersection of Human Rights and Intellectual Property' (2012) 38 Monash Uni L Rev 119.

[8] Ibid; Ruse-Khan (n 1) 255; Ernst-Ulrich Petersmann, 'How to Reconcile Health Law and Economic Law with Human Rights – Administration of Justice in Tobacco Control Disputes' (2015) 10 Asian J WTO Int Health 27.

Disputes.[9] This chapter will argue that the object and purpose expressed in the preamble and Articles 7 and 8 of TRIPS engages human rights concerns when it is applied to the tobacco plain packaging dispute.

II. FRAGMENTATION

A. Importance of Object and Purpose in the Context of Fragmentation

In the absence of explicit incorporation of human rights in intellectual property agreements, there needs to be an interpretive link for human rights to be considered in disputes about trade mark law in international law. Although human rights agreements and intellectual property agreements often have substantially different subject matter, interpretive rules in public international law can be relevant to understanding the relationship between the agreements where they appear to conflict with each other.[10] This may assist states to observe their obligations under treaties binding upon them in good faith.[11] The potential for conflicts resulting from the fragmentation of international law has been recognised in the international community.[12] Interpretive tools can also be useful for addressing fragmentation between intellectual property and other fields of law.[13] Object and purpose is a relevant tool for interpretation of treaties which can be useful for identifying other agreements that may have overlapping subject matter and be relevant to the interpretative exercise. These agreements can constitute relevant rules of international law between the parties and be used by treaty interpreters to address

---

9 Panel Report, 'Australia – Certain Measures Concerning Trademarks, Geographical Indications and Other Plain Packaging Requirements Applicable to Tobacco Products and Packaging' (June 2018) WT/DS435/R, WT/DS441/R, WT/DS458/R, WT/DS467/R (Australia – Plain Packaging Measures). See also Australian Department of Foreign Affairs and Trade, 'Integrated Executive Summary of Australia's Submissions' (March 2016) Summary of Arguments <http://dfat.gov.au/trade/organisations/wto/wto-disputes/Documents/integrated-executive-summary-aus-submissions-tobacco-plain-packaging-ds435-441-458-467.pdf>.

10 Ruse-Khan (n 1) 34–44.

11 Vienna Convention on the Law of Treaties (opened for signature 23 May 1969, entered into force 27 January 1980) 1155 UNTS 331 (VCLT). Art 26 of this convention codifies the *pacta sunt servanda* obligation.

12 International Law Commission, 'Fragmentation of International Law: Difficulties Arising from the Diversification and Expansion of International Law' (Report of the Study Group of the International Law Commission) (2006) UN Doc A/CN4/L682.

13 Ruse-Khan (n 1) 31–66.

fragmentation.[14] Recognition of other relevant international agreements in treaty interpretation increases the likelihood that treaty interpretation in one field of international law will be harmonious with other relevant fields of international law. This is important where the subject matter of different treaties is largely separate but the operation of the terms of the treaty impacts on the operation of the separate treaty.

The fields of intellectual property and human rights are examples of two fields of law that have been generally considered to be separate. One of the reasons that the potential link between the fields is not explicitly relevant is their different institutional development. This article focuses on human rights protections found in the International Covenant on Economic, Social and Cultural Rights (ICESCR).[15] The relevant treaty making body is the Committee on Economic, Social and Cultural Rights (CESCR). Multilateral trade marks protection was initially agreed through the Paris Convention for the Protection of Industrial Property.[16] In 1967 the World Intellectual Property Organization (WIPO) became responsible for the administration of the Paris Convention.[17] The Paris Union continued to discuss revisions to the Agreement. Although WIPO is a United Nations institution, it remained separate from the United Nations institutions that were responsible for human rights. These developed following the adoption of the Universal Declaration of Human Rights (UDHR) in 1948.[18] The deliberations of the negotiating teams responsible for the UDHR and ICESCR did not appear to recognise the significance of the potential overlap between the fields.[19] That significance did not crystallise until the development of a separate regime for multilateral intellectual property protection in the WTO as a result of the TRIPS Agreement.[20] Although

---

[14] Henning Grosse Ruse-Khan identifies VCLT (n 11), art 31(3)(c) as part of his interpretive tool box for addressing fragmentation: Ruse-Khan (n 1) 34–36.

[15] International Covenant on Economic, Social and Cultural Rights (opened for signature 16 December 1966, entered into force 3 January 1976) 993 UNTS 3 (ICESCR).

[16] Paris Convention for the Protection of Industrial Property (opened for signature 20 March 1883, entered into force 6 July 1884, revised 14 July 1967, amended 28 September 1979) 828 UNTS 305 (Paris Convention).

[17] Paris Convention (n 16), Stockholm Revision Act, art 15(1)(a).

[18] Universal Declaration of Human Rights (adopted 10 December 1948) UNGA Res 217 A(III) (UDHR).

[19] Lea Shaver, 'The Right to Science and Culture' (2010) 1 Wisconsin Law Rev 121, 149–151.

[20] Laurence Helfer, 'Regime Shifting: The TRIPS Agreement and New Dynamics of International Intellectual Property Lawmaking' (2004) 29 Yale J Int Law 1, 6.

there is some institutional cooperation between WIPO and the WTO,[21] there is very little interaction between the TRIPS Council and human rights institutions.[22]

United Nations human rights institutions, including CESCR, operate quite separately from the WTO and the TRIPS Council but also from WIPO.[23] WIPO remains important for the development of new multilateral intellectual property standards[24] but the enforcement mechanisms provided by TRIPS have meant that the WTO has been the institutional focal point for interpretation of intellectual property standards.[25] TRIPS is interpreted pursuant to the Dispute Settlement Understanding (DSU) by the Dispute Settlement Body (which includes panels and the Appellate Body) although disputes can be resolved through processes of good offices, mediation and conciliation before they reach adjudication.[26] Important features of the process are the remedies available to complainants when breaches of TRIPS are established.[27] These include retaliatory economic sanctions.[28] The threat of sanctions of this nature strengthens the likelihood that TRIPS Agreement standards will be observed.[29] In

---

21 Agreement between the World Intellectual Property Organization and the World Trade Organization (signed on 22 December 1995, entered into force 1 January 2006) 35 ILM 754.

22 Klaus D Beiter, 'Establishing Conformity Between TRIPS and Human Rights: Hierarchy in International Law, Human Rights Obligations of the WTO and Extraterritorial State Obligations under the International Covenant on Economic, Social and Cultural Rights' in Hanns Ullrich, Reto M Hilty, Matthias Lamping and Joseph Drexel (eds), *TRIPS Plus 20: From Trade Rules to Market Principles* (Springer 2016) 497–498.

23 Ibid.

24 For a recent example, see Marrakesh Treaty to Facilitate Access to Published Works for Persons Who Are Blind, Visually Impaired, or Otherwise Print Disabled (adopted 27 June 2013, entered into force 30 September 2016) VIP/DC/8.

25 Laurence Helfer, 'Human Rights and Intellectual Property: Mapping an Evolving and Contested Relationship' in Rochelle C Dreyfuss and Justine Pila (eds), *The Oxford Handbook of Intellectual Property Law* (Oxford University Press 2018) 121–122.

26 WTO, 'Dispute Settlement Rules: Understanding on Rules and Procedures Governing the Settlement of Disputes' (DSU); Marrakesh Agreement Establishing the World Trade Organization (agreed 15 April 1994, entered into force 1 January 1995) 1869 UNTS 40, art 5.1.

27 DSU (n 26), art 22.

28 DSU (n 26), art 22.2.

29 Helfer (n 20) 2; Murumba refers to the command sanction nature of global intellectual property: Murumba (n 7) 133; Matthew Kennedy, *WTO Dispute Settlement and the TRIPS Agreement* (Cambridge University Press 2016).

contrast, human rights claims are governed under separate mechanisms which emphasise consensus-based compliance.[30] Although the Paris Convention provides for dispute resolution through the International Court of Justice, this mechanism has never been engaged.[31]

Increasing intersections between the fields mean that the doctrinal relationship between them can be important. Fragmentation between different fields of international law can mean that states are bound by conflicting obligations which cannot be effectively addressed by interpretive rules such as *lex posterior*[32] and *lex specialis*.[33] However, Article 31 of the Vienna Convention on the Law of Treaties (VCLT) also identifies other tools for interpretation which permit good-faith interpretation of treaties that bind states. This article codifies rules of interpretation found in customary international law. It provides that good-faith interpretation of terms of a treaty shall be in light of the object and purpose of a treaty as well as the ordinary meaning of the terms in their context. Article 31 provides further guidance for this interpretive exercise. The text, including preamble and annexes, is part of the interpretative context.[34] This context also includes agreements made in connection with the conclusion of the treaty.[35] These can be made by all of the parties or made by one or more parties and accepted as related to the treaty by all parties.[36] Article 31(3) identifies further matters to be considered, which include subsequent agreements or practice relevant to the interpretation and relevant rules of international law applicable in the relations between parties. In addition to being part of interpretative exercise set out in Article 31(1), object and purpose can be important to the latter consideration as they indicate rules that are likely to be relevant.

---

[30] Rhona K Smith, *Textbook on International Human Rights* (7th edn, Oxford University Press 2016) 171.

[31] Sam Ricketson, *The Paris Convention for the Protection of Industrial Property* (Oxford University Press 2015) 323.

[32] VCLT (n 11), art 30; *Lex posterior derogat legi priori* refers to the principle that where all parties to a treaty are also parties to a later treaty on the same subject, provisions in the later treaty supersede provisions in the earlier treaty: International Law Commission (n 12) (2006) A/CN4/L702 17.

[33] Henning Grosse Ruse-Khan, 'A Conflict-of-laws Approach to Competing Rationalities in International Law: The Case of Plain Packaging between Intellectual Property, Trade, Investment and Health' (2013) 9(2) J of Priv Int Law 308, 309.

[34] VCLT (n 11), art 31(1).

[35] Ibid, art 31(2).

[36] Ibid, art 31(3).

B. Why Are Human Rights and Trade Marks Fragmented?

There are a number of reasons that human rights and trade marks are considered to be separate fields of international law. The agreements that enshrine legal obligations for states in each field are separate and do not explicitly reference the other field. ICESCR provides possible protection for trade marks.[37] A right to property protection that may apply to trade marks can be found in some domestic constitutions and regional instruments.[38] However, despite this lack of direct crossover between the relevant texts, the instrumental nature of trade marks means that they can be significant to human rights.[39] In addition to Article 15 and right to property considerations, links between trade marks and human rights can be seen in the case of freedom of expression and the human right to health.[40]

Even more so than patents and copyright, trade mark law has generally been considered to address subject matter that is substantially different to human rights. Article 15(1)(c) ICESCR provides that everyone should benefit from the protection of the moral and material rights to any literary, artistic and scientific production they have created. It has been characterised as an alternative system of protection for intellectual property.[41] It can be used to justify some human rights protection for patents and copyright but it is not generally considered to apply to trade marks.[42] Where there is human rights protection for property, this may provide limited protection for the owners of trade marks.[43] However,

---

[37] ICESCR (n 15), art 15(1)(c).

[38] Peter K Yu, 'The Anatomy of the Human Rights Framework for Intellectual Property' (2016) 69 SMU Law Rev 37, 94–95; Helfer and Austin (n 6) 212–220.

[39] For example, the role of trade marks in detecting counterfeit goods has implications for the human right to health: Duncan Matthews, 'Counterfeiting and Public Health' in Christophe Geiger (ed), *Criminal Enforcement of Intellectual Property: A Handbook of Contemporary Research* (Edward Elgar Publishing 2011) 42, 45–58.

[40] Ruse-Khan recognises a relationship between trade marks, plain packaging and the right to health: see generally Ruse-Khan (n 33). Helfer and Austin recognise the relationship between freedom of expression and trade marks (n 6) 283–312.

[41] Committee on Economic, Social and Cultural Rights, 'The Right of Everyone to Benefit from the Protection of the Moral and Material Interests Resulting from Any Scientific, Literary or Artistic Production of which He or She is the Author (article 15, paragraph 1 (c), of the Covenant)' (2005) General Comment No 17 UN ESCOR E/C.12/GC/17; Ruse-Khan (n 1) 212.

[42] Yu (n 38) 85–95.

[43] Megan M Carpenter, 'Trademarks and Human Rights: Oil and Water – Or Chocolate and Peanut Butter' (2009) 99 Trademark Reporter 892, 915–916.

although this protection is available in some regional systems and domestic constitutions, the right to property has not been translated into a binding obligation in the key multilateral human rights agreements.[44] Trade mark rights are not generally considered to be human rights. This does not mean that human rights are not relevant to the operation of agreements concerning trade mark law. This chapter considers the human rights implications of attempts to restrict states in implementing tobacco plain packaging legislation. These attempts have been staged in domestic, bilateral and multilateral environments. Their impact is both direct and indirect as these attempts can have a chilling impact on regulation in states where the legislation has been contemplated but not introduced.

III. HUMAN RIGHTS CONSIDERATIONS AND THE OBJECT AND PURPOSE OF TRIPS

A. The Object and Purpose of TRIPS and Human Rights

This section will argue that each of the preamble, Article 7 and Article 8 permit consideration of states' binding human rights obligations and are relevant to the object and purpose of TRIPS. The object and purpose of TRIPS is a relevant interpretative tool when WTO disputes require interpretation of specific provisions of TRIPS.[45] The WTO Dispute Settlement Body recognises the relevance of customary rules of interpretation of public international law to their deliberations.[46] This is interpreted to mean that the interpretative principles included in the VCLT apply.[47] Article 31(1) provides that '[a] treaty shall be interpreted in good faith in accordance with the ordinary meaning to be given to the terms of the treaty in their context and in the light of its object and purpose'.[48] The object and purpose of an agreement is often found in the preamble of an

---

[44] Ibid.

[45] Frankel explains how international law relevant to public health, including the Framework Convention on Tobacco Control, can be relevant to a VCLT-based interpretation of the meaning of human health in the TRIPS Agreement: Susy Frankel, 'The WTO's Application of "the Customary Rules of Interpretation of Public International Law" to Intellectual Property' (2006) 46 Va J Int Law 365, 420–421. See also Ruse-Khan (n 1) 34–36.

[46] DSU (n 26), art 3.2.

[47] WTO Appellate Body, 'United States-Import Prohibition of Certain Shrimp and Shrimp Products' (1998) WT/DS58/AB/R.

[48] VCLT (n 11), art 31. The VCLT is used to guide treaty interpretation in the WTO: DSU, art 3.2.

agreement.[49] The significance of Articles 7 and 8 as an expression of the object and purpose of TRIPS that is relevant to the interpretation of each provision of the TRIPS Agreement was emphasised by members of the WTO in the Doha Declaration on TRIPS and Public Health.[50] In addition to the ordinary meaning of terms in their context and the object and purpose of the treaty, Article 31 recognises the interpretative relevance of subsequent agreements and practice in relation to the treaty and 'any relevant rules of international law applicable in the relations between the parties'.[51] The object and purpose of a treaty can guide identification of relevance of these rules of international law in specific interpretative exercises.

The Preamble of TRIPS engages human rights considerations because, along with its objectives of protection and enforcement of intellectual property rights, it recognises 'the underlying public policy objectives of national systems for the protection of intellectual property, including developmental and technological objectives.'[52] The importance of harmonious interpretation of state obligations in international law means that it can be assumed that a relevant underlying public policy objective of the intellectual property protection system complies with other international obligations, including binding human rights obligations.[53] Importantly these obligations are not only obligations to respect human rights, but also obligations to protect and fulfil human rights.[54] Some of these protection

---

[49] Isabelle Buffard and Karl Zemanek, 'The "Object and Purpose" of a Treaty: An Enigma?' (1998) 3 ARIEL 311, 322.

[50] WTO Ministerial Conference, 'Declaration on the TRIPS Agreement and Public Health' (November 2001) WT/MIN(01)/DEC/2 (Doha Declaration). Voon and Mitchell argue that this constitutes a 'subsequent agreement between the parties regarding the interpretation of the treaty or the application of its provisions' which VCLT Article 31(3)(a) directs treaty interpreters to consider: Tania Voon and Andrew D Mitchell, 'Implications of WTO law for Plain Packaging of Tobacco Products' in Tania Voon, Andrew D Mitchell and Jonathan Liberman (eds), *Public Health and Plain Packaging of Cigarettes: Legal Issues* (Edward Elgar Publishing 2012) 122. See Panel finding that paragraph 5 of the declaration constitutes a subsequent agreement: Australia – Plain Packaging Measures, para 7.2409.

[51] VCLT (n 11), art 31(3).

[52] TRIPS (n 2), preamble.

[53] International Law Commission (n 12), A/CN4/L702 8. Yu recognises the importance of human rights as exogenous limits to intellectual property rights: Peter K Yu, 'The Objectives and Principles of the TRIPS Agreement' (2009) 46 Houston Law Rev 979, 1008.

[54] United Nations Committee on Economic, Social and Cultural Rights (CESCR), 'General Comment No 14: The Right to the Highest Attainable Standard of Health (Art 12 of the Covenant)' (August 2000) E/C12/2000/4, para 33.

and fulfilment obligations overlap with the object and purpose of TRIPS that is suggested by Articles 7 and 8 of TRIPS.

Article 7 explicitly acknowledges that 'protection and enforcement of intellectual property rights should contribute to a balance of rights and obligations'. Importantly protection and enforcement should also contribute 'in a manner conducive to social and economic welfare'. Other relevant objectives to which protection and enforcement should contribute are technological innovation, transfer and dissemination of technology, and production and use of technological knowledge.[55] Part 1 of Article 8, the principles provision of TRIPS, identifies specific interests that are relevant considerations for states in the implementation of TRIPS, many of which are relevant to human rights concerns. These include necessary public health and nutrition protection measures and public interest in sectors of vital importance to Member States' socio-economic and technological development.[56] The extent to which the final part of Article 8.1, 'provided such measures are consistent with the provisions of this Agreement', restricts the ability of Member States to rely on this article in developing intellectual property policy that emphasises national interests remains contested.[57] Correa argues that the preamble and Article 7 are provisions that interpretation of Article 8 should be consistent with, so social and economic welfare and a balance of rights and obligations should be taken into account.[58] Yu recognises that in any dispute settlement proceedings there are many supportive links between human rights agreements and the objectives and principles identified in Articles 7 and 8, including rights to life, food, health, education, self-determination, freedom of expression, cultural participation and development, and the benefits of scientific progress.[59] Importantly, the relevant human rights provisions will vary, depending on the circumstances of the case, and policy measures need to be effective in meeting their objectives.[60]

---

55 Yu separates Article 7 into five separate objectives: Yu (n 53) 1000.

56 TRIPS (n 2), art 8(1); TRIPS, art 8(2) also provides for further balancing exercises to occur in circumstances restraining trade or technology transfer that constitute an abuse of rights.

57 Susy Frankel and Daniel J Gervais, 'Plain Packaging and the Interpretation of the TRIPS Agreement' (2013) 46(5) Vand J Int'l L 1149, 1202–1203; Yu (n 53) 1014–1015.

58 Yu (n 53) 1014, citing Carlos Correa, *Trade Related Aspects of Intellectual Property Rights: A Commentary on the TRIPS Agreement* (Oxford University Press 2007) 104.

59 Yu (n 53) 1037.

60 Hannu Wager and Jayashree Watal, 'Human Rights and International Intellectual Property Law' in Christophe Geiger (ed), *Research Handbook on*

B. The Object and Purpose of the Paris Convention and Human Rights

In contrast to TRIPS, the Paris Convention does not contain a preamble and there are no specific clauses to guide object and purpose clauses analogous to Articles 7 and 8. Our understanding of object and purpose can be guided by the title, which recognises that the agreement is for the protection of industrial property for foreign nationals of member states.[61] In comparison to the recognition of underlying public policy objectives in TRIPS, as well as the developmental and technological objectives of the agreement, the object and purpose of the Paris Convention appears very narrow.[62]

Like TRIPS, there is no explicit recognition of human rights in the Paris Convention. The Paris Convention does permit recognition of public interest concerns in some provisions which engage human rights concerns. For example, Geiger and Pontes link the permissible exceptions for the requirement of states to register marks already registered in other members of the Paris Union to fundamental rights considerations of freedom of expression and freedom to conduct business.[63] They argue that, in a European context, restrictions on registration pursuant to Article 6(b) of the Paris Convention are subject to fundamental rights obligations and generally consistent with those obligations.[64] However, there are broader freedom of expression considerations, which may be engaged where there is a mixture of commercial and political or artistic opinion and political or artistic message depends on registration.[65] Human rights obligations that constitute 'relevant rules of international law applicable in the relations between the parties' could be argued in disputes regarding the Paris Convention that are brought within the jurisdiction of the International Court of Justice.[66] The recognition of a right to benefit from science and culture in Article 15(1)(c) ICESCR might be used to argue the relevance of that agreement to interpretation of provisions of the Paris Convention: Article 31(3)(c). If human rights obligations and Paris Convention

Human Rights and Intellectual Property (Edward Elgar Publishing 2015) 149–172, 159.

[61] Ricketson (n 31) 148–149.

[62] Ibid 150.

[63] Christophe Geiger and Leonardo Machado Pontes, 'Trade Mark Registration, Public Policy, Morality and Fundamental Rights' (2017) Centre for International Intellectual Property Studies (CEIPI) Research Paper No 2017-01 <https://ssrn.com/abstract=3009170>.

[64] Ibid.

[65] Ibid.

[66] VCLT (n 11), art 31(3)(c).

obligations were argued to be in conflict this could engage questions of hierarchy between the relevant agreements.[67] To date, the jurisdiction of the International Court of Justice in relation to the Paris Convention has not been invoked.[68]

TRIPS Article 2.1 provides that member states 'shall comply with Articles 1 through 12, and Article 19, of the Paris Convention'. Human rights could also be relevant to interpretation of the Paris Convention in WTO dispute settlement processes because the object and purpose of TRIPS will apply in that interpretative exercise.[69] This object and purpose of TRIPS could engage human rights considerations for the reasons set out above.

IV. ARE HUMAN RIGHTS OBLIGATIONS RELEVANT TO PLAIN PACKAGING?

A. What is Australian Plain Packaging Legislation and How Has It Been Disputed?

This section considers the relevance of human rights obligations to Australia's plain packaging legislation, which has been the subject of several disputes in the WTO. The legislation has been alleged not to comply with provisions of TRIPS, including incorporated provisions of the Paris Convention, and the separate WTO Agreement on Technical Barriers to Trade (TBT).[70] The previous section has established that human rights obligations can be relevant to the object and purpose of TRIPS. However, the relevance of human rights will necessarily depend on the nature of the dispute.[71] Plain packaging legislation engages a range of human rights considerations, including the right to health, the right to freedom of expression and the right to benefits of science and culture. Some of these are relevant to the WTO Disputes.

---

[67] For example, United Nations Charter, art 103 could be used to argue that protections for human rights recognised in the agreement have hierarchy over conflicting rights.

[68] Ricketson (n 31) 323.

[69] Ibid 150.

[70] See for example Request for Consultations by Honduras, 'Australia – Certain Measures Concerning Trademarks and Other Plain Packaging Requirements Applicable to Tobacco Products and Packaging' Honduras (April 2014) WT/DS435/1.

[71] Wager and Watal (n 60) 159.

Australia was the first country in the world to completely restrict tobacco advertising on packaging when it introduced tobacco plain packaging legislation in 2011. Packaging has been characterised as one of the last vehicles for tobacco advertising and has been established to influence the initiation of tobacco consumption.[72] Tobacco consumption has been characterised as a global health epidemic.[73] Initiation of tobacco consumption is particularly relevant to young smokers who have been identified as a target market by tobacco companies.[74] Tobacco consumption has significant negative consequences for the right to health. This was recognised multilaterally when states agreed to the World Health Organization (WHO) Framework Convention on Tobacco Control (FCTC).[75] As part of the FCTC, member states participate in the governing body, the Conference of the Parties (COP). One of the functions of the COP is to adopt guidelines for certain provisions of the agreement.

Article 11 of the FCTC requires parties to the treaty to adopt and implement effective packaging and labelling measures within three years of becoming a party, including measures requiring minimum sizing of graphic warnings about the negative health impacts of tobacco on tobacco packaging. The Guidelines to Article 11 were adopted by the COP 2008 to assist states to improve the effectiveness of measures for the packaging and labelling of tobacco-related products in November 2008.[76] Part of the Guidelines recommend that parties adopt plain packaging measures.[77] Contemporaneously, plain packaging was identified as a key priority in reducing rates of tobacco consumption in Australia in a 2008 discussion paper released by the Australian Government National Health Taskforce (the National Health Taskforce Paper).[78]

---

72 National Preventative Health Taskforce, 'Australia: Healthiest Country by 2020: Technical Report 2 Tobacco control in Australia: Making Smoking History Including Addendum for October 2008 to June 2009' (2009) 20.

73 Andrew D Mitchell and Tania Voon, 'Introduction' in Andrew D Mitchell and Tania Voon (eds), *The Global Tobacco Epidemic and the Law* (Edward Elgar Publishing 2014) 1.

74 Brigit Toebes, Marie Elske Gispen, Jasper V Been and Aziz Sheikh, 'A Missing Voice: the Human Rights of Children to a Tobacco-Free Environment' (2018) 27 Tobacco Control 3.

75 WHO Framework Convention on Tobacco Control (opened for signature 21 May 2003, entered into force 27 February 2005) 2302 UNTS 166 (FCTC), preamble.

76 At its third session in November 2008, the COP adopted guidelines for implementation of Article 11 of the WHO FCTC on 'Packaging and Labelling of Tobacco Products' (FCTC/COP3(10)) (Guidelines).

77 Guidelines, para 46.

78 National Preventative Health Taskforce, Australia, 'The Healthiest Country by 2020: Discussion Paper' National Health Taskforce Paper 23–24.

Subsequently, the Tobacco Plain Packaging Act 2011 (Cth), the Trade Marks (Plain Packaging) Act 2011 (Cth) and supporting regulations (plain packaging legislation) introduced broad requirements for the packaging of tobacco-related products. Plain packaging legislation limits advertising. It limits use of trade marks to their traditional function of indicating source of origin and associated quality.[79] The most relevant requirements to intellectual property are those that impact on the ability of owners of tobacco-related trade marks to use their marks on packaging.[80] Relevantly, the restrictions permit only use of word marks in prescribed size, font and colour in a designated position on the packet.[81] Graphics or device marks cannot be used.[82] The Tobacco Plain Packaging Act 2011 (Cth) articulates the primary policy concerns of plain packaging legislation: the protection of public health and the implementation of the FCTC.[83]

What was the impact of this on owners of tobacco-related trade marks? Plain packaging legislation permits word marks to continue to be used by trade mark owners in a restricted way to denote the source of the product.[84] The legislation also permits trade marks to stay on the register, even where they might be susceptible to non-use actions as a result of the legislation, which enabled trade mark owners to continue to exclude others from using the relevant registered marks.[85] Tobacco companies have argued that these restrictions on the use of their trade marks have significant economic consequences.[86] Tobacco-related trade mark owners have claimed breach of their rights in domestic constitutional litigation,[87] investor–state dispute litigation[88] and the dispute settlement mechanisms of the WTO.[89]

In the High Court of Australia, JT International and British American Tobacco unsuccessfully argued that plain packaging legislation constituted

---

79 Tobacco Plain Packaging Act 2011 (Cth), s 21.

80 Ibid s 20.

81 Ibid s 21.

82 Ibid.

83 Ibid s 3.

84 Ibid s 21.

85 Explanatory Memorandum, Tobacco Plain Packaging Bill 2011 (Cth) 15.

86 Notice of Arbitration, Australia/Hong King Investment Agreement for the Promotion and Protection of Investments; *Philip Morris Asia Limited v The Commonwealth of Australia* (2012) UNCITRAL PCA 2012-12 para 8.3.

87 *JT International SA v Commonwealth of Australia; British American Tobacco Australasia Limited v The Commonwealth* (2012) HCA 43.

88 *Philip Morris Asia* (n 86).

89 Australia – Plain Packaging Measures (n 9).

acquisition of their trade mark rights by the government and this was inconsistent with constitutional requirements that the acquisition of property be on just terms.[90] The High Court found that the legislation did not affect the acquisition of the applicants' intellectual property rights so the claim could not be established.[91] Separately, Philip Morris Asia commenced an international investment arbitration action against Australia. Philip Morris Asia argued that changes resulting from plain packaging legislation deprived them of the value of their investment as it was enacted subsequent to their acquisition of intellectual property rights to tobacco.[92] This was alleged to be inconsistent with the Australia-Hong Kong Bilateral Investment Treaty.[93] However, it was found that these rights had been deliberately acquired so as to exploit the investor–state dispute mechanism.[94] The action ended in interlocutory proceedings that determined that the bringing of the claim in these circumstances constituted an abuse of right under international law.[95]

The WTO Disputes were brought against Australia by Cuba, the Dominican Republic, Honduras and Indonesia pursuant to the DSU. The Ukraine also initiated but then suspended a dispute, which has subsequently lapsed.[96] The complaints asserted that Australia's plain packaging legislation breached Article 20 of TRIPS as it contained special requirements that unjustifiably encumbered the use of tobacco-related trade marks in the course of trade.[97] A range of other complaints were also made asserting breaches of TRIPS and the TBT. Australia justified the impugned provisions, citing domestic public health objectives and compliance with the FCTC.[98] Importantly, tobacco companies with interests in the promotion and sale of tobacco have openly acknowledged that they are funding the WTO actions against Australia.[99] This funding relationship is complex in light of human rights obligations for states to

---

90 *JT International SA v Commonwealth of Australia; British American Tobacco Australasia Limited v The Commonwealth* (2012) HCA 43.

91 Ibid 34–35 (French CJ).

92 *Philip Morris Asia Ltd v Australia* (2012) UNCITRAL PCA 2012-12 [48].

93 Notice of Arbitration, Australia/Hong King Investment Agreement for the Promotion and Protection of Investments (*Philip Morris Asia Ltd v Austl*) UNCITRAL PCA 2012-12 [8.3].

94 *Philip Morris Asia Ltd v Australia* UNCITRAL PCA 2012-12, Award on Jurisdiction and Admissibility (17 December 2015).

95 Ibid [586]–[588].

96 Australia – Plain Packaging Measures (n 9), paras 1.51–1.54.

97 Australia – Plain Packaging Measures (n 9).

98 Australian Department of Foreign Affairs and Trade (n 9).

99 Stephanie Nebehay, 'Australia Says Big Tobacco Aiding WTO Challengers'

perform human rights scrutiny of corporate entities operating in their territories.[100] Permitting tobacco companies to fund actions that assert rights to market products that are known to be harmful to health can engage human rights obligations to protect individuals from potential infringements of the right to health that are discussed in the next section.

B. What Human Rights Are Engaged by the WTO Disputes?

Australian plain packaging legislation engages a range of human rights considerations but the disputes have not focused on relevant human rights obligations. The emphasis on discussion has been on health and although the right to health is clearly implicated, the discourse has focused on public health considerations.[101] Commercial speech is a form of expression and restrictions on trade marks have been argued to be a restriction on freedom of expression.[102] Arguably, moral and material rights of creators of certain tobacco-related trade marks can be protected pursuant to ICESCR Article 15(1)(c). Human rights to property not restricted to scientific, literary and artistic productions and rights to development could also be relevant to the disputes. A right to development entitles 'every human person and all peoples to participate in, contribute to, and enjoy economic, social, cultural and political development'.[103] Human rights obligations to property and development are harder to identify as relevant to interpretation of TRIPS obligations in the WTO Disputes as they are less clearly defined in international law.

1. Right to health

Australia is bound by the ICESCR and has acknowledged the relevance of the human right to the highest attainable standard of health

---

(May 2012) <http://www.reuters.com/article/trade-tobacco-idUSL5E8GMHBW20120522>.

[100] General Comment 24 explicitly requires parties to ICESCR to consider measures such as restricting marketing tobacco products to protect public health: Committee on Economic, Social and Cultural Rights, 'General Comment No 24: State Obligations under the International Covenant on Economic, Social and Cultural Rights in the Context of Business Activities' UN ESCOR, UN Doc E/C12/GC/24, para 19.

[101] See generally Voon, Mitchell and Liberman (n 50).

[102] Mariette Brennan, 'Canada's Next Step in Tobacco Control Laws: Is Plain Packaging Legislation a Viable Proposal' (2013) 51 Alberta L Rev 23.

[103] United Nations Declaration on the Right to Development (December 1986) UN GA Res 41/128, UN Doc 41/128, art 1.1.

in explanatory material surrounding plain packaging legislation.[104] Compliance with the FCTC is an objective of the legislation.[105] The FCTC recognises both the human right to health and public health imperatives.[106] There is debate about the extent to which the FCTC Guidelines that require states to implement plain packaging constitute binding obligations in international law,[107] yet the requirement of the ICESCR that states progressively realise the human right to health for individuals is clear.[108] CESCR's General Comment 14 interpreting the right to health identifies tobacco-related measures as relevant to the right to health.[109] A key relevant obligation engaged by plain packaging legislation is Australia's obligation to protect the right to health by taking 'all necessary measures to safeguard persons within their jurisdiction from infringements of the right to health by third parties'.[110] CESCR includes the failure of states to regulate the activities of corporations that will violate the right to health of others and the failure to protect consumers and workers from activities that are detrimental to health, including marketing and consumption of tobacco.[111] There is well-documented evidence of intentional failure to disclose negative health impacts of tobacco by tobacco companies, which engages additional obligations for states to protect individuals.[112] Australia has attempted to address this protection obligation through plain packaging legislation.

A key priority of plain packaging legislation is to reduce the attractiveness and appeal of tobacco products to young people.[113] This also

---

[104] Explanatory Statement 'Tobacco Plain Packaging: Amendment Regulation 2012 (No 1)' (2012) 5LI No 29 of 2012.

[105] Plain Packaging Act 2011 (Cth), s 3.

[106] FCTC (n 75), preamble.

[107] Chang-fa Lo, 'Guidelines and Protocols under the Framework Convention' in Mitchell and Voon (n 73), 32–45; Jonathan Liberman, 'The Power of the WHO FCTC: Understanding Its Legal Status and Weight' in ibid, 48–60.

[108] ICESCR, art 12; United Nations Committee on Economic, Social and Cultural Rights (CESCR), 'General Comment No 14: The Right to the Highest Attainable Standard of Health (Art 12 of the Covenant)' (2000) E/C12/2000/4 (General Comment 14).

[109] Ibid, para 51.

[110] Ibid.

[111] Ibid.

[112] Melissa E Crow, 'Smokescreens and State Responsibility: Using Human Rights Strategies to Promote Global Tobacco Control' (2005) 29 Yale J of Int Law 209, 211; Carolyn Dresler and Stephen P Marks, 'The Emerging Human Right to Tobacco Control' (2006) 28(3) HRQ 599, 633, 644.

[113] Tobacco Plain Packaging Bill 2011, Explanatory Memorandum.

corresponds to Australia's obligations pursuant to the Convention on the Rights of the Child to protect the rights of children to 'the enjoyment of the highest attainable standard of health'[114] and to ensure that the child has 'access to information and material from a diversity of national and international sources, especially those aimed at the promotion of his or her social, spiritual and moral well-being and physical and mental health'.[115] General Comment 4 of the Committee of the Rights of the Child on Adolescent Health and Development interprets this obligation to protect adolescents from information that is harmful to their health and development.[116] States should 'regulate or prohibit information and marketing of . . . tobacco, particularly when it targets children and adolescents'.[117] This obligation is directly relevant to the restrictions on marketing required by plain packaging legislation. These restrictions are supported by scientific evidence regarding adolescents and plain packaging.[118]

The effectiveness of states' measures to achieve progressive realisation of their human right to health obligations is a relevant consideration in assessing compliance with those obligations. In 2008, the National Health Taskforce Report identified that decline rates of tobacco consumption in Australia were 'flattening out'.[119] Plain packaging legislation formed part of the policy that responded to concerns about the negative health impacts of continuing tobacco consumption. The key health claims of plain packaging legislation are that it will

---

[114] Convention on the Rights of the Child (opened for signature 20 November 1989, entered into force 2 September 1990) 1577 UNTS 3 (CRC), art 24.

[115] CRC (n 114), art 17.

[116] UN Committee on the Rights of the Child, 'General Comment No. 4: Adolescent Health and Development in the Context of the Convention on the Rights of the Child' (2003) UN Doc CRC/GC/2003/4, paras 6 and 21–22 <http://www.ohchr.org/Documents/Issues/Women/WRGS/Health/GC4.Pdf>.

[117] Ibid para 21.

[118] Toebes also identifies the packaging of cigarettes and misleading advertising on cigarettes as important issues for governments to address to protect children's rights: Toebes et al (n 74) 4. Sally Dunlop, Donna Perez, Anita Dessaix, and David Currow, 'Australia's Plain Tobacco Packs: Anticipated and Actual Responses among Adolescents and Young Adults 2010–2013' (2017) 26(6) Tobacco Control 617. See also Richard Edwards, Ali Ajmal, Benjamin Healey and Janet Hoek, 'Impact of Removing Point-of-Sale Tobacco Displays: Data from a New Zealand Youth Survey' (2017) 26(4) Tobacco Control 392.

[119] National Health Taskforce Paper (n 78) 21.

(i) reduce the attractiveness and appeal of tobacco products to consumers, particularly young people;
(ii) increase the noticeability and effectiveness of mandated health warnings;
(iii) reduce the ability of the tobacco product packaging to mislead consumers about the harms of smoking; and
(iv) through the achievement of these objectives in the long term, as part of a comprehensive suite of tobacco control measures, contribute to efforts to reduce smoking rates.[120]

The substantial scientific basis for these claims was set out in a technical report accompanying the National Health Taskforce Report.[121] Additional scientific evidence supported the policy.[122] Competing reports questioned the effectiveness of the proposed measure.[123]

Following the introduction of plain packaging legislation, early analysis

---

[120] Tobacco Plain Packaging Bill 2011, Explanatory Memorandum 1.

[121] See Janne Scheffels, 'A Difference That Makes a Difference: Young Adult Smokers' Accounts of Cigarette Brands and Package Design' (2008) 17(2) Tobacco Control 118; M Wakefield, C Morley, J K Horan and K M Cummings, 'The Cigarette Pack as Image: New Evidence from Tobacco Industry Documents' (2002) 11 (Suppl 1) Tobacco Control i73; Becky Freeman, Simon Chapman and Matthew Rimmer, 'The Case for Plain Packaging of Tobacco Products' (2008) 103(4) Addiction 580; MA Wakefield, D Germain and SJ Durkin, 'How Does Increasingly Plainer Cigarette Packaging Influence Adult Smokers' Perceptions about Brand Image? An Experimental Study' (2008) 17(6) Tobacco Control 416; P Beede and R Lawson, 'The Effect of Plain Packages on the Perception of Cigarette Health Warnings' (1992) 106(4) Public Health 315; ME Goldberg, J Liefeld, J Madill and H Vredenburg, 'The Effect of Plain Packaging on Response to Health Warnings' (1999) 89(9) Am J Pub Health 1434; E Strahan, K White, G Fong, L Fabrigar, M Zanna and R Cameron, 'Enhancing the Effectiveness of Tobacco Package Warning Labels: A Social Psychological Perspective' (2002) 11(3) Tobacco Control 183; M Wakefield and T Letcher, 'My Pack Is Cuter than Your Pack' (2002) 11(2) Tobacco Control 154; Morgan Stanley Research Europe, *Tobacco: Late to the Party* (Morgan Stanley Research 2007).

[122] Quit Victoria, Cancer Council Victoria, 'Plain Packaging of Tobacco Products: A Review of the Evidence' (May 2011).

[123] Philip Johnson, 'Trademarks Without a Brand: The Proposals on "Plain Packaging" of Tobacco Products' (2012) 34(7) EIPR 468–469; British American Tobacco, 'British American Tobacco Australia Submission on the Tobacco Plain Packaging Bill 2011' (June 2011) <http://www.ip-watch.org/weblog/wp-content/uploads/2011/06/BATA-Tobacco-Plain-Packaging-Bill-Submission.pdf>; Submission by Philip Morris Ltd on the Tobacco Plain Packaging Bill Exposure Draft, 'Commoditising tobacco products through plain packaging will harm public health, violate treaties, and does not meet the test of "evidence-based policy"' (2011) <http://webarchive.nla.gov.au/gov/20130329051831/http://www.yourhealth.gov.au/internet/yourhealth/publishing.nsf/Content/Phillip-Morris-Limited~Phillip-Morris-Limited-2>.

indicated the success of the measure in reducing the appeal of tobacco packaging for adolescents,[124] influencing decisions to cease smoking in adult smokers[125] and causing smokers to conceal their packs.[126] Although the benefits of plain packaging legislation in effecting a decline in smoking are expected to be long-term benefits,[127] further evidence establishes the short-term effectiveness of the measure.[128] Multiple tobacco control measures in place in Australia contribute to smoking rates,[129] however the 2016 Post-implementation Review concluded that all of the major datasets examined demonstrated sustained drops in national smoking prevalence in Australia.[130] This reduction was expected to have a significant long-term impact on public health outcomes and suggested that the legislation was fulfilling its aims.[131] The Post-implementation Review analysis did not assess whether alternative measures, other than not introducing the legislative measures at all, would have been more effective or equally effective.[132] There have been criticisms of these findings, which partly reflect the fact that tobacco plain packaging is designed to be a long-term measure.[133] At this stage it is difficult to definitively assess the effectiveness of plain packaging legislation in meeting Australia's progressive realisation of the right to health but, if this can be established, repeal of the legislation could

---

124 Victoria White, Tahlia Williams and Melanie Wakefield, 'Has the Introduction of Plain Packaging with Larger Graphic Health Warnings Changed Adolescents' Perceptions of Cigarette Packs and Brands?' (2015) 24 (Suppl 2) Tobacco Control ii42–ii49.

125 Melanie Wakefield, Linda Hayes, Sarah Durkin and Ron Borland, 'Introduction Effects of the Australian Plain Packaging Policy on Adult Smokers: A Cross-Sectional Study' (2013) 3(7) BMJ Open e003175.

126 Meghan Zacher, Megan Bayly, Emily Brennan, Joanne Dono, Caroline Miller, Sarah Durkin, Michelle Scollo and Melanie Wakefield, 'Personal Pack Display and Active Smoking at Outdoor Café Strips: Assessing the Impact of Plain Packaging 1 Year Post Implementation' (2015) 24 Tobacco Control 94–97.

127 Tasneem Chipty, 'Study of the Impact of the Tobacco Plain Packaging Measure on Smoking Prevalence in Australia' (2016) Post-implementation Review <http://www.health.gov.au/internet/main/publishing.nsf/content/491CE0444F7B0A76CA257FBE00195BF3/$File/PIR%20of%20Tobacco%20Plain%20Packaging%20-%20with%20Addendum.pdf>.

128 Ibid appendix A, para 6.

129 Australian Department of Foreign Affairs and Trade (n 9) para 150.

130 Davidson and Da Silva contest some of these. Sinclair Davidson and Ashton de Silva, 'Did Recent Tobacco Reforms Change the Cigarette Market?' (2018) 37(1) Economic Papers: A Journal of Applied Economics and Policy 55, 69–70.

131 Chipty (n 127) 20.

132 Ibid.

133 Davidson and Da Silva (n 130).

constitute a retrogression in Australia progressively realising its human right to health obligations.[134]

2. Freedom of expression

Arguably the freedom of expression rights of tobacco owners are restricted by plain packaging legislation as owners cannot use the marks on packaging as a form of expression.[135] The human right to freedom of expression enshrined in Article 19 of the International Covenant on Civil and Political Rights (ICCPR),[136] as interpreted by the Human Rights Committee in General Comment 34, states that freedom of expression may include commercial advertising.[137] However, the restrictions on the use of trade marks imposed by plain packaging legislation may be permissible restrictions. ICCPR Article 19(3) permits restrictions that are provided in law and necessary for respect of the rights or reputations of others, for the protection of national security, public order, or public health or morals.[138] The Human Rights Committee confirms the finite nature of these restrictions.[139] It states that restrictions other than those specified in paragraph 3 are not allowed 'even if such grounds would justify restrictions to other rights protected in the Covenant'.[140] There needs to be a direct relationship between the specified justification and the application of the restriction.[141]

The content of Australian plain packaging legislation also suggests that it is necessary for the protection of public health.[142] This is one of the permissible restrictions set out in ICCPR Article 19(3). However, a restriction does not meet the test of necessity 'if the protection could be achieved in other ways that do not restrict freedom of expression'.[143] General

---

134 General Comment 14 (n 108), para 48.

135 Explanatory Statement, Tobacco Plain Packaging Amendment Regulation 2012 (No 1) (Cth) 9–13. Brennan considers whether plain packaging legislation would be consistent with the broader freedom of expression protections found in the Canadian Charter: Mariette Brennan, 'Canada's Next Step in Tobacco Control Laws: Is Plain Packaging Legislation a Viable Proposal' (2013) 51 Alta L Rev 23, 35–48.

136 International Covenant on Civil and Political Rights (opened for signature 16 December 1966, entered into force 23 March 1976) 999 UNTS 171 (ICCPR).

137 United Nations Human Rights Committee, 'Article 19: Freedoms of Opinion and Expression' General Comment No 34 (2011) 102nd sess (September 2011) UN Doc CCPR/C/GC/34 (General Comment 34) para 11.

138 ICCPR (n 136), art 19(3).

139 General Comment 34 (n 137).

140 Ibid para 22.

141 Ibid.

142 Tobacco Plain Packaging Act 2011 (Cth), s 3.

143 General Comment 34 (n 137), para 33.

Comment 34 does not provide further specific guidance on public health. General Comment 34 interprets the rights referred to in Article 19(3) to include human rights, so any restriction on freedom of expression posed by plain packaging legislation can be justified as necessary to achieve realisation of the human right to health.[144] The objective of protecting the human right to health has been identified in explanatory materials for plain packaging legislation and its relevance has been explained above.[145] The Human Rights Committee adopts earlier statements that restrictive measures should not be overbroad and should be consistent with the principle of proportionality, which 'must also take account of the form of expression at issue as well as the means of its dissemination'.[146] Policy documents supporting Australian plain packaging legislation, including the National Health Taskforce Report and supporting documentation set out 'in specific and individualized fashion the precise nature of the threat, and the necessity and proportionality of the specific action taken'.[147] If plain packaging legislation constitutes a restriction on freedom of expression, it can be concluded that the restriction is provided by law and does not appear to be discriminatory to any particular group so it should not be a basis to modify or restrict the legislation.

3. Right to benefit from science and culture

Article 15(1)(c) confers limited human rights protection for creators of literary, artistic and scientific productions. Where trade marks constitute literary or artistic productions, ICESCR Article 15(1)(c) could confer moral and material rights on the authors of those trade marks.[148] Tobacco-related device marks and composite marks can constitute artistic productions so creators of trade marks could argue that plain packaging legislation impacts on their moral and material rights. However, it is not clear that the rights protected by Article 15(1)(c) are directly restricted by plain packaging legislation. There is no pre-existing practice of providing moral rights of attribution to trade mark creators.[149] The human right provided in Article 15(1)(c) does not provide for ongoing remuneration[150]

---

144 Ibid.

145 Explanatory Statement, Tobacco Plain Packaging: Amendment Regulation 2012 (No 1) (5LI, No 29 of 2012).

146 General Comment 34 (n 137), para 34.

147 Ibid, para 35.

148 Cf Yu (n 38) 85–95.

149 See generally Trade Marks Act 1995 (Cth).

150 Committee on Economic, Social and Cultural Rights, 'The Right of Everyone to Benefit from the Protection of the Moral and Material Interests

so it may be assumed that creators of trade marks have already been compensated and their material interest in Article 15(1)(c) is not impaired. The legislation does not appear to be the direct cause of the loss of material or moral rights so in the present assessment of interrelated rights it should not be the basis to restrict operation of the legislation to realise the relevant right to health objectives.[151]

4. Human rights to property and development

Human rights to property and development have been recognised as relevant to the WTO Disputes.[152] Neither right is enshrined in binding international human rights agreements. Although development concerns are clearly relevant to the object and purpose of TRIPS, the status of the human right to development also remains unclear.[153] It is arguable that the restrictions imposed by plain packaging legislation impair the economic development of countries who depend on exports of tobacco-related products to Australia for income.[154] Importantly, economic development is itself impacted by the burden of tobacco-related disease.[155] Health concerns related to tobacco consumption are also problematic for countries that are producers of tobacco.[156] Accordingly, Objective 3.a of the United Nations Sustainable Development Goals is to '[s]trengthen the imple-

---

Resulting from Any Scientific, Literary or Artistic Production of which He or She is the Author (article 15, paragraph 1 (c), of the Covenant)' General Comment No 17 (2005) UN ESCOR 35th Sess UN Doc E/C12/GC/17, para 16.

[151] Helfer and Austin argue that when we consider potential conflicts between human rights and intellectual property, it is necessary to recognise if the intellectual property legislation that is alleged to be in conflict with the relevant human rights is in fact the reason for the restriction of the rights: Helfer and Austin (n 6) 520.

[152] Brigit Toebes, 'Human Rights and Public Health: Towards a Balanced Relationship' (2015) 19(4) Int J Human Rights 488, 495; Albert Alemanno and Enrico Bonadio, 'Do You Mind My Smoking? Plain Packaging of Cigarettes under the TRIPS Agreement' (2011) 10 RIPL 449.

[153] TRIPS Preamble; Uvin questions the status of the right to development: Peter Uvin, 'From the Right to Development to the Rights-based Approach: How "Human Rights" Entered Development' (2007) 17(4/5) Dev Pract 597.

[154] Toebes (n 152) 495. In the WTO Disputes, Cuba argued that plain packaging measures were detrimental to its economic development because of the importance of its tobacco industries: Australia – Plain Packaging Measures, Annex B-3, B-62.

[155] Oscar A Cabrera and Lawrence O Gostin, 'Human Rights and the Framework Convention on Tobacco Control: Mutually Reinforcing Systems' (2011) 7(3) Int J Law Context 285, 286.

[156] Oscar A Cabrera and Juan Carballo, 'Tobacco Control in Latin America' in Mitchell and Voon (n 73) 236.

mentation of the World Health Organization Framework Convention on Tobacco Control in all countries, as appropriate'.[157]

Although property concerns are also clearly relevant to disputes concerning plain packaging legislation,[158] the human right to property has been narrowly interpreted in jurisdictions where protection exists.[159] States are generally given a wide margin of appreciation in European jurisprudence considering whether there has been interference with property rights.[160] Relevant considerations are whether a fair balance has been struck between the interests of the community and those of the applicant, placing on the applicant an individual and excessive burden.[161] The right to health concerns outlined above suggest that plain packaging legislation supports the interests of the community and this would be important to a human right to property assessment. Even though rights to property and development may be engaged by plain packaging legislation, the uncertain nature of both rights means that it would be difficult to argue that either right should be considered in the WTO Disputes.[162]

C. Relevance of Human Rights Engaged

Several human rights considerations are engaged by plain packaging legislation. The analysis suggests that the human rights claim that is most relevant to the WTO Disputes is the right to health. The following section will focus on the right to health and the way in which human rights are relevant to the interpretation of TRIPS in the WTO Disputes, even though they have not been the focus of argument.

---

157 United Nations General Assembly (2015). Transforming Our World: The 2030 Agenda for Sustainable Development A/RES/70/1 <http://www.refworld.org/docid/57b6e3e44.html>.

158 *JT International SA v Commonwealth of Australia*; *British American Tobacco Australasia Limited v The Commonwealth* (2012) HCA 43.

159 Marco Ricolfi, 'Trademarks and Human Rights' in Paul Torremans (ed), *IPLHR* (Kluwer Law International 2015).

160 *Anheuser-Busch Inc v Portugal* (2007) 44 EHRR 42, IHRL 3436 (ECHR); Helfer (n 20) 3.

161 See, for example, the reasoning in *Balan v Moldova* (2008) 19247/03 ECHR.

162 Neither is a clearly defined human right in customary international law or protected by a binding international agreement, which lessens the likelihood of their interpretive relevance. See Uvin (n 153); Yu (n 38) 85–95.

V. HOW DO THE OBJECT AND PURPOSE OF TRIPS PERMIT CONSIDERATIONS OF HUMAN RIGHTS IN THE WTO DISPUTES?

A. Interpreting the Term 'Unjustifiably' in the WTO Disputes

In the WTO Disputes, the complainants asserted that plain packaging constituted multiple breaches of TRIPS and the separate TBT.[163] Article 20 of TRIPS requires that '[t]he use of a trademark in the course of trade shall not be unjustifiably encumbered by special requirements'. Plain packaging legislation only permits use of a trade mark on packaging in a prescribed form, in certain locations on the packaging, in combination with health warnings, graphic photographs and the Quitline mark.[164] The Panel found that plain packaging legislation constitutes special requirements that are an unjustified encumbrance on the use of the relevant trade marks in the course of trade.[165] This section will focus on the Article 20 arguments concerning justifiability of plain packaging measures. These provide scope for interpretation of the term 'unjustifiably' using VCLT interpretative tools. As set out above, the VCLT provides guidelines to the WTO Dispute Settlement Body regarding interpretation. The nature of the encumbrance that must be justified is subject to interpretation.[166] In relation to TRIPS, both the preamble and Articles 7 and 8 are provisions relevant to the object and purpose of the treaty, which will guide interpretation of Article 20.[167] This section sets out the approach taken by the Panel and analyses the relevance of human rights to interpretation of the term 'unjustifiably' in Article 20 in the context of the WTO Disputes, applying the interpretive principles found in Article 31 VCLT. This section will argue that human rights can be relevant to the interpretation of 'unjustifiably' in determining whether plain packaging legislation constituted special requirements that unjustifiably encumbered the use of tobacco-related trade marks in the course of trade.

---

163 See generally Australia – Plain Packaging Measures (n 9).

164 Andrew D Mitchell, 'Australia's Move to the Plain Packaging of Cigarettes and Its WTO Compatibility' (2010) 5 Asian J WTO Int Heal 405, 412; Daniel Gervais, 'Plain Packaging and the TRIPS Agreement: A Response to Professors Davison, Mitchell and Voon' (2013) 23 AIPJ 96, 103; Cf Mark Davison, 'The Legitimacy of Plain Packaging under International Intellectual Property Law' in Voon, Mitchell and Liberman (n 50) 94–96.

165 Australia – Plain Packaging Measures (n 9), para 7.2292.

166 Frankel and Gervais (n 57) 1172–1174.

167 Ibid, 1167–1168.

The Panel approached the interpretative exercise by ascertaining the ordinary meaning of 'unjustifiably' then using other provisions of TRIPS to identify the types of reasons relevant to justifiability.[168] A broad range of potential meanings for 'unjustifiably' suggests that further interpretative tools provided by the VCLT are relevant in interpreting its meaning.[169] Ruse-Khan argues that it is most important to refer to balancing provisions when the relevant articles contain terms that are not explicit.[170] He identifies a number of 'broad and open legal concepts' within TRIPS, including normal exploitation, legitimate interests, (un)reasonableness, necessity and *ordre public*.[171] As discussed in Section III.A of this chapter, VCLT Article 31 requires interpretation 'in good faith in accordance with the ordinary meaning to be given to the terms of the treaty in their context and in the light of its object and purpose'. The context of a treaty term or provision includes the text, the preamble, annexes and agreements made in connection with the conclusion of the treaty.[172]

The Panel determined that the term unjustifiably referenced 'the ability to provide a "justification" or "good reason" for the relevant action or situation that is reasonable in the sense that it provides sufficient support for that action or situation'.[173] It then recognised the relevance of the object and purpose of TRIPS to understanding what reasons could be relevant to justifiability and considered the preamble, Article 7 and Article 8 of TRIPS.[174] The preamble notes the importance of protection and enforcement of intellectual property but also recognises public policy objectives underlying domestic systems of intellectual property protection that can be relevant to the object and purpose of the agreement.[175] As part of its analysis, the Panel identified the Doha Declaration on Public Health as a subsequent agreement relevant to interpretation of TRIPS.[176] The Doha

---

[168] Australia – Plain Packaging Measures (n 9), paras 7.2393–7.2431.

[169] Frankel and Gervais have argued that other WTO case law suggests standards ranging from having a rational relationship to the measure to having a substantial or firm evidence base to a near certain correlation: (n 57) 1204–1206.

[170] Henning Grosse Ruse-Khan, 'Proportionality and Balancing within the Objectives for Intellectual Property Protection' in Paul L C Torremans (ed), IPHR (Kluwer Law International 2008) 162–163; this is similar to Land's argument that standards provision and textual silence are types of flexibility mechanisms: Molly Land, 'Rebalancing TRIPS' (2011–2012) 33 Mich J Int'l L 433, 438–442.

[171] Ruse-Khan (n 170) 162–163.

[172] VCLT (n 11), art 31(2).

[173] Australia – Plain Packaging Measures (n 9), para 7.2395.

[174] Australia – Plain Packaging Measures (n 9), paras 7.2398–7.2402.

[175] TRIPS (n 2), preamble.

[176] Australia – Plain Packaging Measures (n 9), paras 7.2409–7.2410.

Declaration identifies the significance of Articles 7 and 8 to understanding the object and purpose of TRIPS and the Panel was guided by this in its assessment that societal interests were relevant to justifiableness.[177] The Panel characterised Article 20 as reflecting an intended balance by drafters of the TRIPS Agreement 'between the existence of a legitimate interest of trademark owners in using their trademarks in the marketplace, and the right of WTO Members to adopt measures for the protection of certain societal interests that may adversely affect such use'.[178] In interpreting the unjustifiableness of the encumbrance posed by plain packaging legislation, the content of Articles 7 and 8 influenced the Panel's identification of public health considerations as relevant to societal interests.[179]

The Panel also considered the relationship between justifiability and necessity in its assessment of the Article 20 claims.[180] Some complainants argued that (particularly in relation to health) 'unjustifiably' can be interpreted to require measures to be necessary, a term that has been interpreted in relation to other WTO Agreements.[181] The Panel found that interpretation of the term 'unjustifiably' was specific to the TRIPS Agreement and a separate term to 'unnecessarily' was deliberately chosen.[182] The use of the term 'necessary' in Article 8.1 may have influenced the emphasis given to Articles 7 and 8 in the Australian arguments.[183] The long-term, integrated nature of the public health measures in plain packaging legislation means that it would be difficult to empirically compare the measure to other reasonably available alternative measures and this may make any assessments of adequacy of the measure by the dispute settlement bodies more complex.[184] Prior to the WTO Disputes there had been limited prior interpretation of Article 8 to clarify whether use of it in interpretation of Article 20 would engage a strict necessity test.[185] Australia provided extensive evidence of the public health justification

---

177 Ibid paras 7.2399–7.2402.

178 Ibid para 7.2429.

179 Ibid paras 7.2406, 7.2588. Ruse-Khan notes that the 'unjustifiability' requirement in Article 20 allows the consideration of competing policies and interests, such as public health: Ruse-Khan (n 33) 344. Frankel recognises 'health' as an open-textured term: Frankel (n 45) 421.

180 Australia – Plain Packaging Measures (n 9) paras 7.2413–7.2431.

181 Ibid paras 7.2299, 7.2322, 7.2309, 7.2326.

182 Ibid paras 7.2419–7.2422.

183 Ibid paras 7.2327–7.2348.

184 Frankel and Gervais identify the likelihood that adequacy could be considered: Frankel and Gervais (n 57) 1204.

185 Ibid para 88; Daniel Gervais, *The TRIPS Agreement: Drafting History and Analysis* (4th edn, Sweet and Maxwell 2008) 240–241.

for plain packaging[186] but it did not characterise this as a necessary public health measure pursuant to TRIPS Article 8.1.[187] Instead it argued that Article 8 expressly acknowledges 'the broad scope that Members retain under the TRIPS Agreement to adopt laws and regulations for public policy purposes'.[188] Instead of explicitly linking this to object and purpose, Australia emphasised that the core object and purpose of TRIPS is 'to ensure that all WTO Members provide a minimum level of exclusive rights to owners of IP'.[189] Linking public policy considerations more explicitly to object and purpose could strengthen the interpretative weight given to these public policy considerations. This may permit WTO members to address the fragmentation between WTO law and other obligations identified in Section II.A of this chapter, using the example of human rights. The following analysis argues that right to health obligations could also be relevant for interpretation of the term 'unjustifiably'.

A human rights-focused analysis contrasts with the emphasis on public health in the arguments engaging Article 20 in the WTO Disputes. Although the Panel recognised the justifiability of the legislation, it did not consider the human rights justifications.[190] This is consistent with the absence of emphasis on human rights by all of the parties in argument, including the failure of Australia to rely on human rights to support plain packaging legislation.[191] However, the reference to health objectives in plain packaging legislation and the recognition of the role of the legislation in furthering the right to health in explanatory legislative materials indicate that protection of the human right to health is a relevant underlying policy objective of the legislation.[192] The decision presents opportunities for future recognition of human rights in TRIPS disputes. In interpreting the unjustifiableness of the encumbrance posed by plain packaging legislation, the Panel considered the object and purpose of TRIPS discernible from the preamble, Articles 7 and 8.[193] Taking this approach, it recognised the relevance of societal interests, including public heath, to assessments of unjustifiableness.[194] In future disputes, societal

---

[186] See Panel's summary: Australia – Plain Packaging Measures (n 9), paras 7.2586–7.2589.

[187] Ibid, para 7.2348.

[188] Ibid, para 7.2346.

[189] Ibid, para 7.2344.

[190] Ibid, para 7.2598.

[191] Ibid, paras 7.2294–7.2392.

[192] Tobacco Plain Packaging Act 2011 (Cth), s 3; Explanatory Memorandum, Tobacco Plain Packaging Bill 2011 (Cth) 15.

[193] Australia – Plain Packaging Measures (n 9), paras 7.2398–7.2411.

[194] Ibid, paras 7.2406, 7.2588.

interests could be interpreted to directly overlap with the protection of human rights that can be linked to the object and purpose of TRIPS such as the right to health.[195] This interpretative approach could be relevant to other 'open-textured' terms in TRIPS[196] and reduce the impact of fragmentation between different fields of law.

The balance of rights and obligations referenced in Article 7 of TRIPS can be linked to the underlying public policy objectives of the Australian system of intellectual property protection, which include compliance with other international obligations.[197] This chapter has set out provisions of the ICESCR and the Convention on the Rights of the Child that can be interpreted to justify the introduction of plain packaging in Australia. Although there continues to be dispute about the extent to which the FCTC Guidelines require the implementation of plain packaging, in the WTO Disputes engaging TRIPS Article 20 Australia's FCTC obligations were identified by the Panel as relevant to its justification for implementing plain packaging legislation.[198] The objective of protecting health by reducing tobacco consumption is not only relevant to understanding underlying policy objectives and a balance of rights and obligations, but is also relevant to social and economic welfare, which is an objective identified in Article 7. Further, in interpreting whether restricting the use of trade marks on tobacco packaging 'unjustifiably' encumbers use of a mark, Australia's obligation to protect the right to health is relevant to a balance of rights and obligations, consistent with the principle articulated in Article 7.

B. The Importance of Articles 7 and 8

The Panel recognised the explicit linkage of the object and purpose of TRIPS to Articles 7 and 8 in the Doha Declaration and identified the Doha Declaration as a subsequent agreement to TRIPS.[199] As a subsequent agreement, the Doha Declaration is relevant to interpretation of

---

195 Yu also identifies other human rights with links to the object and purpose of TRIPS: Yu (n 53) 1037.

196 Frankel has previously characterised TRIPS provisions where 'the treaty language alone does not determine the scope of the provision' as open textured: Frankel (n 45) 421.

197 Australian Government Productivity Commission, 'Intellectual Property Arrangements' (2016) 13 <http://www.pc.gov.au/inquiries/completed/intellectual-property/report/intellectual-property.pdf>.

198 *Australia – Plain Packaging Measures*, paras 7.2595–7.2596, 7.2604.

199 Ibid, paras 7.2407–7.2411.

provisions of TRIPS such as Article 20.[200] This suggests the importance of recognising the principles and objectives they identify, where they are relevant to interpretation. Australia's approach of emphasising the object and purpose of protection of intellectual property rights in TRIPS may correspond with well-considered legal strategy. However, Australia's approach risked diminishing other considerations found in the preamble, Article 7 and Article 8 that are relevant to both object and purpose and the issues raised in a dispute. Arguably, the limited interpretation of Articles 7 and 8 of TRIPS by the dispute settlement bodies has made it difficult for some countries to use them confidently when they wish to rely on them in interpretation of the compatibility of domestic legislation with TRIPS[201] but the Panel Decision in the WTO Disputes provides further, significant interpretation.[202] This is particularly important in cases such as tobacco plain packaging legislation where the multiplicity of disputes can be characterised as a coordinated attack on the introduction of plain packaging legislation worldwide. Together with Philip Morris's attack on Uruguay's less restrictive tobacco legislation, the disputes regarding plain packaging legislation have been cited as barriers to the introduction of this legislation in other countries.[203] In this way the actions of tobacco companies can have a chilling regulatory impact on efforts to address the link between package advertising and tobacco consumption.[204]

This has special significance in the context of the right to health because states' obligations include the responsibility to protect individuals against the actions of third parties that constitute threats to health. Evidence suggests that tobacco companies are the type of third parties that states need to protect against.[205] Problematically, where there are potential conflicts between fragmented human rights obligations and intellectual property obligations, attacks on legislation in multiple, expensive dispute resolution fora can give strong economic incentives for states to give primacy to their intellectual property obligations. Recognising the importance

---

200 VCLT (n 11), art 31(3)(a).

201 Susy Frankel, 'Some Consequences of Misinterpreting the TRIPS Agreement' (2009) 1 WIPO Journal 35, 41–42.

202 Australia – Plain Packaging Measures (n 9), paras 7.2413–7.2431.

203 Lukasz Gruszczynski, 'Australian Plain Packaging Law, International Litigation and Regulatory Chilling Effect' (2014) EJRR 242, 244; Eric Crosbie and George Thomson, 'Regulatory Chills: Tobacco Industry Legal Threats and the Politics of Tobacco Standardised Packaging in New Zealand' (2018) 131(14) NZMA 1473.

204 See Jennifer L Tobin, 'The Social Cost of International Investment Agreements: The Case of Cigarette Packaging' (2018) 32(2) Ethics Int Aff 153.

205 Crow (n 112) 211; Dresler and Marks (n 112) 633, 644.

of Article 7 and Article 8 arguments and linking them to human rights obligations will not specifically address the problems posed by plurilateral and bilateral trade agreements.[206] However, such arguments may at least partially mitigate the potentially chilling impact of non-state actors on human rights-supportive legislation to the extent that they build a culture in the WTO of recognising the links between human rights and the object and purpose of TRIPS. Frankel has identified the potential utility of non-violation complaints to address the cumulative negative impact of TRIPS-plus standards found in bilateral trade agreements on the structure and purpose of TRIPS.[207] If human rights objectives are recognised as relevant to Articles 7 and 8 and the object and purpose of TRIPS, this may also be a relevant consideration if non-violation complaints are used to address the impact of bilateral and plurilateral trade agreements in the future.

C. Rules of International Law Relevant to Interpretation of 'Unjustifiably'

The relevance of human rights to interpretation of Article 20 in the WTO Disputes can be strengthened by analysis of relevant rules of international law applicable to some or all parties to the dispute. VCLT Article 31(3)(c) engages separate consideration of relevance and applicability. One of the reasons that directly addressing the relevance of Articles 7 and 8 to interpretation of TRIPS is important is that the object and purpose of TRIPS can assist our understanding of what 'relevant rules of international law applicable between the parties' can guide treaty interpretation.[208] Human right to health obligations bind Australia and are relevant to the object and purpose of TRIPS so it is arguably not necessary to reference Article 31(3)(c).[209] However, identifying treaties which bind the relevant parties

---

[206] Some of these complex issues are considered in Cynthia Ho, 'Sovereignty Under Siege: Corporate Challenges to Domestic Intellectual Property Decisions' (2015) 30(1) BTLJ 213; Rochelle Dreyfuss and Susy Frankel, 'From Incentive to Commodity to Asset: How International Law is Reconceptualizing Intellectual Property' (2015) 36 Mich J Int Law 557, 565–566.

[207] Susy Frankel, 'Challenging Trips-Plus Agreements: The Potential Utility of Non-Violation Disputes' (2009) 12(4) JIEL 1023, 1043.

[208] VCLT, art 31(3) guides the treaty interpreter to consider 'any relevant rules of international law applicable between the parties'.

[209] McLachlan notes that use of VCLT, art 31(3)(c) is part of a broader process of interpretation and 'some of the issues where reference to external sources of international law may be helpful may be better resolved as part of an enquiry into either the ordinary meaning of the words in their context, or the object and purpose

reaffirms the existence of these potentially competing international obligations and that dispute resolution fora should recognise and address these obligations.[210]

The relevant international laws applicable to interpreting Article 20 pursuant to Article 31 of the VCLT can depend on the interpretation of 'parties' in Article 31(3)(c).[211] This can refer to the parties in dispute or all of the parties to the TRIPS Agreement or it recognises a balance between obligations that bind one party to the dispute and a significant number of WTO members.[212] There is dispute as to whether, when these rules are external to the agreement being interpreted, they must be binding on all of the parties to the agreement, or, in cases of dispute, to parties who are in dispute with each other, or simply for at least one of the parties to the agreement or dispute.[213] The approach that other rules can be relevant if the parties to the dispute will be bound by them contributes to systemic integration of international law, although that integration can be limited to agreements between the overlapping parties.[214] These rules guide our understanding of how the protection and enforcement of intellectual property contributes to the relevant balance of rights and obligations recognised in Article 7 of TRIPS.

Section 4 has identified the right to health as the most important human right engaged by plain packaging legislation. Right to health obligations can be found in the ICESCR and other human rights agreements, including the Convention on the Rights of the Child. Arguably the FCTC interprets right to health obligations found in the ICESCR that are relevant to health obligations related to the consumption of tobacco.[215] Compliance with certain obligations in each of these agreements constitutes a justification for restrictions on trade mark rights that can guide treaty interpretation as to the meaning of 'unjustifiably' in each of the disputes. Table 7.1 sets out the status of each of the parties in relation to each of these agreements.

---

of the treaty': Campbell McLachlan, 'The Principle of Systemic Integration and Article 31 (3)(c) of the Vienna Convention' (2005) 54(2) ICLQ 279, 291.

210 Ruse-Khan proposes a conflict rule of integration approach that recognises the value of a forum which can best integrate other laws: Ruse-Khan (n 33).

211 Cf Benn McGrady, who emphasises relevance: Benn McGrady, *Trade and Public Health: The WTO, Tobacco, Alcohol, and Diet, Trade and Public Health* (Cambridge University Press 2011) 45–78.

212 Ruse-Khan (n 1) 143.

213 See for example the different approaches taken by McGrady and Ruse-Khan. See McGrady (n 211) 45–78; Ruse-Khan (n 1) 142.

214 Ruse-Khan (n 1) 143.

215 Cabrera and Gostin (n 155) 293.

Table 7.1 Ratification of agreements relevant to the right to health by WTO disputants

Party	Convention on the Rights of the Child	ICESCR	FCTC
Australia	Ratified	Ratified	Ratified
Honduras	Ratified	Ratified	Ratified
Cuba	Ratified	Signed	Signed
Indonesia	Ratified	Acceded	Not signed
Dominican Republic	Ratified	Acceded	Not signed

The FCTC only applies to the dispute between Australia and Honduras but it is quite widely ratified amongst members. The Convention on the Rights of the Child is an agreement that binds all of the parties to the disputes and is very widely ratified. The ICESCR is a relevant agreement in disputes between Australia and Honduras, Indonesia and the Dominican Republic, respectively. Although Cuba is not bound by the ICESCR as a signatory that has not yet ratified the agreement, it is obliged 'to refrain, in good faith, from acts that would defeat the object and the purpose of the treaty'.[216] It is also relevant that, at the time of signing, Cuba's foreign minister stated that Cuba had always applied the principles enshrined in the agreement.[217] Arguably, the provisions of the ICESCR could constitute a relevant rule of customary international law that would also be relevant to the dispute between Australia and Cuba, pursuant to Article 31(3)(c).[218]

Where international agreements outside the WTO are relevant to both the dispute and the object and purpose of TRIPS, considerations of systemic integration are engaged when they also bind parties to the dispute. Ruse-Khan argues that interpretation of the term 'parties' should arguably favour a normative environment which binds a significant number of other WTO members as opposed to smaller normative environments such as bilateral investment treaties.[219] The decisions of the Appellate Body in *EC-Aircraft* suggest that there should be a balance between agreements that balance all WTO members and agreements that bind individual

216 VCLT (n 11), art 18.

217 James C McKinley Jr, 'Cuba signs 2 Human Rights Treaties' New York Times (February 2008).

218 Ruse-Khan (n 1) 35.

219 Ibid 143.

members.[220] Benn McGrady characterises the approach of requiring parties to the dispute to be parties to extraneous agreements for them to be relevant as a restrictive approach to interpretation of Article 31(3)(c).[221] He argues that a more appropriate approach for WTO disputes is to consider rules of international law relevant to the issues in dispute.[222] If this broader approach were taken, it is arguable that Convention on the Rights of the Child, ICESCR and FCTC rights are relevant laws.

VI. CONCLUDING OBSERVATIONS

Human rights obligations engaging the right to health can justify plain packaging legislation and can be relevant to the interpretive tools of object and purpose and Article 31(3)(c). These concerns are relevant to interpretation of the term 'unjustifiably' even if they are not necessary public health measures. Accepting the relevance of the right to health to the WTO Disputes, interpretation of that right by the CESCR raises additional relevant considerations. The right to health requires states to recognise the importance of international cooperation and assistance between states to permit all states to recognise minimum core obligations identified by the CESCR in relation to the right. Related to this is the obligation of state parties to 'ensure that their actions as members of international organizations take due account of the right to health'.[223] Arguably the WTO members who are bringing these actions are not taking due account of the right to health. The CESCR interprets violations of the obligation to respect the right to health to include 'the failure of the State to take into account its legal obligations regarding the right to health when entering into bilateral or multilateral agreements with other States, international organizations and other entities, such as multinational corporations'.[224] If Articles 7 and 8 are not sufficiently broad to recognise right to health obligations this obligation might be engaged. Problematically, limited emphasis on these provisions limits interpretation of them by WTO

---

[220] Appellate Body Report, 'European Communities – Measures Affecting Trade in Large Civil Aircraft' (2011) WT/DS316/AB/R, 363.

[221] McGrady (n 211) 45–78.

[222] Ibid. See Benn McGrady, 'Fragmentation of International Law or Systemic Integration of Treaty Regimes: EC-Biotech Products and the Proper Interpretation of Article 31 (3)(c) of the Vienna Convention on the Law of Treaties' (2008) 42 J World Trade 589.

[223] General Comment 14 (n 108), para 39.

[224] Ibid, para 50.

dispute settlement bodies. This means that it is difficult to understand how they can be used to protect human rights.

There are interpretative justifications for considering human rights concerns in IP-related WTO disputes. Recognition of this may permit greater systemic integration of international laws for intellectual property and for human rights and strengthen arguments that the WTO is the venue for dispute resolution best equipped to address conflicts between intellectual property and human rights.

PART III

Innovation and enforcement objectives in the European Union

8. Patents, supplementary protection certificates and data exclusivity at the service of pharmaceuticals

Żaneta Pacud*

I. THE FRAMEWORKS OF HARMONISED PHARMACEUTICAL AND PATENT REGULATIONS IN EUROPE

After World War II modern technologies allowed for large-scale chemical syntheses resulting in new molecules that were believed to have therapeutic effects. Many medicaments were introduced into markets after very simplistic examination. It was only in the late 1950s that a scandal with Thalidomide made European health authorities aware of the danger of unpredictable side-effects of pharmaceuticals that were not properly tested.[1]

The first European Economic Community (EEC) pharmaceutical initiative, Directive 65/65/EEC,[2] obliged the founding six member states of the EEC to enact requirements concerning safety and efficacy of medicinal products. As a result no proprietary medicinal product[3] could be placed on the market in the EEC unless it was authorised by a national health authority on the grounds of the Directive's provisions, which demanded specified pharmaceutical data. The most burdensome requirement lay in the necessity of presenting results of preclinical tests and clinical trials.[4] For ethical reasons, especially connected to clinical trials being repeated

* All online sources were last accessed on 27 December 2018.

1 Alan Heaton, *The Chemical Industry* (Springer 1994) 40.

2 Council Directive 65/65/EEC of 26 January 1965 on the approximation of provisions laid down by law, regulation or administrative action relating to proprietary medicinal products [1965] OJ EC 369/65.

3 Proprietary medicinal product was denoted as any ready-prepared medicinal product placed on the market under a special name and in a special pack; Art 1(1) of Directive 65/65/EEC.

4 Directive 65/65/EEC, arts 2, 3 and 4.

in relation to the same pharmaceutical, this requirement was eased in case of products with an established use where the results of the said tests and trials could then be substituted by published references.[5] That was the one exception to providing full data, known today as a well-established use application. That first Directive did not provide for additional protection for innovative medicines to be introduced in the market.

There was no common European patent policy for medicinal products in the 1960s. Many national legal systems did not provide for patentability of medicinal products as such. Exceptions were Great Britain, which allowed the patenting of pharmaceuticals from 1949, followed by France and Germany, where it became possible from 1968.[6] This situation changed in 1973 when the Convention on the Grant of European Patents[7] was signed and came into operation in 1978. It provided uniform criteria for patentability in all contracting states. Medicinal products became patentable as such.[8] Countries could, however, make reservations for a limited period of time to preclude claims to pharmaceutical products, but not the processes of their manufacture.[9]

Importantly, the European Patent Convention (EPC) introduced patentability of first medical use, being a claim category directed to an already known substance when used for the first time in a medical method.[10] This type of claim was quite revolutionary as it is contrary to the commonly accepted requirement of absolute novelty. It was, however, deemed justified as necessary to answer the needs of a pharmaceutical industry

---

5 Directive 65/65/EEC, art 4(8) (a)–(b).

6 Dieter Schneider, 'Patenting of Pharmaceuticals – Still a Challenge?' (2008) 39 IIC 511, 511–512.

7 Convention on the Grant of European Patents of 1973, amended in 2000. The revised text of the Convention, as adopted by decision of the Administrative Council of 28 June 2000, is referred to as EPC 2000, whereas its earlier version is denoted as EPC 1973 see <https://www.epo.org/law-practice/legal-texts/html/epc/2016/e/cl_iv.html>.

8 EPC 2000 (n 7), art 52(4), stating clearly that the exclusion of medical method from patentability shall not apply to products, in particular substances or compositions, for use in any of these methods.

9 EPC 1973 (n 7), art 167. Austria used this option to prohibit direct protection of pharmaceuticals until 1987. Spain and Greece used this option to prohibit such protection until 1992. See also Trevor Cook, *Pharmaceuticals, Biotechnology and the Law* (LexisNexis 2016) 80; Kieran Bradley, Noel Travers and Anthony Whelan, *Of Courts and Constitutions: Liber Amicorum in Honour of Nial Fennelly* (Bloomsbury Publishing 2014) 156.

10 EPC 2000 (n 7), art 52(5).

searching for new drugs among already known chemical substances.[11] Increasing difficulties in synthesis of completely new compositions and the availability of better diagnostic tools led to expansion of the scope of patentability for medical uses within the next decade.[12]

Another regional agreement – the Community Patent Convention – was signed in 1975. This never came into force. It contributed, however, to the substantial harmonisation of national provisions concerning patent infringement[13] and – which is less known – also of those concerning indirect protection of product and the burden of proof related to it.[14]

As regards data exclusivity, after almost two decades of Directive 65/65/EEC being in force, it was assessed critically in a European Commission Report.[15] The Commission indicated a likelihood of abuse of the well-established use application resulting in an unduly facilitated access of follow-on drugs to the market. As protection for natural substances or subsequent indications of known substances was not always available, the Commission proposed a new instrument of a 10-year period of *data exclusivity for innovative medicinal products* entering the market. This instrument was intended to be independent from patent protection.[16] As a counterbalance for the generic industry the Commission recommended that it should be possible for a generic producer to refer to the data in a pharmaceutical dossier of an innovative drug after the said exclusivity period had expired. These proposed rules were modified because of a critical opinion of the Economic and Social Committee that pointed out that such a long period of exclusivity could considerably impair public health interests in some member states.[17]

---

[11] Lionel Bentley and Brad Sherman, *Intellectual Property Law* (4th edn, Oxford University Press 2014) 546.

[12] On average about 80% of R&D expenditure was spent on examining known substances, with only 16–20% spent on synthesis of new substances. Cf Gerhard Klöpsch, 'Patentability of Pharmaceuticals According to the European Patent Convention (EPC)' (1982) 13 IIC 461.

[13] Ansgar Ohly and Justine Pila, *The Europeanization of Intellectual Property Law* (Oxford University Press 2013) 28.

[14] Cook (n 9) 78.

[15] Report from Commission to the Council concerning the adoption of certain urgent measures intended to facilitate the development and marketing of medicinal products in the Community COM (84) 437 final. See also ibid 561–562.

[16] European Commission Proposal on the Project of the Directive 87/21/EWG, COM (84) 437 final.

[17] The primary project of the Committee opinion, approving the 10-year period of data exclusivity as an incentive for research and development in the pharmaceutical area as being necessary for the future of European innovative potential. This version was rejected and substituted with the critical opinion. See Opinion of the

In its eventual shape, Directive 87/21/EEC improved the regime of well-established use application[18] and introduced two further exceptions to the general rule requiring that an application for a marketing authorisation includes full data.[19] The first allowed for the usage of reference data of an authorised medicine with the consent of the marketing authorisation holder. The second created the possibility of usage of the said reference data by a generic entrant without the consent of a marketing authorisation holder. At the same time it constituted a period during which the data could not be referred to.

The basic data exclusivity period was for six years. The Community member states could opt for a stronger protection, providing 10 years of independent data exclusivity for any kind of authorised medicinal products or they could weaken the protective regime by rendering the six-year period dependent on the validity period of patent protection for a relevant product.[20] In the case of high-technology medicines, especially biotechnological pharmaceuticals, the data exclusivity period lasted for 10 years and could not be linked to a patent.[21] The majority of EEC countries chose the six-year period; eight countries opted for longer data exclusivity.[22] Different periods of data protection resulted in varying dates on which generic drugs could access the market.[23] It also caused difficulties in executing a decentralised or a mutual recognition procedure.[24]

Economic and Social Committee of 27 March 1985 on the Proposal for a Council Directive amending Directive 65/65/EEC on the approximation of provisions laid down by law, regulation or administrative action relating to proprietary medicinal products, with appendices [1985] OJ C/160/08.

[18] See art 4(8)(a)(ii) of Directive 65/65/EEC, amended by Directive 87/21/EEC [1987] OJ L 15.

[19] See Directive 65/65/EEC, amended art 4(8)(a)(i) and (iii).

[20] See Directive 65/65/EEC, amended art 4(8)(a)(iii).

[21] Products of high technologies were indicated in List A and List B of the Annex to Council Directive 87/22/EEC of 22 December 1986 on the approximation of national measures relating to the placing on the market of high-technology medicinal products, particularly those derived from biotechnology [1987] OJ L 15.

[22] A six-year period of data exclusivity was chosen in Austria, Denmark, Finland, Ireland, Portugal, Spain, Greece, Poland, the Czech Republic, Hungary, Latvia, Lithuania, Slovakia, Malta, Estonia, Cyprus, Bulgaria, Romania and three EFTA countries. The 10-year period was accepted in Belgium, Germany, France, Italy, the Netherlands, Sweden, the United Kingdom and Luxembourg.

[23] European Medicine Agency, 'Notice to Applicants' 40.

[24] Under these two procedures of a national type a generic product could be authorised for the market only after expiry of the 10-year period of data exclusivity, if such was provided in the law of the authorising country, even if the referring country opted for the shorter, 6-year period.

After expiry of the data exclusivity period, any follow-on entrants to the market could refer to the pharmaceutical dossier of the reference product instead of presenting their own results of preclinical tests and clinical trials.[25] Access to the market was, however, limited in most cases primarily by patents. The provisions concerning generic applications could be applied only after the relevant patents had expired, which as a rule lasted longer than the data exclusivity period. Hence, the latter was especially important when patent protection was unavailable or weak, or when it was about to expire shortly after a marketing authorisation had been achieved.

The European data exclusivity legislation followed and was influenced by its US counterpart – the Drug Price Competition and Patent Term Restoration Act 1984, known commonly as the Hatch-Waxman Act. The US law was not only about data exclusivity, rather it was presented as providing society with a variety of price-effective and innovative medicines through balancing interests between the innovative and generic industries by means of several legal instruments introduced at once. These were patent term extension[26] and data exclusivity periods for new chemical entities[27] for the sake of innovative industry and an abridged procedure for approving follow-on drugs,[28] data exclusivity for the first generic market entrants[29] and Bolar exemption[30] for the generic sector. An important

[25] Directive 65/65/EEC, art 4(8) amended by Directive 87/21/EEC [1987] OJ L 15/36, art 1.

[26] Patent term extension aims to compensate for the loss of effective patent protection due to the approval procedure. It covers the exact period between the filing of the application for approval and its grant, whereas the maximum length of the extended patent cannot be more than 14 years. At the moment of its introduction patent term extension was seen also as a trade-off for the innovative industry losing their informal post-patent exclusive right based on the period of time generic companies had to spend for the follow-on approval procedure. See 35 USC s 201(a). See also Francesca Papadopoulou, 'Legal Transplants and Modern Lawmaking in the Field of Pharmaceutical Patents – A Way to Achieve International Harmonisation or the Source of Deeper Divergences' (2016) 47 IIC 901.

[27] The data exclusivity for new chemical substances lasts five years and it is independent of patent protection. See 35 USC, s 271.

[28] The abridged procedure aimed at facilitating generic entries into market by limiting the scope of required tests to confirmation of bioequivalence between the original and generic medicines.

[29] The instrument of the 180-day period of exclusivity is related to generic applications, filed in a so-called abridged procedure when challenging a patent for a relevant innovative medicinal product. Its commencement is connected either with the first commercial marketing of the generic product or with a court decision holding the relevant patent either invalid or not infringed. See 35 USC, s 271.

[30] The name of this provision is derived from *Roche Products v Bolar*

solution for reasons of legal certainty was a common register of marketing approvals of medicinal products and patents referring to them, known as the Orange Book. Whereas legal instruments corresponding to data exclusivity and patent term extension were transplanted to Community legislation relatively soon – in 1987 and 1992 respectively – the changes beneficial for the generic industry were introduced there only partially; the abridged procedure for generic applications was enacted in 1987 and the regulatory testing exception, equivalent to the Bolar exemption, in 2004.[31]

II. PATENTS FOR PHARMACEUTICAL INNOVATIONS

Subsequently, the rules of patent protection based on the EPC were modified. Many of these changes were connected to pharmaceuticals. The EPC was amended only once and most legal developments were introduced via the decisions of the European Patent Office (EPO), the Implementing Rules to the EPC or through various acts of law of the EU.

The first important change was related to patentability of the so-called *second and subsequent medical uses* in 1984, the *Eisai* case.[32] Since there was no legal basis for this type of invention in the EPC, the Enlarged Board of Appeal recognised this as a lacuna that had to be closed, by reference to an ancient Roman praetorian practice.[33] Because of the *Eisai* decision, claims for second medical use became allowable, benefitting from a fiction of novelty in the new use. These claims were designed in a

---

Pharmaceutical Co Inc (1984) 733 F2d 858 (Fed Cir). The Bolar provision, situated in 35 USC, s 271(e)(1), states that it shall not be an act of infringement to make, use, or sell a patented invention solely for uses reasonably related to the development and submission of information under a Federal law which regulates the manufacture, use, or sale of drugs.

31 For the consequences thereof, see Papadopoulou (n 26) 891.

32 Decision of the Enlarged Board of Appeal G 5/83 [1985] OJ EPO 3 64.

33 See the Reasons for the Decision G 2/08 [2010] OJ EPO 10 456, point 5.10.2. According to the Board, as the Convention did not preclude patentability of a second medical use but at the same time did not provide for it, the *Eisai* decision filled this loophole in the patent system. However, introduction of the second medical use claims in the so-called Swiss form was contrary to art 54(5) of the EPC 1973 (n 7) and was based, until the entry into force of the Revising Act of 2000, on an interpretation *contra legem*. Moreover, the recognition by the Board that the *Eisai* decision is an expression of a praetorian way of filling a legal vacuum questions the separation of legislative and executive powers in the system based on the EPC.

Swiss form referring to a process of manufacture rather than to a method of treatment and thus avoiding the prohibition on such methods.[34]

Patentability of second medical uses was obviously seen as a step in favour of the research-based industries and difficulties they have with inventing new active substances. The *Eisai* decision did not, however, only address this problem – it was also an attempt to catch up with the level of protection for medicines available under US law for patent protection for therapeutic methods by means of new use of a known substance.[35] The European pharmaceutical industry has been under constant competitive pressure from US enterprises, where innovative pharmaceutical companies have seen the legal environment as a condition *sine qua non* of making competition successful.[36] However, it should be underlined that the exemption of medical practitioners from patent infringement, which constitutes an integral part of the framework of patent protection for pharmaceuticals in the US, was not followed in Europe.[37] On the one hand it creates systemic contradiction between prohibition on patents for medical methods and liability of medical practitioners for using patented substances in medical methods. On the other hand, the second medical use patent protection against physicians, pharmacists or health insurance

---

[34] Article 52(4) excluded therapeutic, surgical and diagnostic methods from patentability. In the EPC 2000 (n 7) this provision was moved to art 53(c), without any change in merit.

[35] The general basis for patent protection in the US is provided in 35 USC, s 101, which states: 'Whoever invents or discovers any new and useful process, machine, manufacture, or composition of matter, or any new and useful improvement thereof, may obtain a patent therefor, subject to the conditions and requirements of this title.' A further basis for patentability of a new use of an old compound may specifically be found in 35 USC, s 100(b), which states that 'the term "process" means process, art, or method, and includes a new use of a known process, machine, manufacture, composition of matter, or material'.

[36] For a discussion of the rationale of second medical use see Stephan Gruber and Jürgen Kroher, 'Patentability of Pharmaceutical Inventions – A Comparison of the Legal Situation in Germany and Some Common Law Countries, Part One' (1984) 5 IIC 591, 592; Jean Miller, 'Patentability of a Second Indication of a Pharmaceutical in Europe' (1986) 26 IDEA 17, 18.

[37] Such an exemption could not be introduced to the EPC itself as it does not regulate the scope of right resulting from European patents. The EPO clarified in its *Genentech* decision that in order to protect physicians from being sued for patent infringement the contracting states should introduce appropriate provisions in their national laws. See decision *Genentech* T/1030 [2006] OJ EPO 9, point 16. This exemption has not been regulated in the proposed unitary patent package either. See 35 USC, s 287(c), stating that the relevant patent provisions shall not apply against the medical practitioners or against a related care entity with respect to such medical activity.

agencies may be very illusory,[38] which is observable in the set of *Bristol Mayer Squibb* cases[39] and more recently in *Warner Lambert*[40] and *Novartis*.[41]

The TRIPS Agreement[42] established global minimum standards of intellectual property rights, requiring patents to be available for any inventions, whether products or processes, in all fields of technology.[43] For several World Trade Organization (WTO) members, including European jurisdictions, this required introduction of *product patent protection* for the first time.[44] For developing countries that were permitted to delay the introduction of direct patent protection for pharmaceuticals there was a requirement to provide pipeline protection.[45] The uniform, strong patent protection, supplemented by provisions limiting compulsory licences to domestic markets, resulted in an 'access to essential medicines' controversy. In order to lessen the negative impact on availability of drugs in the least developed countries there were several measures undertaken: the Doha Declaration was adopted in 2001,[46] a modification of the TRIPS

---

38 See Hans-Reiner Jaenichen, Jurgen Meier and Niels Hoelder (eds), 'Medical Use Claims: EPC 2000 and Its Impact on Prosecution and Patent Enforcement' in Wolrad Prinz zu Waldeck und Pyrmont, Martin J Adelman, Robert Brauneis, Josef Drexl and Ralph Nack, *Patents and Technological Progress in a Globalised World* (Springer 2009) 269–271.

39 *Bristol-Myers Squibb Co v Baker Norton Pharmaceuticals Inc* [2001] RPC 45 (CA).

40 *Warner-Lambert Company LLC v Actavis Group PTC EHF & Ors* (High Court of Justice, 21 January 2015) EWHC 2015, 72 (Pat).

41 *Novartis AG v Sun Pharmaceutical Industries BV* (Hague Court of Appeal, 27 January 2015).

42 Agreement on Trade-Related Aspects of Intellectual Property Rights (opened for signature 15 April 1994, entered into force 1 January 1996) 1869 UNTS 299 (TRIPS).

43 Ibid art 27.

44 Ibid arts 65 and 66 provided for transitional periods allowing 'developing' and 'least developed countries' to delay providing product patent protection – among others – in the area of pharmaceuticals. Whereas the first provisions had already expired, the transitional periods for the least developing countries were extended several times and will be in force until the end of 2032.

45 It was known as a mailbox system or a black box system. See Pires de Carvalho, *The TRIPS Regime of Patent Rights* (Alphen aan den Rijn 2002) 310–311. The matter was subject to the first dispute before the Dispute Settlement Body concerning TRIPS (n 42), see: Pakistan, 'Patent Protection for Pharmaceutical and Agricultural Chemical Products' WT/DS36/4.

46 On 14 November 2001, the Fourth Ministerial Conference of the WTO adopted the Doha Declaration on the Agreement on Trade Related Aspects of Intellectual Property Rights and Public Health. The Declaration recognises, especially in the context of public health needs, that each WTO Member has the

Agreement concerning compulsory licences was signed in 2005[47] and completed in 2017. These were addressed in Europe – allowing export of pharmaceuticals to certain countries under certain conditions.[48]

Another development relates to inventions derived from biotechnology, especially genetic engineering, which were deemed as inadequately protected by that time. Directive 98/44/EC[49] sanctioned *patentability of biotechnological inventions*, employing the already existing practice of the EPO.[50] By decision of the Administrative Board of the European Patent Organisation, its most important provisions were transposed to the EPC system as part of the Implementing Regulation.[51] Hence, this Directive not only contributed to harmonising national patent laws, but also influenced a normative shape of the European patent system.

The new millennium started with revision of the EPC.[52] In order to eliminate any legal uncertainty over the patent protection of subsequent medical uses the former practice of the EPO was codified, providing for their *patentability in product-by-use claim* form.[53] While it was a mere codification measure, it turned out to have influence on the scope of second medical use patents, conferring likely broader protection than would have resulted from the Swiss claim construction. In the view of the Enlarged Board of Appeal it could, in particular, lead to possible restrictions on the freedom of medical practitioners to prescribe or to administer generics.[54]

---

right to grant compulsory licences, and the freedom to determine the grounds upon which such licences are granted.

47 See decision of the WTO General Council of 6 December 2005 and its Protocol amending the TRIPS (n 42) by adding art 31*bis*.

48 Regulation (EC) no 816/2006 of the European Parliament and of the Council of 17 May 2006 on compulsory licensing of patents relating to the manufacture of pharmaceutical products for export to countries with public health problems [2006] OJ EC L 157/1.

49 Directive 98/44/EC of the European Parliament and of the Council of 6 July 1998 on the legal protection of biotechnological inventions [1998] OJ EC L 213/13. It refers in Recital 5 of the Preamble to differences existing in the legal protection of biotechnological inventions as offered by the laws and practices of the different Member States and possibly resulting in barriers to trade and impediments to the proper functioning of the internal market.

50 Cook (n 9) 240.

51 See Chapter V of the Implementing Regulation, titled 'Biotechnological Inventions', Rules 23b–23j.

52 See Act revising the Convention on the Grant of European Patents of 29 November 2000 (n 7).

53 See EPC 2000, art 54(5).

54 See Case G 2/08 *Dosage regime* [2010] OJ EPO 456, point 6.5 of the Reasons.

Medical use inventions were also subject to a 2010 decision of the EPO – *Genentech.*[55] The case sanctioned the availability of patent protection for second medical indications, with a dosage regime being the only claimed feature not found in the state of the art. These dosage regime patents also confirmed patentability of a whole range of subject matter, including the group of patients being treated;[56] a new route or mode of administration;[57] and a different technical effect leading to a truly new application.[58] *Genetech* also influenced the formal aspect of pharmaceutical claims by abolishing the Swiss form of second medical indications as not needed anymore after the introduction of product-by-use format on the ground of new art 54(5) EPC 2000.

Seen as a consequence of a long process aiming at full availability of patent protection for medical uses the *Genetech* decision was the culmination of the process which began with *Eisai* in 1984.

Subsequent legislative initiatives in the patent area in Europe are related to a unitary patent system within the European Union and provide for the same effects of national, European and unitary patents.[59] Given the controversies over enforcement of pharmaceutical patents in different European countries, discrepancies in interpretation of patent claims and various judicial traditions, this system might be of paramount importance for the European pharmaceutical industry.

Other changes evolve through case law, such as a judgment of the German Federal Supreme Court confirming a grant of compulsory licence for an antiviral drug.[60] It seems to be a landmark decision for several reasons; it deals with a compulsory licence for a pharmaceutical product for the supply to the domestic market; it is granted beyond the framework of competition proceedings;[61] and it acknowledges the significance of public health interest in European countries.

---

55 Case G 2/08 *Dosage regime* [2010] OJ EPO 456.

56 See EPO decisions: T 19/86 [1989] OJ EPO 24; T 893/90 of 22 July 1993, not published; T 233/96 of 4 May 2000, not published.

57 EPO decisions T 51/93 of 8 June 1994; T 138/95 of 12 October 1999.

58 T 290/86 [1992] OJ EPO 414; T 254/93 [1998] OJ EPO 285; T 1020/03 [2007] OJ EPO 204.

59 This system is based on three legal acts: Regulations 1257/2012/EU; Regulation 1260/2012/EU; and Agreement on the Unitary Patent Court.

60 Case X ZB 2/17 *Raltegravir* (FCJ, 11 July 2017).

61 Earlier compulsory licences for medicinal products were granted on the basis of abuse of a dominant position in two known cases in Italy: *Glaxo-Principi Attivi Provvedimento* n 15175, A 363 *L'autorita Garante della Concorenza e del Mercato* (8 February 2006) and *Merck-Principi Attivi Provvedimento* n 14388, A 364, *L'autorita Garante della Concorenza e del Mercato* (15 June 2005).

Supplementary protection certificates (SPCs) are intellectual property rights formally separate from patent rights although factually constituting their extensions. As was pointed out in the Commission proposal, as a consequence of a cumbersome and time-consuming authorisation procedure the basic patent term of 20 years was reduced in the case of pharmaceuticals to an average of eight years.[62] Such a period of so-called 'effective patent protection' for innovative drugs was seen by the research-based industry as inadequate to recoup investment and meet competition with foreign enterprises benefitting from longer protection and to prevent research centres being relocated from the Community.[63] Introduction of the SPC system was opposed by the generic sector as delaying the moment of a follow-on drug entry into the market. It was also expected to produce an increase of costs and expenditure on medicinal products by consumers and health insurance institutions.[64]

According to Regulation 469/2009[65] an SPC comes into effect on expiry of a patent and is valid for a period not exceeding five years, rendering the maximum protection not more than 15 years.[66] The scope of the SPC protection is limited to an active ingredient covered by a basic patent[67]

---

62 Proposal of 11 April 1990 concerning the creation of Council Regulation (EEC) 1768/92 of 18 June 1992 concerning the creation of a supplementary protection certificate for medicinal products [1992] OJ EU L 182/1. A supplementary protection certificate for medicinal products, COM (90)101FINAL -SYN 255. See also Christopher Brückner, *ESZ/SPC* (2nd edn, Carl Heymanns 2015) 13.

63 According to the Proposal an SPC would extend the period of patent by the lesser of 10 years from patent expiry and 16 years from the date of the first marketing in any of the Community member states. See Cook (n 9) 455. In order to balance the interests between the researching industry and the health system, the respective periods of time were shortened. Cf Detlef Schennen, *Die 0110 Verlängerung der Patentlaufzeit für Arzneimittel in gemeinsamen Markt* (1993) 26; Katarzyna Zbierska, 'Relation between SPC and Data Exclusivity' (2014) 16 Pharm Pol & L 85.

64 Opinion 91/C 69/06 on the proposal for a Council Regulation (EEC) concerning the creation of a supplementary protection certificate for medicinal products [1991] OJ EU C 69/22.

65 Regulation (EC) 469/2009 of the European Parliament and of the Council of 6 May 2009 concerning the supplementary protection certificate for medicinal products [2009] OJ EU L 152/1. According to Recital 1 of the ITS Preamble, the formerly binding Regulation 1768/92 was substantially amended several times, which was the reason for the recodification.

66 See SPC Regulation, art 13.

67 'Basic patent' means a patent which protects a product as such, a process to obtain a product or an application of a product, and which is designated by its holder for the purpose of the procedure for grant of a certificate. On the possible interpretation of the notion, see below.

and by a marketing authorisation of a corresponding medicinal product and to any use of that ingredient as a medicinal product that has been authorised before the expiry of the certificate.[68] The criteria of protective ability, and especially the dependence on both patent and marketing authorisation, are the subject of consecutive judgments of the Court of Justice of the European Union (CJEU). It explained that a product is protected by a basic patent when it is 'specified/identified in the wording of a claim' (*Medeva*),[69] 'protected as such' (*Georgetown University*),[70] 'related implicitly but necessarily and specifically to an active ingredient in question' (*Eli Lilly*)[71] and finally 'constituting the sole subject-matter of the invention' (*Actavis*).[72] Together with an earlier ruling sanctioning SPC for a second medical indication (*Neurim*),[73] the CJEU case law opened the way to achieving more than one SPC for one basic patent and shifted the SPC function from a necessary compensation for lost time of marketing exclusivity towards the protection of an investment in research to discover a new therapeutic use of a product.

III. DATA EXCLUSIVITY

Data exclusivity, as established on the grounds of Directive 87/21/EEC,[74] evolved subsequently in two directions. First, the existing regime was subject to major amendments; second, it involved new instruments of data exclusivity for specific kinds of pharmaceuticals: orphan drugs and paediatric medicines.

The first decade of the data exclusivity regime gave rise to questions

---

68 According to a later ECJ judgment this rule has been interpreted so that an SPC covers the active ingredient, as a medicinal product, in any of the forms enjoying the protection of the basic patent. See Case C-392/97 *Farmitalia Carlo Erba Sr* [1992] OJ EU L 182/1.

69 C-322/10 *Medeva BV v Comptroller General of Patents, Designs and Trade Marks* (CJEU, 24 November 2011).

70 C-484/12 *Georgetown University v Octrooicentrum Nederland* [2014] OJ EU C 52/33.

71 C-493/12 *Eli Lilly and Company Ltd v Human Genome Sciences Inc* [2014] OJ EU C 45/24.

72 Case C-577/13 *Actavis Group PTC EHF, Actavis UK Ltd v Boehringer Ingelheim Pharma GmbH & Co KG* [2015] OJ EU C 146/04.

73 Case C -130/11 *Neurim Pharmaceuticals* [2012] OJ EU C 295.

74 Council Directive 87/21/EEC of 22 December 1986 amending Directive 65/65/EEC on the approximation of provisions laid down by law, regulation or administrative action relating to proprietary medicinal products [1987] OJ EU L 15.

about exclusivity for new variations of an already authorised drug. The innovative industry strived for securing a full period of data exclusivity not only for the new chemical substances, but also for new indications thereof. In 1998 the European Court of Justice (ECJ) clarified this issue,[75] stating that a medicinal product, when essentially similar to a product which had been authorised for no less than six or 10 years in the Community, might be authorised under an abridged procedure for all dosage forms, doses and dosage schedules already authorised for that product. The practical consequence of this judgment was that the data exclusivity periods for pharmaceutical variations authorised later than the basic medicine became substantially shorter than six or 10 years.[76] The innovative pharmaceutical industry claimed this left them without any incentive to undertake line extension work, especially close to or after expiry of a relevant patent or SPC.[77] The rule was nevertheless adopted in the amendments of 2004 and denoted as global marketing authorisation.[78] The concerns of innovative industry were taken into consideration and resulted in one additional year of data exclusivity. In 2001, Directive 65/65/EEC was replaced by Directive 2001/83/EC, codifying the hitherto pharmaceutical legislation within the European Community.[79] However, it did not result in modifications on the merits as far as data exclusivity was concerned. The regime was subject to crucial changes only in 2004 when Directive 2004/27/EC was enacted.[80]

Directive 2004/27/EC established a new timeframe for data and market exclusivity, known commonly as the 8+2+1 scheme, distinguishing between data protection and market exclusivity periods. The hitherto optional six- or 10-year periods of data protection were replaced by the

---

75 Case C-368/96 *Generics UK v Glaxo-BMS* (ECJ, 3 December 1998).

76 According to para 53 of this ruling, a medicinal product that is essentially similar to a product which has been authorised for not less than six or 10 years and is marketed in the member state for which the application is made may be authorised, under the abridged procedure, for all therapeutic indications already authorised for that product, even if those indications have been authorised for less than six or 10 years.

77 See Cook (n 9) 572.

78 See Amended Directive 2001/83/EC, art 6.

79 Directive 2001/83/EC of the European Parliament and of the Council of 6 November 2001 on the Community code relating to medicinal products for human use [2001] OJ EU L 311.

80 Directive 2004/27/EC of the European Parliament and of the Council of 31 March 2004 amending Directive 2001/83/EC on the Community code relating to medicinal products for human use [2004] OJ EU L 136/34. It obliged the Community Member States to implement its provisions by 30 October 2005.

uniform eight-year period, which treated innovative products all the same and did not depend on patent protection. Additionally, after the eight years of data protection, another two-year period of market exclusivity was provided. As a consequence, a generic entrant may refer to the innovative dossier after the eight years from the first marketing authorisation, but the generic authorisation may be effective not earlier than before the end of the 10th year from that moment. On a one-off basis another year of market exclusivity may be obtained if during the eight-year period the authorisation holder has obtained authorisation for a new therapeutic indication of the same medicinal product which shows a significant clinic benefit. A non-cumulative period of one year of data exclusivity may be granted for a new indication of a well-established substance when significant preclinical or clinical studies were carried out in relation to this indication.[81] And lastly, a one-year period of data exclusivity may be granted in support of a change of legal classification of a medicament, from subject to medical prescription to an over-the-counter product.[82]

The 2004 Directive also introduced new notions of reference and generic medicinal products[83] and sanctioned the rule of global marketing authorisation, which provides now that a marketing authorisation for a new product includes all its additional strengths, pharmaceutical forms, administration routes presentations as well as any variations and extensions which are authorised later.[84] Moreover, the Directive established further rules concerning marketing authorisation in the case of combination products,[85] biosimilars,[86] and a hybrid procedure.[87] Last but not least, two important regulations, situated at the intersection of pharmaceutical regulatory regime and patent law, were introduced.

The first is the regulatory test exemption allowing for the optimal usage of the abridged procedure for generic entrants. The generic industry tried to invoke a research exemption as a basis for its bioequivalence tests

---

[81] Amended Directive 2001/83/EC, art 10(5).

[82] See art 74(a) of the amended Directive 2001/83/EC. Over-the-counter (OTC) products are not subject to medical prescription. See arts 72 and 71 of this Directive.

[83] See respectively arts 10 and 6 of the amended Directive 2001/83/EC. Reference product is denoted as authorised in accordance with the requirement of Directive 2001/83, whereas a generic medicinal product is defined as having the same qualitative and quantitative composition in active substances, the same pharmaceutical form and being bioequivalent to the reference product.

[84] Amended directive 2001/83/EC, art 6(1).

[85] Ibid art 10(b).

[86] Ibid art 10(4).

[87] Ibid art 10(3).

and trials but only with partial success.[88] After the 2000 decision of the WTO panel,[89] confirming compatibility of Canadian Regulatory Review provision with TRIPS and, in the light of the needs of innovative pharmaceutical industry to clarify the admissibility of Bolar-like activities, the exemption was introduced into EU legislation. It states that conducting the necessary studies and trials with a view to the application of provisions concerning generic, biosimilar and hybrid files and the consequential practical requirements thereof shall not be regarded as contrary to patent or SPC rights.[90] The provision does not enumerate the types and scope of allowed activities and in comparison to the US version it lacks detail.[91] Moreover, being implemented into national laws in various ways[92], it became even less clear what third-party activities[93] and types of products are covered.[94]

The second regulation is commonly known as skinny labelling.[95] According to amended art 11 *in fine* of Directive 2001/83/EC[96] the parts

---

88 For details see Manuel Campolini and Ignace Vernimme, 'Bolar and Experimental Use Exemptions in the EU: How the Landscape Has Changed for Generic and Biotech Drug Makers' (2014) 12 Scrip Regulatory Affairs 1.

89 WTO, 'Canada – Patent Protection for Pharmaceutical Products' (2000) WT/DS114/13.

90 Amended Directive 2001/83/EC, art 10(6).

91 The US provision of Bolar exemption indicates directly the types of exempted activities, which are making, using and selling the invention. As such it also covers activities of third parties as an inevitable consequence of any sale.

92 A narrow scope of the Bolar exemption was accepted in Sweden, Belgium, Cyprus and Poland. A broad scope was accepted in Germany, Spain, France, Estonia, Italy and Finland. See Papadopoulou (n 26) 903.

93 See *Polpharma SA v Astellas Pharma Inc* (1992) IV CSK 92/13 (Polish Supreme Court). The Court interpreted the exemption narrowly, stating that it may not be applied to sale of active substance for the reasons of conducting necessary tests and trials. See also the *Polpharma v Astellas Pharma* (1968) I-2 U 68/15 (Düsseldorf Higher Regional Court) considering if a sale of limited quantities of the active substance to a generic company, allowing it to conduct the necessary studies, may be covered by Bolar exemption. The request for a preliminary ruling has, however, been withdrawn before a ruling of the CJEU.

94 See Campolini and Vernimme (n 88) 2 arguing that the Bolar exemption, especially as implemented into the German Patent Act, also covers necessary tests and trials in case of reference product, i.e. marketed on the ground of full application.

95 See for example Ravi Srinivasan, 'Chris Milton, EPO Second Medical Use Claims: The Skinny ScPC Loophole' (October 2011) Managing Intellectual Property <http://www.managingip.com/Article/2918674/EPO-second-medical-use-claims-The-skinny-SmPC-loophole.html>.

96 See Amended Directive 2001/83/EC on the Community code relating to medicinal products for human use.

of the summary of the product characteristics of the reference medicinal product that refer to indications or dosage forms, which were still covered by patents at the time when a generic medicine was marketed, need not be included. This mechanism may lessen the effectiveness of patents for second medical use inventions, especially in countries where a pharmacy substitution of innovative drug has been introduced.[97] In the small number of cases of infringement of second medical use patents courts have adjudicated in favour of generic producers. They have successfully argued that there was no evidence of a conscious and intentional preparation of a drug to be used in a patented indication[98] or no evidence of an introduction of a drug to the market for the patented use.[99] The literary reading of a Summary of Product Characteristics and of leaflets accompanying medicinal products seems crucial in rulings about potential infringement.[100] Deleting the patented indications from both makes the second medical use claims effectively unenforceable against prescribing and selling drugs for off-label use.[101]

Data exclusivity for orphan drugs was established in 2000, in Regulation 141/2000.[102] It was dedicated solely to medicinal products used for treatment of rare illnesses, defined as occurring in the Community in fewer than five out of every 10,000 persons and which were treated as having no economic impact amounting to an incentive for research under the normal market conditions. There were several foreign laws that were apparently successful, with protective systems for orphan medicines.[103] They inspired

---

[97] See for instance art 44 of the Polish Act on Reimbursement of Medicines, Foodstuffs Intended for Particular Nutritional Purposes and Medical Devices [2011] OJ 122, 696.

[98] *Hospira UK Ltd v Genentech Inc* [2014] EWHC 1094 (Pat).

[99] *Warner-Lambert Company LLC v Actavis Group PTC EHF & Ors* [2015] EWHC 72 (Pat). Differently, in a similar, but not identical case between the same parties in *Novartis AG v Sun Pharmaceutical Industries BV* ECLI:NH:HR:2017:692.

[100] See especially decisions of the German court in Düsseldorf: 4a O 12/03 *Ribavirin* GRUR-RR (2004) 193 2U 54/11 *Cistus Incanus* and 4a O 145/12 *Chronische Hepatits C.*

[101] Christian Fackelman, *Patentschutz und ergänzende Schutzinstrumente für Arzeimittel im Spannungsfeld von Wettbewerb und Innovation* (Carl Heymmans 2009) 149.

[102] Regulation (EC) 141/2000 of the European Parliament and of the Council of 16 December 1999 on orphan medicinal products [2002] OJ UE L 18/1.

[103] In the US, a system of incentives for development of orphan medicinal products was introduced in 1983, known as the 'Orphan Drug Act'. All designated orphan products are eligible for a federal tax credit equal to 50% of the clinical research expenditure; orphan products are exempted from the application fee for FDA approval, and the first product authorised for a specific indication gets a

the Community legislation, which offers for drugs that treat rare illnesses a period of 10 years of both data and market exclusivity as well as several secondary incentives: fee redundancy, scientific consultation and the possibility of conditional marketing authorisation. The orphan exclusivity initiated much stronger protection than the regime of data exclusivity for reference products: its 10-year period of data protection means that any generic application may be submitted only after it expires, which de facto prolongs the period of monopoly by several more months. Within this 10-year period of market exclusivity it is not possible to apply for either a generic or other innovative authorisation for the same or even a similar product for the same therapeutic indication. Hence, the market exclusivity for an orphan drug provides an absolute monopoly for its marketing authorisation holder.[104]

Data exclusivity for paediatric drugs is based on Regulation 1901/2006.[105] It introduced the requirement to carry out tests and trials of medicinal products for children and youths under 18 years old. As a reward for the tests conducted according to the so-called Paediatric investigation plan – irrespective of their outcome – the Regulation provided for extension of already existing exclusivities or establishment of new ones. The Regulation includes a basic privilege of a six-month extension of the SPC period. However, it does not apply when an applicant has already secured a one-year extension for a new therapeutic indication with significant clinical benefit.[106] In the case of orphan drugs the respective reward means an extension of market exclusivity from 10 to 12 years.

For those medicinal products that do not benefit from a patent or SPC protection a paediatric use marketing authorisation (PUMA) was enacted.[107] In the first nine years of Regulation 1901/2006 being in force

---

seven-year marketing exclusivity period. A similar regime was introduced in Japan in 1995, in Singapore in 1997 and in Australia in 1998. See Proposal for a European Parliament and Council Regulation (EC) on orphan medicinal products (1998) COM 450 final.

[104] The period of orphan exclusivity may be reduced to six years if the economic or prevalence criteria of designation are not fulfilled anymore. See art 8.2 of the Orphan Regulation.

[105] Regulation (EC) 1901/2006 of the European Parliament and of the Council of 12 December 2006 on medicinal products for paediatric use and amending Regulation (EEC) 1768/92, Directive 2001/20/EC, Directive 2001/83/EC and Regulation (EC) 726/2004 [2006] OJ EU L 378/1.

[106] See art 10(1) of Directive 2001/83/EC and art 14(11) of Regulation 726/2004.

[107] Art 38 of Regulation 1901/2006 on medicinal products for paediatric use.

only two authorisations for off-patent paediatric products were granted.[108] Data exclusivity alone is unlikely to be enough of an incentive to stimulate a development of a new drug, especially in the paediatric area.[109]

When analysing the evolution in the legal environment of pharmaceutical innovations it is visible that its dynamics varies as regards particular regimes.

As concerns the regulatory exclusivities it can be observed that there are two important periods of time, with two blocks of regulations changing the rules of data and market exclusivity.

First was the legislation passed around the middle of the 1980s. It was initiated by the US legal acts: 1983 Orphan Drug Act and 1984 Hatch-Waxman Act with its data exclusivity provisions. In Europe the EC submitted a critical report on malfunctioning practices within protection of pharmaceutical data, which resulted eventually in Directive 87/21/EEC, with the first European format of data exclusivity. The second block of regulations was passed in the first decade of the 21st century, starting with the 2000 Regulation on orphan drugs; Directive 2004/27/EC creating the current regime of data and market exclusivity and introducing regulatory test exemption and skinny labelling provisions; progressing to the 1901/2006 Regulation on paediatric uses; and eventually to the 2009 Biologic Price Competition Act in the US.

The SPC system has been based on Regulation 1768/1992. This act was amended on the merits only with regard to paediatric extensions.[110] Gradual modifications of the legal structure of SPC, especially in the context of premises of protective ability, have, however, been made on the grounds of consecutive judgments of the ECJ. When analysing the evolution in the legal environment of pharmaceutical innovations it is visible that its dynamics variy as regards particular regimes (see Figure 8.1).

---

[108] They were granted for Buccolam in 2011 and for Hemangiol in 2014. See European Medicines Agency, '10-year Report to the European Commission' (October 2016) EMA/231225/2015 16.

[109] See Tereq Mukattash, Jeff Millership, Paul Collier and James McElnay, 'Healthcare Professional Experiences and Attitudes on Unlicensed/Off-Label Paediatric Prescribing and Paediatric Clinical Trials' (2011) Eur J Clin Pharmacol 67, 449–461.

[110] Some minor modifications of Regulation 1768/1992 were related to acts of accession of new member states of the EC.

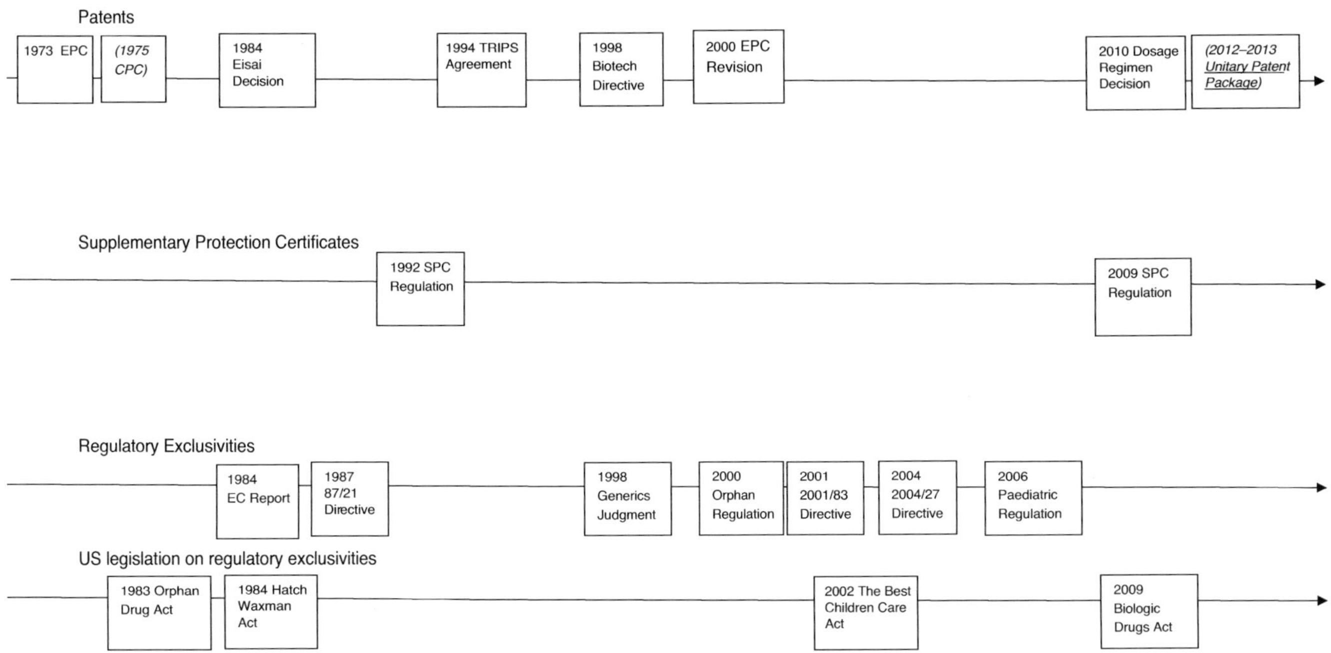

Figure 8.1 Time scheme of legislation and case law referred to above

IV. CONCLUDING OBSERVATIONS

Patent law is under constant reconstruction by means of legislative measures and case law, both occurring at international, EU and national level. This dynamic of constant change is visible especially when one takes into account the number of laws that have been proposed but not enacted. The reason for this may be quite prosaic; it is still the patent system which is of major significance for pharmaceutical industry, and as such it is subject to the utmost political, social and economic tension.

Other conclusions that might be drawn from developments within the three protective regimes concern their rationale. The general purpose of all three regimes is to promote development of new medicines by means of temporary monopoly allowing the originators to recoup their investments. One may, however, distinguish several specific reasons lying behind particular legislative and case law milestones.

First, there are reasons that concern catching up with changes in chemistry and biotechnology. This kind of rationale is visible mostly in patent law. It was reflected primarily in securing patentability of pharmaceutical products as such, addressing the rapid progress in modern chemistry. Later, due to technical limitations in synthesis of new moieties, patentability of first and subsequent medical uses was introduced, with a view to providing protection for results of research among the already known medically active substances. This development was accompanied by new technologies in diagnosis which allowed for distinguishing new illnesses to be cured.[111] Access to advanced genomics, combinatorial chemistry and biology, as well as many other highly advanced techniques, led to progress in biotechnological medicines which was reflected in specific provisions on patentability of biotechnological inventions.[112]

The second type of justification for instruments of legal protection for pharmaceuticals is related to the improvement of market conditions for certain types of medicinal products. In Europe this is the case with orphan

---

[111] There are about 30,000 illnesses differentiated in official worldwide statistics, however the total number of drugs approved by the US FDA is only 1,453. See respectively Christian Thielscher, *Medizinökonomie: Band 2: Unternehmerische Praxis und Methodik* (Springer-Verlag 2012) 9 and Michael Kinch, Austin Haynesworth, Sarah Kinch and Denton Hoyer, 'An Overview of FDA-Approved New Molacular Entities (NMEs): 1823–2013' (2014) 19 Drug Discov Today 8.

[112] Another development here is connected to biologic drugs, which benefit from a special data exclusivity regime only in the US, Canada and Japan. See Andreas Hübel, Thilo Schmelcher and Ulrich Storz, *Biopatent Law: Patent Strategies and Patent Management* (Springer 2012) 33.

drugs and paediatric medicinal products. Orphan drugs were given a special regime of exclusivity to facilitate research on new medicines for treatment of rare diseases. Paediatric indications were provided with extensions for both SPC and orphan exclusivity, or – as regards off-patent paediatric drugs – with data and market exclusivity. Both extensions and exclusivity function as incentives to carry out tests on the paediatric population, which are otherwise underestimated.

The third kind of rationale is providing a better legal environment for development and competitiveness of the European research-based pharmaceutical industry. Such reasons are visible in improvements in rules of patent protection comprising product patents, protection of first and second medical indications and liberal criteria of patentability of the latter.[113] SPCs, intended to compensate for the time lost for delay in authorisation, were introduced as a response to US patent term extensions. Data exclusivity regulations, with their general aim to recoup investments in R&D activities, also followed the relevant American legislation. The significance of data exclusivity for reference drugs is that of supplementing or strengthening the protection resulting from patents and SPC, especially in the case of weak patents that can be circumvented easily or that may be nullified.[114]

And last, another kind of *ratio legis* may be distinguished, namely balancing interests in the pharmaceutical market through legal measures advantageous for generic industry or for the public health. A good example is the abridged procedure of marketing authorisation, with its rationale concerning both ethical aspects and economic reasons focusing on easier access to medicines. Subsequently, the regulatory testing exemption and skinny labelling regulation both prevented patent-based delays in generic entries into market. The concept of global marketing authorisation achieved an analogous goal within the pharmaceutical regulatory framework.

Most changes in the European legal regime were directed to expanding protection for innovative drugs, with the general aim of European industry being a leader in development of new products, i.e. based on new chemical entities. Legal measures directed to support the generic industry are not so significant and were introduced much later than in the US.

The situation may change as the European authorities see the need to

---

[113] Graham Dutfield, 'Healthcare Innovation and Patent Law's "Pharmaceutical Privilege": Is There a Pharmaceutical Privilege? And If So, Should We Remove It?' (2017) 12 Health Econ Policy Law 454.

[114] Paul Garland and Haflidi Kristjan Larusson, 'Data Exclusivity, Bolar Exemptions and Generic Drugs in the EU' (2007) 4 EIPR 128.

strengthen the balance in the pharmaceutical systems in the EU and its member states for economic reasons.[115] Whereas in the beginnings of pharmaceutical and patent legislation generic producers were seen merely as free-riders, nowadays they are considered to play an important role in the market.[116] This approach is even more observable in the health policy of particular countries relating to drug reimbursement, substitution of medicines in pharmacies and off-label use.[117] Another reflection of this tendency may be seen in the use of instruments of compulsory licence for pharmaceuticals for the sake of public health interest.

An open question remains as to whether this entire system of legal protection of pharmaceuticals can be shaped as balanced also in relation to economic and social interests of particular EU member states, bearing in mind differences among them in their stage of development, market size and the prevalence of innovative or generic industry.[118]

---

[115] See Council conclusions on strengthening the balance in the pharmaceutical systems in the European Union and its Member States (2016/C 269/06) with its observations, among many others, on inappropriate market behaviour of some manufacturers, access to medicinal products being endangered and consequences of public investment in development of new medicines.

[116] Papadopoulou (n 26) 908.

[117] See for example art 44(2)–(3) of the Polish Law on reimbursement of medicinal products (OJ [2011] 122/696) providing rules for pharmacy substitution of innovative medicines with cheaper generic ones. See also Zbierska (n 63) 85.

[118] See Susy Frankel and Jessica Lai, *Patent Law and Policy* (LexisNexis NZ 2016) 10.

9. Developing policies that leverage research and innovation to retain socio-economic benefits – the strategic use of intellectual property*

Helen Yu**

I. INTRODUCTION

The EU has identified research and innovation (R&I) as key pillars of its strategy to create sustainable growth and prosperity in Europe.[1] Policies that prioritise R&I as being core to EU and economic development are well demonstrated in the Responsible Research and Innovation policy (RRI)[2] and Research and Innovation Strategies for Smart Specialisation (RIS3).[3] The underlying premise that implicitly drives these policies is that certain local dynamics are conducive, and therefore can be leveraged, to foster innovation, growth and development through collaboration with local stakeholders.[4] However, the assumption that increased innovation

* All online sources were last accessed on 27 December 2018.

** This chapter is supported by the CoNeXT project (http://conext.ku.dk) under the University of Copenhagen's Excellence Program for Interdisciplinary Research. All online sources were last accessed on 29 December 2018.

1 EC, 'Europe 2020 – A Strategy for Smart, Sustainable and Inclusive Growth' COM(2010) 2020 final; EC, 'Research and Innovation – Pushing Boundaries and Improving the Quality of Life' (2014); EC, 'Horizon 2020 – First Results' (2015).

2 EC, 'Responsible Research and Innovation – Europe's Ability to Respond to Societal Challenges' (2012); EC, 'Options for Strengthening Responsible Research and Innovation' (2013).

3 EC, 'Guide to Research and Innovation Strategies for Smart Specialisations' (2012); EC, 'Connecting Smart and Sustainable Growth through Smart Specialisation' (2012).

4 Ugo Fratesi and Lanfranco Senn, 'Regional Growth, Connections and Economic Modelling: An Introduction' in Ugo Fratesi and Lanfranco Senn (eds), *Growth and Innovation of Competitive Regions* (Springer 2009) 3; James Karlsen, Arne Isaksen and Olav R Spilling, 'The Challenge of Constructing Regional Advantages in Peripheral Areas: The Case of Marine Biotechnology

will necessarily lead to *local* economic development and growth remains to be proven.[5] Not all regions have the capacity, resources, infrastructure, or access to enable it to reap the socio-economic benefits arising from the development and commercialisation of locally created innovations. In fact, it is conceivable that local innovation can lead to growth in another region, such as a nearby metropolitan city better suited to develop the social and economic potential of an innovation, and actually harm the region through migration of intellectual capital to follow the development of the innovation.[6]

RIS3 appears to address, or at least mitigate, the urban bias of past innovation policies by focusing on the often neglected regional dimensions of innovation.[7] However, other EU-wide innovation policies (such as RRI) are developed by policy-makers from metropolitan cities where there remains a potential for big-city bias, implemented under the assumption that innovation strategies are universally applicable to metropolitan and non-metropolitan areas when research shows not all regions are alike in their ability to innovate and seize the benefits arising from locally developed innovations.[8] The key question is how the various EU policies can and strategies on innovation and growth leverage local R&I activity to foster regional development. One of the core objectives of RRI and RIS3 is to conduct collaborative research with and for society so that

---

in Tromsø, Norway' (2011) 23(3–4) Entrep Region Dev 235; Antti Pelkonen and Mika Nieminen, 'How Beneficial is a Knowledge-Based Development Strategy for Peripheral Regions? A Case Study' (2016) 24(2) Eur Plan Stud 364.

[5] Richard Shearmur and Nicolas Bonnet, 'Does Local Technological Innovation Lead to Local Development? A Policy Perspective' (2011) 3(3) RSPP 249; Andrew Caragliu and Peter Nijkamp, 'Space and Knowledge Spillovers in European Regions: The Impact of Different Forms of Proximity on Spatial Knowledge Diffusion' (2016) 16(3) J Econ Geogr 749.

[6] Mario Polèse and Richard Shearmur, 'Why Some Regions Will Decline: A Canadian Case Study with Thoughts on Local Development Strategies' (2016) 85(1) Reg Sci 23, regarding the case of ALCAN, an aluminium producer with production facilities in the city of Saguenay in Quebec, Canada.

[7] EC, 'Smart Specialisation and Innovation in Rural Areas' (2014) S3 Policy Brief Series No 09/2014.

[8] Vernon Henderson, 'Urbanization and the Geography of Development' (2014) World Bank Policy Research Working Paper 6877; Jari Kolehmainen, Joe Irvine, Linda Stewart, Zoltan Karacsonyi, Tunde Szabó, Juha Alarinta and Anders Norberg, 'Quadruple Helix, Innovation and the Knowledge-Based Development: Lessons from Remote, Rural and Less-Favoured Regions' (2016) 7(1) J Knowledge Econ 23; Mervi Rajahonka, Toni Pienonen, Riikka Kuusisto and Jari Handelberg, 'Orchestrators of Innovation-Driven Regional Development: Experiences from the INNOFOKUS Project and Change2020 Programme' (2016) 5(10) TIM Review 52; Caragliu and Nijkamp (n 5).

the value of publicly funded research can be maximised and returned to benefit society.[9] However, while RRI and RIS3 encourage innovation through societal engagement, they can give rise to complex issues, making it challenging for regions to capture and retain the socio-economic benefits arising from local R&I activity. If R&I is to function as an efficient driver of growth, it is imperative that policies support the efficient development of academic discoveries into products and technologies that can address societal challenges and achieve socially desirable outcomes. Translation and commercialisation are essential mechanisms to ensure research can be transformed into innovations and introduced into the market for the benefit of society. Stakeholders involved in the innovation process (i.e. industry, researchers, government, etc.) participate and collaborate with others to fulfil their own agenda.[10] Without intellectual property (IP) to safeguard investments in R&I, potential stakeholders may be discouraged from contributing to the translation and commercialisation of discoveries into innovations if there is no incentive to collaborate and share. This chapter contributes to the debate on local socio-economic development by introducing an IP strategy aimed at attracting and retaining investment and intellectual capital to regions that have a higher education institution and/or research infrastructure. As this chapter will show, because local innovation does not necessarily lead to local development, indiscriminate application of innovation and development initiatives such as RRI and RIS3 may not necessarily lead to the desired results.

II. REGIONAL DEVELOPMENT AND INNOVATION POLICIES

Key international organisations, including the World Economic Forum, the International Monetary Fund, the World Bank and the Organisation for Economic Co-operation and Development, have all urged governments to create a climate that promotes innovation, supports investment and stimulates competitiveness.[11] Similarly, the

---

9 See (n 2) and (n 3).

10 Helen Yu, 'Redefining Responsible Research and Innovation for the Advancement of Biobanking and Biomedical Research' (2016) 3(3) Oxford JLB 611.

11 Klaus Schwab (ed), 'The Global Competitiveness Report 2016–2017' (2016) World Economic Forum; Stefanie Fabrizio et al, 'From Ambition to Execution: Policies in Support of Sustainable Development Goals' (2015) International Monetary Fund SDN/15/18; World Bank, 'Global Economic Prospects: A Fragile

European Commission (the 'Commission') has explicitly stated that Europe 'needs to ensure that the conditions necessary for the competitiveness of the Community's enterprises exist, including facilitating adjustment to structural changes, encouraging a favourable environment for entrepreneurship and SMEs, encouraging an environment favourable to enterprise cooperation, and fostering better exploitation of the innovative potential of enterprises'.[12]

But what is 'regional competitiveness' and can the concept of 'competitiveness' of regions be understood in the same way as it is applied in the business context? Regions can enhance and improve their local appeal, assets and advantages (i.e. housing, infrastructure, standard of living, communications, networks) to attract investment and businesses to the region. However, regions are not usually direct economic actors like businesses with independent control over their activities to compete, grow and be profitable in the market.[13] Regional actors include public sector institutions as well as industry, making economic success of businesses in the region only one of several objectives of regional development agendas. In other words, regional competitiveness is about creating a sustainable environment conducive to achieving regional socio-economic prosperity where all regional actors (public and private) play a role in contributing to local growth and development.

Some regions are more innovative than others because of certain local characteristics.[14] The focus on such endogenous development suggests that regions need to and can build up the capacity to develop from within by leveraging their local resources and competencies to facilitate regional

---

Recovery' (2017) World Bank Group Flagship Report; OECD, *Promoting Growth in All Regions* (OECD Publishing 2012); OECD, *Regional Outlook: Productive Regions for Inclusive Societies* (OECD Publishing 2016).

[12] EC, 'Better Regulations for Innovation-Driven Investment at EU level' (2016) Commission Staff Working Document.

[13] Edward J Malecki, 'Jockeying for Position: What It Means and Why It Matters to Regional Development Policy When Places Compete' (2004) 38(9) Regional Studies 1102; Evan Cleavea, Godwin Arku, Richard Sadler and Jason Gillilanda, 'The Role of Place Branding in Local and Regional Economic Development: Bridging the Gap between Policy and Practicality' (2016) 3(1) RSRS 207; Ann Markusen, 'Sticky Places in Slippery Space: a Typology of Industrial Districts' (1996) 72 Econ Geogr 293; Mercado Delgado, Michael E Porter and Scott Stern, 'Clusters, Convergence, and Economic Performance' (2014) 43(10) Research Policy 1785.

[14] Philip Cooke, Martin Heidenreich and Hans-Joachim Braczyk (eds), *Regional Systems of Innovation: The Role of Governance in a Globalized World* (Routledge 2004).

development through internal processes.[15] However, endogenous growth requires that regional actors align their respective interests and share a common sense of enterprise and desire to create local mechanisms to drive regional success.[16] In other words, endogenous drivers of regional development depend on both the regional actors and the wider social, economic and institutional interaction between the regional actors to shape and create attributes that make a region competitive. As such, reports and analyses on best practices drawn from case studies of successful regions may have limited applicability to other regions if the unique dynamics of the successful region do not exist in other regions or are difficult or impossible to reproduce due to cultural, political or jurisdictional reasons. The pursuit of a 'one size fits all' approach to regional development may prove to be rather impracticable, especially given the accepted premise that drivers of regional competitiveness are endogenous and unique to the region.[17] However, a set of policy tools directed at improving a region's competitive advantage and quality as a location to discover, develop and commercialise innovations may be more successful at facilitating local development. More concretely, policies that focus on the effective use of knowledge derived from a region's innovation capacity through beneficial relationships with the public and private sector may be better able to achieve the objective of fostering local socio-economic development.

The quadruple helix model of innovation places a greater focus on the interests of the public and encourages direct involvement of society in the innovation process in order to support and pursue initiatives that aim to improve socio-economic conditions to the benefit of the public, whether such initiatives are technological, social, commercial or non-commercial

---

15 Robert E Lucas, 'On the Mechanics of Economic Development' (1998) 22(1) JME 3.

16 Andres Rodríguez-Pose, 'Do Institutions Matter for Regional Development?' (2013) 47(7) Regional Studies 1034; Ronald L Martin, 'A Study on the Factors of Regional Competitiveness: A Draft Final Report for the European Commission Directorate-General Regional Policy' (2003); Cecilia Pasquinelli, 'Competition, Cooperation and Co-Opetition: Unfolding the Process of Inter-Territorial Branding' (2013) 6(1) Urban Res Pract 1.

17 Peter Maskell and Anders Malmberg, 'Localised Learning and Industrial Competitiveness' (1999) 23 Cambridge J Econ 167; Michael Stuetzer, Martin Obschonka, Udo Brixy, Rolf Sternberg and Uwe Cantner, 'Regional Characteristics, Opportunity Perception and Entrepreneurial Activities' (2014) 42(2) SBE 221; Harald Bathelt and Patrick Cohendet, 'The Creation of Knowledge: Local Building, Global Accessing and Economic Development – Toward an Agenda' (2014) 14(5) Econ Geogr 869.

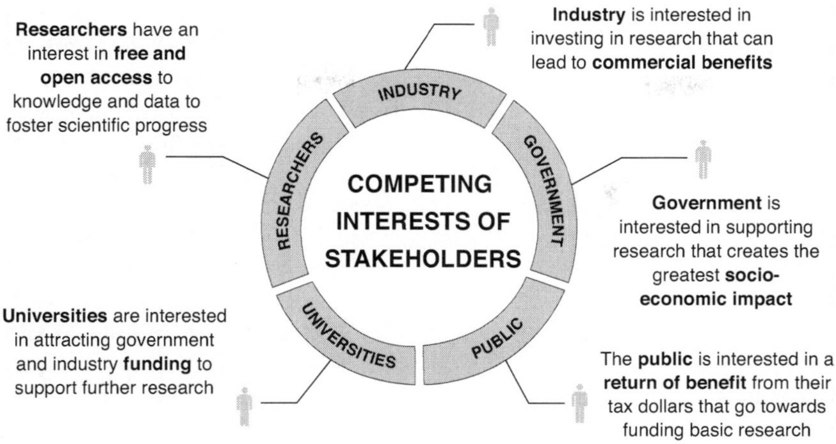

Figure 9.1 Interconnected stakeholder interests

in nature.[18] However, translation and commercialisation may result in tension, for example between the interests of industry and those of researchers, because collaborations incentivised by commercial interests may have the effect of compromising research integrity.[19] Although the advancement of scientific research involves the participation of a number of stakeholders, each with different interests and motivations, the parties share at least one common desired outcome: the discovery of new innovations for the betterment of society. The Commission refers to outcomes that benefit the public good as the ultimate objective of responsible R&I practices.[20] To realise the public benefit objective, innovation policies must therefore consider the interests of *all* stakeholders involved in the translation and commercialisation of knowledge (see Figure 9.1). In order for a region to benefit from innovation, not only is it necessary for it to

---

[18] See (n 3).

[19] Justin E Bekelman, Yan Li and Cary P Gross, 'Scope and Impact of Financial Conflicts of Interest in Biomedical Research: a Systematic Review' (2003) 289(4) JAMA 454; Joel Lexchin, Lisa A Bero, Benjamin Djulbegovic and Otavia Clark, 'Pharmaceutical Industry Sponsorship and Research Outcome and Quality: Systematic Review' (2003) 326 BMJ 1167; Mohit Mhandari, Jason W Busse, Dianne Jackowski, Victor M Montori, Holger Schünemann, Sheila Sprague, Derek Mears, Emil H Schemitsch, Dianne Heels-Ansdell and PJ Devereaux, 'Association Between Industry Funding and Statistically Significant Pro-Industry Findings in Medical and Surgical Randomized Trials' (2004) 170(4) CMAJ 477.

[20] See (n 2).

possess innovation inputs, the region must also have the appropriate absorptive capacities and internal resources that enable collaborations to turn into innovations.

On the one hand, Europe's 2020 strategy calls for 'smart growth' by developing the economy based on knowledge and innovation and 'inclusive growth' by fostering a high employment economy.[21] On the other hand, RRI policy mandates open access and open science to improve knowledge circulation at the expense of IP rights.[22] Then there is RIS3, which advocates for regions to develop from within by leveraging their local resources and competencies. However, in order for a region to benefit from local innovations, there needs to be 'something' to ground the development and commercialisation of the innovations locally, or at least a tool that enables the benefits to flow back to the region that originally invested the resources to discover and research the potential of the innovation.

Philosophers, social scientists, and policy-makers have recommended interdisciplinary research 'to attune research and innovation processes to societal needs'.[23] Empirical studies show how interdisciplinary research can address societal and ethical aspects at the R&D stage,[24] contributing to an increased reflexivity among scientists. In the context of fostering local socio-economic development, an interdisciplinary approach to understanding innovation, productivity and competitiveness would be helpful to shape policy related to building critical mass to facilitate cluster formation. Clusters have been defined as 'geographical concentrations of interconnected companies, specialized suppliers, service providers, firms in related industries, and associated institutions (e.g. universities, standards agencies and trade associations) that compete but also co-operate'.[25] Cluster policy aims to encourage regional innovation, cross-pollination of ideas, and knowledge spillovers by supporting the agglomeration of regional actors through collective and collaborative efforts to achieve

---

[21] See (n 1).

[22] See (n 2).

[23] Daan Schuurbiers, Neelke Doorn, Ibo Van de Poel and Michael E Gorman, 'Mandates and Methods for Early Engagement' in Neelke Doorn, Daan Schuurbiers, Ibo van de Poel and Michael E Gorman (eds), *Early Engagement and New Technologies: Opening Up the Laboratory* (Springer 2014) 3–15.

[24] Steven Flipse, Joric Oude Vrielink and Maarten van der Sanden, 'Building Interactive Communication Tools to Support Interdisciplinary Responsible Innovation' (2016) 3(4) JIM 119; Sjoerd D Zwart, Ibo van de Poel, Harald van Mil and Michael Brumsen, 'A Network Approach for Distinguishing Ethical Issues in Research and Development' (2006) 12(4) Sci Eng Ethics 663.

[25] Michael E Porter, *On Competition* (Harvard Business School Press 1998) 197.

greater regional prosperity.[26] Public research organisations and research infrastructures now play an increasing role in attracting intellectual capital and organisations as contributors to the local economy.[27] Policies that link research and business to facilitate cluster formation therefore require an attractive business environment that supports an innovation-oriented culture and makes a place 'sticky' to embed the innovation, intellectual capital, and investment to the region.[28] As will be explained in greater detail, IP may be used as a tool to create 'stickiness'.

III. LOCAL INNOVATION ≠ LOCAL DEVELOPMENT

The primary objective of regional development policies is to facilitate and enable innovation, which presumes that productivity will increase and therefore lead to local economic growth, improved standards of living, job creation, and other associated socio-economic benefits. Regional policies are increasingly being implemented on the assumption that local innovation leads to local development.[29] While there are examples of successful regions arising from local innovation,[30] these may be examples of well-located regions benefiting from external linkages that their location provides.[31] The causal mechanism is not necessarily one connected with locality such as in non-metropolitan regions where there is less accessibility[32]

---

26 Emily Wise, James Wilson and Madeline Smith, 'In Search of Indicators to Support the "Perfect Cluster": Where Evaluation Theory Collides with Policy Practice' (2016) OECD Blue Sky Forum on Science and Innovation Indicators.

27 Andrew Johnston and Robert Huggins, 'Drivers of University–Industry Links: The Case of Knowledge-Intensive Business Service Firms in Rural Locations' (2016) 50(8) Regional Studies 1330.

28 Markusen (n 13).

29 Claudia Werker, 'An Assessment of the Regional Innovation Policy by the European Union Based on Bibliometrical Analysis' (2006) Max Planck Institute of Economics, Evolutionary Economics Group.

30 Fratesi and Senn (n 4); Giuseppe Folloni, 'A Model of Local Development' in Ugo Fratesi and Lanfranco Senn (eds), *Growth and Innovation of Competitive Regions* (Springer 2009) 45.

31 Richard Shearmur, 'Not Being There: Why Local Innovation is Not (Always) Related to Local Factors' in Knut Ingar Westeren (ed), *Foundations of the Knowledge Economy* (Edward Elgar Publishing 2012) 117.

32 Gilles Duranton and Diego Puga, 'Nursery Cities: Urban Diversity, Process Innovation, and the Life-Cycle of Products' (2003) 91(5) Am Econ Rev 1454.

and urban agglomeration.[33] The assumption of a link between localities and innovation suggests that regions possess certain assets and that drawing on these assets by local stakeholders will generate innovation, growth and regional competitiveness. There are surveys that attempt to understand how firms draw upon their environment to innovate[34] in order to develop policies to increase levels of innovation. However, these surveys do not help understand the conditions under which local innovation leads to local development. Causality is assumed and policies based on this assumption will not ensure that economic activity and employment opportunities remain in the region.[35] Local characteristics such as clusters, research institutions, and active industry are only a part of the innovation landscape. Other geo-structural factors such as density, accessibility to major markets and human capital, agglomeration, location relative to other regions, and availability of infrastructure all have a strong effect on local growth, irrespective of local particularities.[36] A region may take advantage of its local opportunities and dynamics, leading to innovation and socio-economic growth, but such development may in large part be because of the region's proximity to a metropolitan area, allowing it to borrow or access non-local resources from its larger neighbour. Thus, local dynamics alone do not necessarily lead to local growth and innovation.[37] Innovation can lead to job loss through relocation in order to gain better access to resources and infrastructure in order to support growth resulting from successful development of innovations. Employment and job creation is one of the primary concerns of local communities.[38] In other words, regional innovation policies do not necessarily lead to local economic benefit and may even lead to economic decline if spin-off companies and

---

33 Philip McCann, 'Sketching Out a Model of Innovation, Face-To-Face Interaction and Economic Geography' (2007) 2(2) Spatial Econ Analysis 114.

34 OECD, 'Community Innovation Statistics: From Today's Community Innovation Surveys to Better Surveys Tomorrow' (2006).

35 See (n 5).

36 Richard Shearmur and Mario Polese, 'Do Local Factors Explain Local Employment Growth? Evidence from Canada 1971–2001' (2007) 45(4) Regional Studies 453; Masahisa Fujita and Tomoya Mori, 'Frontiers of the New Economic Geography' (2005) 84(3) Pap Reg Sci 377; Shearmur (n 31).

37 Harald Bathelt, Anders Malmberg and Peter Maskell, 'Clusters and Knowledge: Local Buzz, Global Pipelines and the Process of Knowledge Creation' (2004) 28(1) Prog Hum Geogr 31; Ron Boschma, 'Proximity And Innovation: A Critical Assessment' (2005) 39(1) Regional Studies 61; Andre Torre, 'On the Role Played by Temporary Geographical Proximity in Knowledge Transmission' (2008) 42(6) Regional Studies 869; McCann (n 33) 114–134; Duranton and Puga (n 32).

38 Ron Martin and Peter Tyler, 'Regional Employment Evolutions in the European Union: A Preliminary Analysis' (2000) 34(7) Regional Studies 601.

intellectual capital follow the development of the innovation and move out of the region. As such, regional policies focusing primarily on innovation itself may not capture the long-term economic benefits of successfully developing local innovations. There needs to be an equal emphasis on mechanisms to internalise economic processes in order to keep development local. As stated in the literature: 'Regional innovation policies . . . must not be confused with regional development policies: a regional innovation policy will encourage local firms to establish new routines and spinoffs. A regional development policy will focus on ensuring that these new routines and spinoffs are captured locally.'[39]

IV. REGIONAL UNIVERSITIES AND RESEARCH INFRASTRUCTURES AS 'ANCHOR TENANTS'

The literature suggests that local innovation can only lead to local development if the innovation is sufficiently locally embedded.[40] In other words, the local environment contributes to and strongly influences both the innovation process and the extent to which regions can reap the benefits from local innovation. Given that it has become increasingly accepted that regions must rely on their own institutions, resources and capital to achieve sustainable socio-economic growth and become competitive,[41] regional development policies should focus on identifying local competencies to create strategies that leverage and develop such local capacities.[42] For example, universities and research institutions are bedrock institutions that can attract and develop intellectual capital to be introduced into the local workforce and highly skilled workers.

Traditionally, an anchor tenant is used to describe a large retail store with a dedicated client base, which assures a certain amount of traffic to where the retail store is located. Taking advantage of this client base, the co-location of other shops near the anchor tenant has a greater likelihood

---

39 See (n 5).

40 Fratesi and Senn (n 4).

41 Michael Storper and Richard Walker, *The Capitalist Imperative: Territory, Technology and Industrial Growth* (Wiley 2009); Trevor Barnes, Jamie Peck, Eric Sheppard and Adam Tickell, 'Methods Matter: Transformations in Economic Geography' in Adam Tickell, Eric Sheppard, Jamie Peck And Trevor Barnes (eds), *Politics And Practice in Economic Geography* (SAGE 2007) 1.

42 C R Bryant, 'Urban and Rural Interactions and Rural Community Renewal' in Ian Bowler, C R Bryant and C Cocklin (eds), *The Sustainability of Rural Systems* (Springer 2002) 247.

of indirectly increasing the business of these co-located stores. Applied to the context of innovation and regional development, universities and public research infrastructures, as anchor tenants, attract researchers to conduct basic research. However, because they do not develop and commercialise research, innovative firms have an opportunity to take advantage of the science and research being conducted in order to improve their prospects of commercial success by establishing themselves in the region. Research institutions have a role to play in building 'knowledge economies' beyond knowledge creation and technology transfer activities by contributing to entrepreneurship through university–industry interactions.[43] The anchor tenant theory has been used to explore the relationship between regional innovation and the co-location of university research as a source of knowledge spillover that can lead to the development of new innovations.[44] However, the theory has not been applied to examine universities or research infrastructures as anchor tenants to *attract businesses to the region as consumers of university research*. As discussed in the previous section, because local innovation does not necessarily lead to local development, the question is whether universities and/or research infrastructures can anchor an innovation and sufficiently locally embed it to facilitate and encourage local development. In other words, can geographic concentration of research activity be used as a foundation to build critical mass for cluster formation and encourage and attract industrial R&D to the region? If yes, by applying RIS3 policies, regional universities and research infrastructures can build upon existing regional characteristics and competencies and foster research activities in these areas to attract investment and intellectual capital to the region, which can then be converted into socio-economic benefit to the region.

The literature has long recognised the advantages for innovative firms to be geographically located near leading universities and public research organisations[45] and that the presence of innovative firms in a region is an

---

43 OECD, *Higher Education in Regions: Globally Competitive, Locally Engaged* (OECD Publishing 2007); Qiantao Zhang, Niall G Mackenzie, Dylan Jones-Evans and Robert Huggins, 'Leveraging Knowledge as a Competitive Asset? The Intensity, Performance and Structure of Universities' Entrepreneurial Knowledge Exchange Activities at a Regional Level' (2016) 47(3) Small Bus Econ 657; Radzivon Marozau, Maribel Guerrero and David Urbano, 'Impacts of Universities in Different Stages of Economic Development' (2016) J Knowledge Econ 1.

44 Ajay Agrawal and Iain M Cockburn, 'The Anchor Tenant Hypothesis: Exploring the Role of Large, Local, R&D-Intensive Firms in Regional Innovation Systems' (2003) 21 IJIO 1227.

45 Bart Clarysse, Mike Wright, Johan Bruneel and Aarti Mahajan, 'Creating

attractor for university R&D.[46] However, there is significant variation across regions and countries in the local capacity to convert upstream research into downstream innovation and local commercial activity.[47] In other words, the flow of knowledge from universities and research infrastructures does not necessarily lead to local development and the development of a business ecosystem to support commercial activity is not an automatic consequence of setting up innovative firms around universities and research infrastructures. However, if the focus changes to viewing universities and research infrastructures as anchor tenants to attract intellectual capital and innovative firms, by applying RIS3 principles to research and innovate around regional competencies or characteristics, the resulting innovations become further embedded in the region, making the region well known for particular fields of R&I. Supporting services and resources will have greater confidence in co-locating and contribute to developing a business ecosystem to support the innovative firms if the region is known to have core R&I competencies or strengths in a particular field.

There are several models for how university–industry engagement might impact regional innovation: the knowledge factory; the relational university; the entrepreneurial university; the systemic university; and the engaged university.[48] The most discussed aspect of university engagement has been encouraging greater and more effective transfer and application of knowledge between universities and the business sector.[49]

Value in Ecosystems: Crossing the Chasm between Knowledge and Business Ecosystems' (2014) ERC Research Paper No 22, 1–45.

46 Charlie Karlsson and Martin Andersson, 'The Location of Industry R&D and the Location of University R&D: How are they related?' in Charlie Karlsson, Ake E Andersson, Paul C Cheshire and Roger R Stough (eds), *New Directions in Regional Economic Development: Advances in Spatial Science* (Springer 2009) 267.

47 See Agrawal and Cockburn (n 44).

48 Elvira Uyarra, 'Conceptualizing the Regional Roles of Universities: Implications and Contradictions' (2010) 18(8) Eur Plan Stud 1227.

49 Philip McCann and Raquel Ortega-Argilés, 'Smart Specialization, Regional Growth and Applications to European Union Cohesion Policy' (2015) 49(8) Regional Studies 1291; Markus Perkmann, Riccardo Fini, Jan-Michael Ross, Ammon Salter, Cleo Silvestri and Valentina Tartari, 'Accounting For Universities' Impact: Using Augmented Data to Measure Academic Engagement and Commercialization by Academic Scientists' (2015) 24(4) Research Evaluation 380; Michaela Trippl, Tanja Sinozic and Helen Lawton Smith, 'The Role of Universities in Regional Development: Conceptual Models and Policy Institutions in the UK, Sweden and Austria' (2015) 23(9) Eur Plan Stud 1722; James K Woodell, 'The Fountain of Knowledge: The Role of Universities in Economic Development' (2016) 20(3) J High Educ Outreach Engagem 196.

Commercialisation of university research, commonly understood and defined as 'efforts to sell the work of universities for a profit'[50] emphasises the economic impact of university research at the expense of the social value of returning the benefit of publicly funded research to society.[51] Empirical studies have found evidence of considerable impact of university activities on regional economic development, including fostering regional competitiveness through policies that leverage the competitive position and advantage of a region.[52] In other words, universities and research infrastructures have key roles to play in the development and articulation of regional strategies, including: participating with regional stakeholders in the 'entrepreneurial discovery process' through knowledge generation and active engagement in innovation and governance; defining strategic regional smart specialisation priorities that match the scientific research strengths of the region; and providing connections and access to external sources of knowledge through academic networks.[53] Understanding this active, strategic role for universities and research infrastructures in shaping local socio-economic development strongly suggests that innovation policies focused on advancing the transfer of science, technology and innovation alone is not enough to bring about societal change and growth but requires the social sciences (i.e. law, economics, public policy) to support collaboration and engagement of regional actors.

Case studies have examined successful endogenous growth in different regions. For example, in the Basque Country, academic institutions as agents for proactively shaping regional socio-economic development have recently been explored.[54] Located on the north coast of Spain, the Basque

---

50 Derek Bok, *Universities in the Marketplace: The Commercialisation of Higher Education* (Princeton University Press 2003).

51 Sascha Friesike, Bastian Widenmayer, Oliver Gassman and Thomas Schildhauer, 'Opening Science: Towards an Agenda of Open Science in Academia and Industry' (2015) 40(4) J Technol Transfer 581; Helen Yu, 'Bridging the Translational Gap: Collaborative Drug Development and Dispelling the Stigma of Commercialization' (2016) 21(2) Drug Discovery Today 299.

52 Joshua Drucker and Harvey Goldstein, 'Assessing the Regional Economic Development Impacts of Universities: A Review of Current Approaches' (2007) 30(1) Int Reg Sci Rev 20; Dominique Foray, 'The Economic Fundamentals of Smart Specialisation' (2013) 83(2) Ekonomiaz 55; Jesus Valdaliso and James Wilson, *Strategies For Shaping Territorial Competitiveness* (Routledge 2015).

53 John Goddard, Louise Kempton and Paul Vallance, 'Universities and Smart Specialisation: Challenges, Tensions and Opportunities for the Innovation Strategies of European Regions' (2013) 83(2) Ekonomiaz 83.

54 Mari Jose Aranguren, Jose Maria Guibert, Jesus M Valdaliso and James R Wilson, 'Academic Institutions as Change Agents for Territorial Development' (2016) 30(1) Indust Higher Ed 27; James Karlsen, Miren Larrea, James R Wilson

Country is a region recognised for its successful economic transformation from an industrial region to an innovative and competitive region through adopting a technology and cluster policy focused on the region's advantages and competitive position.[55] One of the academic institutions that has played a key role in facilitating the transfer of academic knowledge and research to society is Orkestra – Basque Institute of Competitiveness (Orkestra).[56] Created as one of three University Development Units of the Deusto Foundation, Orkestra is integrated into the San Sebastian campus of Deusto University and has been instrumental in providing qualitative and quantitative evidence to the region on strategies for the co-generation and development of knowledge through engagement with regional stakeholders to generate local socio-economic benefits.[57] As an advisory organisation, Orkestra aligns policy strategies and provides empirical evidence on the benefits of regional academic engagement with the explicit objective of influencing regional socio-economic development. Through a shared vision of making a region competitive and successful, institutions like Orkestra can drive regional actors to participate in regional networks of innovation and governance and provide a bridge for external sources of knowledge through international connections and networks.

An example of where socio-economic growth has developed exogenously is Sofia Antipolis. Founded in 1969 and developed in a vacant space absent any knowledge base or factors typically associated with the successful creation of an innovation ecosystem, Sophia Antipolis was built based on the concept of cross-fertilisation and the idea that 'if you build it, they will come'.[58] Cross-fertilisation and collective learning relates to

---

and Mari Jose Aranguren, 'Bridging the Gap between Academic Research and Regional Development in the Basque Country' (2012) 47(1) Eur J Ed 122.

[55] Ibid; OECD, *OECD Reviews of Regional Innovation: Basque Country, Spain* (OECD Publishing 2011); Mari Jose Aranguren, James Karlsen, Miren Larrea and James R Wilson, 'The Development of Action Research Processes and Their Impacts on Socio-Economic Development in the Basque Country' in Roger Sudgen, Marcela Valania and James R Wilson (eds), *Leadership and Cooperation in Academia: Reflecting on the Roles and Responsibilities of University Faculty and Management* (Edward Elgar Publishing 2013); Michael E Porter, Christian Ketels and Jesus M Valdaliso, 'The Basque Country: Strategy for Economic Development' (2013) Harvard Business School Case 713-474.

[56] See Orkestra <http:www.orkestra.deusto.es>.

[57] Orkestra – Basque Institute of Competitiveness, 'The Basque Country Competitiveness Report 2015: Productive Transformation in Practice' (2015) Deusto University Press.

[58] Christian Longhi, 'Networks, Collective Learning and Technology Development in Innovative High-Tech Regions: The Case of Sophia-Antipolis' (1999) 33(4) Regional Studies 333.

the process whereby innovative behaviour is facilitated by members of a productive network through shared and accumulated knowledge.[59] This typically requires relationships between various economic actors, both private and public, within a geographic area, to establish an environment that is mutually reinforcing to foster innovation and development.[60] Funded by private and public resources, including key industry players, a technology park was developed with priority given to innovative and high-technology enterprises to create a culture that facilitates collective learning and cross-fertilisation.[61] Driven by private sector vision and supported by political will, Sophia Antipolis became a technology hub within 20 years with the accumulation of innovative firms to grow endogenously and create local competencies. Despite the high level of innovative activity in the technology park, it initially lacked local absorptive capacity of the resulting technology and highly skilled workers to support the local development of innovation, so firms had to rely on external relations and even consider relocation.[62] During the period 1987–1991, close to 60 firms left the region, causing the loss of over 650 jobs, indicating that the region lacked the ability or certain synergies to embed these particular firms.[63] The opening of the University of Nice, Sophia Antipolis campus, in 1986 enabled the region to train qualified workers, create a labour market and encourage spin-off development. The positive economic outcome arising from the Sophia Antipolis innovation ecosystem therefore depended on the accumulation of local specific advantages favouring the creation and absorption of new innovations.[64] There is emerging evidence that science and technology parks alone are insufficient to drive an innovation strategy and that local regional dynamics are also an important element to provide

---

[59] Clive Lawson and Edward Lorenz, 'Collective Learning, Tacit Knowledge and Regional Innovative Capacity' (1999) 33(4) Regional Studies 305; Elvira Uyarra, 'What is Evolutionary about "Regional Systems of Innovation"? Implications for Regional Policy' (2010) 20(1) J Evol Econ 115; Catherine L Wang and Harveeb Chugh, 'Entrepreneurial Learning: Past Research and Future Challenges' (2014) 16(1) Int J Manag 24.

[60] Lawson and Lorenz (n 59).

[61] Michael Storper, 'Regional "Worlds" of Production: Learning and Innovation in the Technology Districts of France, Italy and the USA' (1993) 27(5) Regional Studies 433; Roberta Capello, 'Collective Learning and the Spatial Transfer of Knowledge: Innovation Processes in Italian High-Tech Milieux' in David Keeble and Clive Lawson (eds), *Collective Learning Processes and Knowledge Development in the Evolution of Regional Clusters of High-Technology SMEs in Europe* (ESRC Centre For Business Research, University of Cambridge 1998) 19.

[62] Longhi (n 58).

[63] Ibid.

[64] Ibid.

strategic innovation support and develop local synergies for creative innovation.[65] Whether regional development is endogenous or exogenous, the examples of Sofia Antipolis and the Basque Country identified a common factor to successful regional growth: locally embedding innovations so that development remains in and to the benefit of the region.[66]

V. INNOVATION MANAGEMENT: STRATEGIC USE OF INTELLECTUAL PROPERTY

The relationship between economic development, IP protection and innovation reveals great inconsistency.[67] Early literature on the optimal level of IP protection and level of innovation revealed an inverted U-curve, demonstrating the trade-off between the positive, such as the ability to appropriate R&D investment-based profits and incentivise further innovation, and the negative, such as reduced competition and higher transaction costs.[68] Industry has long recognised IP, particularly patents, as both legally and strategically important.[69] For example, patents can

---

65 Cooke, Heidenreich and Braczyk (n 14).

66 Ibid; Aranguren et al (n 54); Martin and Tyler (n 38). See also Longhi (n 58).

67 Walter G Park and Juan Carlos Ginarte, 'Intellectual Property Rights and Economic Growth' (1997) 15(3) Contemp Econ Policy 51; Rod Falvey, Neil Foster and David Greenaway, 'Intellectual Property Rights and Economic Growth' (2006) 10(4) Rev Dec Econ 700; Yee Kyoung Kim, Keun Lee, Walter G Park and Kineung Choo, 'Appropriate Intellectual Property Protection and Economic Growth in Countries at Different Levels of Development' (2012) 41(2) Research Policy 358; Kausik Gangopadhyay and Debasis Mondal, 'Does Stronger Protection of Intellectual Property Stimulate Innovation?' (2012) 116(1) Economic Letters 80; Claude Henry and Joseph E Stiglitz, 'Intellectual Property, Dissemination of Innovation and Sustainable Development' (2010) 1(3) Global Policy 237; Ellen Enkel, Oliver Gassmann and Henry Chesbrough, 'Open R&D and Open Innovation: Exploring the Phenomenon' (2009) 39(4) R&D Management 311; Bronwyn H Hall, 'Does Patent Protection Help or Hinder Technology Transfer' in Sanghoon Ahn, Bronwyn H Hall and J Lee (eds) *Intellectual Property for Economic Development* (Edward Elgar Publishing 2014) 11–32.

68 Yuichi Furukawa, 'Intellectual Property Protection and Innovation: An Inverted-U Relationship' (2010) 109(2) Economic Letters 99; Ryo Horii and Tatsuro Iwaisako, 'Economic Growth with Imperfect Protection of Intellectual Property Rights' (2007) 90(1) Journal of Economics 45.

69 Wesley M Cohen, Richard R Nelson and John P Walsh, 'Protecting their Intellectual Assets: Appropriability Conditions and Why US Manufacturing Firms Patent (or Not)' (2000) National Bureau Of Economic Research Working Paper No 7552; Anne Kelley, 'Practicing in the Patent Marketplace' (2011) 78(1) Univ

be used as bargaining chips,[70] as a management tool in negotiations with strategic or financial partners,[71] and to generate revenue through licensing[72] or from sales.[73] There is extensive literature on the reasons why companies patent and acquire patents,[74] but there is only limited literature on the strategic use of patents by non-corporate owners.

A patent portfolio is a collection of patents, typically owned by a corporate entity. Regardless of motive and use, patent portfolios can be used strategically to manage the economic and technological value of innovations.[75] Complex innovations usually require access to essential patents owned by third parties to secure market access and patents therefore become a form of currency to negotiate the exchange of complementary technologies through cross-licensing between firms.[76] As such, patent portfolios can be leveraged externally in the technology market by granting access to otherwise protected technologies so that a third party can realise

---

Chic Law Rev 115; M Smith and F Hansen, 'Managing Intellectual Property: A Strategic Point of View' (2002) 3(4) J Intell Capital 366.

70 Nicolas Van Zeebroeck and Bruno Van Pottelsberghe, 'Filing Strategies and Patent Value' (2011) 20(6) EINT 539.

71 Wesley M Cohen, Akira Goto, Akiya Nagata, Richard Nelson and John P Walsh, 'R&D Spillovers, Patents and the Incentives to Innovate in Japan and the United States' (2002) 31(8) Research Policy 1349.

72 Robert H Pitkethly, 'Intellectual Property Strategy in Japanese and UK Companies: Patent Licensing Decisions and Learning Opportunities' (2001) 30(3) Research Policy 425.

73 Kevin Rivette and David Kline, *Rembrandts in the Attic: Unlocking the Hidden Value of Patents* (Harvard Business Press 2000).

74 Georg Von Graevenitz, Bronwyn H Hall, Dietmar Harhoff, Stefan Wagner, Alfonso Gambardella, Paola Giuri and Karin Hoisl, 'The Strategic Use of Patents and Its Implications for Enterprise and Competition Policies' (2007) Report For The European Commission; Knut Blind, Jakob Edler, Rainer Frietsch and Ulrich Schmoch, 'Motives to Patent: Empirical Evidence from Germany' (2006) 35(5) Research Policy 655; Ahn, Hall and Lee (n 67).

75 Michele Grimaldi, Livio Cricelli, Martina Di Giovanni and Francesco Rogo, 'The Patent Portfolio Value Analysis: A New Framework to Leverage Patent Information for Strategic Technology Planning' (2015) 94 Technol Forecast Soc Change 286; Ulrich Lichtenthaler, 'Leveraging Technology Assets in the Presence of Markets for Knowledge' (2008) 26(2) EMJ 122.

76 Paolo Giuri et al, 'Inventors and Invention Processes in Europe: Results from the Patval-EU Survey' (2007) 36(8) Research Policy 1107; William W Fisher and Felix Oberholzer-Gee, 'Strategic Management of Intellectual Property' (2013) 55(4) Calif Manag Rev 157; Christoph Grimpe and Katrin Hussinger, 'Resource Complementarity and Value Capture in Firm Acquisitions: The Role of Intellectual Property Rights' (2014) 35(12) SMJ 1762; Markus Reitzig, 'The Private Values of "Thickets" and "Fences": Towards an Updated Picture of the Use of Patents Across Industries' (2004) 13(5) Econ Innovat New Tech 457.

the value of the invention. For example, instead of abandoning unused patents or patents that have application in innovations outside the core competency of the owner, they can be leveraged and used as a bargaining chip to generate financial and non-financial value by finding application in other useful innovations.[77] Licensing is recognised as one of the most significant methods of technology transfer as it facilitates dissemination and exploitation of discoveries and establishes a foundation for synergistic collaboration between parties to create mutually beneficial results.[78]

Firms can also benefit from external innovation and R&D activities of universities derived from publicly funded research, for example to reduce R&D costs and fill the development pipeline.[79] There are also examples of firms referred to as non-practising entities that acquire patents but do not produce goods or services based on the acquired patent.[80] Within the category of non-practising entities, there are technology market intermediaries or brokers, referred to as patent aggregating companies, that help innovative firms leverage their patent portfolio by matching their supply of

---

[77] David Kline, 'Sharing the Corporate Crown Jewels' (2003) 44(3) MIT Sloan Management Review 89.

[78] EC, 'Innovation: How to Convert Research into a Commercial Success Story – Part 3: Innovation Management for Practitioners' (2013); Henry Chesbrough, 'From Open Science to Open Innovation' (2015) ESADE Institute for Innovation and Knowledge Management (ESADE); Knowledge Transfer Working Group of the European Research Area Committee, 'European Research Area Guidelines on Intellectual Property (IP) Management in International Research Collaboration Agreements between European and Non-European Partners' (2012). See (n 2).

[79] Donald S Siegel, David Waldman, Leanne E Atwater and Albert Link, 'Commercial Knowledge Transfers from Universities to Firms: Improving the Effectiveness of University–Industry Collaboration' (2003) 14(1) J High Tech Manag Res 111; Helen Yu, *Achieving Proof of Concept in Drug Discovery and Development: The Role of Competition Law in Collaborations between Public Research Organizations and Industry* (Edward Elgar 2016); Markus Perkmann, Valentina Tartari, Maureen McKelvey, Erkko Autio, Anders Broströmix, Pablo D'Este, Riccardo Fini, Aldo Geuna, Rosa Grimaldi, Alan Hughes, Stefan Krabel, Michael Kitson, Patrick Llerena, Franceso Lissoni, Ammon Salter and Maurizio Sobrero, 'Academic Engagement and Commercialisation: A Review of the Literature on University–Industry Relations' (2013) 42(2) Research Policy 423; Organisation for Economic Co-Operation and Development, 'OECD Principles and Guidelines for Access to Research Data from Public Funding' (2014); Manuel Crespo and Houssine Dridi, 'Intensification of University–Industry Relationships and Its Impact on Academic Research' (2007) 54(1) Higher Education 61.

[80] Robert P Merges, 'The Trouble with Trolls: Innovation, Rent-Seeking, and Patent Law Reform' (2009) 24(4) Berkeley Tech L J 1583; Markus Reitzig, Joachim Henkel and Christopher Heath, 'On Sharks, Trolls, and their Patent Prey: Unrealistic Damage Awards and Firms' Strategies of "Being Infringed"' (2007) 36(1) Research Policy 134.

patents with demand in the market for access to protected technologies.[81] These technology brokers are differentiated from other non-practising entities, referred to as patent trolls, who acquire patents for the purpose of enforcing against potential infringers to obtain profit.[82] However, there is no reference in the literature on universities or publicly funded institutes, as owners of patent portfolios, to locally embed innovations derived from local discoveries. Intellectual property management of knowledge transfer activities by universities is discussed,[83] but not how public research organisations can strategically exploit patents derived from publicly funded research. Specialised public institutions, like Centres of Excellence (CoE),[84] work directly with specific industry sectors to explore new ways to integrate and apply university research to develop new innovations.[85] Evidence indicates that the public has greater trust in public research institutions, even if the institution receives some private funding,[86] suggesting that publicly funded, not-for-profit independent institutions involved in the translation of research may be the type of organisation best suited to maintain public trust and manage the development and commercialisation of research and discoveries.[87] With their unique knowledge of the particular dynamics associated with the scientific field and multi-disciplinary team of professionals that possess an understanding of the academic environment as well as industry, these independent research organisations could act as 'guardians' of a patent portfolio and decide on how best to use patent rights to achieve the most desirable socio-economic outcome for the region. Because of the mission and core competencies of research organisations such as CoE, they may be in the best position to assess technological uncertainties and identify opportunities for the application of discoveries

---

81 Reitzig et al (n 80).

82 Merges (n 80).

83 Rejean Landry, Malek Saïhi, Nabil Amara and Mathieu Ouimet, 'Evidence on How Academics Manage their Portfolio of Knowledge Transfer Activities' (2010) 39(10) Research Policy 1387; Martin Meyer and Puay Tang, 'Exploring the "Value" of Academic Patents: IP Management Practices in UK Universities and Their Implications for Third-Stream Indicators' (2007) 7(2) Scientometrics 415.

84 EC, 'Action for "Centres of Excellence" with a European Dimension' <http://ec.europa.eu/research/era/pdf/centres.pdf>.

85 IMEC <www.imec.org> and ATTRACT <www.attract-eu.org>.

86 Christine Critchley and Dianne Nicol, 'Understanding the Impact of Commercialization on Public Support for Scientific Research: Is It About the Funding Source or the Organization Conducting the Research?' (2011) 20(3) Public Underst Sci 347; FA Miller, M Painter-Main, R Axler, P Lehoux, M Giacomini and B Slater, 'Citizen Expectations of "Academic Entrepreneurship" in Health Research: Public Science, Practical Benefit' (2015) 18(6) Health Expectations 2356.

87 See Yu (n 10).

in new technologies and innovations. Furthermore, for the same reasons technology market intermediaries can be effective 'matchmakers' to facilitate technology transfer,[88] public institutions can fulfil the same function but with a view to advancing local socio-economic development.[89] Unlike patent brokers and patent aggregating companies, CoE have an extensive knowledge of both academia and industry, giving them the credibility to effectively interact with and relate to the interests of both communities to facilitate the translation of basic research into marketable innovations.[90] Certain CoE actively search and identify new research being conducted at public research organisations and match the technological potential of the discovery with the core competency and commercial interest of industry partners.[91] In this manner, CoE can build a patent portfolio around discoveries derived from publicly funded research to (a) facilitate knowledge transfer through licensing or assignment of patent rights to industry while generating revenue for further research; and (b) ensure freedom to operate by granting access to protected technologies to enable further R&I. As such, the strategic and economic value of patents derived from publicly funded research can be optimally managed and leveraged with a view to the socio-economic benefit of the region.

VI. UNIVERSITY–INDUSTRY COLLABORATIONS TO OPTIMISE USE OF PUBLIC RESEARCH

Over the last few decades, the position of universities and public research organisations has evolved considerably.[92] They have become more active

---

88 See Fisher and Oberholzer-Gee (n 76); Kelley (n 69); Mario Benassi and Alberto Di Minin, 'Playing in Between: Patent Brokers in Markets for Technology' (2009) 39(1) R&D Management 68.

89 Gregor Trencher, Masaru Yarime, Kes B McCormick, Christopher N H Doll and Stephen B Kraines, 'Beyond the Third Mission: Exploring the Emerging University Function of Co-Creation for Sustainability' (2013) 41(2) Sci Public Policy 151; Perkmann et al (n 79); Maribel Guerrero, James A Cunningham and David Urbano, 'Economic Impact of Entrepreneurial Universities' Activities: An Exploratory Study of the United Kingdom' (2015) 44(3) Research Policy 748; Glenda Kruss, Simon Mcgrath, Il-haam Petersen and Michael Gastrow, 'Higher Education and Economic Development: The Importance of Building Technological Capabilities' (2015) 43 Int J Educ Dev 22.

90 Yu (n 79).

91 Ibid.

92 Bart Van Looy, Paolo Landoni, Julie Callaert, Bruno van Pottelsberghe de la Potterie, Eleftherios Sapsalis and Koenraad Debackere, 'Entrepreneurial

in transferring technology to industry since placing publicly funded research in the public domain is no longer seen as sufficient to generate the full benefits of innovation.[93] University–industry collaborations are recognised as a pragmatic means to pool resources and reduce duplication efforts.[94] However, if collaborative partnerships are to be supported as a means to facilitate the innovation process, cooperation between stakeholders involved in the innovation process requires a setting that supports and fosters collaboration to conduct research with and for society. To realise the socio-economic benefit objective of publicly funded research and/or publicly funded research infrastructures, the interests of all stakeholders involved in the translation and commercialisation of knowledge must be considered. Stakeholders need to find ways to forge closer ties through partnerships and research collaborations while preserving academic and societal core values and providing industry and government with the incentive required to justify investment of public and private funds in basic research. It is conceivable to anticipate polarisation between, for example, institutions that want to partner with industry as a means to secure research funds and those who view collaboration with industry as a betrayal of academic objectives and principles.[95] However, the relationship is mutually beneficial: academia requires funding to conduct research and industry can provide it. Industry requires innovative research to commercialise and academia can provide cutting-edge early-stage research and discoveries. University policies and European Research Area guidelines on IP management in international research collaborations urge researchers to protect the commercial potential of their research by patenting and forming close partnerships with industry to facilitate the translation of knowledge into products.[96] The World Intellectual Property Organization also provides guidelines to universities and research organisations on developing policies related to managing IP

Effectiveness of European Universities: An Empirical Assessment of Antecedents and Trade-Off' (2011) 40(4) Research Policy 553.

[93] Mike Wright, Bart Clarysse, Phillipe Mustar and Andy Lockett (eds), *Academic Entrepreneurship in Europe* (Edward Elgar Publishing 2007) 1.

[94] See Yu (n 51).

[95] John P Walsh, Wesley M Cohen and Charlene Cho, 'Where Excludability Matters: Material versus Intellectual Property in Academic Biomedical Research' (2007) 36(8) Research Policy 1184; H Ledford, 'Drug Buddies' (2011) 474 (7352) Nature 433.

[96] Knowledge Transfer Working Group of the European Research Area Committee (n 78); Timothy Caulfield, 'Commercialization Creep' (2012) 34 Policy Option 20; Crespo and Dridi (n 79).

rights in research findings and academic discoveries.[97] The intention of the guidelines is to facilitate greater collaboration and lay the foundation for knowledge-based economic development.[98]

Different drivers and regulatory structures impact each industry sector. Because translation organisations operate in the R&D and the private sector of a particular sector, such organisations are arguably in the most neutral and informed position to balance the best level of 'openness' and IP protection to de-risk the translation and commercialisation of research while ensuring that the most desirable socio-economic outcome can be achieved.[99] In addition to the proprietary rights associated with IP, the transactional function of patents can be seen as an incentive to facilitate collaboration by providing a system by which the parties can organise collaborative R&D in a manner that is most efficient based on their unique knowledge of market dynamics.[100] By reducing transactional hazards associated with creating a relationship between stakeholders, discoveries have a greater likelihood of being translated into innovations for the benefit of the public. As long as industry involvement in the translation of basic research is necessary to achieve this outcome, financial motives associated with commercialisation are an undeniable fact, whether or not there is empirical evidence to support the notion that patents are essential to stimulate innovation.[101]

VII. BALANCING OPEN INNOVATION AND IP

As previously alluded to, scholars have criticised the impact of IP protection on innovation and economic development. The literature largely supports the contention that openness and access to knowledge fosters competition and access to knowledge for more efficient science and innovation.[102] According to the Commission, the basic premise of

---

[97] World Intellectual Property Organization (WIPO), 'Model Intellectual Property Policy for Universities and Research Institutions' <http://www.wipo.int/edocs/pubdocs/en/wipo_pub_transition_2_a.pdf>.

[98] Ibid.

[99] Yu (n 10).

[100] Nancy Gallini and Suzanne Scotchmer, 'Intellectual Property: When Is It the Best Incentive System? (2002) 2 Innovation Policy and the Economy 51; Bronwyn H Hall and Deitmar Harhoff, 'Recent Research on the Economics of Patents' (2012) National Bureau of Economic Research, <https://www.nber.org/papers/w17773.pdf >.

[101] Ibid.

[102] Carl Shapiro, 'Competition and Innovation: Did Arrow Hit the Bull's Eye?'

open innovation is to 'open up the innovation process to all active players so that knowledge can circulate more freely and be transformed into products and services that create new markets, fostering a stronger culture of entrepreneurship'.[103] Open innovation therefore advocates for the purposive use of available knowledge to accelerate the introduction of new innovations into the market. However, open access during the *discovery phase* may preclude subsequent patent protection if the novelty and/or inventiveness of future innovations are inadvertently destroyed through dissemination.[104] As previously discussed, IP rights are critically important in incentivising and inducing industry to undertake the risk of development and invest in the commercialisation of knowledge to introduce new innovations to the market. Theoretically, knowledge arising from the development and translation phase of the innovation process relating to the practical application of scientific discoveries should be protected by IP while background knowledge that supports the application remains open to the scientific community. However, the delineation between early-stage research (where open science is encouraged to foster the advancement of science) and applied research (where the preservation of IP rights becomes relevant to preserve translation and commercialisation potential) is not clear and particularly difficult for scientists to determine, not that they are trained to do so, nor should they be burdened with such a role. But the reality is that as pioneers at the forefront of discovering new technologies, they are the ones saddled with the initial decision of sharing or protecting.

The Commission's vision of an open innovation ecosystem in Europe includes:

(i) combining the power of ideas and knowledge from different actors (whether private, public or civil society/third sector) to co-create new products and find solutions to societal needs;
(ii) creating shared economic and social value, including a citizen and user-centric approach;
(iii) capitalising on the implications of trends such as digitalisation, mass participation and collaboration.[105]

---

in Josh Lerner and Scott Stern (eds), *The Rate and Direction of Inventive Activity Revisited* (University of Chicago Press 2011) 361; Chesbrough (n 78).

[103] EC, 'Open Innovation, Open Science, Open to the World – a Vision for Europe' (2016).

[104] Zachary Quinlan, 'Hindsight Bias in Patent Law: Comparing the USPTO and the EPO' (2013) 37(6) Fordham Int'l L J 1787; The Royal Society, 'Keeping Science Open: The Effects of Intellectual Property Policy on the Conduct of Science' (2003) <https://royalsociety.org/topics-policy/publications/2003/keeping-science-open/>.

[105] EC (n 103) 14.

While the Commission states 'it is essential to ensure that intellectual property is protected before making knowledge publicly available',[106] it fails to provide concrete recommendations on how to manage IP rights when opening up R&I. The assertion of IP rights, however, does not necessarily mean that they will be exercised in an exclusionary manner. Patent donations, patent pledges and open source patents are examples of the way in which patent rights can be exercised in a manner that does not negatively impact the advancement of research and knowledge.[107] Although patenting and its driving effects on innovation have been strongly challenged,[108] the Commission continues to recognise that 'boosting cooperation on innovation entails putting in place adequate framework conditions and a level playing field, including fair and equitable treatment of intellectual property'.[109]

With the trend towards open innovation, it is necessary to assess the role of traditional patent systems in an environment largely built on shared knowledge and collaborative innovation. The merits of open approaches such as open source methodologies were first widely used and explored within the software industry.[110] The concept of 'copyleft' (in contrast to copyright) arose from the Free and Open Source community to support open accessibility of software source code.[111] Copyleft essentially requires licensees that modify code to offer access and grant unrestricted rights to redistribute the modified code to third parties as a means to promote development and sharing of IP rights.[112] Applied to the patent system, the concept of 'patentleft' emerged as a means to leverage patent rights for defensive purposes while preserving the freedom to innovate and extract rights and privileges that will benefit parties who elect to participate in the

---

106 Ibid 42.

107 Nicole Ziegler, Oliver Gassmann and Sascha Friesike, 'Why Do Firms Give Away Their Patents for Free?' (2014) 37 World Patent Inform 19; Timothy Caulfield, Robert M Cook-Deegan, F Scott Kieff and John P Walsh, 'Evidence and Anecdotes: An Analysis of Human Gene Patenting Controversies' (2006) 24(9) Nat Biotechnol 1091.

108 William D Carey, 'Patent Policy Versus Innovation' (1978) 200(4349) Science 1439; M Boldrin and DK Levine, 'The Case against Patents' (2012) Federal Reserve Bank of St. Louis Working Paper No 2012-035A, 1–25; Gastón Llanes and Stefano Trento, 'Patent Policy, Patent Pools, and the Accumulation of Claims in Sequential Innovation' (2012) 50(3) Economic Theory 703.

109 EC (n 103) 76.

110 Eric S Raymond, 'The Cathedral and the Bazaar' (1999) 12(3) Phil Tech 23.

111 Guillaume Ménage and Yann Dietrich, 'Do We See The Emergence of "Patent Left"?' (2010) Les Nouvelles 42.

112 Ibid.

open source system. The notion of open source applied to patents appears paradoxical at first but the concept of 'open patents' essentially modifies the accessibility and usage of patented technology. The act of sharing explicitly implies the existence of property that can be exchanged between parties. Econometric studies seem to indicate that R&D collaborations may even be associated with more patenting as they allow companies to enter collaborations without giving up on proprietary claims on the innovations arising from the partnership.[113] In other words, patent rights do not necessarily contradict open innovation as they can be used as a tool to allow firms to grant access to their proprietary knowledge while preserving the incentive function of IP to pursue R&I. However, traditional use of patent rights does not necessarily improve the broader access to technology. The question is whether the innovation process can be improved through the adoption of the concept of 'open source patents' or 'patent pledges' to foster innovation and growth in technology.[114]

A creative commons[115] and open source system typically found in the software and copyright context may have benefits that can contribute to a successful open patent system. Creative commons and open source are systems through which creators of works can share all or part of the rights to their works with third-party users, including those in the fields of scientific research.[116] Generally, the protected material is not 'free' in terms of cost, but the material is free to third parties to use, modify and share.[117] For example, under a General Public License, any software derived from software distributed under this licence inherits the public licence and restricts third-party users from claiming proprietary rights in modifications made to open source software.[118] Instead, the resulting, modified software must also be free to users and carry the same terms as the original licence. One of the elements common to both creative commons and open innovation

---

113 Carine Peeters and Bruno van Pottelsberghe, 'Innovation Strategy and the Patenting Behavior of Firms' (2005) 16(1) J Evol Econ 109; Hanna Hottenrott and Cindy Lopes-Bento, 'Quantity or Quality? Knowledge Alliances and Their Effects on Patenting' (2005) 24(5) ICC 981.

114 Stephanie Vu, 'Pledging Patents Effectively: Copyright and Open Source as a Framework for Patent Pledges' (2015) 14 JTHTL 437.

115 Creative Commons, 'About the Licenses' <https://creativecommons.org/licenses/>.

116 Andres G Gonzalez, 'Open Science: Open Source Licenses in Scientific Research' (2005) 7(2) NC JOLT 321.

117 Open Source Initiative <http://www.opensource.org>.

118 GNU Operating System, 'What is Copyleft?' <https://www.gnu.org/copyleft/copyleft.html>; see also GNU General Public License <https://www.gnu.org/copyleft/gpl.html>.

is a community of stakeholders dedicated to the belief that sharing of resources and ideas will lead to more innovation. By pledging access to IP on the condition that all third-party users will use the IP for a specific purpose, such a patent pledge would restrict IP owners from asserting their patent rights against legitimate third-party users but they would still retain the right to assert their rights against third-party users using the IP for anything other than the specified purpose.

VIII. CONCLUSION

The existing research and literature on fostering socio-economic development, although vast and of a high quality, often elucidates and focuses on isolated aspects of growth and loses site of the bigger regional development picture on a more holistic and interdisciplinary level.[119] Furthermore, much of the research focuses on 'best practices' based on what worked elsewhere, in the hope of developing a 'one size fits all' regional development policy.[120] However, instead of a general 'checklist', many of the identified factors are endogenous to the region and specific to the culture and institutional environment of the particular successful region.[121] Within the checklist, one ubiquitous factor emerges: the innovative capacity of the region and the effective use of such available knowledge through relationship with the business community.[122] Collaboration

---

[119] Ann R Markusen, 'Studying Regions by Studying Firms' (1994) 46(4) Prof Geogr 477; Ron Martin and Peter Sunley, 'Deconstructing Clusters: Chaotic Concept or Policy Panacea?' (2003) 3(1) J Econ Geogr 5; C Unwin, 'Urban Myth: Why Cities Don't Compete' (2006) Centre for Cities, Institute for Public Policy Research Discussion Paper No 5.

[120] Edward J Malecki, 'Jockeying for Position: What It Means and Why It Matters to Regional Development Policy When Places Compete' (2004) 38(9) Regional Studies 1101; Surabhi Pancholi, Tan Yigitcanlar and Mirko Guaralda, 'Place Making Facilitators of Knowledge and Innovation Spaces: Insights from European Best Practices' (2015) 6(3) IJKBD 215; Ron Boschma, 'Constructing Regional Advantage and Smart Specialisation: Comparison of Two European Policy Concepts' (2014) 13(1) Scienze Regionali 51.

[121] Iain Deas and Benito Giordano, 'Conceptualising and Measuring Urban Competitiveness in Major English Cities: An Exploratory Approach' (2001) 33(8) Environ Plan, 1411; Karl Kresl and Balwant Singh, 'Competitiveness and the Urban Economy: Twenty-Four Large US Metropolitan Areas' (1999) 36(5–6) Urban Studies 1017; Costia Hadjimichalis and Ray Hudson, 'Contemporary Crisis across Europe and the Crisis of Regional Development Theories' (2014) 48(1) Regional Studies 208.

[122] Robert Hassink, 'Regional Innovation Policies Compared' (1993)

creates value.[123] As part of creating a favourable environment to attract and retain highly mobile resources such as capital investments and intellectual capital, patent portfolios of local discoveries held by research institutions can be used to embed the innovation and create 'stickiness' to the region as a foundation for cluster formation. A research centre with a particular expertise, such as a CoE, will attract intellectual capital to the region in order to have access to world-class research and research infrastructures,[124] especially if the expertise is proprietary or unique to the region. Firms will also want to move and co-locate in the region where they can have access to leading-edge technology and access to young minds looking to develop a career, thereby grounding the intellectual capital and skilled workers to the region.[125] This in turn encourages the region to invest in building infrastructure to provide the foundations for a range of economic activities in support of locally developing innovations and upgrade amenities to enhance liveability and make the region attractive to skilled workers and firms.[126] This grounds the firms to the region and creates the foundation to build critical mass for cluster formation.

By taking a more holistic view of regional socio-economic development, there are natural synergies unique to each region that can be enhanced rather than trying to replicate success by following some template of another region.[127] Not all regions have the same attributes and substan-

---

30(6) Urban Studies 1009; Corrine Autant-Bernard, 'The Geography of Knowledge Spillovers and Technological Proximity' in Maryann Feldman and Nadine Massard (eds), *Institutions And Systems In The Geography Of Innovation* (Springer 2002) 181; Paul Benneworth, Romulo Pinheiro and James Karlsen, 'Strategic Agency and Institutional Change: Investigating The Role of Universities in Regional Innovation Systems (RISS)' (2017) 51(2) Regional Studies 235; OECD, 'Building Competitive Regions: Strategies And Governance' (2005).

[123] See (n 1) and (n 3). Kristel Miller, Rodney Mcadam, Sandra Moffett, Allen Alexander and Pushyarag Puthusserry, 'Knowledge Transfer in University Quadruple Helix Ecosystems: An Absorptive Capacity Perspective' (2016) 46(2) R&D Manag 383; Oscar Alfonso, Sara Monteiro and Maria Thompson, 'A Growth Model for the Quadruple Helix Innovation Theory' (2010) 13(5) J Bus Econ Manag 849.

[124] Henry Etzkowitz and Carol Kemelgor, 'The Role of Research Centres in the Collectivisation of Academic Science' (1998) 36(3) Minerva 271.

[125] Ivan Turok, 'Cities, Regions and Competitiveness' (2004) 38(9) Regional Studies 1069.

[126] OECD (n 122).

[127] Michael Kitson, Ron Martin and Peter Tyler, 'Regional Competitiveness: An Elusive yet Key Concept?' (2004) 38(9) Regional Studies 991; Christian Ketels, 'Recent Research on Competitiveness and Clusters: What Are the Implications for Regional Policy?' (2013) 6(2) Camb J Regions Econ Soc 269.

tive differences between the regions also means deliberately creating such attributes in an attempt to reproduce conditions of a successful region where the same attributes developed organically may not lead to the same results.[128] A narrow focus on the role of the private sector and its interests ignores other important non-economic factors with which regional development policies should be equally concerned, such as the well-being of individuals or communities. As such, regional development policies that are heavily dependent on large corporations or multinational firms become vulnerable to having policy shaped or influenced by economic interests instead of regional interests.

As discussed in this chapter, some of the key factors associated with successful regional development can be proactively fostered by effectively shaping, leveraging and attuning endogenous variables and circumstances unique to the region. Developing policies that leverage local R&I activity to retain socio-economic benefits requires the collaboration and alignment of public and private interests. This is not to suggest that public research organisations and research infrastructures need to transform their core mandate from knowledge creation to entrepreneurial knowledge transfer and become a 'science factory'. However, pursuing 'purposeful' scientific research and discovery and teaching excellence with a view to contributing to the socio-economic benefit of society would not alienate public trust or academic core values as higher research and education institutions. Promoting the understanding of translation and commercialisation of science into innovations through policy objectives and strategies will help the relevant stakeholders in the innovation process to understand the role they each play in the larger innovation ecosystem. The role of public research organisations and research infrastructures should neither be centrifugal to spin out R&I to industry, nor centripetal and take from industrial research and development to drive university research. An interdisciplinary approach to developing policies relating to fostering innovation and socio-economic development will hopefully redirect discussions away from single perspectives of individual disciplines and encourage a more holistic consideration instead.

---

[128] Gillian Bristow and Peter Wells, 'Innovative Discourse for Sustainable Local Development: a Critical Analysis of Eco-Industrialism' (2005) 1(1–2) Int J Innovat Sustain Dev 168.

10. Patent invalidation and legal certainty*

Christoph Ann**

I. INTRODUCTION

In Europe, patents are utilised frequently. Within the European Patent Office (EPO) they are taken out mostly by German industry. It is important to note that patents can only justify their cost if they are valid and (thus) enforceable. Only then can patents perform their function, which is to ensure their holders exclusive rights to an invention.

For the past 15 years, there has been much talk about patent enforcement in the EU. The risk of patent invalidation, however, was only debated more recently. The risk of patent invalidation is real because anyone can file a nullity action as long as the patent is in force. Theoretically, numerous plaintiffs can lodge identical nullity actions against the same patent until one claim is successful. Here, I shall discuss the success rates of these nullity actions and the insights that they may yield.

II. PATENT VALUE: NULLITY ACTION AND SYSTEMIC HYGIENE

All considerations must start with the fact that in any market economy, patent protection must comply with an unconditional requirement of quality. All proceedings before patent offices (grant/objection) and patent courts (appeal/nullity suits) must aim to grant only patents that satisfy all substantive patentability requirements. Only then does a claim to a German or European patent exist[1] and can such patent be granted.

* All online sources were last accessed on 27 December 2018.

** The chapter is based on various presentations on the topic that the author gave in 2015 and 2016: at a public workshop at Bardehle Pagenberg on patent invalidation; at the German VPP's (German Association of Intellectual Property Experts) Spring Conference 2016 in Berlin; at Ericsson; and at ATRIP 2017.

If patentability is assessed incorrectly, a patent can be revoked for a number of reasons.[2] A patent may be revoked because the patent's subject matter was completely or partially non-patentable, because the patent did not adequately disclose the protected invention, because the essential content of the patent had constituted the usurpation of a third party's invention, or because the subject matter patented was amended after the filing of the application and thus constituted an inadmissible extension of the applied subject matter or its scope of protection; the latter being prohibited by the German Patent Act, s 123 paras 2 and 3, EPC, art. 38.

Given that grounds for revocation are not (and cannot be) identified in the grant proceedings, patent grants happen that should not have. Then, the patent grant was unlawful. Unlike under German general administrative law, which only permits (unlawful) favourable administrative acts (*Verwaltungsakte*) to be withdrawn, if strict conditions are met, granted patents can always be revoked, if grounds for revocation exist. The nullity suit's subject matter is not the administrative act of patent grant, but the result of the patent itself. Nevertheless, one cannot disregard the close relationship between the two and the patent applicant's interests in the outcome of nullity proceedings. These interests indisputably deserve (some) protection if the patent system is to be kept open to SMEs instead of increasingly becoming an arena only for deep pockets.

Regardless of any systemic hygiene, which patent nullity suits should guarantee, and which is fundamentally correct because inferior patents distort competition, their continued admissibility does come at the price of reducing legal certainty. This uncertainty may reduce incentives to innovate because affluent competitors can use nullity actions as a tool to create cost risks for competitors with flawless patents. This became evident in the infringement trial *IPCom v Nokia*.[3] Nokia was said to have reacted to IPCom's infringement actions by filing a large number of nullity actions to exert financial pressure on IPCom. If nullity actions are primarily filed as competition tactics, the purpose of systemic hygiene ceases to apply and the abusive assertion of rights comes into view.

A further problem of patent nullity actions is that the textbook case of printed novelty-destroying materials overlooked by the examiner is the rare exception. More frequently, disputes occur as to whether the office

---

1 This right also constitutes an entitlement under substantive law; cf correctly Tobias Bremi and Dieter Stauder, *Singer/Stauder Europäisches Patentübereinkommen* (7th edn, Carl Heymanns 2016) art 60, no 1.

2 Cf art 138 European Patent Convention (EPC); ss 21, 22 German Patent Act (PatG).

3 *IPCom v Nokia* (2012) EWCA 567.

should not have assessed available patent documents differently.[4] Also, examination standards come into play, as shown by the 'person skilled in the art'. This person is known to be fictitious and his or her expertise and average skills can be decided only on an ad hoc basis. Views on this can differ.

For patent court judges, this is likely to be even more valid, given that they are disadvantaged not only by routine, but also by the problem of hindsight. Hindsight may make something seem banal, which at its time was a true breakthrough. German Federal Court of Justice (BGH) patent judge von Albert, in 1981, pointed to the danger to which patent court judges are particularly prone: 'Nullity proceedings are to help ensure that patents which for lack of substantive patentability were granted incorrectly do not last. This, however, may not lead to this question being decided by petty argumentation.'[5]

III. SYSTEM CRITIQUE: SUCCESS RATE OF NULLITY ACTIONS

A. The Patent Litigation Dilemma

Before addressing the success rate of patent nullity actions and the conclusions to be drawn from them, one needs to revisit the German system of bifurcation. Unlike most other European jurisdictions, this system allocates patent validity and patent infringement to different jurisdictions.

Bifurcation was introduced in the first patent statute to apply throughout the German Reich of 1871,[6] and as plausible as it was then, it now causes problems with patent enforcement where patent validity is in dispute. The untenable state that, statistically, nullity suits in their first instance before the Federal Patent Court (BPatG) take almost as long as infringement suits (in the patent infringement courts) before the Regional

4 Rudolf Kraßer and Christoph Ann, *Patentrecht* (7th edn, CH Beck 2016) § 26 no 220.

5 Hans-Joachim von Albert, 'Probleme des Nichtigkeitsverfahrens im Hinblick auf das neue europäische Patentsystem' (1981) 83(7) Gewerblicher Rechtsschutz und Urheberrecht 451, 458.

6 Details in Christoph Ann, 'Technische Richter in der Patentgerichtsbarkeit – ein Modell mit Perspektive?' in Achim Bender, Klaus Schülke and Volker Winterfeldt (eds), *Festschrift 50 Jahre Bundespatentgericht* (Carl Heymanns 2011) 109, 114.

Court (trial court level) and the Higher Regional Court (appeal),[7] again is leading German infringement courts into an unpleasant patent litigation dilemma.

On the one hand, as only the German Patent and Trade Mark Office (DPMA), EPO and BPatG at first instance can rule on *patent validity*, German patent infringement courts as a matter of law must respect patents in force and base their infringement rulings upon them. Thus, infringement judgments may be handed down that subsequently prove incorrect if the enforced patents do not hold up before the German Federal Patent Court. The effects this may have upon enforcement are evident.

On the other hand, what should infringement courts do? Were they to venture too far into patent review, they would overstep their jurisdiction. So, they have little choice. Consequently, there is a considerable level of unease among patent litigation judges when they have before them matters that depend on patent validity.[8] In particular:

(a) infringement decisions shall be declared provisionally enforceable (*vorläufig vollstreckbar*),
(b) proceedings shall be stayed under § 148 German Code of Civil Procedure, and
(c) preliminary injunctive shall be granted.

The resulting patent litigation dilemma is related to the conclusions that can be drawn from the success rates of patent nullity suits filed with the German Federal Court of Justice (BGH) because overall infringement cases are tried much more quickly than nullity cases before the BPatG.

Were enforced patents indeed largely invalidated by the BPatG, public confidence in patent validity would be in jeopardy. Such a loss of confidence could result in it becoming more efficient for potential infringers to simply rely on the success of a potential nullity action rather than avoiding infringement by expensively inventing around or taking on licences. Such

---

[7] According to Thomas Kühnen and Rolf Claessen, 'Die Durchsetzung von Patenten in der EU – Standortbestimmungen vor Einführung des europäischen Patentgerichts' (2013) Gewerblicher Rechtsschutz und Urheberrecht 592, 595, patent nullity proceedings before the BPatG took an average of 24.6 months in 2012.

[8] Cf on this matter also Tobias Wuttke and Peter Guntz, 'Wie weit reicht die Privilegierung des Klägers durch das Trennungsprinzip?' (2012) Mitteilungen der deutschen Patentanwälte 477, 483; Tobias Wuttke, 'Die aktuelle gerichtliche Praxis der einstweiligen Unterlassungsverfügung in Patentsachen – zurück zu den Anfängen' (2011) Mitteilungen der deutschen Patentanwälte 393.

a development would be the kiss of death for the patent system, given that patent protection and licensing only makes sense if patents are valid and enforceable.

B. Bifurcation Critique

In 2014, Hess, Müller-Stoy and Wintermeier[9] rightly criticised the success rates of patent nullity suits before the BPatG. Out of 143 nullity actions against patents in International Patent Classification (IPC) classes G and H (software and telecommunication), for the period 2010–2013, 60 per cent of patents were held to be totally invalid. Another roughly 30 per cent were partially invalidated. Only 10 per cent were upheld as valid.[10] Based in particular on 60 per cent invalidations compared to validity of 10 per cent, the authors suggested a system failure. They concluded this even though annulment had only been sought for an insignificant quantity of all patents in force. In its 2014 annual report, the BPatG explicitly addressed this criticism,[11] noting that on average out of all challengeable patents only 0.02 per cent are annulled by the court.

When, however, Hess, Müller-Stoy and Wintermeier point out that challengeable patents have an above-average chance of being declared invalid, this appears questionable. Even nullity plaintiffs do not consider the lion's share of all enforced patents amenable to invalidation. Rather, they obviously select which patents they want to challenge. Kühnen and Claessen confirm this from the infringement perspective: 'Astonishingly, the validity of allegedly infringed industrial property rights is challenged only in approximately half of all infringement proceedings.'[12] Moreover, the basic hypothesis that enforced patents constitute a positive selection of all patents in force appears questionable. There is no indication why enforced patents should have above-average legal validity. Infringement actions are not so much contingent on right holders' validity prognoses, but rather on the existence of infringement and on patent value, which justifies the considerable cost that parties incur in infringement proceedings.[13]

Remarkably, neither Hess, Müller-Stoy and Wintermeier nor Kühnen and Claessen criticise the work of the two patent offices that grant patents

---

[9] Peter Hess, Tilman Müller-Stoy and Martin Wintermeier, 'Sind Patente nur "Papiertiger"?'(2014) Mitteilungen der deutschen Patentanwälte 439.

[10] Ibid 439, 441.

[11] Bundespatentgericht, *Jahresbericht* (2014) 62.

[12] Kühnen and Claessen (n 7) 592, 594.

[13] Also cf Section IV.2 below.

for Germany. Hess, Müller-Stoy and Wintermeier consider it unlikely that examiners' errors are the main cause for high invalidation rates because in 2010–2013, most invalidations (complete as well as partial) were based upon lack of inventive step (>50 per cent) and of novelty (20 per cent). In contrast, non-permissible extension (11 per cent) and non-reproducibility (2 per cent) were insignificant as grounds for annulment.[14]

The textbook case of a publication that destroys novelty, but was overlooked by the examiner, actually is rare. Even though prior art was often introduced in nullity proceedings, it mostly was not newly-found, but had existed in patent documents – and had been reinterpreted. This was plausible considering nullity plaintiffs without large patent departments and search services are unlikely to perform better research than the better qualified and considerably more specialised office examiners.[15]

Hess, Müller-Stoy and Wintermeier conclude that if patents were largely invalidated because BPatG judges interpreted known materials differently than examiner/patent departments (DPMAs) or examining divisions/boards of appeal (EPO) had done initially, this meant that BPatG judges were deciding identical questions differently than patent examiners had done. This was allegedly the statement of a BPatG judge, who claimed actual examination to be taking place only before his court.

Should the BPatG indeed regard itself as Germany's 'ex-post patent catenaccio', this would be highly problematic. After all, the patent system is about incentivising innovation, including R&D funding. In addition, it would raise the legal question of how 'routines of dissenting' in patent review were compatible with the property guarantee under Art 14 of the German constitution (GG).[16]

C. Patent Critique

Henkel and Zischka[17] take a different approach in their slightly more recent working paper: they conclude that high invalidation rates before the BPatG indicate shortcomings in patent quality and, thus, in office grant proceedings. Thus, Henkel and Zischka imply that patent value is expectedly low because of patents no longer being fit for enforcement – but rather being targets for infringers to be sued out their ways.

---

14 Hess, Müller-Stoy and Wintermeier (n 9) 439, 441.

15 Hess, Müller-Stoy and Wintermeier (n 9) 439, 450.

16 Grundgesetz für die Bundesrepublik Deutschland 1949.

17 Joachim Henkel and Hans Zischka, 'Why Most Patents are Invalid – Extent, Reasons, and Potential Remedies of Patent Invalidity' (2015) <https://journals.aom.org/doi/abs/10.5465/ambpp.2015.17115abstract>.

In regard to the BPatG's statistical argument that only a fraction of patents were challenged, Henkel and Zischka, like Hess, Müller-Stoy and Wintermeier, reject this and conclude that if enforced patents were challenged more than others, there must be a positive selection.[18] Henkel and Zischka extrapolate the empirically confirmed invalidation rate by adding all settled nullity suits. They conclude that nullity suits are settled only for patents that otherwise would also have been invalidated. This was why right holders were willing to settle. Also settlements were beneficial to both parties because they saved costs and prevented third parties from using patented inventions – against the public interest in sound competition.[19]

Unlike Hess, Müller-Stoy and Wintermeier, who claim that the problem was patents' inadequate legal certainty, which undermines confidence in their validity, Henkel and Zischka criticise patent grant procedures at large, essentially reverting to Bessen and Meurer's[20] and Lemley's[21] criticism of the United States Patent and Trademark Office (USPTO) (in the early 2000s) as 'rationally ignorant'.

Henkel and Zischka do have a point that patent quality is of overarching significance for any patent system, and that in any good system more than only 20–30 per cent of all patent nullity suits should be rejected.

D. Are the Critics Right?

1. High invalidation rates are not new to Germany

Looking at the outcome of nullity proceedings, German invalidation rates have been surprisingly stable throughout the years. Roughly, the outcomes can be broken down into equal thirds: complete invalidation (plaintiff's

---

18 Ibid 1, 20.

19 Ibid 2, 18f. It can be doubted whether this correctly depicts practice, given that it is by no means the case even before the German courts that actions are only lodged where the plaintiff is convinced of their prospects of success. An action can in fact be filed for a number of reasons, such as to demonstrate that the plaintiff means business, and hence to accelerate negotiations that are being held back, or which they consider are being held back, or quite simply in order to create pressure by creating cost risks. German procedural law does its utmost to try to prevent this unlike in the United States, cf Christoph Ann, 'Klägerfreundlichkeit im US-Zivilprozess' in Markus Gloe and Volker Reinhardt (eds), *Politikwissenschaft und Politische Bildung* (VS Verlag für Sozialwissenschaften 2010) 157, 159, but this is easier said than done since moneyed parties are simply better able to enforce their interests than others. The best procedural law cannot change this.

20 James Bessen and Michael J Meurer, *Patent Failure: How Judges, Bureaucrats, and Lawyers Put Innovators at Risk* (Princeton University Press 2009).

21 Mark A Lemley, 'Rational Ignorance at the Patent Office' (2001) 95 Nw U L Rev 1495.

victory), partial invalidation (plaintiff's partial victory), and dismissal of the nullity action (defeat). Even though one-third of all challenged patents being invalidated would not sound spectacular,[22] at the end of the day, partial invalidations are key. Whether nullity plaintiffs succeed depends on whether patents' surviving parts still hold value.[23]

Patent professionals often claim that partial invalidations happen because in nullity proceedings patents are cut back to the invention's core, in other words that an application's 'fat' was cut away, not the 'prime cut'. For partial invalidation cases, it is plausible to assume that the right holder chose not to surrender the patent, but maintained it for a reason despite rising annuities.[24]

Equating partial and total invalidations as forms of 'impairment' does not appear to be the right approach. It would mean neglecting that partially invalidated patents might hold considerable value for their holders – depending on the invalidated part's relevance. This can only be determined separately for each case. Hüttermann[25] rightly called for a distinction in this regard.

2. Enforced patents stronger than average?

Whether enforced patents are indeed particularly strong has already been touched on above, and there is doubt. Even though only a relatively small number of patents are challenged before the BPatG, most of these are enforced patents because they are more vulnerable to such (expensive) challenges than patents where enforcement is not a problem.

However, by no means all enforced patents are challenged. Rather, their validity remains uncontested in roughly 50 per cent of all infringement proceedings.[26] Even from the perspective of the infringement defendant, who would benefit from a patent invalidation, the validity of at least 50 per cent of all enforced patents is so far beyond doubt that they are not even challenged. This is remarkable because were the rates calculated by the critics (>70 per cent) correct, patent nullity suits would have success rates, which should make them no-brainers: patents then should be sued, not respected.

As a result, this is likely to mean two things: first, infringement defendants select nullity suits and obviously do not presume their chances of

---

22 Cf Aloys Hüttermann, 'Patente – Papiertiger oder wirkliche Tiger' (2016) Mitteilungen der deutschen Patentanwälte 101, 102.

23 Kühnen and Claessen (n 7) 592, 594.

24 Cf only Bundespatentgericht (n 11) 62 left-hand column.

25 Hüttermann (n 22) 101.

26 Kühnen and Claessen (n 7) 592, 594.

success to be around 80 per cent. Secondly, not only strong patents are enforced, but ones that are infringed and that are valuable. Patent enforcement and patent quality, thus, appear to be decoupled more than Hess, Müller-Stoy and Wintermeier and Henkel and Zischka allege.[27]

3. Lack of an inventive step as grounds for revocation

As said above, the BPatG largely invalidates patents for lack of inventive step. Invoked prior art primarily stems from patent documents, which nullity plaintiffs have interpreted differently than either the DPMA's examiners or the EPO's examining divisions.[28]

The significance of inventive step and the problems of developing authoritative examination standards have been an ongoing patent law topic for decades.[29] These difficulties culminate in the 'person skilled in the art' that Art 56 EPC uses as a benchmark. This person consists of a cognitive as well as a creative component. The former describes what the person skilled in the art *can realise*, the latter what he/she *can imagine*, i.e. how far his or her (average) understanding reaches beyond his or her (average) ability.

Obviously, there is room for assessment, and nullity suits at the BPatG reflect that – to begin with because they imply that the understanding and ability of the person skilled in the art (theoretically) needs to be assessed for a particular case when looking back up to 20 years.

4. What legal certainty do patent holders need?

Hess, Müller-Stoy and Wintermeier discuss how leaving interpretation of legal terms to patent offices and courts can raise issues of legal certainty.[30] This is not about demanding legal force for patents as for administrative acts in general administrative law. However, one may ask how the right to file nullity actions, and the possibility of having an authority that does not grant patents (such as the BPatG) invalidate them because of a lack of inventive step is in harmony with the patent system's purpose of promoting innovation and with a patent holder's legal status.

Incentives to innovate cannot work without a minimum of legal certainty because this is what any applicant will demand. Inventors will

---

[27] That valuable patents rather than strong patents are enforced is true for patent assertion entities (PAEs) even more than for manufacturing industry.

[28] Section 4 of the Patent Act: 'if, having regard to the state of the art, it is not obvious to a person skilled in the art'.

[29] Dieter Liedel, *Das deutsche Patentnichtigkeitsverfahren – eine Bestandsaufnahme* (Carl Heymanns 1979) 198.

[30] Kraßer and Ann (n 4) § 26 no 244.

reveal their invention (and to commit to the considerable cost of a patent application) only if they receive a minimum of reliability; at least in the sense they can mostly rely on the examination of the patent office rather than it being superfluous because the 'real examination' takes place only after the right holder has taken further risks.[31]

On the one hand, legal certainty cannot mean unconditional investment protection for applicants and no risk for patents, which should not have been granted, to be invalidated. On the other hand, patent holders must be protected against arbitrary revisions of justifiable patent office rulings; for at least three reasons.

First, every patent invalidation should consider the patent system's purpose: to incentivise inventive activity and to enable sound risk management for R&D investments. Secondly, the patent system must be kept open for applicants who are short on capital, such as individuals and SMEs. Office examination, therefore, must not be replaced by BPatG as a 'Super Patent Office'. Thirdly, side-effects triggering loss of confidence in office actions must be avoided. Otherwise, willingness to take out FRAND (fair, reasonable, and non-discriminatory) licences might be made contingent on the judicial 'post-validation' of patents, or 80 per cent portfolio discounts being claimed on grounds that 80 per cent of all patents were latently invalid according to scholarly findings.[32]

E. What Do Invalidation Rates Tell Us About Patent Value?

Statistics are useful but they cannot contribute to the resolution of any individual case. For example, even though it is undisputed that many German taxpayers evade income tax, this does not mean anything about the individual taxpayer. After all, not all German taxpayers are guilty of tax evasion.

This consideration is important, because statements of about 70–80 per cent validity of all patents in force for Germany will foreseeably be misunderstood. Even if many patents were to be declared invalid, for the time being individual patents would still have to be regarded as valid. After all,

---

31 Kraßer and Ann (n 4) § 26 nos 37–43.

32 Cf, for example, Intel, whose representative at the Fordham IP Conference in 2016 suggested that injunctions in patent litigation only be granted on condition of their proportionality, even though Intel for a long time had been particularly known for its robust patent enforcement. Fordham Intellectual Property Law Institute and Emily C & John E Hansen Intellectual Property Institute, '24th Annual Intellectual Property Law & Policy Conference Program' (2016) <http://fordhamipconference.com/wp-content/uploads/2010/08/Detailed-Program-4.1.16-1.pdf>.

not even the fiercest critics of the patent system say that *all* patents in force for Germany were invalid.

Also, only very few nullity verdicts are handed down every year. As the BPatG reported for 2014, only about 0.02 per cent of all patents in force for Germany are invalidated.[33] In 2010–2013, figures were even smaller: only 171 patents were completely invalidated and 139 in part.[34]

Both aspects reduce the value of statistics, particularly since the BGH's patent panel only confirms 58 per cent of all BPatG nullity rulings.[35] Out of these decisions, two-thirds favour patent holders so that BPatG nullity verdicts are withdrawn, fully or in part. Thus, the BGH's patent panel is more likely to rule in favour of right holders than the BPatG – raising the question whether the BPatG invalidates patents too quickly.

Admittedly, the BPatG is right when it points out that partial invalidations differ substantially from total invalidations, in quantity as well as quality.[36] Treating both the same does not correctly reflect patent practice and hence is inadequate.[37]

F. Remedies

Any readjustment of patent nullity proceedings must accept that there cannot be legal force for patents as under administrative law. Nevertheless, patents, too, need some legal certainty because otherwise they cannot carry out their role of incentivising inventive activity. Therefore, it is not acceptable that the 'real' patent examination is being outsourced to the BPatG. This makes patent offices and their work dispensable and inflates applicants' and right holders' costs. For this very reason, examination standards, too, should not vary. Rather, they must be consistent.

As a result, BPatG nullity examination should be rethought and diverging examination standards should be tackled. After all, this is where the problems lie. This would also be in line with modern US patent examination procedures (*ex parte* re-examination, post-grant review, *inter partes* review), which are characterised by materiality thresholds for accessing proceedings: for instance, the motion for re-examination requires submission of a substantial new issue of patentability, and nullity plaintiffs

33 Bundespatentgericht (n 11) 62 right-hand column.
34 Hess, Müller-Stoy and Wintermeier (n 9) 439, 440.
35 Confirmations also include actions rejected by the BPatG where the nullity plaintiff files an appeal on points of fact and law and the BGH rejects this appeal.
36 Bundespatentgericht (n 11) 62 left-hand column.
37 Cf also Hüttermann (n 22) 101.

are estopped with arguments they could have put forward in previous proceedings. Conversely, for newly discovered prior art no estoppel exists.

Access to BPatG nullity suits in revised German patent review proceedings should be shaped so that DPMA objection proceedings are revitalised. Here, numbers have decreased for 15 years. While in 2004, 841 objections were filed against DPMA grant rulings, that number decreased to a mere 257 in 2014. This is worrying because the shift from DPMA objection proceedings to BPatG nullity proceedings appears to be tactically motivated. If parties settled and the nullity plaintiff withdrew his action, the patent would remain in force and the nullity plaintiff would be favourably licensed – at the expense of competitors. In objection proceedings before the offices, this would not be possible. Here, the objection's withdrawal only terminated the objecting party's standing, but did not end the examination. So even after the objection's withdrawal, offices could continue scrutinising the objected office decision to grant.[38]

IV. CONCLUSION

Concluding, it needs to be said that all considerations of legal certainty for patent holders must begin with true legal force not being an option for patents. Nonetheless, patents, too, need a minimum of legal certainty because 'real' patent examination taking place only before the BPatG (with an option for infinite relaunch) would be untenable. Less so because it would reduce the relevance of patent office work, but because a patent system that would first generate patents and then, after grant, burden them with a latent nullity rate of up to 80 per cent, would lose purpose.

However, there is no disputing the fact that success rates of nullity suits against German patents and for European patents valid for Germany are considerable; even though this is not new and has not changed for over 50 years. Also, even though most nullity suits are filed against patents that are being enforced, enforcement of patents and patent quality are largely decoupled. Otherwise, nullity suits would not be filed against a mere 50 per cent of all patents enforced.

Whether high success rates of nullity actions are a result more of inadequate patent quality or of differing examination standards for inventive step is doubtful. Not only does inventive step constitute the most

[38] Kraßer and Ann (n 4) s 26, no 172 and s 30, no 44; Frédéric Bostedt, *Singer/Stauder Europäisches Patentübereinkommen* (7th edn, Carl Heymanns 2016) art 101 nos 87–90.

significant grounds for patent revocation before the BPatG, but a large number of cases are settled (which is no superior form of nullity) and the numbers of partial as well as total invalidations are roughly the same. Partial invalidation before the BGH is reduced in favour of patent holders in a high percentage of cases so that right holders in the end retain more than the BPatG had been willing to give them.

All in all, this discussion should be a reason for further addressing legal certainty for patents as a topic. Even though patents can never enjoy unconditional legal force, the patent system must continue to incentivise inventive activity, must stay open for SMEs, and must avoid dangerous side-effects.

The question of how patent nullity and hence patent value should be addressed further will stay with us for years to come – irrespective of the UK leaving the European Union and of the EU's Unitary Patent and Unified Patent Court System (UP/UPC) getting off the ground.

11. Intellectual property rights in a digital environment: an EU-wide mapping of available legislative enforcement measures

Ana Nordberg and Knud Wallberg*

I. INTRODUCTION

The rationale for intellectual property rights (IPRs) primarily emerged from two different logics. Legal protection for intellectual creations or immaterial goods has been justified based on views of (1) intellectual property as a manifestation of personality, and as an exterior actualisation/extension of personality and thus inherently linked to personality rights; and (2) intellectual property as a means to protect the creative and innovative results of human endeavour, in other words, as an economic asset that is capable of being considered an immaterial form of property. Historically, both personality and utilitarian-based justifications for IPRs were developed based on observations and by reference to the then material world.[1]

Today, however, we live in a world where material reality is complemented by a dematerialised space, or a digital ecosystem; a space where traditional market barriers and transaction costs, by default, either do not exist or are substantially reduced. Simultaneously, the digital ecosystem, made possible by the internet, has become so much more than a mere tool for work and leisure. It has become a primary space of socialisation, information sharing, free expression of opinions, and global cultural and educational exchange. Finally, and most importantly in this context, the

* All online sources were last accessed on 27 December 2018.

[1] See Lyman Ray Patterson, *Copyright in Historical Perspective* (Vanderbilt University Press 1968); Josef Kohler, *Das Recht des Markenschutzes* (Stahel 1885); Franck I Schechter, 'The Rational Basis of Trade Mark Protection' (1927) 40 (6) Harv L Rev 813ff; Franck I Schechter, *The Historical Foundations of the Law Relating to Trade Marks* (Columbia University Press 1925).

internet has developed to become a dominant forum for commercial trade and continuous development of new businesses and business models.

The (still) widespread vision of the digital world as a space of freedom, without national borders and (little) regulatory supervision, contrasts with the basic notion and function of IPRs as private entitlements over artistic and commercial creations of the mind, which is based on detailed legislation and is linked to national or regional territories. It is thus not surprising that the enforcement of IPRs has faced constraints and difficulties. Online infringements are at the outset enforced under the countries' general procedural rules concerning jurisdiction and evidence that are applicable to all types of infringements. There is an inherent tension in applying the same procedures and normative frameworks to a global digital world. The online infringements of IPRs raise difficult challenges, especially regarding territoriality, jurisdiction and other trans-border issues. Moreover, online infringements of IPRs are often of a dematerialised nature and are difficult to subsume under rules that were drafted with off-line infringements in mind.

Legislators have, however, been aware of these difficulties and steps have been taken towards adapting and applying the legislative measures aimed at the enforcement of IPRs in the digital era. A number of legislative measures that aim at facilitating online enforcement have thus already been adopted. The measures do not always specifically target IPRs, but do also encompass them. At the European Union (EU) level, examples of such legislative measures are the Enforcement Directive,[2] the Regulation on Customs Enforcement of Intellectual Property Rights,[3] and the Electronic Commerce Directive.[4] There are no specific EU instruments of harmonisation on administrative or criminal enforcement of IPRs. However, the European Arrest Warrant,[5] the European Evidence Warrant[6] (and

---

2 Corrigendum to Directive 2004/48/EC of 29 April 2004 on the enforcement of intellectual property rights [2004] OJ L157/16.

3 Council Regulation (EU) 608/2013 of 12 June 2013 concerning customs enforcement of intellectual property rights and repealing Council Regulation (EC) 1383/2003 [2013] OJ L181/15.

4 Council Directive 2000/31/EC of 8 June 2000 on certain legal aspects of information society services, in particular electronic commerce, in the Internal Market [2000] OJ L178/1 (E-commerce Directive).

5 Council Framework Decision 2002/584/JHA of 13 June 2002 on the European arrest warrant and the surrender procedures between Member States [2002] OJ L190/1.

6 Council Framework Decision 2008/978/JHA of 18 December 2008 on the European evidence warrant for the purpose of obtaining objects, documents and data for use in proceedings in criminal matters [2008] OJ L350/72.

the European Investigation Order, under implementation)[7] as well as money laundering legislation[8] can, at least to some extent, be applied in IPRs infringement situations. Moreover, at the international level, the TRIPS Agreement[9] provides an international basis for enforcement of IPRs, and the Council of Europe Cybercrime Convention[10] has created a number of tools with relevance to the enforcement of IPRs. The World Intellectual Property Organization (WIPO) has also been active in this field, with the adoption of the WIPO Copyright Treaty (WCT)[11] and the WIPO Performances and Phonograms Treaty,[12] as well as the adoption of the Joint Recommendation Concerning Provisions on the Protection of Marks, and Other Industrial Property Rights in Signs, on the Internet.[13]

In this chapter, we will present the main findings of a recent research project on legislative measures related to the online infringement of IPRs[14] that we had the pleasure to conduct for and in cooperation with the European Union Intellectual Property Office (EUIPO).[15]

---

[7] Council Directive 2014/41/EU of 3 April 2014 regarding the European Investigation Order in criminal matters [2014] OJ L130/1.

[8] Council Directive 2005/60/EC of 26 October 2005 on the prevention of the use of the financial system for the purpose of money laundering and terrorist financing [2005] OJ L309/15; Council Directive (EU) 2015/849 of 20 May 2015 on the prevention of the use of the financial system for the purposes of money laundering or terrorist financing, amending Council Regulation (EU) No 648/2012, and repealing Council Directive 2005/60/EC and Commission Directive 2006/70/EC [2015] OJ L141/73.

[9] Agreement on Trade-Related Aspects of Intellectual Property Rights (opened for signature 15 April 1994, entered into force 1 January 1996) 1869 UNTS 299 (TRIPS).

[10] Council of Europe, Convention on Cybercrime, Budapest (November 2001) CETS 185.

[11] WIPO Copyright Treaty (adopted 20 December 1996, entered into force 6 March 2002) 2186 UNTS 121.

[12] WIPO Performances and Phonograms Treaty (adopted 20 December 1996, entered into force 20 May 2002) 2186 UNTS 203.

[13] Joint Recommendation Concerning Provisions on the Protection of Marks and Other Industrial Property Rights in Signs, on the Internet (Adopted by the Assembly of the Paris Union for the Protection of Industrial Property and the General Assembly of the World Intellectual Property Organization (WIPO) at the Thirty-Sixth Series of Meetings of the Assemblies of the Member States of WIPO 24 September to 3 October 2001) 845(E) <www.wipo.int/publications/en/details.jsp?id=345&plang=EN>.

[14] Study on legislative measures related to online IPR infringements, commissioned by the European Union Intellectual Property Office (2018) <https://euipo.europa.eu/ohimportal/en/web/observatory/observatory-publications>.

[15] Former Office for Harmonization of the Internal Market (OHIM).

II. BACKGROUND, METHODOLOGY AND APPROACH

Infringements of IPRs have taken and do increasingly take place on the internet. This trend has been widely identified and has raised concerns among multiple stakeholders and has led to a number of recent initiatives at EU level.[16]

Even before these recent initiatives, a number of legislative measures had been adopted at the international level as well as in the EU with the overall aim of reinforcing and further harmonising the protection of IPRs. These measures include provisions aimed at enabling right holders and law enforcement authorities (public prosecutors, police forces and administrative authorities) to enforce IPRs in an improved and effective manner.[17] However, as already the titles of the aforementioned legislative measures indicate, the legislation was for the most part drafted to apply generally and not with the specific purpose of addressing the need to prevent, deter or disrupt infringements of IPRs in the digital environment. Furthermore, the legislative measures were for the most part drafted as minimum requirements that leave room for the countries to adopt and apply additional national measures. The main purpose of the study was therefore to investigate the availability and the actual application of a number of very specific enforcement measures that may be used to prevent, disrupt or sanction infringements of IPRs in the online environment.

In geographical terms, the study was designed to cover all Member States of the EU at the relevant date.[18] As far as the material scope is concerned, the study focused on enforcement measures that may be used to immediately prevent or disrupt online infringement of trade marks, and copyright and related rights, and thus damages and compensation measures were not considered.

A number of transversal topical issues were initially identified in literary sources and through consultation with relevant stakeholders and the members of the expert group that was established to serve as an

---

16 Most notably the 2013 Europol Serious and Organised Crime Threat Assessment (SOCTA); the EU Customs Action Plan to combat IP infringements for the years 2013–2017; the Commission Communication on a Digital Market Strategy for Europe COM(2015) 192 final; and the joint Europol and EUIPO Situation Report on Counterfeiting in the EU, the latest report being from 2017.

17 See Study on legislative measures (n 14) chapter 8.

18 The study was conducted during 2017, and the likely future exit of the UK and its potential repercussions were not taken into consideration for the purposes of designing its scope.

advisory committee for the study. From among these numerous topics, the following eight were selected, namely: legislative measures capable of allowing right holders and authorities to obtain account information of the suspected infringer; measures blocking access to websites; measures suitable for actions targeted at domain names; measures suitable for actions targeted at hosts; judicial cooperation in investigation including the European Investigation Order; extradition procedures including the European Arrest Warrant; measures on money laundering provisions; and lastly criminal sanctions.

The reasons for choosing these eight topics followed a decision that the study should investigate legal measures from the perspective of those seeking enforcement, and thus the study focuses on legal measures that are able to provide 'practical solutions to practical problems'. These entail, for example, the possibility to obtain from an online service provider the disclosure of the identity of a customer/user based on the suspicion of infringement of IPRs, and the possibility of the European Investigation Order applying to specific categories of substantive conducts involving IPRs.[19]

From a research perspective, the project followed an empirical approach. The initial part of the study consisted of a mapping exercise, seeking to identify the available legislative measures in each EU Member State. The main tool that was applied for this purpose consisted of two questionnaires: the first concerning civil measures and a second concerning criminal measures.

There were two main methodological justifications for such a division. First, from a practical enforcement perspective, de facto applicability, availability and viability of enforcement measures depends largely on national procedural rules. Rules on judicial procedure will tend to have a very different configuration depending on whether the judicial enforcement is conducted under civil or criminal law.[20] Second, having in mind the national diversity in such matters, and because the study was intended to have a practice-oriented perspective, it was necessary to resort to two

---

[19] Previous Observatory studies have looked into IPR infringements in the online environment but none of them deal with the issue of which concrete, existing, legislative measures can be used to prevent or combat online infringements of IPRs. See for example Study on voluntary collaboration practices in addressing online infringements of trade mark rights, design rights, copyright and rights related to copyright (2016).

[20] We were made aware that some measures may have an administrative or hybrid nature.

different groups of respondents with enforcement experience and technical expertise.

The questionnaires were presented and debated with the expert group that was established for the study and which functioned as an advisory board, after which they were sent out to representatives of all EU Member States through two different networks of practitioners.[21] These networks agreed to select and recruit individual respondents with practical experience and expertise in national enforcement matters.

Replies were received on most of the detailed questions and from the vast majority, albeit not all, EU Member States,[22] which is a methodological limitation that was taken into account in the analysis and conclusions. It was not within the scope of the empirical investigation to independently verify each reply in light of theoretical legal knowledge and academic debates. In other words, the information that was retrieved presented the views of the respondents and thus reflects the legal interpretation of the current legislation as seen from the practical perspective of persons who deal with infringement cases regularly, and in the national jurisdictions concerned. Both of these conditions are important in the following analysis, particularly as far as country-specific examples are concerned. These limitations should be kept in mind but do not affect the core goal of the project – to draw an overall picture of the availability of the legislative measures in the EU Member States seen from a practical rights enforcement perspective, rather than drawing a detailed picture of the legislation and legal debates in each Member State.

III. COMMON IPR-INFRINGING ACTIVITIES IN THE DIGITAL ENVIRONMENT

In addition to our own literary surveys, the selection of topics was carried out in close cooperation with the EUIPO and the established expert group. As part of this exercise it was expedient to first identify and describe the types of online infringement activities that were considered to be the most relevant in relation to the study. Since IPR-infringing activities in the online environment are heterogeneous both regarding the substantive

---

21 The questionnaire on civil measures was distributed to the members of ECTA's Internet Committee. The questionnaire on criminal measures was sent to the various national authorities through EUROJUST. As members of the original project team, the present authors wish to acknowledge the importance of the contributions and express our gratitude to all the respondents.

22 See Study on legislative measures (n 14) chapter 4.

actions or material content of the infringements and regarding the technological means that are used,[23] the below-mentioned list of activities is not, and is not intended to be, an exhaustive one.

A. Illegal Sharing and Distribution of Copyright-protected Works

Illegal copying, communication and distribution of copyrighted works in the digital environment occurs in many different ways. The first and still widely applied way to distribute illegal copies of copyright-protected works consists of file sharing. File sharing is the practice of distributing or providing access to digital files such as computer programs, multimedia files, documents or e-books. In this context, digital files are files that include or consist of material protected by copyright or related rights. File sharing is also carried out in several ways. The original method consisted in manual sharing of files copied to a CD-ROM or similar movable storage devices, later methods take place completely online and include the use of dedicated file hosting servers of cyberlockers or the use of peer-to-peer (P2P) networking.[24]

In more recent years, streaming has become a major means of copyright infringement. This is particularly visible in unauthorised streaming of live events, but also of popular TV series. 'Streaming' refers to a technique for transferring data in a steady and continuous stream. Streaming technology allows the client's browser or plug-in to start displaying the data before the entire file containing the material is transmitted.[25] This constitutes an advantage for those users that do not have access to an internet connection fast enough to download large multimedia files quickly.

The lack of national barriers on the internet, and the territoriality artificially maintained by the continued existence of national systems for licensing and managing rights has created factual barriers to portability and EU-wide offers of licensed content.[26] This fact has been considered

---

23 EUIPO, 'Research on Online Business Models Infringing Intellectual Property Rights' (2016).

24 Wording based on the description of file sharing found at <www.techopedia.com/definition/16256/file-sharing>. See Canvas 24 in the above mentioned EUIPO study for a description of the use of cyberlockers for IPR infringing activities.

25 Based on the definition found at <www.webopedia.com/TERM/S/streaming.html>.

26 De Wolf & Partners, 'Report on Contractual Clauses for the Online Distribution of Content: Final Report A Study Prepared for the European Commission DG Communications Networks, Content & Technology' Ref Ares (2017) 5134801 8–10 <https://ec.europa.eu/digital-single-market/en/news/report-contractual-clauses-online-distribution-content>; European Commission, 'Travel

to be at least partly responsible for some of the cultural attitudes that are less favourable to the legitimate interests of artists and other right holders.[27]

B. Sale and Distribution of IPR-infringing Goods

According to recent figures from Eurostat, during 2015, about 65 per cent of EU internet users shopped online.[28] A considerable portion of this trade takes place through known online marketplaces[29] but online commerce also takes place and through ordinary web shops, i.e. web shops that operate under their own dedicated domain names, and also to some extent via social media platforms. This growth in legitimate online trade is, however, being paralleled by a similar increase in illicit trade. Digital marketplaces are used often as a market channel for illicit goods such as counterfeited software, clothes and mobile phones.[30] Similar situations occur on social media platforms.[31]

Another infringement trend is the creation of websites selling counterfeit goods, designed to induce the consumer to believe they are using an official website of a particular brand owner. These websites often use domain names that include a third-party trademark and reproduce the content and design of the brand owner website.[32]

---

with your digital subscriptions: Joint statement by the European Commission, the European Parliament and the Bulgarian Presidency of the Council of the EU' STATEMENT/18/2341 of 27 March 2018 <http://europa.eu/rapid/press-release_STATEMENT-18-2341_en.htm>.

[27] See recent EU legislative initiatives of the EU to tackle these issues, such as Council Regulation (EU) 2017/1128 of 14 June 2017 on cross-border portability of online content services in the internal market [2017] OJ L168/1.

[28] See the Digital Agenda Scoreboard (2016) <https://ec.europa.eu/digital-single-market/en/digital-scoreboard>.

[29] An overview of marketplaces across Europe can be found at <www.bvoh.de/overview-of-online-marketplaces-across-europe/>. A list of the top 20 marketplaces by traffic is listed in 'Commission Staff Working Document: Online Platforms' (2016 SWD 172) 17 – 18.

[30] An illustrative example can be found in Canvas 8 in 'Research on Online Business Models Infringing Intellectual Property Rights' EUIPO (2016).

[31] An illustrative example can be found in Canvas 9 in 'Research on Online Business Models Infringing Intellectual Property Rights' EUIPO (2016).

[32] See 'Research on Online Business Models Infringing Intellectual Property Rights – Phase 2 Suspected trade mark infringing e-shops utilizing previously used domain names' EUIPO (2017).

C. Fraud, Extortion and Other Traditional Cybercriminal Offences

The above-mentioned types of infringements of IPR frequently reach a scale where the infringements may also constitute criminal offences, meaning that the penal provisions in national IPR legislation or in the relevant penal codes may apply.[33] In addition, trade marks are used for acts that are classified as criminal offences from the outset, as for example in the widespread 'phishing scams'. The term 'phishing' is generally used to describe malicious attempts to acquire money and sensitive information or to install malware. Phishing attempts are initiated through contact with victims via chat and text services, e-mails and postings on social media platforms or blogs. The victim is often redirected to a third-party website. The contact will immediately appear to be sent in good faith and for a legitimate purpose. Because the sender address makes use of a domain name that resembles the genuine domain name of a company (or institution) it will thus create the impression that it originates in such legitimate entity.

Spear phishing is an advanced and focused form of phishing that targets specific individuals and requires a larger and more focused effort from the attacker.[34] A more recent variation of spear phishing is boss phishing or CEO fraud in which the sender of the mail impersonates a manager or leader of an organisation and persuades an entry- or middle-level employee to transfer money, internal documents or other types of assets to the sender.[35]

Common to these infringing models is the establishment of a spoofing website, i.e. a website that is a close imitation of the official website of the impersonated company or person. The use of spoofing websites explains why a visit to the website does not necessarily create any suspicion about the malicious circumstances.[36] The phishing communication will often contain a hyperlink to the spoofing website but these websites can also be visited independently. Once visiting the spoofing website, the victim will be prompted to reveal personal data and similar sensitive information

---

[33] EUIPO, 2017 Situation Report on Counterfeiting and Piracy in the European Union (2017) <www.europol.europa.eu/publications-documents/2017-situation-report-counterfeiting-and-piracy-in-european-union>.

[34] Definition adopted in Business Model study.

[35] See *inter alia* 'CEO Phishing Scams Up the Identity Theft Stakes' <www.idtheftcenter.org>.

[36] See EUIPO, 'Canvas 16 in 'Research on Online Business Models Infringing Intellectual Property Rights' (2016).

under various false pretexts, such as updating credit card information, confirmation of passwords, or enabling security features.

Depending on the exact scope of what the user is lured into doing, such acts may result in one or more criminal offences: for example, such conduct may be classified as fraud if the attacker manages to lure the victim into paying a sum for a non-existent obligation or a non-existent product or service. If the attack results in installation of ransomware, it may amount to extortion, and the installation of malware may amount to vandalism.[37] Having their trade marks and trade names involuntarily associated with such criminal activities naturally causes right holders concern regarding their trade marks and company reputation.

D. Cybersquatting and Other Trademark-infringing Uses of Domain Names

Domain names play a key role in a number of IPR-infringing activities. Cybersquatting was the first widespread type of IPR-infringing use of domain names and covers situations where the registration and use of a domain name that is identical or confusingly similar to a third party's trade mark is done in bad faith and with the intention to profit.[38] A variation of cybersquatting is 'typosquatting', where a registrant acquires misspellings of domain names with the intention of misleading internet users and thus diverting and exploiting the internet traffic that was originally intended for the genuine websites. Both phenomena continue to occur frequently,[39] arguably due to not only the implementation of the many new generic top-level domains such as .xyz and .top,[40] but also because of the continuous development of ways to gain revenue from such registrations such as 'pay-per-click' revenues and revenues based on affiliate advertising schemes.[41]

---

37 Because there are differences in penal laws, the terms fraud, extortion and vandalism are here used in a generic sense, and not as legal definitions of specific types of illicit acts and behaviour.

38 There does not seem to be a uniform definition of the term. The term stems from the US Anti-Cybersquatting Consumer Protection Act (ACPA) 15 USC, s 1125 (D) but is used in many other contexts and with different meanings.

39 WIPO, 'WIPO Cybersquatting Cases Hit Record in 2016, Driven by New Top-Level Domain Names' <www.wipo.int/pressroom/en/articles/2017/article_0003.html>.

40 See the press release from WIPO, 'WIPO Cybersquatting Cases Reach New Record in 2017' <www.wipo.int/pressroom/en/articles/2018/article_0001.html>.

41 See the description of such revenue schemes in EUIPO, 'Research on Online Business Models Infringing Intellectual Property Rights' para 5.3.2 (2016).

The domain name system is also being used for other types of infringing use of trade marks, such as the above-mentioned fraudulent e-mail phishing scams.[42]

IV. ENFORCEMENT OF INTELLECTUAL PROPERTY RIGHTS IN THE DIGITAL ENVIRONMENT: SOME TRANSVERSAL ISSUES

Right holders facing an infringement of their copyright and trade marks may rely on a variety of civil and criminal remedies in order to disrupt infringements and obtain compensation.

Traditionally, trade mark proprietors, authors and other right holders will enforce their IPRs through litigation or resorting to law enforcement authorities. Typically, such actions are initiated against a suspected infringer, which may be either the producer, the distributor or the vendor of the infringing goods, services or materials. It is, however, widely recognised that such actions often fall short when it comes to effectively tackling infringing conduct online. Aware of such difficulties, both right holders and enforcement authorities have searched for alternative models to investigate and enforce rights infringed in a digital environment and with the traditional difficulties of cross-border enforcement. Increasingly, using the position of online intermediaries as 'natural points of control' is how effective enforcement has developed.[43] This study reflects this trend by including analyses of whether and to what extent existing legislative measures may be used and employed both in relation to the immediately suspected infringer and to the relevant intermediaries.

These factors and the fact that the types of infringement conduct are multiple and heterogeneous made it necessary to limit the scope of

---

[42] See the business models involving use of others' trademarks in domain names described in Canvasses 3, 4, 5, 16, 17 and 19 of EUIPO, 'Research on Online Business Models Infringing Intellectual Property Rights' (2016). For reference to examples of recent case law, see Knud Wallberg, 'Recent Developments in Domain Name Law and Practice under the .dk Top Level Domain' (2017) 1 Nordiskt Immateriellt Rättsskydd 40.

[43] Maayan Perel (Filmar) and Niva Elkin-Koren, 'Accountability in Algorithmic Copyright Enforcement' (2016) 19 Stan Tech L Rev 473 https://ssrn.com/abstract=2607910 (it is put in the following way: 'Online intermediaries have acquired an important role in managing online behaviour and enforcing the rights of Internet users. They offer a natural point of control for monitoring, filtering, blocking, and disabling access to content, which makes them ideal partners for performing civil and criminal enforcement').

the study. Therefore, a limited number of horizontal issues linked to enforcement were selected. Selection criteria focused on measures that play a crucial role in determining the existence of an infringement; allow the direct infringer and other participants in the infringing activities to be identified; allow relevant evidence of such infringing conduct to be obtained; disrupt the infringement activities; ensure that the infringers can effectively be brought to trial in the concerned jurisdiction; and finally ensure that (custodial) sentences can be executed. In this regard, eight horizontal topics were identified (see Table 11.1) and will be the object of analysis in the following sections.

As the following sections will illustrate, the mapping and the analysis of the legislative measures that are available in the responding EU Member States in relation to the above-listed topics showed both EU-wide commonalities and national plurality of approaches to enforcement.

A. Obtaining Information on the Identity of the Suspected Infringer

Establishing the identity of the suspected infringer is most often a necessary precondition to legal proceedings susceptible of stopping or at least disrupting the infringement conduct. In cases of sharing of files or streaming of copyright-protected material, it is often relatively simple to determine the Internet Protocol (IP) address used, except when the IP address is concealed by technical means. It is also often the case that the alleged infringement takes place by means of use of a third-party IP address.

When the infringing activity takes place on an open online platform, such as an online market place or a social network, it is possible to identify the 'account' of the alleged infringer. However, the identification of the holder of the account is privy to the operator of the platform.

Often infringement occurs on a dedicated website, i.e. a website that uses a specific domain name as its internet address. Websites that are used to promote or distribute infringing products, services or materials seldom contain reliable information on the party controlling the website. Although the domain registries maintain publicly available WHOIS databases in relation to the registrants, the accuracy of the information in these databases is largely dependent on the correctness of the information provided by the registrants.[44] On certain top-level domains, registrants can

---

[44] The issue of false contact information is often mentioned in the literature. See WIPO, 'WIPO Jurisprudential Overview 3.0' (overview of WIPO Panel Views on Selected UDRP Questions) <http://www.wipo.int/amc/en/domains/search/overview3.0/>; For an illustrative example, see WIPO Case DNL2017-0068 *Dr*

Table 11.1 Enforcement of IPRs in an online environment: horizontal topics

TOPIC	KEY ISSUES
Obtaining account information	• Retrieval of information from online intermediaries on: • the account holder contact information (the challenge of false contact information) • the IP-addresses that are used for the infringing actions • WHOIS-information related to the domain name
Blocking access to websites	• Websites hosted in the Member State itself • Websites hosted in other EU Member States • Websites hosted in non-EU Member States
Domain name actions	• Types of actions (suspension, transfer, etc.) • Towards the Registry • Towards the Registrar • Towards the Registrant
Actions targeted at hosts	• Actors hosting or advertising infringing material: • Takedown of concrete listings • Suspension, blocking etc. of specific vendor accounts • Suspension, blocking etc. of future accounts of a specific account holder
European Investigation Order	• Its application to online infringements of IPR, and if so its application to: • requesting information on bank accounts • freezing or confiscation of the deposits of such accounts • locating and seizing servers used for suspected infringements • interception and seizing of counterfeited products before they reach the consumer
Extradition European Arrest Warrant	• Its application to online infringements of IPRs, and if so its application to: • extradition of infringers or suspected infringers from other EU Member States
Money laundering	• Its application to online infringements of IPR
Criminal sanctions	• Maximum sentences • Time limits for prosecution • Infringements at a non-commercial scale • Objective liability • Liability for companies

rely on the use of a privacy or proxy service that results in concealing their identity in the WHOIS register. How this database should be modelled in the future is not clear. An interim model was created[45] in order to ensure compliance with the General Data Protection Regulation;[46] however, since it has been the object of regulatory criticism, further changes are likely to occur.[47]

It is therefore very important to determine whether the different online intermediaries can be ordered to disclose the information in their possession on a customer/user, upon suspicion that the customer is using the intermediary services for conducting IPR-infringing activities. Legislative measures that concern the disclosure of information on a suspected infringer are available as a starting point in all EU Member States. The legal basis for the diverse national measures has been harmonised to a certain extent by the relevant articles in the Enforcement Directive (IPRED).[48]

1. Disclosure of the identity of the holder of a particular account

The right holders' right to information in IPR infringement cases is stipulated in Article 8(1) of the IPRED but it does not specifically address the right to obtain account information. The Directive does allow Member States to grant right holders 'rights to receive fuller information'[49] than those cited. The mapping showed that national legislation in most Member States[50] can in general be applied by the competent judicial authority[51] to order an internet intermediary to disclose such account information, provided that the request meets general procedural requirements of being 'justified and proportionate'.[52] Specifically concerning criminal enforcement

---

Martens International Trading GmbH Dr Martens Marketing GmbH v Olga Olga s 6B concerning the domain name <doktermartens.nl>.

45 See <www.icann.org/resources/pages/gtld-registration-data-specs-en>.

46 Council Regulation (EU) 2016/679 of 27 April 2016 on the protection of natural persons with regard to the processing of personal data and on the free movement of such data, and repealing Directive 95/46/EC (General Data Protection Regulation) [2016] OJ L119/1.

47 See Data Protection Working Party to the ICANN, Brussels (April 2018) art 29 <https://www.icann.org/en/system/files/correspondence/jelinek-to-marby-11apr18-en.pdf>.

48 Enforcement Directive (n 2).

49 Ibid art 8(3)(a).

50 Except for example Malta and Slovenia.

51 Usually the courts or in criminal proceedings the public prosecutor. Some Member States reported that other authorities may also require this information, for example in Spain the Intellectual Property Commission.

52 Or similar wording to that effect.

measures, in almost all EU Member States an online intermediary can be asked to disclose account information on a particular customer, with the exception of Germany, where survey replies indicated this was not possible and Spain, where the matter is unresolved. Procedural requirements may apply, such as the measure being requested by a competent authority and authorised or validated by a judicial authority, and that the order fulfils general requisites and procedural guarantees.

2. Contact information on the holder of a specific account

In relation to contact information on the holder of a specific account, in a given online network or platform, the mapping suggests that it is possible through civil procedures to get a judicial decision ordering these intermediaries to disclose such information. In criminal proceedings, in those Member States that allow the possibility of ordering an intermediary to disclose account information on specific costumers, there is also the possibility of obtaining the individual contact information of the account holder.

3. Contact information on persons or entities using an IP address for intellectual property rights-infringing activities

IP addresses and associated information may be personal data, which means that the rules and principles of data protection must also be observed.[53] Such may be the case for static IP addresses[54] as well as for dynamic IP addresses.[55] The overall picture, regarding the contact information of a person or an entity that uses an IP address or makes a server available under an IP address provided by its access provider, is that it is generally possible in all Member States to get a judicial decision that orders the provider of the online service to disclose this information, both in civil and criminal procedures.[56]

---

[53] Council Regulation (EU) 2016/679 of 27 April 2016 on the protection of natural persons with regard to the processing of personal data and on the free movement of such data, and repealing Directive 95/46/EC (General Data Protection Regulation) [2016] OJ L119/1; Council Directive (EU) 2016/680 of 27 April 2016 on the protection of natural persons with regard to the processing of personal data by competent authorities for the purposes of the prevention, investigation, detection or prosecution of criminal offences or the execution of criminal penalties, and on the free movement of such data, and repealing Council Framework Decision 2008/977/JHA [2016] OJ L119/89.

[54] See Case C-70/10 *Scarlet Extended SA v SABAM* (2011) ECLI:EU:C:2011:771, [51].

[55] See Case C-582/14 *Patrick Breyer v Bundesrepublik Deutschland* (2016) ECLI:EU:C:2016:779.

[56] Notable exceptions are reportedly Greece and Spain, where this issue was

4. Contact information of the registrant of a domain name

If the registrant of a domain name is an individual person, that person may[57] invoke the applicable rules on the protection of personal data and request that registrant information[58] not be publicly accessible in the WHOIS database. In addition, as mentioned above, some registries allow registrants to use privacy services or proxy holders. However, in civil and criminal proceedings in all EU Members States[59] such information may, in principle,[60] be disclosed, albeit the specific procedures to obtain such information vary across Member States.

B. Blocking of Access to Websites

If an IPR-infringing activity takes place on or through a dedicated website it is immediately evident that an effective way to disrupt and to prevent such activities from taking place is to prevent internet users from accessing the website.[61] The defendants in these cases are the intermediaries, established companies that can be immediately identified, and thus be the subject of legal actions. Blocking orders have therefore become a legal remedy that is frequently used.[62]

Blocking of the access to a website is, however, a limited and targeted legal measure. The website will not cease to exist and may be accessible via access providers not covered by the blocking order, namely providers in other jurisdictions. These may voluntarily agree to follow such an order and it is noteworthy that major providers in a number of EU Member States have agreed to implement blocking orders against a specific website or a specific service even when a blocking order formally only obliges one of the signatory access providers.[63]

---

reported as being unresolved or debatable as far as criminal proceedings are concerned.

[57] The issue is not settled yet at EU level.

[58] Which usually includes name, address, telephone number and e-mail address.

[59] See <https://eurid.eu/en/register-a-eu-domain/domain-name-disputes/>.

[60] The matter is listed as unresolved in six Member States.

[61] See EUIPO-commissioned study, section 8.4 regarding inactivation of a website by targeting the website's domain name and section 8.5 regarding measures targeted at the hosts of the infringing activities.

[62] See *inter alia* the recurring Europol operation 'In Our Sites' <https://www.europol.europa.eu/activities-services/europol-in-action/operations/operation-in-our-sites-ios-vi>.

[63] Some illustrative examples are the 2015 Portuguese 'Memorando de Entendimento' (Memorandum of Understanding), which is published in Portuguese at <https://paulasimoesblog.files.wordpress.com/2015/09/memorando.

The general rule on the exemption of the liability of access providers in civil matters[64] is set out in Article 12(1) of the E-commerce Directive and provides that the access provider is not liable for the information transmitted by its customers, in specified conditions. This provision does not affect courts or the administrative authorities of the Member States, requiring access providers to terminate or prevent infringements, in accordance with national rules.[65]

Injunctions in the form of blocking orders are in principle available in all Member States,[66] except Slovenia.[67] Injunctions are available both in civil and criminal proceedings.[68] It is common ground that a blocking order can only be issued if it is found to be a both effective and proportionate remedy in the specific case.[69] It is noteworthy that both the substantive and procedural requirements vary among Member States.[70]

C. Domain Name Actions

As mentioned above in Section III D, domain names play a key role in various types of online infringements and have done so for the past two decades. Partly because of the comprehensive harmonisation within the EU of the laws on trade marks and on copyright and neighbouring rights, there are some clear rules. If a domain name is used for activities that infringe copyrights or trade marks, a court may order the infringer to

---

pdf>, and the 'Code of Conduct for Handling Decisions to Block Access to Services which Infringe Intellectual Property Rights' adopted by the members of the Telecom Industry Association, Denmark, <https://rettighedsalliancen.dk/wp-content/uploads/2017/04/CoCrev_dec16_UK.pdf>.

64 The issue of liability in criminal matters is not subject to harmonisation at EU level.

65 Cf E-commerce Directive, art 12(3).

66 Council Directive 2001/29/EC on the harmonisation of certain aspects of copyright and related rights in the information society [2001] OJ L167/10 (INFOSOC Directive), art 8(3); Enforcement Directive (IPRED) (n 2) art 11. However, during our survey, the matter was reported as 'unresolved' in Bulgaria, Cyprus and Poland.

67 Blocking orders have been issued in relation to illegal online gambling websites.

68 Hungary reports that the remedy is only available in criminal proceedings.

69 The two said criteria are explicitly stated in art 3(2) of the Enforcement Directive (n 2).

70 The IPRED is a minimum harmonisation directive and the relevant provisions are worded in rather broad terms. It follows from general EU law that each Member State decides how to implement directives. Further, there is no harmonisation of the rules on civil and criminal procedures at EU level.

cease the infringing activities under the domain name, just as the court may impose damages, fines and other sanctions, whether civil, criminal or both in accordance with the general provisions of the relevant legislation.

It is, however, important to establish whether there are additional legal measures that can be applied to prevent resumption of an infringing use of a domain name. Therefore, the study focused on enquiring whether the suspension, deletion, transfer and seizure of domain names were available in the EU Member States, and to what extent these measures can be applied towards the registrants, the registrars and the registries respectively.[71]

The domain name system is not governed by any international treaty,[72] nor are the country code top-level domains (ccTLD) specific for each EU Member State subject to harmonisation at the EU level. Consequently, the specific requirements for registration, transfer and other activities relating to domain names under the ccTLDs vary among Member States, and there are also variations of legal measures available when a domain name is used for IPR-infringing activities.

The subject of a civil or criminal action that involves use of a domain name will be, as a starting point, the registrant of the domain name since it is justified to presume that the registrant is also the entity that is responsible for the actual use of the domain name.[73] However, it is important to consider whether the legal measures apply to the other key players in the legal and practical setup of the domain name system, primarily the ccTLD registries and the registrars in their capacity as 'name server managers' (NSMs).

The main outcome from the surveyed legislative measures (suspension, deletion, transfer and seizure) is that some of these are available in most Member States. However, none of them are available in all Member States. By way of example, it may be possible to obtain a court order that transfers infringing domain names from the holder of the domain names to the right holder in most Member States, while this will not be possible in some Member States (for example Germany, Austria[74] and the Czech Republic).[75]

---

[71] Reference is made to the description of the role of these actors in the description of the domain name system above in Section III.

[72] See the explanation of the domain name system above in Section III.

[73] This is, however, not always the case. Regarding anonymous or concealed registrants, see EUIPO Study (n 14).

[74] Supreme Court Case (2013) ZIR 2014/1 74.

[75] Supreme Court Case (2012) 23 Cd 3407/2010.

D. Actions Targeted at Hosts

The study mapped and focused on three different types of legal measures that are particularly relevant in relation to intermediaries that act as hosts for the infringing activities: first, takedowns of IPR-infringing offers or advertisements; secondly, blocking or suspension of existing accounts that are used to disseminate or distribute infringing goods and services; and finally, the possibility to block or otherwise prevent suspected infringers from opening future accounts.

The mapping and analysis of this topic also revealed a rather fragmented overall picture. On the one hand, the exemption from liability of hosting providers is covered by Article 14(1) of the E-commerce Directive.[76] However, the actual standard of secondary liability is not harmonised and relies on national law. Article 14(1) of the E-commerce Directive implies that the provider is not liable for the content that it hosts for its customers, unless the host knew that the content was illegal or does not act expeditiously to take down (i.e. remove or disable access to) the content as soon as it is made aware of the illegal content. Thus, while a hosting provider typically is not liable for infringing material, it is possible to get a court order that requires a host to take down IPR-infringing content from its platform in all Member States.

On the other hand, the possibility of demanding that a hosting provider suspends an existing account of a suspected infringer is not subject to specific EU legislation, and the mapping showed that this legal measure is either not available or the availability is unresolved in almost half of the Member States. The situation is even more fragmented when it comes to the possibility of preventing a suspected infringer from opening a new account with a hosting service when a previous account has been suspended. This legal measure is either not available or its availability is unclear or subject to legal debate in well over half of the Member States.

E. European Investigation Order

Infringements of IPRs in the digital environment come with a delocalisation of the infringing activities and of the suspected infringers. Infringing activities may take place in several Member States simultaneously, while the suspected infringers may be located in one or more Member States.

---

[76] Council Directive 2000/31/EC of 8 June 2000 on certain legal aspects of information society services, in particular electronic commerce, in the Internal Market (E-commerce Directive) [2000] OJ L178/1.

Investigative judicial cooperation between the Member States therefore plays an important role in enforcement of IPRs.

The European Investigation Order (EIO)[77] is a legislative measure of judicial cooperation between the Member States, replacing a previous more fragmented framework.[78] It is based on mutual recognition of decisions, which means that each Member State is obliged to recognise and carry out the request of another Member State, as it would do with a decision coming from its own authorities. Counterfeiting and piracy of products is included in the list of offences that are covered by the EIO, provided that the offence is subject to a maximum penalty of at least three years' imprisonment in the issuing country. However, not every type of IPR infringement is considered to be 'counterfeiting and piracy' under national law, and the maximum sentence in cases of counterfeiting and piracy is not three years in all Member States. Both factors limit the application of the EIO by the competent authorities in the Member States in relation to IPR infringements.

F. Extradition – European Arrest Warrant

The European Arrest Warrant (EAW)[79] is another simplified cross-border procedure for the purpose of prosecuting or executing a custodial sentence or detention order. The EAW may be applied in cases where infringing conduct takes place in several Member States simultaneously, while the suspected infringer or infringers may freely circulate or reside in other Member States. Needless to say, cross-border judicial cooperation plays an important role in such cases.

An EAW consists of a request issued by a judicial authority in one Member State (the issuing state) to detain a person located in another Member State (the executing state) and to surrender the said person for prosecution in the issuing Member State. 'Counterfeiting and piracy of products' as well as 'computer related crimes' are included in the list of

---

[77] Council Directive 2014/41/EU of 3 April 2014 regarding the European Investigation Order in Criminal Matters (EIO Dir) [2014] OJ L130/1.

[78] The EIO Directive is intended to create a comprehensive system to replace all the existing instruments in this area, including Council Framework Decision 2008/978/JHA on the European evidence warrant for the purpose of obtaining objects, documents and data for use in proceedings in criminal matters [2008] OJ L350/72, and it should cover 'as far as possible all types of evidence, containing time-limits for enforcement and limiting as far as possible the grounds for refusal' (recital 6 EIO Dir).

[79] Council Framework Decision 2002/584/JHA on the European arrest warrant and the surrender procedures between Member States (EAW) [2002] OJ L190/1.

offences which do not require that the offence is also a criminal act in the executing state.[80] This is a derogation from the general requirement of double criminality, which entails that the offence that forms the background for the EAW is punishable in both the issuing state and in the executing state.

However, the absence of the double criminality requirement is limited to situations where the offence is punishable by a custodial sentence or a detention order for a maximum period of at least three years by the law of the issuing Member State.[81] Similar to the EIO, this limitation precludes the application of the EAW in some Member States for a number of IPR infringements. In such cases an EAW may, however, still be issued, provided that the IPR infringement is punishable in the issuing Member State with at least 12 months' imprisonment, in addition to which the executing state may then require that the criminal offence, on which the EAW is based, also constitutes an offence under their national law.[82]

G. Money Laundering

Commercial scale IPR infringements are, by definition, motivated by profit. The latest figures concerning the EU alone mention annual values of about 85 billion EURO, and although precise figures are not available, it is presumed that a vast and growing part of these activities take place online.[83]

Legal measures tackling money laundering can indirectly be a tool to disrupt organised, large-scale activities that involve IPR infringements. Money laundering is a process by which proceeds originating in illicit activities are converted into property such as assets or values with the purpose of hiding their provenance.[84]

The 'follow the money' approach is regarded as an important way to prevent and disrupt illicit activities, including IPR infringements. This

---

80 Ibid art 2(2).

81 Ibid.

82 Ibid art 2(1) and (4).

83 See the Observatory publications on the economic cost of IPR infringements in various sectors. Reference is also made to the report by RAND Europe, 'Measuring IPR Infringements in the Internal Market' (2012) for the European Commission, Internal Market and Services Directorate-General.

84 For the definition in EU law, see Council Directive (EU) 2015/849 of 20 May 2015 on the prevention of the use of the financial system for the purposes of money laundering or terrorist financing, amending Council Regulation (EU) No 648/2012, and repealing Council Directive 2005/60/EC and Commission Directive 2006/70/EC (Money Laundering Directive) [2015] OJ L141/73, art 1(3).

approach not only enables the authorities to identify, seize and confiscate the money, but also enables, or at least facilitates, establishing the identity of the perpetrators.

The current anti-money laundering framework consists of two legal instruments: the 'Fourth Anti-Money Laundering Directive'[85] and the 'Fund Transfers Regulation',[86] both adopted on 20 May 2015. The instruments, in principle, cover proceeds originating from online IPR infringements. Recital 18 explains that the money laundering Directive is intended to apply to online activities of the obliged entities.[87] The Directive has been transposed by 20 Member States,[88] including the UK, where the future of judicial cooperation is uncertain until the exit of the UK from the EU is resolved.[89]

The Swedish case *SweFilmer*[90] illustrates how anti-money laundering enforcement measures can be used. The case involved streaming of unlicensed audio-visual works and underlying money laundering activities that were central to the investigation. The main defendant was charged both with copyright infringement and laundering the profits of such illicit activity. The case ended at first instance with both a custodial penalty and payment of damages to the right holders because money laundering carries higher penalties (six months to six years' imprisonment)[91] than copyright infringement (fine or up to two years' imprisonment).[92] The 'follow the money' approach was not only instrumental to unravelling the illicit activities and the persons responsible, but also essential to the use of international cooperation investigative measures.

---

85 Money Laundering Directive (n 84).

86 Council Regulation (EU) 2015/847 of 20 May 2015 on information accompanying transfers of funds and repealing Regulation (EC) No 1781/2006 [2015] OJ L141/1.

87 The entities obliged by the Directive are defined in art 2 of the Money Laundering Directive (n 84).

88 At the time the report was written, the following Member States had not transposed the directive: Bulgaria, Ireland, Greece, Cyprus, Luxembourg, the Netherlands, Poland and Romania.

89 Advocate General Szpunar argues that the UK's decision to leave the EU should not affect the execution of a European arrest warrant issued by it as long as the UK is a Member State. Opinion of the Advocate General in the Case C-327/18 *PPU* ECLI:EU:C:2018:644.

90 Varberg Regional Court Case n T 1463-15 and Göta Appeal Court.

91 Act on Penalties for Money Laundering Offences 2014 (Sweden), s 3.

92 Act on Copyright in Literary and Artistic Works 1960 (Sweden), s 53.

H. National Criminal Sanctions

Criminal sanctions are not subject to harmonisation at EU level but, as illustrated above, the type of penalties and the maximum penalties do at the same time play an important role in the actual applicability of EU law-based enforcement mechanisms for online IPR infringements, namely the EIO and the EAW.

The study therefore also included a mapping and analysis of the following issues related to the national criminal sanctions of the individual Member States: (1) the maximum sentence for online IPR infringements under the national legislation of each Member State; (2) whether national law entails accessory or alternative penalties; (3) whether national law punishes negligent infringements; (4) whether infringements at a non-commercial scale are punishable; (5) whether Member States' national penal law entails objective criminal liability; and finally (6) whether legal persons (including intermediaries) can be held criminally liable for online IPR infringements.

Previous studies and surveys have demonstrated that national definitions of counterfeiting and piracy, and the conducts typified as crimes, vary considerably and are difficult to compare.[93] Concerning the maximum penalties, the mapping revealed a pattern of substantive national differences as the maximum possible imprisonment sentences range from two years to ten years. In the vast majority of Member States, the available penalties are organised in a broad range, usually starting with non-custodial sentences. Furthermore, many replies indicated that maximum penalties are only considered in a limited number of cases where there are aggravated circumstances, such as commercial or large scale of the infringements, organised crime, or links to other criminal activities.

Accessory penalties or non-custodial sentences are possible in all Member States. These appear under different titles and denominations and include, for example: confiscation, forfeiture, seizure, destruction or removal from the channels of commerce of counterfeited and pirated goods; confiscation, forfeiture, seizure, destruction of objects or materials used in counterfeiting and piracy of goods; publicity of the decision and public admission of guilt; liquidation (legal entities) and prohibition of future business (managers). For example, the latter remedy was applied

---

[93] International Trademark Association, 'Criminal Prosecution of counterfeiting and Piracy in Member States of the European Union' (2010).

in the Spanish *Bajatetodo* case[94] in which the defendant was banned from creating or administering any website for three years.

National criminal law requires a certain 'state of mind' or *mens rea* in order for an infringement of an intellectual property right to be criminally sanctioned. National jurisdictions approach negligence and intent differently. Only a minority of Member States have reported that national law criminalises negligent[95] online conduct that constitutes IPR infringements. Similarly, concerning objective criminal liability, only four EU Member States reported that their national legislation allows IPRs infringements to be penalised in such circumstances.

Furthermore, a considerable number of Member States completely exclude criminal liability if the infringement is not conducted on a commercial scale. 'Commercial scale' is here used as an umbrella term to describe a variety of requirements found in national laws such as: infringement in the course of trade, large-scale infringement, counterfeiting of a defined or undefined number of goods; infringement committed in the course of trade or as a commercial activity, for profit. In such jurisdictions, small-scale counterfeiting and pirating limited to a small number of goods will not be subject to criminal enforcement.

Legal entities, in particular intermediaries, play an important role in the digital environment. The majority of responses confirmed that legal entities could be criminally liable for IPR infringements. A number of accessory penalties and non-custodial penalties were also mentioned as applicable to IPR-infringing entities, such as fines, foreclosure and prohibition of doing business.

V. FUTURE CHALLENGES FOR ENFORCEMENT AND THE NEED FOR FURTHER STUDIES

Increasing digitalisation is pervasive in all spheres of society. The digital ecosystem has developed as a dominant forum for commercial trade. We witness the constant and continuous development of new businesses models based on licensed IPRs. However, side by side with these, new infringing models are emerging.

The enforcement of IPRs has faced constraints and difficulties due to problems in applying the same procedures and normative frameworks both to the analogic, national world and to the global, digital world.

---

94 426/2014 of 2014-11-12 (Criminal Court of Appeal).

95 For example the laws in Germany and Denmark require 'gross negligence'.

Enforcement of IPRs faces particular difficulties regarding territoriality, jurisdiction and other trans-border issues. Moreover, online infringements of IPRs are often of a dematerialised nature and are difficult to subsume under rules that were drafted with off-line infringements in mind.

Emerging technologies such as Artificial Intelligence (AI), machine learning, automated prediction tools and block chain technology may create further difficulties, but also opportunities for more effective and timely enforcement of IPRs.[96]

The main purpose of this study was to investigate whether and to what extent a number of existing legislative measures that can be applied to prevent or combat infringements of IPRs in the online environment are available in the EU Member States. The research followed an approach of focusing on legislative measures that can be characterised as providing 'practical solutions to practical problems' and the study is primarily based on the replies to two questionnaires obtained from practitioners in the field.

While this approach is suitable to provide policy makers, civil society and private businesses with an overview of the current situations in the EU and its Member States, it does not give an in-depth insight into each individual topic. In order to gain such insight, further and more targeted studies will be necessary and such studies seem to be particularly interesting for those topics where the existing analysis shows that the legal situation is either unresolved or is fragmented.

Because technological development is notoriously difficult to predict and legislation has a tendency to 'lag behind' such developments, further studies may be very useful. A number of observed trends illustrates this challenge. First, there is a continued growth of the internet user base and expanding interface between the analogic and digital world with the pervasive increase of objects and devices connected to the internet (Internet of Things). Secondly, in the legal field, there is an acknowledgment of the need to adapt to technology, and thus we witness an evolving legal framework with several legislative initiatives currently being considered e.g. new initiatives such as the European Commission's proposals around copyright in the Digital Single Market or concerning the novel nature of works generated by AI. Thirdly, concerning the mechanisms for enforcement, the tendency is to develop further the privatisation of enforcement mechanisms in particular notice-and-takedown procedures; automated identification and/or enforcement using machine learning and

---

96 An example of the latter was the '#EUBlockathon2018' event <https://euipo.europa.eu/ohimportal/da/web/observatory/blockathon>.

AI; decentralisation of enforcement e.g. by use of block chain technology. Finally, on the infringement side there is a growing development of parallel infrastructures such as the notorious Darknet and the Telegram Open Network.

These factors will arguably result in an increased complexity and difficulty in enforcing IPRs in emerging e-ecosystems, such as the automation of infringing conducts that may create 'dynamic' infringement models with very short cycles. These are often connected with abuse of safeguards, such as privacy/personal data protection rules and freedom of speech.

Legal uncertainty also makes it difficult for internet users to adhere to licit conduct as often users in good faith may find it difficult to identify the right holders, assert the scope of rights and thus conform to the legal norms.

The dynamic nature of fast technological development and of the evolution of legitimate business models may also play in favour of infringers and thus continuous efforts and research to adapt legal interpretation and find improved legal solutions will remain a challenge for the intellectual property community.

PART IV

Aspects of copyright and their relationship to overall purpose

12. Use and abuse of neighbouring rights and the growing need for a sound understanding: the case of online news protection in Europe*

Valentina Moscon

I. INTRODUCTION

The proposed Directive on Copyright in the Digital Single Market[1] introduces a new neighbouring right for press publishers calling for reflection on features of neighbouring rights, including in particular their subject matter of protection and relationship to copyright law. Invoking these rights as an answer to various issues including organisation of sporting events[2] appears to be an ongoing trend, which is not, however, based on a sound understanding of problems and their best legal solution. In this respect, analysis of the Commission's proposal might provide more general background to the question of whether and when it is appropriate to introduce new neighbouring rights. Therefore, this chapter focuses on this category of intellectual property (IP) rights. While investigating whether online news protection as outlined in the proposal may be a task for neighbouring rights, this chapter will look at the object and purpose of neighbouring rights.

The issue of news protection in the interests of press publishers has arisen at various times in history. Both copyright and neighbouring rights have been taken into account as means for protecting news. However,

* All online sources were last accessed on 27 December 2018.

1 Proposal for a Directive of the European Parliament and of the Council on Copyright in the Digital Single Market COM (2016) 593. At the time this chapter was written, the Directive was not adopted.

2 A new art 12a protecting sport event organisers was introduced at a late stage by the European Parliament within the September 2018 amendments. According to art 12a, 'Member States shall provide sport event organisers with the rights provided for in Article 2 and Article 3 (2) of Directive 2001/29/EC and Article 7 of Directive 2006/115/EC'.

during the Berne Convention negotiations and subsequently in the debate prior to the adoption of the Rome Convention in 1961, the news protection was explicitly excluded from the copyright and neighbouring rights area.[3] This historical background suggests focusing on specific aspects of the Commission's proposal, inquiring in particular whether the provision identifies the specific achievement to be rewarded by means of the proposed neighbouring right and what it is.

The chapter is structured as follows. The second section deals with neighbouring rights in international law. The third section proposes a possible systematic understanding of neighbouring rights. The fourth section introduces the background to the Commission proposal, exploring the content of the provision. The proposal is placed in the current context where the tendency is to resort to IP for the protection of intangible assets which are not attributable to the traditional catalogue of IP rights. Section five takes a historical perspective. The preparatory work before the Berne Convention states that the subject falls into the area of unfair competition rather than IP law. Thus, the distinction between IP law and unfair competition law is developed further in Section six as a background for assessing whether the subject matter of the proposed neighbouring rights is attributable to the area of IP law (Section seven). Finally, after concluding that neighbouring rights are inadequate legal instruments for news protection, Section eight focuses on four legal instruments – copyright law, *sui generis* database protection, competition law and trade mark law – which may safeguard the interests of press publishers, at the same time as enhancing news circulation through multiple channels and the quality of the information made available to the public.

II. NEIGHBOURING RIGHTS IN INTERNATIONAL LAW

In the first half of the last century, a broad international debate led to the introduction of special rights for subject matter such as sound recordings, broadcasts and live performances that, for different reasons, do not meet

---

[3] International Convention for the Protection of Performers, Producers of Phonograms and Broadcasting Organisations (signed on 26 October 1961, entered into force 18 May 1964) 496 UNTS 43 (Rome Convention). This treaty was adopted under the auspices of three international organisations: the World Intellectual Property Organization (WIPO, formerly the United International Bureaux for the Protection of IP), the United Nations Educational, Scientific and Cultural Organization (UNESCO) and the International Labour Organization (ILO).

the requirements for copyright protection.[4] Separate rights, analogous to those of authors but outside authors' rights regimes altogether, emerged as 'neighbouring rights'. This first occurred in the Rome Convention of 1961, granting protection to sound recordings, broadcasts and live performances. A further development of these rights occurred with TRIPS and the WIPO Performances and Phonograms Treaty.[5] These rights – whose legal character appears not yet to be entirely clarified – have been treated as 'neighbouring' as each of them is connected, albeit in different ways, with the exploitation of authors' rights.

A neighbouring right for press publishers was proposed too to protect 'press news'.[6] However, the protection of publishers' investments was seen as unconnected to authors' rights and the unfair competition law was indicated as the best suited area where to find legal tools to regulate this matter.[7] Even the Post-Samedan international agenda has excluded press publishers' rights to news from a neighbouring right formulation. These rights are indeed not even located in the 'norm formulation agenda of WIPO'.[8]

Copyright and neighbouring rights are in close relationship and very often both rights converge into a single product (e.g. a phonogram incorporates rights of authors, producers and performers). Therefore the regulation of one affects the regulation of the other as well as the exploitation of one has an impact on the exploitation of the other.[9] In this context the

---

4 See Sam Ricketson, 'Rights on the Border: The Berne Convention and Neighbouring Rights' in Ruth Okediji (ed), *Copyright Law in the Age of Limitations and Exceptions* (Cambridge University Press 2017) 342–374; Rasmus Fleischer, 'Protecting the Musicians and/or the Record Industry?' (2015) 5(3) QMJIP 327; Sam Ricketson and Jane Ginsburg, *International Copyright and Neighbouring Rights* (2nd edn, vol 2, Oxford University Press 2006) 1205.

5 Agreement on Trade-Related Aspects of Intellectual Property Rights (opened for signature 15 April 1994, entered into force 1 January 1996) 1869 UNTS 299 as Annex 1C to the Marrakesh Agreement (TRIPS).

6 The most thorough and accessible account of the work of the Samedan Committee is to be found in the October, November and December 1940 issues of Le Droit d'auteur, DA 109–111, 121–125, 133–138. The minutes of the meeting are recorded as being in the UNIDROIT archives. See also Sam Ricketson and Jane Ginsburg, 'Intellectual Property in News? Why Not?' in Sam Ricketson and Megan Richardson (eds), *Research Handbook on Intellectual Property in Media and Entertainment* (Edward Elgar Publishing 2016) 12–13.

7 Ricketson (n 4) 366.

8 Ibid.

9 A good example of the problematic relationship between copyright and neighboring rights is that emerged in the German case "Metall auf Metall". The reference arises from a long – running lawsuit in Germany which has already been

question of how to solve conflicts between neighbouring rights and those of the authors brought to the creation of a taxonomy of rights. According to the Rome Convention[10] and *WIPO Performances and Phonograms Treaty* (WPPT),[11] neighbouring rights must leave intact and in no way affect the protection of copyright. Indeed, while assuring protection for the contribution of performers, phonogram producers and broadcasters, the drafters at the various meetings sought to achieve a taxonomy of rights that kept authorship at the centre. The hierarchy of involved interests starts with creation of works, which accordingly has the largest claim to recognition.[12] Performers, phonogram producers and broadcasters build on these initial contributions, either through performance or interpretation, in the case of performers, or through fixation and dissemination, in the case of phonogram producers and broadcasters.

considered by the Bundesgerichtshof (German Federal Court of Justice) in 2008 and 2012 and the Bundesverfassungsgericht (German Federal Constitutional Court, Supreme Court in matters of constitutional law) in 2016. The underlying claim was brought by the German electronic music pioneers, Kraftwerk. They asserted copyright and phonogram producer rights against the unauthorized use of a rhythmic sound fragment of two seconds in a continuous rhythmic sequence of Sabrina Setlur's song "Nur mir". The sound fragment stemmed from the piece "Metall auf Metall" in Kraftwerk's 1977 album "Trans Europa Express". In "Nur mir", the sound fragment is slowed down (by 5%) and repeated. The case has been brought before the CJEU to whom various questions have been submitted. One of those questions is whether Member States can enact a provision which – in the manner of Paragraph 24(1) of the Gesetz über Urheberrecht und verwandte Schutzrechte (German Law on Copyright and Related Rights) – inherently limits the scope of protection of the phonogram producer's exclusive right to reproduce (Article 2(c) of Directive 2001/29/EC) and to distribute (Article9(1)(b) of Directive 2006/115/EC) its phonogram in such a way that an independent work created in free use of its phonogram may be exploited without the phonogram producer's consent. For a more detailed discussion of the Metall auf Metall decisions in Germany, see Rupprecht Podszun, 'Postmoderne Kreativität im Konflikt mit dem Urheberrechtsgesetz und die Annäherung an "fair use"', Zeitschrift für Urheber-und Medienrecht 2016, 606; Matthias Leistner, 'Die "Metall auf Metall"- Entscheidung.

10 Rome Convention (n 3) , art 1.

11 World Intellectual Property Organization Performances and Phonograms Treaty (adopted 20 December 1996, entered into force 20 May 2002) (1997) 36 ILM 76 (WPPT), art1(2).

12 Ricketson (n 4) 372–373.

III. IN SEARCH OF A SYSTEMATIC APPROACH FOR NEIGHBOURING RIGHTS

International law does not preclude nation states from including in their own legal systems new neighbouring rights, which, indeed, have been introduced at the national level to protect different subject matters.[13] While it is known that there are two different approaches in the common law and civil law systems,[14] neighbouring rights – when adopted – replicate to a large extent copyright protection. It is not the aim of this chapter to carry out a comparative analysis of national implementations of neighbouring rights. However, in general terms, the three main drivers of these rights can be summarised as follows.[15]

The first driver concerns achievements which, although similar to copyright works, differ from them in that they lack a minimum degree of creativity.[16] Falling into this category might be theatrical sketches; photographs; engineering projects; and scientific editions of works in the public domain. A special position is occupied by the *sui generis* database protection provided for by the European law.[17] In Europe there is a special regime for non-creative databases for which qualitatively and/or quantitatively substantial investments are made in either obtaining, verifying or presenting the content. This right is often dealt with separately from other neighbouring rights because – unlike the neighbouring rights mentioned above – the protected subject matter is clearly defined as the investment in a database. Nevertheless, it seems reasonable to include *sui generis* rights on a database in this group since protection concerns a non-creative database. If the database were creative it would be a copyrighted work.[18] The second driver has to do with performances which, despite their artistic character, do not result in works. Performances make works available to the public and allow them to be marketed. The third driver refers to

---

13 Alexander Peukert, 'Related Rights' in Jurgen Basedow, Klaus J Hopt and Reinhard Zimmermann (eds), *The Max Planck Encyclopedia of European Private Law* (OUP 2012) 1443–1446.

14 Ibid 1445.

15 Valeria Falce, *La modernizzazione del diritto d'autore* (Giappichelli 2012) 68–71.

16 Alberto Musso, *Diritto d'autore sulle opere dell'ingegno letterarie e artistiche* (Zanichelli 2008) 299.

17 Directive 96/9/EC of 11 March 1996 on the legal protection of databases (Database Directive).

18 P Bernt Hugenholtz, 'Directive 96/9/EC (Database Directive)' in Thomas Dreier and P Bernt Hugenholtz, *Concise European Copyright Law* (2nd edn, Wolters Kluwer 2016) 379.

phonograms, radio and television broadcasts, and videograms. These neighbouring rights are triggered by financial investments from market players who develop their business models mostly based on pre-existing works. The subject matter of protection is, however, a specific achievement of an industrial nature, which clearly differ from works. Moreover, those investments are most of the time functional to full exploitation of the works in question.[19]

IV. THE EUROPEAN COMMISSION'S PROPOSAL

A. A Complex Background

> [T]he digital journalism produced by many news organizations has become less and less meaningful. Publishers that are funded by algorithmic ads are locked in a race to the bottom in pursuit of any audience they can find – desperately binge-publishing without checking facts, pushing out the most shrill and most extreme stories to boost clicks. 'Where once we had propaganda, press releases, journalism, and advertising', the academic Emily Bell has written 'we now have content'. Readers are overwhelmed: bewildered by the quantity of 'news' they see every day, nagged by intrusive pop-up ads, confused by what is real and what is fake, and confronted with an experience that is neither useful nor enjoyable.[20]

These words mirror a complex background. Social media platforms and technology companies are having a greater effect on press publishers than even the shift from print to digital and the growth of the commercial Internet. The transition from print to digital did not initially change the basic business model for many news publishers – that is, selling advertisements to fund the journalism delivered to readers. For a time, it seemed that online audiences might potentially compensate for the decline in print readers and advertisers. But that business model is facing a crisis, which is partly related to the powerful rise of third-party market players such as social media platforms and technology companies[21] which have influenced

---

19 Ricketson and Ginsburg (n 6) 1206.

20 Katharine Viner, 'A Mission for Journalism in a Time of Crisis, The Long Read' (November 2017) The Guardian <https://www.theguardian.com/news/2017/nov/16/a-mission-for-journalism-in-a-time-of-crisis>.

21 Globally there are over 40 different social media sites and messaging apps through which news publishers can reach segments of their audience. As shown by empirical studies such as the one reported in Reuters Institute Digital News Report 2017 <https://reutersinstitute.politics.ox.ac.uk/>, the news and technology industry is partly different in the US and Europe. The Apple News app, for example, is only

the news market.[22] These companies are much more than mere distribution channels. They can control what audiences see, who gets paid for their attention, and what format and type of journalism succeeds. In particular, social media platforms and search companies lead the distribution and presentation of news as well as the monetisation of publishing and their relationship with the audience. Indeed, many platforms actively select, rank and classify news publications with the aim of getting as many people as they can to use their platforms. To some extent this has incentivised the spread of low-quality content provided that it attracts readers. At the same time, the rapid adoption of smartphones has transformed news consumption, turning technology companies, with their apps and operating systems, into the gatekeepers of information.[23]

Therefore, the distribution and presentation of news, the monetisation of publishing and the relationship with the audience, in the forms briefly mentioned above, tend to be concentrated in the hands of a few companies.[24] This concentration is partly related to companies' ability to collect and use data on readers' habits and preferences.[25]

Against this multifaceted background, news publishers are struggling to understand whether and how to rethink their processes and structures. Reactions have hitherto been varied, also depending on the market

---

available in the US, the UK and Australia. Apple's News app, which aggregates digital news media, launched in the UK in 2015 with a range of publishing partners including the BBC, *The Telegraph*, *The Guardian*, *The Sun* and Sky News. Some magazine companies are also on board. A similar service is provided by Snapchat's Discover portal, which offers publishers like *Le Monde*, CNN and *The Wall Street Journal* the opportunity to reach a younger audience. Snapchat Discover has been available in the US, the UK and Australia, with the first non-English-speaking versions in France (September 2016), Norway and Germany (in early 2017).

[22] See Emily Bell and Taylor Owen, 'The Platform Press: How Silicon Valley Reengineered Journalism' (2017) Columbia Graduate School of Journalism <https://www.cjr.org/tow_center_reports/platform-press-how-silicon-valley-reengineered-journalism.php/>.

[23] See Reuters Institute Digital News Report 2017 (n 21) 10. Apple News has been one of the biggest gainers over the past year. Apple's News app, for example, which launched in the UK in 2015 with a range of publishing partners including the BBC, The Telegraph and The Guardian, aims to be a news aggregation service. A similar service is provided by Snapchat's Discover portal.

[24] For example, Facebook owns WhatsApp and Messenger, the two most popular messaging apps, along with Instagram, which has been incorporating many of Snapchat's most popular features. Alongside Google, the company has acquired and is maintaining enormous power over the discovery and distribution of content, including news. See Reuters Institute Digital News Report 2017 (n 21) 12.

[25] Ibid.

they cover.[26] Various methods have been used to give new life to press publishing; refocusing on quality of journalism for which perhaps people would be prepared to pay and focusing on audience engagement are some trends, though these are not universal.[27]

Groups of press publishers have been seeking to achieve legal protection of their interests. They argue that the new ways of consuming content facilitate free riding by third parties that would profit from using content in a variety of ways without sharing the value generated from them, thereby preventing publishers from receiving market compensation for their production activities. In some European countries – Germany[28] and Spain[29] are examples – press publishers have managed to procure special laws within national copyright regimes, while similar laws have been proposed without success in other countries – for example, in Austria,[30] Italy,[31] Sweden,[32] and France with respect to images.[33] In other

---

26 Viner (n 20).

27 Ibid.

28 Section 87f-g Copyright Act 1965 (Germany), as last amended by Section 8 of the Copyright Act 2013. This provision raised many criticisms that are summarised, among others, in M Stieper, 'Abschnitt 7 Schutz des Pressverlegers', in G Schricker/U Loewenheim (eds), *Urheberrecht: Kommentar* (5th edn, CH Beck 2017) 2096–2121.

29 Ibid. See Boletín Oficial de las Cortes Generales, Congreso de los Diputados, Informe de la Ponencia: Proyecto de Ley por la que se modifica el Texto Refundido de la Ley de Propriedad Intelectual, aprobado por Real Decreto Legislativo 1/1996, de 12 de abril, y la Ley 1/2000, de 7 de enero, de Enjuiciamiento Civil, No 81-3 (July 2014) <http://www.congreso.es/public_oficiales/L10/CONG/BOCG/A/BOCG-10-A-81-3.PDF>. See also Raquel Xalabarder, 'The Remunerated Statutory Limitation for News Aggregation and Search Engines Proposed by the Spanish Government; Its Compliance with International and EU Law' InfoJustice (2014) <http://infojustice.org/archives/33346>. 'Press Publisher Rights in the New Copyright in the Digital Single Market Draft Directive' (2016) CREATe Working Papers 2016/15, 20.

30 Urheberrechts-Novelle 2015, available at <https://www.ris.bka.gv.at/Dokument.wxe?Abfrage=Begut&Dokumentnummer=BEGUT_COO_2026_100_2_1102902>. See Tom Hirche, 'Surprising Turn in Austria' <http://ancillarycopyright.eu/news/2015-06-15/surprising-turn-austria>.

31 Decree Law 3 October 2006 no 262 – cancelled upon conversion – proposed a change to art 65 of Law no 633 of 1941 (Italian Copyright Act). See Valeria Falce and Maria L Bixio, 'Verso un nuovo diritto connesso a favore degli editori on line. Brevi note su recenti derive (iper)-protezionistiche' (2017) <http://www.dimt.it/wp-content/uploads/2016/09/Paper-Ancillary-copyright.pdf>.

32 See Greg Sterling, 'Sweden the Latest to Consider Google "Link Tax" For Newspapers' (November 2014) <https://searchengineland.com/sweden-latest-consider-google-link-tax-207706>.

33 Brad Spitz, 'Thumbnails: French Proposal for Payment of Royalties by

European countries, pressure from publishers has brought about negotiated solutions, as in Belgium, France and Italy.[34] Moreover, negotiated solutions appear to be the preferred approach for press publishers in the US.[35]

B. Content and Purposes of the European Proposal

In heeding press publishers' claims, the European Commission, following the German legal intervention, has proposed a new neighbouring right for press publishers.[36] Article 11 of the proposed Directive on Copyright

---

Search Engines' Kluwer Copyright Blog (April 2014) <http://copyrightblog.kluweriplaw.com/2014/04/28/thumbnails-france/>.

34 The Italian, Belgian and French solutions are compared in Maria L Bixio, 'Google-Fieg, tregua per l'info-mediazione' (2016) <http://www.dimt.it/index.php/it/notizie/15166-28google-fieg-tregua-per-l-info-mediazione>.

35 See David Chavern, 'Protect the News From Google and Facebook. A Partial Exemption from Antitrust Laws would help Publishers and Readers' (2018) Wall Street Journal <https://www.wsj.com/articles/protect-the-news-from-google-and-facebook-1519594942>; Madeline Purdue, 'Newspapers Want Anti-Trust Pass to Handle Facebook, Google' (July 2017) USA TODAY <https://www.usatoday.com/story/tech/news/2017/07/10/newspapers-want-anti-trust-pass-handle-facebook-google/465379001/>; David Chavern, 'How Antitrust Undermines Press Freedom' (July 2017) Wall Street Journal <https://www.wsj.com/articles/how-antitrust-undermines-press-freedom-1499638532>; Jim Rutenberg, 'News Outlets to Seek Bargaining Rights Against Google and Facebook' (July 2017) New York Times <https://www.nytimes.com/2017/07/09/business/media/google-facebook-news-media-alliance.html?_r=0>.

36 The proposal has been widely criticised in the literature. See Christophe Geiger, Oleksandr Bulayenko and Giancarlo Frosio, 'The Introduction of a Neighbouring Right for Press Publisher at EU Level: The Unneeded (and Unwanted) Reform' (2017) EIPR 39(4) 202; Falce and Bixio (n 23); Alexander Peukert, 'An EU Related Right for Press Publishers Concerning Digital Uses: A Legal Analysis' (2016) Research Paper of the Faculty of Law, Goethe University Frankfurt No 22/2016 <https://ssrn.com/abstract=2888040>; Martin Senftleben, Maximilian Kerk, Miriam Buiten and Klaus Heine, 'New Rights or New Business Models? An Inquiry into the Future of Publishing in the Digital Era' (2017) 48(5) IIC 538; Reto M Hilty and Valentina Moscon (eds), 'Modernisation of the EU Copyright Rules: Position Statement of the Max Planck Institute for Innovation and Competition' (2017) Max Planck Institute for Innovation and Competition Research Paper No 17-12 <http://pubman.mpdl.mpg.de/pubman/item/escidoc:2470998:11/component/escidoc:2479390/E-Book%20-%20Hilty%20-%20Moscon%20-%2018.09.2017.pdf>; Raquel Xalabarder, 'Press Publisher Rights in the New Copyright in the Digital Single Market Draft Directive' CREATe Working Paper 2016/15; Eleonora Rosati, 'Neighbouring Rights for Publishers: Are National and (Possible) EU Initiatives Lawful?' (2016) IIC 569; Lionel Bently et al, 'Strengthening the Position of Press Publishers and Authors

in the Digital Single Market states that 'Member States shall provide publishers of press publications with the rights provided for in Article 2 and Article 3(2) of Directive 2001/29/EC for the digital use of their press publications'. The mentioned provisions provide for exclusive rights of reproduction and the right of making available to the public.

The protected press publication is defined as a 'fixation of literary works of a journalistic nature, which may also comprise other works or subject matter and constitute an individual item within a periodical or regularly updated publication under a single title'. In addition, this publication must have 'the purpose of providing information related to news or other topics and published in any media under the initiative, editorial responsibility and control of a service provider'.[37]

The EU Commission explains in the Recitals[38] that a free and pluralistic press is essential to ensure the quality of journalism and citizens' access to information, and that the organisational and financial contribution of publishers must be recognised and rewarded so that the industry can be sustainable.[39]

According to the Commission, the introduction of a new neighbouring

---

and Performers in the Copyright Directive' (2017) Study for the Policy Department for Citizens' Rights and Constitutional Affairs <http://www.europarl.europa.eu/thinktank/en/document.html?reference=IPOL_STU%282017%29596810Z>; Richard Danbury, 'Is an EU Publishers' Right a Good Idea?' (2016) Report on the AHRC Project; Taina Pihlajarinne and Juha Vesala, 'Proposed Rights of Press Publishers: A Workable Solution?' (2017) 13(3) JIPLP 220–228; Fabian Zuleeg and Iva Tasheva, 'Rewarding Quality Journalism or Distorting the Digital Single Market? The Case For and Against Neighbouring Rights for Press Publishers' (2017) European Policy Centre – Discussion Paper; Ana Ramalho, 'Beyond the Cover Story – An Enquiry into the EU Competence to Introduce a Right for Publishers' (2017) 48(1) IIC 71; Christophe Caron, 'Legal Analysis with Focus on Article 11 of the Proposed Directive on Copyright in the Digital Market' (2017) Briefing Paper for the JURI Committee <http://www.europarl.europa.eu/thinktank/en/document.html?reference=IPOL_BRI(2017)596834>; Mireille van Eechoud, 'A Publisher's Intellectual Property Right: Implications for Freedom of Expression, Authors and Open Content Policies' (2017) OpenForum Europe, 32 <http://www.openforumeurope.org/wp-content/uploads/2017/01/OFE-Academic-Paper-Implications-of-publishers-right_FINAL.pdf>.

37 See art 2(4).

38 See Recitals 31 and 32.

39 The text of the negotiating mandate that Member States agreed on in Council has been available since 25 May 2018. The amendments provided for by the Council, however, do not exclude the introduction of a neighbouring right for press publishers. The Council has deleted the word 'fixation', defining in Article 2(4) press publication as 'a collection composed mainly of literary works of journalistic nature'. Such amendment does not change the critical position taken in this

right in favour of press publishers would grant remuneration to press publishers for the services they provide to the general public. Other declared reasons for introducing new neighbouring rights are:[40] to strengthen press publishers' bargaining position vis-à-vis online platforms; to facilitate exploiting and enforcing their rights against online infringement; to facilitate the sharing of the compensation for uses under exceptions between authors and publishers; to avoid different approaches to the protection of publishers at the national level (e.g. Spanish and German legislation) resulting in fragmentation in the single market.

C. The Increasing Recourse to Neighbouring Rights

The Commission's proposal appears to be just the tip of the iceberg, to be observed as a case study for a general reflection on neighbouring rights. Over recent years, indeed, the tendency has been to resort to IP for protection of intangible assets whose connection to the traditional catalogue of IP rights is far from obvious.[41]

Some 'atypical' exclusive rights are ascribed to the category of neighbouring rights despite the fact that the neighbourhood of these rights to copyright is difficult, if not impossible, to determine. This is the case, for example, with exclusive rights recognised by some European countries in favour of organisers of sporting events.[42] The French legislature, for instance, enacted a specific provision for organisers of sporting events[43] on the organisation and promotion of sporting and physical activities, subsequently amended and now codified in Article L333-1 of the French Sports Code.[44] This provision establishes that sports federations and

---

chapter. At the time of writing, the Parliament has not yet agreed on its proposal. On 5 July 2018 the Parliament voted against the Voss's JURI Proposal.

40 Commission, 'Staff Working Document, Impact Assessment on the Modernisation of EU Copyright Rules, accompanying the Proposal for a Directive on Copyright in the Digital Single Market and the Proposal for a Regulation on the Exercise of Copyright and Related Rights Applicable to Certain Online Transmissions of Broadcasting Organisations and Retransmissions of Television and Radio Programmes' SWD (2016) 302 final, 156 and Annex 3A (Impact Assessment).

41 For a more detailed analysis see Alexander Peukert, *Güterzuordung als Rechtsprinzip* (Mohr Tübingen 2008).

42 On the protection of sports events in the EU, see Thomas Margoni, 'The Protection of Sports Events in the EU: Property, Intellectual Property, Unfair Competition and Special Forms of Protection' (2016) 47(4) IIC 386–417.

43 See Loi relative à l'organisation et à la promotion des activités physiques et sportives 1984 (France), art 18-1.

44 See Code du Sport, created by Ordonnance no 2006-596 du 23 mai 2006

organisers of sporting events are proprietors of the exploitation rights of the sporting events or competitions they organise. The nature of this right is not explicitly defined by the law. However, some sources classify it as a type of neighbouring right to copyright.[45] Although the reasons advanced for protection emphasise principled arguments (such as promoting sporting and physical activity), the subject matter of protection is economic investments as such.[46]

Similarly, in Italy a new neighbouring right was introduced in 2007 by a legislative decree amending the Italian Copyright Act and creating a new Article 78-*quater* entitled 'audio-visual sports rights'.[47] Audio-visual rights are defined as exclusive rights lasting 50 years from the date of the event covering the fixation and the live or delayed, temporal or permanent reproduction, in any manner or form, of the event, its communication and making available to the public, distribution to the public; rental and lending, and the fixation, elaboration or reproduction of the broadcast of the event. According to the Sports Decree,[48] the competition and event organisers are joint owners of audio-visual rights to a sporting event.

---

relative à la partie législative du code du sport, as amended.

45 Vivant Michel and Bruguière Michel, *Droit d'auteur et droits voisins* (2nd edn, Dalloz 2012) 1053; Lucas André and Lucas Henri-Jaques, *Traité de la propriété littéraire et artistique* (4th edn, Litec 2012) 934. See also Christophe Geiger, *Droit d'auteur et droit du public à l'information* (Litec 2004).

46 See Conseil d'État (France) 5ème et 4ème sous-sections réunies (March 2011) 342142 <http://www.juricaf.org/arret/FRANCE-CONSEILDETAT-20110330-342142>.

47 The new neighbouring right is based on Law 19 July 2007 no 106, 'Diritti televisivi sugli eventi sportivi nazionali: delega per la revisione della disciplina' and on the decrees implementing the framework act, mainly the legislative decree 'Sport e diritti audiovisivi' Legislative Decree, 1 January 2008 no 9. For a detailed account see L Ferrari, 'Rights to Broadcast Sporting Events under Italian Law' (2010) ISLJ 65. For a critical analysis, see Vincenzo Zeno-Zencovich, 'La statalizzazione dei diritti televisivi sportivi' (2008) XXXVI(6) Il diritto dell'informazione e dell'informatica 695–710; G Resta, *Diritti esclusivi e nuovi beni immateriali* (1st edn, Kluwer 2010).

48 See Legislative Decree, 1 January 2008 no 9.

V. PUBLIC INTERNATIONAL LAW AND NEWS PROTECTION

A. Premise

The right proposed by the European Commission falls within the scope of rights regulated by international treaties outlining regimes that are collectively called 'intellectual property'.[49] The establishment of new neighbouring rights must therefore be consistent with international IP regimes to be interpreted – as stated by Article 31 of the Vienna Convention on the Law of Treaties (VCLT) – 'in their context and in the light of its object and purpose'.[50] According to Article 32 VCLT, the preparatory work for the treaty and the circumstances of its conclusion provide relevant support for any possible interpretation of treaties.

The starting point for the issue at hand is the Berne Convention (BC),[51] which states in Article 2(8) that 'the protection of this Convention shall not apply to news of the day or to miscellaneous facts having the character of mere items of press information'. This wording has been part of Article 2 since the Stockholm Revision of 1967[52] but the issue was discussed at a national level even before the first BC of 1886.[53]

B. News Stories and Press Publishers' Investments: An Old Issue

Legal proposals for 'property rights' in news circulated in the then Australian colonies as early as the 1870s.[54] The growing popularity of newspapers in this period was linked to the advent of the telegraph, which made communication of news from one place to another (sometimes overseas) easier and quicker than before. However, protection of news included in telegrams was difficult to achieve under both imperial

---

[49] See Sam Ricketson, 'The Public International Law of Copyright' in Isabella Alexander and H Tomas Gomez-Arostegui (eds), *Research Handbook on the History of Copyright Law* (Edward Elgar Publishing 2016).

[50] Vienna Convention on the Law of Treaties (opened for signature 23 May 1969, entered into force 27 January 1980) 1155 UNTS 331 (VCLT).

[51] See Berne Convention for the Protection of Literary and Artistic Works (signed on 4 May 1896, entered into force 5 December 1887, revised on 24 July 1971) 1161 UNTS 3 (Berne Convention).

[52] See Berne Convention (n 51), as revised in Stockholm on 14 July 1967 (Stockholm Act).

[53] Ricketson and Ginsburg (n 6).

[54] Lionel Bently, 'Copyright and the Victorian Internet: Telegraphic Property Laws in Colonial Australia' (2004) 38 Loy J Pub Int L 71.

copyright and Australian copyright.[55] The inference drawn was that there was no copyright in the news itself, but there may have been copyright in its mode of expression.[56] In this context, the Australian Associated Press pressured the legislators of the Australian colonies to establish property rights in news.[57]. A similar debate took place in the US where, until the middle decades of the 1800s, newspapers were partisan organs mostly supported by political sponsors and government subsidies. Towards the end of the 19th century technological changes narrowed the lead-time advantage that newspapers traditionally had and exposed them to competition from which they had previously been geographically isolated. Therefore, news companies began pressuring legislatures[58] and courts, obtaining protection only from the latter. The issue was debated in *International News Service v Associated Press*,[59] which has now lost its importance as a precedent in the United States but is worth mentioning as the court stated two relevant principles. First, the majority opinion recognised that the information found in the Associated Press news was not copyrightable, and free access to and use of information per se could not be called into question.[60] Second, regulation of the news market does not concern the field of copyright, but rather the area of law which regulates relations among competitors. The Associated Press was entitled to an injunction against International News Service because its use of news copied from bulletin boards and early editions of the Associated Press member papers constituted misappropriation, a kind of unfair competition. The majority opinion described the defendant's interest in its news as 'quasi-property', which, however, is good only for a short period (less than one day) and only against a direct competitor of the plaintiff. This doctrine 'postpones participation by complainant's competitor in the processes of distribution

---

[55] Ibid 88.

[56] *Walter v Steinkopf* (1892) 3 Ch 489 (Eng).

[57] Bently (n 57).

[58] The one serious attempt in Congress took place on 4 March 1884, where Senator John Sherman of Ohio introduced 'A Bill Granting Copyright in Newspapers' (S 1728, 48th Cong). Six days later, Representative John Randolph Tucker of Virginia introduced an identical bill in the House (HR 5850, 48th Cong). The story is reconstructed in detail in Robert F Brauneis, 'The Debate over Copyright in News and its Effect on Originality Doctrine' in Robert F Brauneis (ed), *Intellectual Property Protection on Fact-based Works. Copyright and Its Alternatives* (Edward Elgar Publishing 2009) 54.

[59] *International News Service v Associated Press* (1918) 248 US 215 (SCOTUS); see Eric Easton, 'Who Owns the First Rough Draft of History? Reconsidering Copyright in News' (2004) 27 Column JL & Arts 561.

[60] *International News* (n 59), 234.

and reproduction of news that it has not gathered, and only to the extent necessary to prevent that competitor from reaping the fruits of complainant's efforts and expenditure'.[61]

C. The Line Between Copyright and other Regulatory Tools in the Berne Convention

As mentioned above, Article 2(8) BC denies copyright protection to 'news of the day' or 'miscellaneous facts', provided that such articles are mere news items. A provision in that form has been part of Article 2 since the Stockholm Revision of 1967.[62] The Stockholm study group report made clear, first, that the provision intended to exclude facts from copyright protection but not the copyrightable articles in which the facts were contained. The study group highlighted further that this provision works as a reminder of the freedom of information and constitutes the expression of a principle from which legislation and jurisprudence can exclude mere facts or information from copyright protection. This principle suggests something similar – albeit limited to the press – to the idea/expression dichotomy that was later developed and expanded in TRIPS[63] and WIPO Copyright Treaty.[64]

Secondly, according to the study group, the provision draws a demarcation line between copyright and other means of protection. This point had already been raised in the context of the Berlin revision[65] where it was stated that the commercial interests of press publishers do not fall within the province of copyright. According to the Berlin working group, commercial questions regarding news reproduction should be regulated in the field of competition law.[66] Indeed, the issue was debated during the Paris Convention. However, various attempts to introduce a provision in the Convention that could guarantee effective protection of news all failed.[67] The subject has, therefore, not been regulated at an international level and has remained in the hands of nation states. At the same time, however,

---

[61] Ibid, 241.

[62] WIPO, *Records of the Intellectual Property Conference of Stockholm* (Stockholm Intellectual Property Conference 1971) vol 1, 115.

[63] TRIPS (n 5) art 9(2).

[64] WIPO Copyright Treaty (signed on 20 December 1996, entered into force on 6 March 2002) 2186 UNTS 121, 36 ILM 65 (1997), art 5 2.

[65] Berlin Act, art 9(3). See further International Union for the Protection of Literary and Artistic Works, *L'Union internationale littéraire et artistique, 1886–1936: sa fondation et son développement* (1936) 249.

[66] Actes de la Conférence no 27 (1908) 251–252.

[67] For a historical reconstruction, see Ricketson and Ginsburg (n 6).

the international debate on the issue offers guiding principles for national states.[68]

VI. INTELLECTUAL PROPERTY AND COMPETITION LAW

The history of the international debate on news protection allows us to dwell on two areas of law which play complementary but different roles. From an economic perspective two main (interrelated) arguments form the basis of IP exclusive rights. On the one hand, exclusive rights are intended to create incentives for production of intellectual works. On the other hand, these rights serve to avoid potential market failure. Given the role played by IP in market regulation, contemporary commentators recognise that IP performs functions complementary to unfair competition law, which is by nature devoted to regulating competitor relations.[69] Along this line, although legal approaches protecting IP and competition are considered as a whole,[70] it is important not to lose sight of the particularities of each field.[71]

Focusing on the European landscape, in most national unfair competition law systems, subject matter worthy of protection consists of investments in products and services to be marketed. However, unfair competition law does not protect investments as such, at least not unconditionally. The requirements for and characteristics of protection vary to a significant extent in the various states, but generally speaking protection

---

[68] See Stephen P Ladas, *Patents, Trademarks, and Related Rights: National and International Protection* (2nd edn, vol 3, Harvard University Press 1975) 1724–1725.

[69] Among others, see Annette Kur, 'Funktionswandel von Schutzrechten: Ursachen und Konsequenzen der inhaltlichen Annäherung und Überlagerung von Schutzrechtstypen' in Gerhard Schricker, Thomas Dreier and Annette Kur (eds), *Geistiges Eigentum im Dienst der Innovation* (Nomos 2001) 23–50; Annette Kur, 'A New Framework for Intellectual Property Rights – Horizontal Issues' (2004) IIC 35(1) 1–21; RH Weber, 'Dritte Spur zwischen absoluten und relativen Rechten?' in Heinrich Honsell, Wolfgang Portmann, Roger Zäch and Dieter Zobl (eds), *Aktuelle Aspekte des Schuld- und Sachenrecht*s, *Festschrift für Heinz Rey* (Schulthess Juristische Medien 2003) 583–595.

[70] See Reto M Hilty, 'The Law against Unfair Competition and its Interfaces' in Reto M Hilty and F Henning-Bodewig (eds), *Law against Unfair Competition. Towards a New Paradigm in Europe? MPI Studies on Intellectual Property, Competition and Tax Law* (Springer 2007) 1–52.

[71] See Reto M Hilty, '*Gedanken zum Schutz der nachbarrechtlichen Leistung – einst, heute und morgen*' (1991) 116 UFITA 35.

of investments is related to the behaviour of the competitor taking over the investment.[72] The question must be asked whether the behaviour of a competitor taking over investments is likely to squeeze the original competitor out of the market and whether this leads to market failure in the long run.[73] Moreover, unfair competition law is normally based on 'liability' rules and on the technique of balancing of interests: competition as such is not prohibited or penalised – but the methods used by competitors may be. Presumptions of liability may be applicable in some cases but this does not change the nature of things, namely that the legal protection places itself in the domain of competition law. IP focuses instead on the result of the investment (such as a work or a patent) which will be given protection based on an exclusive right. In fact, although IP protection (whatever theory one may follow) results in market regulation, the aim of protection goes further than mere market regulation and has a different function from protection of investments.[74] In other words, IP – which entails exclusive rights *erga omnes* enforceable – is aimed at rewarding the right holder for a particular achievement. The achievement may consist in a creation that exhibits a qualitative advance in existing knowledge. Examples of this type of right are patents, copyright, design rights, etc. The key element of IP law is that the subject matter of protection has special characteristics and special requirements of protection, in particular in qualitative terms.

VII. THE EUROPEAN PROPOSAL

A. Subject Matter of Protection

According to Article 2(4) of the Proposed Directive, the press publication to be protected is a 'fixation of a collection of literary works of a journalistic nature which may also comprise other works or subject-matters'.[75] However, such a definition remains rather obscure. Given that the information embedded in the newspaper is in the public domain and can be rewritten and summarised an infinite number of times, one may first

---

72 Ibid 16–19.

73 See Hilty (n 71). Similarly, see, Giorgio Resta, 'Nuovi beni immateriali e *numerus clausus* die diritti esclusivi' in Giorgio Resta (ed), *Diritti esclusivi e nuovi beni immateriali* (Kluwer 2010) 3–25.

74 Ricketson (n 4).

75 As mentioned above, the Commission proposal is still on the table of the European Parliament and Council at the time of writing.

wonder whether the provision refers to arranging a particular layout.[76] But, if that were the case, the provision would be poorly worded. Also, if the protection of the layout were the objective of Article 11, it would be worth considering whether and to what extent this may be covered by the trade mark law as an element of the publisher branding and the quality of press publishing by means of trademark law. A brand can be a publisher's key asset in strengthening its position in the market.[77]

Also, one might wonder whether fixation may be intended as the transfer of the work onto carriers. However, a distinction between text or images and their fixation is hardly feasible.[78] Fixation is made in the first instance by the author, who fixes the work during writing, drawing or photographing. And it is this sort of fixation by the author – assuming grounds for protection exist – that enjoys copyright protection. Press publishers can hardly be compared with phonogram producers: a recording made by the producer – which consists in fixation of performance of the musical work on the carrier – is distinguishable from the work which incorporates it. In fact, a musical work can be performed and recorded multiple times, resulting in different phonograms. In other words, the fixation of the musical work on the carrier is just one of the possible channels of use and exploitation of the work which may be enjoyed without being fixed in a phonogram.

Furthermore, in most European legal systems newspapers enjoy copyright protection as collective works. Therefore, even assuming that the European Commission with the definition at hand refers to the selection and editing of articles, the new right for press publishers overlaps with copyright protection. For example, Article 3 of the Italian Copyright Act[79] – similarly to German,[80] French[81] and Spanish[82] laws – states that '[c]ollective works . . ., shall be protected as original works . . .'. According

---

76 In some countries, for example the UK, the publisher will also have copyright in the published edition, the typographical arrangement of the publication – design, layout and typeface.

77 See Martin Senftleben, Maximilian Kerk, Miriam Buiten and Klaus Heine, 'New Rights or New Business Models? An Inquiry into the Future of Publishing in the Digital Era' (2017) 48(5) IIC 538.

78 On this, see Ansgar Ohly, 'Ein Leistungschtutzrecht für Pressverleger' (2012) Wettbewerb in Recht und Praxis, 41.

79 Law for the Protection of Copyright and Neighbouring Rights 1941.

80 Copyright Act 1965 (Germany); see for example Thomas Dreier, 'S 4 Sammelwerke und Datenbankwerke' in Gernot Schulze and Thomas Dreier (eds), *UrhG* (5th edn, CH Beck 2015) s 4, paras 8–15.

81 See French Intellectual Property Code, art L113-2.

82 See Spanish Royal Legislative Decree, art 12.

to the Italian Copyright Act, the author is the person who organises and directs the creation of the collective work. In addition, according to Article 38, publishers have the right to use the work, unless otherwise stipulated.[83] Moreover, in most cases press publishers acquire authors' rights by direct individual contract, being therefore in the position to claim effective protection as derivative rightholders. In conclusion, under many national European laws, newspapers, including online newspapers, are already protected by copyright law to a far-reaching extent.

Yet the proposal appears to differentiate the objectives of the new neighbouring right from that of copyright. As mentioned above, Recital 32 states that Article 11 intends to protect press publishers' 'organizational and financial contribution'. This stated purpose, however, does not answer the question of what the subject matter of protection is. Setting up the objectives of the provision does not equate to outlining the subject matter and the related requirements of protection. If the subject of protection is the publishers' investment this should be openly stated by the European legislator, which should also design the contours of protection. Both the objective and the subject matter of protection need to be clarified to enable implementation and application of the provision consistently with the legislators' intention. At the same time, without a definition of the threshold of protection even minimal or insignificant investments may be sufficient to provide publishers with an exclusive right.

In this context a parallel can be drawn with the *sui generis* right for databases. First, although objectionable from several perspectives,[84] EU legislators specified the purpose, subject matter and threshold requirements for protection.[85] The *sui generis* right explicitly aims at protecting the investment of the database producer. In order to be protected under the *sui generis* database right, a database qualitatively and/or quantitatively requires a substantial investment in obtaining, verification or presentation of the content.[86] Secondly, the achievement of the investor is precisely identified in the Database Directive. Moreover, assuming that the subject matter of protection of the proposed right is the investment

---

[83] According to the majority of commentators this right is subsequent to the original one of the author; parties can indeed differently agree on the use of rights. See B Cunegatti, 'Le rassegne stampa on-line tra esclusive d'autore e divieti di concorrenza sleale' (2007) Dir Internet 3.

[84] See Peter K Yu, 'The Political Economy of Data Protection' (2010) 84 Chi Kent L Rev 777–801.

[85] Database Directive (n 17).

[86] Ibid art 7(1).

of the publisher, there may be an overlap between *sui generis* database protection and the new neighbouring right. Press publications might be considered databases within the meaning of the database Directive when requirements of protection are met.

B. Inadequacy of the Proposed Neighbouring Rights

The historical background outlined in the previous Sections suggests that protecting press publishers' commercial interests through copyright law and copyright-related rights is not in keeping with the 'spirit' of international law. This history further indicates that the protection of those interests – whenever needed – falls within the area of unfair competition regimes.

In addition, a subject matter of protection that distinguishes itself from the one of copyright or other IP rights such as database right and trade mark right (with regard to the branding of publishers) is not identifiable. Such indeterminacy cause, among other consequences, a potential conflict between press publishers' neighbouring rights and copyright of authors (who play a central role in creating news stories). A journalist may have an interest in having an article found and linked by a search engine content aggregator, however the decision whether this linking should be done might remain in the publishers' hands if the neighbouring right on the 'fixation of a collection of literary works of a journalistic nature' was exclusively attributed to publishers. In fact, merely stating that this right should not be exercised against the interests of the authors and other rightholders[87] – does not resolve the possible conflict of interests. One may argue that, even in the current situation where authors transfer their right to press publishers, authors' interests might be negatively affected by those of publishers. However, this is a question of copyright contract law and might be solved by regulating this matter in a way that fosters synergies between authors and press publishers.

---

87 As established in the Impact Assessment of the European Commission, see Commission, 'Staff Working Document, Impact Assessment on the Modernisation of EU Copyright Rules, Accompanying the Proposal for a Directive on Copyright in the Digital Single Market and the Proposal for a Regulation on the Exercise of Copyright and Related Rights Applicable to Certain Online Transmissions of Broadcasting Organisations and Retransmissions of Television and Radio Programmes' SWD (2016) 302 final, 156 and Annex 3A (Impact Assessment).

VIII. FOUR COMPLEMENTARY DRIVERS FOR A HOLISTIC APPROACH

In order to evaluate both the 'an' and the 'quomodo' of any legal intervention, at least two dimensions should be considered: on the one hand, the economic perspective concerning market functioning; on the other, the regulatory perspective inspired by social values. Dealing with both dimensions requires adopting a holistic approach based on the consistent and complementary application of four legal instruments: copyright law, *sui generis* database protection, competition law and trade mark law.

For copyrighted news, press publishers enjoy copyright as subsequent rightholders. In this respect, the position of press publishers might be strengthened, focusing on publishers' need to easily license, enforce their rights and participate in the statutory remuneration for copyright permitted uses, rather than on creating new rights. With regard specifically to the European context, the legislator could amend Article 5 'Presumption of authorship or ownership' of the European Enforcement Directive[88] to create the presumption that a press publisher must be regarded as entitled to enforce copyright in any item if that publisher's name appears in the news publication.[89]

Furthermore, *sui generis* database protection might play an important role. Digital publishing might be encouraged to develop new business models based on a content platform.[90] Indeed, the value of a business model based on developing content platforms that allow users to benefit from added value compared to a mere online magazine is connected to the functionality of the platform and the organisation of content.[91] A platform can be defined as an 'integration layer that combines and organizes multiple inputs into a single access point for the user'.[92] On a platform, the various inputs interact with each other and create value for the consumer

---

[88] Directive 2004/48/EC of the European Parliament and of the Council of 29 April 2004 on the Enforcement of Intellectual Property Rights.

[89] Alexander Peukert, 'An EU Related Right for Press Publishers Concerning Digital Uses: A Legal Analysis' (December 2016) Research Paper of the Faculty of Law, Goethe University Frankfurt No 22/2016 <https://ssrn.com/abstract=2888040>.

[90] Senftleben et al (n 77) 538–561.

[91] Ibid. In particular the authors raise the question whether adopting an additional layer of IP protection in the publishing sector can be deemed an appropriate instrument to stimulate and reward investment in this field. See also Peukert (n 89).

[92] See Senftleben et al (n 77) 545. See also David S Evans and Richard Schmalensee, 'The Industrial Organization of Markets with Two-Sided Platforms' (2007) 3(1) Compet Policy Int 151–179.

as well as for the provider. Hence, platforms – including platform functionality and infrastructure – have become a key to a successful business model in today's publishing market.

The third instrument to focus on is competition law. The expression 'competition law' is used in this context by reference to its substantive and broad meaning concerning market regulation including unfair competition law. Although there are at European level rather different regimes in this area of law, these policies share 'family ties' mirroring the overarching aim of protecting the welfare of individuals in the market economy.[93] With regard to the press publishing market a harmonised European policy may be desirable.[94] Focusing more specifically on unfair competition law, different national legal conceptions and regulations as to what are permissible and non-permissible commercial practices may threaten the

---

[93] See Francisco Costa-Cabral and Orla Lynskey, 'Family Ties: the Intersection between Data Protection and Competition in EU Law' (2017) 54 Common Mark L Rev 21. The core provisions of EU competition law have been primary law since the Treaty of Rome, art 106(1). The Treaty on the Functioning of the European Union (TFEU) extended the scope of application of EU competition rules to State-owned undertakings and public entities operating in the market: 'In the case of public undertakings and undertakings to which Member States grant special or exclusive rights, Member States shall neither enact nor maintain in force any measure contrary to the rules contained in the Treaties, in particular to those rules provided for in Article 18 and Articles 101 to 109'. Art 101 TFEU sanctions anti-competitive agreements, while Art 102 TFEU sanctions abuses by dominant companies. The text of these two provisions has not changed since the Treaty of Rome in 1957. Art 35(1) Reg 1/2003 required EU Member States to designate a National Competition Authority in charge of enforcing arts 101–102 TFEU. Although Reg 1/2003 did not harmonise the powers and the institutional structure of the NCAs, every Member State has established an administrative or a judicial authority in charge of enforcing EU competition law at the national level. In addition, national courts have a growing role in private enforcement of competition law. National civil courts of the EU Member States have jurisdiction to hear damage and injunction cases linked to breaches of arts 101–102 TFEU. The 2014 Damages Directive has partially harmonised for the first time the national procedural rules applicable to damages cases in EU competition law.

[94] See Protocol No 27 on Internal Market and Competition annexed to the Treaty on European Union, which states: 'Considering the Internal Market as set out in Article 3 of the Treaty on European Union includes a system ensuring that competition is not distorted, have agreed that to this end, the Union shall, if necessary, take action under the provisions of the Treaties, including under Article 352 of the Treaty on the Functioning of the European Union.' Moreover, art 3(1)(b) TFEU states that one of the areas in which the Union has exclusive competence is 'the establishing of competition rules necessary for the functioning of the Internal Market'.

functioning of the digital single market.[95] Various forms of regulation within this area of law might be introduced. In this regard it is worth mentioning, as a possible approach, Article 101 of the Italian Copyright Act. According to Article 101, reproduction and distribution of news are free (if not protected by copyright), as long as they are not conducted in ways that go against the honest use of journalistic news.[96] This provision clearly contains an unfair competition rule specifying a general ban based on the conduct of the one using the news.[97]

The fourth path to enhance the value of press publishers' services might be aimed at promoting branding and, as explained above, the quality of press publishing by means of trade mark law. In following this path, press publishers are called upon to work on their own business models to create added value for their products,[98] promoting the quality of the service. At the same time, advertisers might prioritise investing in more attentive and responsible platforms, thereby promoting a virtuous circle of growth. In turn investment in advertising on platforms that publish unreliable content might significantly decrease.[99]

Finally, as in many other areas of the digital economy, a significant role in digital press publishing is played by accessibility to data as 'digital resources'.[100] It is not the aim of this work to dissect the issues of a complex subject that stands at the centre of academic and legislative

---

95 The Single Market refers to the EU as one territory without any internal borders or other regulatory obstacles to the free movement of goods and services. A functioning Single Market stimulates competition and trade, improves efficiency, raises quality, and helps cut prices. The Single Market is at the heart of the European project. The documents delivered toward fostering the digital single market strategy are available on the EU Commission website <https://ec.europa.eu/growth/single-market/strategy_en>.

96 On this point see P Gaetano Marchetti and Luigi Carlo Ubertazzi (eds), *Commentario breve alle leggi su proprietà intellettuale e concorrenza* (Wolters Kluwer 2016) 1897–1901; Cass civ 10 maggio 1993, no 5346 with commentary by Mario Fabiani, 'Sui limiti di protezione delle notizie e informazioni di stampa' (1994) Dir Aut 76. See also Cunegatti (n 83) 251.

97 This is regulated in Italy by art 2598 of the Civil Code.

98 See Senftleben et al (n 77) 538–561.

99 Indeed, one of the largest advertisers in the world recently announced that they would reduce investment on platforms or environments that create division in society and promote anger or hate. See Christopher Carbone, 'Unilever Threatens Facebook, Google with Online Advertising Cuts' Fox News (February 2018) <http://www.foxnews.com/tech/2018/02/12/major-advertiser-threatens-to-pull-ads-from-google-facebook-over-trash-content.html>.

100 See Gintare Surblyte, 'Data as a Digital Resource' (October 2016) Max Planck Institute for Innovation & Competition Research Paper No 16-12 <https://ssrn.com/abstract=2849303>.

debate.[101] However, it is enough to highlight in this context that data is a fundamental digital resource in a data-driven economy: all companies, including publishers, compete over data.

IX. CONCLUSION

Although the European proposal is anchored to the social value attributed to press publishers' activities, the chosen method of regulation is barely justifiable on a systematic and policy level. First, the creation of new neighbouring rights for press publishers does not fit properly within the 'spirit' of international IP law. As has emerged from the historical development of international law, copyright and neighbouring rights have been expressly excluded as means of legal protection for press publishers' commercial interests. The debate leading up to this exclusion suggested that the subject fell outside the scope of IP law. The pure commercial interests of press publishers, it was stated, fall under the scope of unfair competition law. In fact, the rationale for protecting competitors in the market is primarily the functioning of the market. Conversely IP does not only aim at regulating the functioning of the market; it focuses indeed on the achievement of investment (e.g. a work, patent or design).

This differentiation does not have a purely speculative value but is a cornerstone from a systematic perspective. The systematic placement of the legal instruments allows for an interpretation of them that is consistent with their objectives. Conversely, a wrong systematic placement of the legal instruments may reflect negatively on their application, causing legal uncertainty and undesirable effects on both market functioning and the social values pursued by the legal system.

Also, in the case at hand the European Commission has not identified a subject matter of protection which allows the protection of the publishers' interests to be subsumed within the area of IP law. In addition, the new right would overlap with existing IP rights such as copyright law and the *sui generis* database protection.

---

[101] Ibid; Josef Drexl, 'Designing Competitive Markets for Industrial Data – Between Propertisation and Access' (October 2016) Max Planck Institute for Innovation & Competition Research Paper No 16-13 <https://ssrn.com/abstract=2862975>; Josef Drexl et al, 'Position Statement of the Max Planck Institute for Innovation and Competition of 26 April 2017 on the European Commission's "Public Consultation on Building the European Data Economy"' (April 2017) Max Planck Institute for Innovation & Competition Research Paper No 17-08 <https://ssrn.com/abstract=2959924>.

Thus, rather than inappropriately relying on neighbouring rights, this chapter suggests a holistic approach. This is inspired by market-functioning needs, but also by values such as diversification of information channels and quality of information. In enhancing digital press publishing, a proper regulation should aim at promoting development of new business models triggered by the quality of services and content offered. To these ends, four complementary drivers have been addressed: copyright law, *sui generis* database protection, competition law, and trade mark law. Furthermore, since digital press publishing relies on data and publishers compete over data, regulation of accessibility to data as 'digital resources' is the fifth pillar on which the suggested comprehensive approach is based.

13. Making derivative works without authorisation and the interpretation of originality and creativity under Thailand's copyright law*

Chongnang Wiputhanupong

I. INTRODUCTION

Making derivative works without authorisation of the copyright owner is a significant issue in the digital world. In many cases it is difficult to search for authorisation. Therefore, despite the risks of copyright infringement lawsuits, many online creators often use online digital prior-arts to create subsequent online digital works or derivative works without authorisation from the copyright owner.

Generally 'derivative works' means those works the creation of which is based on other works.[1] The work is recognised under Article 2(3) of the Berne Convention as 'derivative work', which includes but is not limited to translations, adaptations, arrangements of music, and other alterations of a literary or artistic work.[2] The Berne Convention requires that such derivative works are protected, without prejudice to the copyright in the original work, when the derivative work is also original.

Although it is internationally required that copyright does not protect

* All online sources were last accessed on 27 December 2018.

1 J Adrian Sterling, *World Copyright Law: Protection of Authors' Works, Performances, Phonograms, Films, Video, Broadcasts and Published Editions in National, International and Regional Law* (3rd edn, Sweet & Maxwell 2008) 279.

2 Berne Convention for the Protection of Literary and Artistic Works (signed on 4 May 1896, entered into force 5 December 1887, revised on 24 July 1971) 1161 UNTS 3 (Berne Convention) (art 2(3) ('Derivative works; Translations, adaptations, arrangements of music and other alterations of a literary or artistic work shall be protected as original works without prejudice to the copyright in the original work . . .'). See also Sam Ricketson and Jane C Ginsburg, *International Copyright and Neighbouring Rights: The Berne Convention and Beyond* (2nd edn, Oxford University Press 2006) paras 8.79–8.83.

facts or ideas,[3] it is not explicitly stated, on the international level, that a work has to possess a certain degree of originality and creativity in order to be protected under copyright law.[4] Nevertheless, according to Article 2(5)[5] of the Berne Convention there is a requirement for the 'collections of literary or artistic works' in the sense that the works can be protected by copyright only if they meet the criterion of 'intellectual creation'.[6]

Even though this context of 'intellectual creation' is specified only for those works under Article 2(5) of the Berne Convention, it could be presumed that this is as an implicit requirement for the protection of other works mentioned under Article 2 as well.[7] The requirement is emphasised explicitly for the works of collections under Article 2(5) because in many cases the authorship inherent in those works may not be obvious compared to those in the primary works protected under Article 2(1).[8]

Additionally, originality and creativity have also been mentioned as a criterion of copyright protection in the European Union. According to the ECJ's decision of the European Court of Justice (ECJ) in *Infopaq International A/S v Danske Dagblades Forening*, the scope of protection[9] was given a broad interpretation and a strong meaning that a work will qualify for copyright protection if it contains or expresses 'the author's own intellectual creation'.[10] Therefore, a sentence or parts of sentence, even though it is comprised of only 11 consecutive words,[11] are also eligible for copyright protection under Article 2 of Directive 2001/29.

---

3 Agreement on Trade-Related Aspects of Intellectual Property Rights (opened for signature 15 April 1994, entered into force 1 January 1996) 1869 UNTS 299 (TRIPS), art 9 ('Copyright protection shall extend to expressions and not to ideas, procedures, methods of operation or mathematical concepts as such').

4 Sterling (n 1) 337.

5 Berne Convention 1971 (n 2), art 2(5) ('Collections of literary or artistic works such as encyclopaedias and anthologies which, by reason of the selection and arrangement of their contents, constitute "intellectual creations" shall be protected as such, without prejudice to the copyright in each of the works forming part of such collections').

6 Sterling (n 1) 337; Ricketson and Ginsburg (n 2) 448.

7 Ricketson and Ginsburg (n 2) 488.

8 Ibid.

9 Council Directive 2001/29/EC of 22 May 2001 on the Harmonisation of Certain Aspects of Copyright and Related Rights in the Information Society [2001] OJ L 167 (Copyright Directive), art 2.

10 Case C-5/08 *Infopaq International A/S v Danske Dagblades Forening* [2009] ECR I-6569 (ECJ) 48.

11 Ibid.

One popular form of online digital works is parody. Parody could be categorised as a kind of 'derivative work'[12] which is eligible for copyright protection under the Berne Convention.[13] According to Hutcheon[14] and Rose,[15] the nature of parody involves the displacement, the 'imitation with critical irony' and the 'comic incongruity', which distinguishes it from other kinds of derivative works or works that borrow from existing works and amounts to plagiarism.[16] Parody always contains parts of the original work, creating the possibility of copyright infringement.[17] Online digital parody also creates some questions about copyright protection and the status of unauthorised online digital derivative works.

In order to explore the copyright protection given to these unauthorised online digital derivative works, this chapter will begin with a comparison between US and UK law (Section II). Section III will explore the interpretations of the Thai Supreme Court regarding originality and creativity and copyright protection granted to original and derivative works. This includes an analysis of the meaning of 'author' under the Thai Copyright Act. An appendix to the chapter concludes with an overview of the meaning of author and the protection granted to unauthorised derivative works in the laws of some other Asian countries.

II. COPYRIGHT PROTECTION ON UNAUTHORISED DERIVATIVE WORKS IN THE US AND UK

At the national level, copyright protection of derivative works will be granted according to different standards and degrees of originality. This section compares the US and UK approaches.

---

12 Sterling (n 1) 641.

13 Berne Convention 1971 (n 2) art 2(1). (3) Translations, adaptations, arrangements of music and other alterations of a literary or artistic work shall be protected as original works without prejudice to the copyright in the original work.

14 Linda Hutcheon, *A Theory of Parody: The Teachings of Twentieth-Century Art Forms* (Methuen 1985) 6.

15 Margaret A Rose, *Parody: Ancient, Modern, and Post-Modern* (Cambridge University Press 1993) 52.

16 Ellen Gredley and Spyros Maniatis, 'Parody: A Fatal Attraction? Part 1: The Nature of Parody and Its Treatment in Copyright' (1997) 19 EIPR 339, 340.

17 Sterling (n 1) 641.

A. US Law

US copyright law clearly separates the exclusive right of reproduction from the right of making derivative work.[18] The definition of derivative work includes that which is based on one or more pre-existing works.[19] For this purpose, the 'pre-existing work' must be consistent with the general subject matter of copyright set forth in section 102, regardless of whether it is or was ever copyrighted.[20]

Under section 103(a) and (b), there are four conditions for protection of a derivative work: (1) the protection does not extend to any part of the work in which another's copyrighted material has been used unlawfully; (2) the protection extends only to the material contributed by the author of such work; (3) the work which employs the pre-existing work would not be granted protection; and (4) the copyright protection granted to such work will not affect or enlarge the scope, duration, ownership, or subsistence of any copyright protection in the pre-existing material. The House Report notes that, even when the consent of the copyright owner had not been obtained 'the unauthorized reproduction of a work might be "lawful" under the doctrine of fair use and if so the work incorporating it could be copyrighted'.[21]

Feist[22] held that a work needs to bear a 'modicum of creativity' in order to meet the criterion of originality and thus be eligible for copyright protection. Similarly, the same standards and conditions apply to derivative

---

[18] 17 USC, s 106 ('Subject to sections 107 through 122, the owner of copyright under this title has the exclusive rights to do and to authorize any of the following: (1) to reproduce the copyrighted work in copies or phonorecords; (2) to prepare derivative works based upon the copyrighted work').

[19] 17 USC, s 101 A ('"derivative work" is a work based upon one or more pre-existing works, such as a translation, musical arrangement, dramatization, fictionalization, motion picture version, sound recording, art reproduction, abridgment, condensation, or any other form in which a work may be recast, transformed, or adapted. A work consisting of editorial revisions, annotations, elaborations, or other modifications which, as a whole, represent an original work of authorship, is a "derivative work"').

[20] According to the House Report, a 'derivative work' would also require a process of recasting, transforming, or adapting 'one or more preexisting works' and the 'preexisting work' must be consistent with the general subject matter of copyright set forth in section 102, regardless of whether it is or was ever copyrighted. United States House of Representatives, House Report No 91-1476 (1976) Copyright Law Revision 57.

[21] House Report No 94-1476 (n 20) 57–58.

[22] *Feist Publications Inc v Rural Telephone Service Co* (1991) 499 US 340 (SCOTUS) [51].

works. In *L Batlin & Son Inc v Snyder*[23] and *Durham Industries Inc v Tomy Corp*[24] the courts denied protection for derivative works (a plastic Uncle Sam Bank and the three Disney figures) on the basis that they were merely the reproduction of the prior work of art, and therefore were insufficiently original for copyright protection.

In *Anderson v Stallone*,[25] upon considering whether Anderson's appropriation of the Rocky characters could be granted protection as derivative works, it was noted that the holder of a copyright has the exclusive right to prepare derivative works based upon his copyrighted work. The court then cited the decision in *Litchfield v Spielberg*[26] that a work is derivative 'only if it would be considered an infringing work if the material which it had derived from a prior work had been taken without the consent of the copyright proprietor of the prior work'.[27] The court therefore

---

23 *L Batlin & Son Inc v Snyder* (1976) 536 F2d 486 (2nd Cir) ('This court has examined both the appellants' plastic Uncle Sam bank made under Snyder's copyright and the uncopyrighted model cast iron mechanical bank which is itself a reproduction of the original public domain Uncle Sam bank . . . The substance of appellee's expert's testimony on which the district judge evidently relied was that the variations found in appellants' plastic bank were merely "trivial" and that it was a reproduction of the metal bank made as simply as possible for the purposes of manufacture . . . [t]here were no elements of difference that amounted to significant alteration or that had any purpose other than the functional one of making a more suitable (and probably less expensive) figure in the plastic medium.') See also *Alfred Bell & Co v Catalda Fine Arts Inc* (1951) 191 F2d 99 (2nd Cir).

24 *Durham Industries Inc v Tomy Corp* (1980) 630 F2d 905 (2nd Cir) ('The three Tomy figures are instantly identifiable as embodiments of the Disney characters in yet another form: Mickey, Donald and Pluto are now represented as small, plastic, wind-up toys. Neither party contests the fact that Walt Disney created the three characters at issue. Tomy acknowledges Disney's ownership of copyrights on these characters and concedes that without a license from Disney Tomy's publication of its Disney figures would constitute infringement. That Tomy's creations are derivative works is in itself, of course, no bar to copyrightability. But this principle is subject to two important and related limitations. First, to support a copyright the original aspects of a derivative work must be more than trivial. Second, the scope of protection afforded a derivative work must reflect the degree to which it relies on preexisting material and must not in any way affect the scope of any copyright protection in that preexisting material. Thus the only aspects of Tomy's Disney figures entitled to copyright protection are the non-trivial, original features, if any, contributed by the author or creator of these derivative works . . . Lacking even a modest degree of originality, Tomy's Disney figures are not copyrightable').

25 *Anderson v Stallone* (1989) 11 USPQ2d 1161 (CD Cal) [25].

26 *Litchfield v Spielberg* (1984) 736 F2d 1352 (9th Cir) 1354.

27 Melville B Nimmer and David Nimmer, *Nimmer on Copyright: A Treatise on the Law of Literary, Musical and Artistic Property and the Protection of Ideas* (Revised edn, M Bender 1978) s 3.01.

examined whether Anderson's treatment was an unauthorised derivative work. It found that Anderson's characters in Rocky IV were not merely substantially similar to Stallone's but they were Stallone's characters as Anderson had copied and appropriated Stallone's Rocky characters in his treatment.[28] The appropriation therefore infringes upon the protected expression of Stallone in the Rocky characters and renders Anderson's work an unauthorised derivative work.[29]

In the next issue where Anderson sought copyright protection for the non-infringing portions of his treatment, the plaintiff relied upon the content of 17 USC, s 103(a) and the House Report[30] as support for his position that the non-infringing parts are entitled to copyright protection.

The judgment concluded that even though Congress intended to provide protection for the non-infringing portions of derivative works, the House Report language is ambiguous:

> It makes a general statement that non-infringing portions of a work should be granted protection if these portions do not employ the pre-existing work. The report then provides two examples: one involving a compilation where the non-infringing portion was deemed protected, and another involving a derivative work where no part of the work could be protected. The general statement, when taken in the context of the comparison of compilations and derivative works in the section and the two examples given, is best understood as applying only to compilations. Although it is not crystal clear, it appears that the Committee assumed that in a derivative work the underlying work is 'employed' throughout. . . . Both then appear to conclude that no part of an infringing derivative work should be granted copyright protection. Only if a derivative work is assumed to employ the infringing work throughout do these passages read coherently. . . . However, in dicta the court opined on what result would be warranted if the derivative work had been made without the permission of the original author. The Court cited to the aforementioned passages from Professor Nimmer's treatise and the House Report and assumed without discussion that the 'derivative copyrights would be invalid, since the pre-existing illustration used without permission would tend to pervade the entire work'.[31]

---

28 *Anderson v Stallone* (n 25) [24].

29 In *Anderson v Stallone* (n 25) the court focused on the originality test but did not consider the fair use exceptions for purposes of granting copyright protection to derivative works.

30 House Report No 94-1476 (n 20).

31 *Anderson v Stallone* (n 25). See also *Eden Toys Inc v Florelee Undergarment* (1982) Co697 F2d 27 (2nd Cir) 34–35; *Gracen v Bradford* (1983) 798 F2d 300 (7th Cir) 302–303; and *Schrock v Learning Curve Int'l Inc* (2009) 586 F3d 513 (7th Cir).

In *Tempo Music Inc v Famous Music Corp*,[32] the United States District Court had to decide whether or not the harmony and revised melody of the song 'Satin Doll' added to the earlier musical work, when used or performed without the lyrics, was a derivative work. Determining that question would decide whether Billy Strayhorn's estate, who had collaborated in their creation, had an interest in 'Satin Doll' when it was used or performed without lyrics.[33]

In effect, the court disagreed with the assertion of the Ellington Estate, who claimed that a harmonic progression alone could not support a claim of copyright interest in a derivative musical work. Instead, the court relied on the test from *Batlin*[34] and Nimmer[35] and first held that the substantially similar harmony in the 1953 recording of 'Satin Doll' had not yet entered the public domain. In some other cases,[36] un-copyrighted works were found to be in the public domain and therefore copyright protection for those elements of the subsequent works containing material from the earlier works was not possible. However, in this particular case, the 1953 records did not restrain copyright protection for the elements of the subsequent works containing substance from the earlier works. Hence, the harmony remained eligible for full copyright protection.

Second, regarding the similar bars of harmony found in the original works, the complainant (Ellington Estate) argued that subsequent harmony was non-original and did not qualify for copyright protection. The court cited *Levine*[37] and rejected this argument, finding that there were various ways to compose the song but the author had chosen to perform in this particular expression. The court was not persuaded that, in composing the derivative work, the authors did not, as a matter of law, 'create a protectable work by combining various common elements so as to produce a unique expression of music'.[38] Therefore, the disputed work was an original work and was copyrightable.

---

[32] *Tempo Music v Famous Music Corp* (1993) 838 F Supp 162 (SDNY); Massimo Pavolini, 'Derivative Musical Works: Protection and Royalties in the Balance' (1994) 5(3) ELR101.

[33] *Tempo Music v Famous Music* (n 32) [167].

[34] *Batlin v Snyder* (n 23).

[35] Nimmer (n 27) s 4.05.

[36] *Shaw v Lindheim* (1992) 809 F Supp 1393 (CD Cal); *Silverman v CBS Inc* (1989) 870 F2d 40 (2nd Cir).

[37] *Levine v McDonald's Corp* (1990) 735 F Supp 92 (SDNY).

[38] Ibid.

Accordingly, there are two approaches[39] to the protection of a derivative work under US law. In the first approach, the standard and requirement of originality is somewhat low and tends to favour derivative authors.[40] In the second approach, more contribution than a modicum of originality is required from the author of the derivate work. Under the higher standard of 'non-trivial' or 'substantial originality', the author of derivative work applies substantial contribution so that the work is distinguishable from the original.[41]

According to the United States District Court in *Moore Publishing Inc*,[42] which compared the *Batlin*[43] and *Gracen*[44] judgments:

> [Both cases] initially recognize that the quantum of originality required for copyright protection is modest and that the contributions [of the derivative author] need only rise above the minimal or trivial to be protected. But both opinions then continue on to require that the contributions be 'substantially' different from the preexisting work. It would appear that a contribution could be more than trivial, but still not substantially different from the preexisting work. Would such a contribution be entitled to protection?

Generally, it could be concluded that even though the first approach may require at least a modicum of originality for a derivative work to be protected, the court applying that standard will also consider what has been added to the prior work and whether the contribution is sufficient to enable audiences to distinguish between the derivative and the original work.[45]

This approach, however, contradicts Nimmer, who relies mainly on the standard of 'substantially different':

> In general, the applicable standard in determining the necessary quantum of originality is that of a 'distinguishable variation' that is more than 'merely trivial.' Any variation will not suffice, but one that is sufficient to render the derivative work distinguishable from its prior work in any meaningful manner will be sufficient. [46]

---

39 Natalie Heineman, 'Computer Software Derivative Works: The Calm Before the Storm' (2008) 8 JHTL 235, 243.

40 *Tempo Music v Famous Music* (n 32).

41 *Batlin v Snyder* (n 23).

42 *Moore Publishing Inc v Big Sky Marketing Inc* (1991) 756 FSupp 1371 (D Idaho).

43 *Batlin v Snyder* (n 23).

44 *Gracen v Bradford Exchange* (1983) 698 F2d 300 (7th Cir).

45 Heineman (n 39) 244.

46 Nimmer (n 27) ss 3.03[A], 3-12 and 3-13.

B. UK Law

There is no explicit meaning of 'derivative work' provided under the Copyright, Designs and Patents Act 1988 (United Kingdom). The relevant rights of the original owner include adaptation which is relevant to derivative works.[47]

A mere copy from the prior work will not be granted copyright protection. However, even if a subsequent work contains parts of the earlier works, that work can still be copyrightable if sufficient and independent skill, labour and judgement have been applied.[48] There are three limitations before a work would be treated as original and therefore be protected as derivative work: (1) the labour applied to the work must be of the right kind; (2) the effort contributed must bring about a material change in the work; and (3) the change of the work must be of the right kind, which could be discussed further as follows.[49]

The test of labour appeared in *Interlego AG v Tyco Industries Inc*[50] when Lord Oliver stated that 'only certain kind of skill, labour and judgment confer originality'. Furthermore, in *Macmillan v Cooper*[51] the Privy Council also emphasised that a subsequent work will fail to meet the standard of originality if the material contained therein could not be distinguished from the prior work.[52] Finally, it could be seen in *Sawkins*

---

[47] Copyright, Designs and Patents Act 1988 (United Kingdom) (hereinafter CDPA (UK)), s 16(1) ('The owner of the copyright in a work has . . . the exclusive right to do the following acts in the United Kingdom– (e) to make an adaptation of the work or do any of the above in relation to an adaptation'); CDPA, s 21(3) ('In this Part "adaptation" – (a) in relation to a literary work, other than a computer program or a database, or in relation to a dramatic work, means – (i) a translation of the work; (ii) a version of a dramatic work in which it is converted into a non-dramatic work or, as the case may be, of a non-dramatic work in which it is converted into a dramatic work; (iii) a version of the work in which the story or action is conveyed wholly or mainly by means of pictures in a form suitable for reproduction in a book, or in a newspaper, magazine or similar periodical; (ab) in relation to a computer program, means an arrangement or altered version of the program or a translation of it; (ac) in relation to a database, means an arrangement or altered version of the database or a translation of it; (b) in relation to a musical work, means an arrangement or transcription of the work').

[48] Hugh I L Laddie, Peter Prescott and Mary Vitoria, *The Modern Law of Copyright and Designs* (4th edn, LexisNexis 2011) 87.

[49] Lionel Bently and Brad Sherman, *Intellectual Property Law* (3rd edn, Oxford University Press 2009) 99–104.

[50] *Interlego AG v Tyco Industries Inc* [1989] 1 BLR 271 (PC).

[51] *Macmillan v Cooper* (1924) 40 TLR 186 (PC).

[52] Ibid 188. The Privy Council stated that 'to secure copyright for this product it is necessary that labour, skill and capital should have been expended sufficiently

v Hyperion[53] that the court granted copyright protection to Sawkins' musical works providing that the effort, such as the time and labour spent on creating the new editions, was sufficient and therefore met the criterion of originality, even though those musical works were based on the works of Lalande.

In summary, the two jurisdictions provide some degree of difference towards the concept of originality and the protection of derivative work, but both jurisdictions generally require a sufficient degree of originality for a derivative work to be protected.[54]

C. A Comparison Between the US and UK Laws

Fundamentally, a derivative work must be dependent on another prior or original work.[55] Under US law a subsequent work is derivative when it contains a 'substantial' amount of components from the underlying work.[56] When a work borrows a 'substantial amount of components' from a prior work, there may be some circumstances where parts of those derivative works could not be easily distinguished from the original work. This could happen regardless of whether the author of the subsequent derivative work has permission from the author of the pre-existing work.

In general, according to Nimmer, if the author of the subsequent work uses substantial parts of the original work with authorisation from the original author regardless of whether those parts are distinguishable from the original work, the author of the derivative work will be able to acquire copyright protection on the work based on an agreement or licence with the original author.[57] Using parts of the prior work outside the scope of the licence could constitute copyright infringement.[58]

Where use is without permission it will be copyright infringement. According to Goldstein, in the absent of proper consent, the copyright

---

to impart to the product some quality or character which the raw material did not possess, and which differentiates the product from the raw material' and therefore denied copyright protection for the reduction of the Life of Alexander.

53 *Sawkins v Hyperion* [2005] EWCA 565.

54 The concept and scope of originality is different between both jurisdictions as discussed earlier, however.

55 17 USC, s 101 ('A "derivative work" is a work based upon one or more pre-existing works'). Although there is no explicit meaning of 'derivative work' under the CDPA (UK), the meaning could be inferred from those given under the Berne Convention (n 2), art 2(3).

56 See Heineman (n 39).

57 Nimmer (n 27) s 3.04 [A].

58 Heineman (n 39).

owner does not have the chance to license the acts of the infringer.[59] The unauthorised use of substantial parts of the prior work could amount to copyright infringement[60] regardless of whether those parts are distinguishable or indistinguishable from the original work.

In order to focus on copyright protection granted to derivative works, rather than infringement, there are two issues to note. First, when infringement occurs from the use of a substantial part, there could be a distinction where either the derivative work is distinguishable or indistinguishable from the prior work. In both situations, both the US and the UK will not grant copyright protection to parts of derivative works which are merely slavish copies of the earlier work.[61] One fundamental reason is because those copied parts do not meet the criteria of originality and violate the right of reproduction of the original author. Also the infringer of the subsequent copied work certainly has not created the new work or the new market.[62]

Second, the copyright protection granted to derivative works, which are unauthorised uses of substantial parts of prior works could be divided and analysed as follows.

1. Derivative works which are indistinguishable from the prior work in the UK

It is likely that the work would be protected and infringing the right of making adaptation at the same time. Even though a derivative work draws substantially on a prior work, a court may allow copyright protection to the whole derivative work if a sufficient degree of skill, labour and judgment is proven.[63] This applies to both authorised and unauthorised uses of the prior work.

In some cases where those unauthorised uses are indistinguishable from the prior work, such as an unauthorised translation of a novel, the unauthorised translation of the entire novel could qualify for copyright protection if the translation required skill, labour and judgement. UK copyright law may grant copyright protection to the translator in such a case notwithstanding that the act of translating might create a dispute of copyright infringement because it violates the exclusive right of making

---

[59] Paul Goldstein, 'Derivative Rights and Derivative Works in Copyright' (1982–1983) 30 CSUSA 209, 240 (citing *Baker v Seldon* (1870) 101 US 99 (SCOTUS)).

[60] A significant issue which will not be discussed in this chapter.

[61] Nimmer (n 27) s 3.06; Laddie, Prescott and Vitoria (n 48) 87.

[62] Goldstein (n 59) 217.

[63] Laddie, Prescott and Vitoria (n 48) 87.

adaptation[64] guaranteed under section 16(1)(e) of the Copyright, Designs and Patents Act 1988 (UK).[65]

Furthermore, since the limitations and exceptions of copyright infringement under UK copyright law are more restrictive than the fair use in the US,[66] the author of the translation might own copyright in the translation but infringe the right to make an adaptation of the work.[67] This means that any copyright in the translation cannot easily be exploited if at all.

2. Derivative works which are indistinguishable from the prior work in the US

It is likely that derivative works which are indistinguishable from the prior work would not be protected in the United States. Also, it would be infringing the right to make derivative works (not the right of reproduction) of the original author.

Under US law, the translated version of the novel falls into the scope of 'derivative work'[68] and the exclusive right to make a derivative work is guaranteed to the copyright owner.[69] Therefore, the unauthorised translation of the entire novel would be an infringement.

The US Copyright Act explicitly states that the copyright in a compilation or derivative work 'does not extend to any part of the work in which such [pre-existing] material has been used unlawfully'.[70] By virtue of this

---

64 Ibid.

65 CDPA (UK), s 16 (1)(e) ('The acts restricted by copyright in a work. (1) The owner of the copyright in a work has, in accordance with the following provisions of this Chapter, the exclusive right to do the following acts in the United Kingdom – (e) to make an adaptation of the work or do any of the above in relation to an adaptation (see section 21); and those acts are referred to in this Part as the "acts restricted by the copyright"').

66 Chongnang Wiputhanupong, 'Copyright for the Digital Era: Are We Aiming at Individuals?' (Doctorate Dissertation, University of Nottingham 2016).

67 CDPA (UK), ss 16 and 21.

68 17 USC, s 101 ('A "derivative work" is a work based upon one or more preexisting works, such as a translation, musical arrangement, dramatization, fictionalization, motion picture version, sound recording, art reproduction, abridgment, condensation, or any other form in which a work may be recast, transformed, or adapted. A work consisting of editorial revisions, annotations, elaborations, or other modifications which, as a whole, represent an original work of authorship, is a "derivative work"').

69 17 USC, s 106 (2) ('Subject to sections 107 through 122, the owner of copyright under this title has the exclusive rights to do and to authorize any of the following: (2) to prepare derivative works based upon the copyrighted work').

70 Copyright Act 1976, s 103(a).

provision, the US would usually deny copyright protection on the portion of derivative work which employs the original work unlawfully.[71]

Generally, under US copyright law, the unauthorised use of parts of copyrighted work could possibly be regarded as lawful under the fair use doctrine. Therefore, according to the example given above, first of all, the translation of the entire novel is an infringement of the right to create derivate works of the original author. Secondly, the author of the unauthorised translated version of the full novel in the US would not be granted copyright protection unless evidence had been proven that the act of translating and incorporating the original work was lawful under the fair use doctrine.[72] In this case, the translation of the entire novel is unlikely to meet the criteria of fair use. This is simply because, according to Goldstein, the sole translation of a novel from one language into another is nothing but a change of the prior expression from one into another different though equivalent form.[73] Therefore, the unauthorised translation of the full novel would not be granted copyright protection under the US law.[74]

3. Derivative works which are distinguishable from the prior work such as parodies and satires

When a derivative work contains unauthorised use of substantial parts of the prior work, there are many cases where those uses could be distinguishable from the original work; for example in the work of satires[75] and parodies.[76] In such cases, the subsequent works will generally contain parts which contain (a) originality of the author of the derivative works, and (b) substantial similarity borrowed from the underlying work.

In cases where the derivative works are distinguishable from the underlying works, and where those creations have sufficient originality, those separable parts are eligible for copyright protection in both US[77] and

---

[71] Nimmer (n 27) s 3.06.

[72] Ibid.

[73] Goldstein (n 59) 226.

[74] At the early stage judges posited that a work could not be both original and infringing. Therefore a translation would not be regarded as infringing because of 'the creative originality' of the subsequent author contributed during the act of translation. See also Pierre N Leval, 'Nimmer Lecture: Fair Use Rescued' (1997) 44 UCLA L Rev 1449, 1452.

[75] Satires may be monologues, parodies or narratives. Gilbert Highet, *The Anatomy of Satire* (1st edn, Oxford University Press 1962) 13–14.

[76] Wiputhanupong (n 66).

[77] See 17 USC, s 103 (b).

UK jurisdictions and therefore the subsequent author of those parts will be able to be granted copyright protection as well.

Copyright infringement usually takes place when the author of a derivative work borrows substantial parts from the earlier work without authorisation from the original author. Those borrowed parts, if distinguishable from the first work, will not be able to acquire copyright protection under both jurisdictions. In addition, in some other cases an unauthorised use of the prior works could possibly be lawful if those works were available in the public domain as well.[78]

The requirement of lawful use of the original work in the US has two approaches: the 'Pervades' and the 'Infringement'.[79] The 'Pervade Standard' means that a derivative work will not be nullified unless the underlying work tended to 'pervade' it.[80] In other words, even if there is no consent, a derivative work would be considered as 'lawful' as long as it does not pervade the prior work. As stated in *Pickett v Prince* '. . . the creator of a derivative work would not require authorization if the pre-existing work does not "pervade" the derivative work, but would require authorization if the pre-existing work does "pervade"'.[81] This approach has some uncertainties since it would persuade the authors of the derivative work to create a subsequent work without the permission of the original author given that that work does not pervade the original work. And that would undermine the value of the exclusive right of the original copyright owner.[82]

While the infringement approach is at odds with the pervades approach, it assumes that the subsequent work would be a justified derivative work only if that work would be 'an infringement' of the prior work when lacking the consent of the original author.[83] If using the infringement approach, a court must first identify whether there are substantial similarities between the original work and the subsequent work. In most cases there will likely be infringement because the derivative work needs to incorporate a substantial amount of the underlying work.[84] The act of taking substantial parts could possibly be lawful as fair use.[85] This could

---

78 Heineman (n 39) 250.

79 Ibid 250–251.

80 See *Eden Toys Inc v Florelee Undergarment Co* (1982) 697 F2d 27 (2nd Cir) and *Pickett v Prince* (1999) 52 F Supp 2d 893 (ND Ill). See also Heineman (n 39).

81 *Pickett v Prince* (n 80) [903].

82 Nimmer (n 27) s 3.06.

83 Heineman (n 39) 251–252.

84 Nimmer (n 27) s 3.03[A]; See also Heineman (n 39).

85 17 USC, s 107 ('The factors to be considered for fair use shall include – (1)

lead to another problem where the protection of the rights of the two authors of the work (the author of the original work and the author of the subsequent work) conflict.[86] One possibility suggested in *Steward v Abend*[87] is that 'Congress simply intended that a derivative work author may not employ a copyrighted work without the author's permission, although of course he can obtain copyright protection for his own original additions'. Nimmer also indicates that 'the right to claim copyright in a non-infringing derivative work arises by operation of law [section 106 and section 103(a)], not through authority from the copyright owner of the underlying work'.[88]

Both approaches in the US support protection of derivative works if they are original, regardless of whether the consent of the original author has been given. In other words, the author of an unauthorised derivative work which incorporates the original work could be granted copyright protection only if able to show that the act of using the prior work is legitimate.[89]

It is worth noting that even though the US fair use doctrine is more flexible than the standard of UK fair dealing, the result in this example is eventually the same. This is, in particular, for those substantial similarity parts which are borrowed and used to create a derivative work that is distinguishable from the prior work, such as parodies and satires.

In conclusion, Nimmer emphasised that '[a] work is not derivative unless it has substantially copied from a prior work'.[90] Also the act of 'taking substantial parts' of the original work and making derivative work 'without authorisation' of the original author is against the exclusive right of making adaptation guaranteed under the right of preparing derivative work[91] and the right of making an adaptation of the work[92] of the original

the purpose and character of the use, including whether such use is of a commercial nature or is for non-profit educational purposes; (2) the nature of the copyrighted work; (3) the amount and substantiality of the portion used in relation to the copyrighted work as a whole; and (4) the effect of the use upon the potential market for or value of the copyrighted work').

86 Heineman (n 39) 252.

87 *Stewart v Abend* (1990) 495 US 207 (SCOTUS) 232.

88 Nimmer (n 27) s 3.06, n 4 and Heineman (n 39) 253.

89 See *Gracen v Bradford Exchange* (1983) 698 F2d 300 (7th Cir); *Pickett v Prince* (n 80) citing *Dynamic Solutions Inc v Planning & Control Inc* (1986) 646 F Supp 1329 (SDNY).

90 Nimmer (n 27) s 3.01.

91 17 USC, s 106(2).

92 CDPA (UK), s 16(1)(e) and s 21.

Table 13.1 Copyright protection on derivative work: a comparison between the US and UK laws

Derivative works which are indistinguishable from the prior work	Derivative works which are distinguishable from the prior work such as parodies and satires
UK = protected + infringe the right of making adaptation US = not protected + infringe the right of making derivative work (not the right of reproduction)	Parts with Originality – UK = protected – US = protected Substantial similarity parts UK = the whole work will not be protected + will be infringement right of making adaptation US = (1) the whole work will not be protected + will be infringement right of making derivative work (2) the whole work will attract copyright + will not be infringement (fair use i.e. transformative or parody, satire, criticism or comments)

author.[93] Therefore, making derivative work without authorisation of the original author could constitute copyright infringement in both jurisdictions as appears in Table 13.1.

Nevertheless, generally, the author of the derivative work (either in the US or UK) will probably have copyright protection. The protection will be given based on two different approaches, which result in similar consequences.

In general there are three fundamental considerations before a subsequent work could be protected by copyright as derivative work.

(1) Such a work needs to be qualify under the definition of derivative work in Article 2(3) of the Berne Convention, i.e. a translation, adaptations, arrangements of music and other alterations of a literary or artistic work.
(2) Whether the author of such subsequent work receives authorisation from the original author, or the work is adapted by the original author.
(3) The second condition will lead to the third question about originality and creativity.

93 Nimmer (n 27) s 3.01.

According to Goldstein,[94] because copyright's underlying economic principles aim to attract private investment in the creation of original expression, the structure of copyright for derivative works intentionally provides the original author with two incentives: (1) the right to use elements in the prior work to prepare a derivative work; and (2) protection for the original elements of a derivative work.

In other cases where derivative authors copy substantial parts of the prior work there will be a copyright infringement unless the maker of the new version, or any other third-party copier, licenses use of the original.[95] Any copyright protection for a derivative work will only be for those parts which are original.

Finally, it is noteworthy that originality and creativity are the basic principles or legal framework that are the law of both countries. However, although the word 'original' is specified in the law, there is no explicit or clear definition of it or of creativity. The courts interpret 'originality and creativity' in accordance with their cultural context.

III. COPYRIGHT PROTECTION ON UNAUTHORISED DERIVATIVE WORKS: THAILAND

Unfortunately, under Thailand's copyright law,[96] protection vests only in a derivative work that was created with authorisation of the copyright owner. There is a question about what happens to derivative works or online digital derivative works which were created without authorisation of the copyright owner. This section explores the interpretations of the Thai Supreme Court regarding originality and creativity, and the copyright protection granted to original and derivative works according to those interpretations. The meaning of author as specified under the Thai Copyright Act will also be analysed and identified.

A. Protection on a Work of Creation under the Thai Copyright Act: Originality and Creativity

Section 11 of the Copyright Act 1994 (Thailand) specifies that[97]

---

94 Goldstein (n 59) 216–217.
95 Bently and Sherman (n 49) 99.
96 Copyright Act 1994 (Thailand).
97 Ibid.

> [c]opyright in a work which is an adaptation of a copyright work under this Act, made with the consent of the owner of copyright shall vest in the person who makes such an adaptation, but without prejudice to the owner of the copyright in the work created by the original author that is adapted.

The provision requires the copyright owner's consent and so an adaptation of an original copyright work which is made without that consent will not be protected.

Therefore, according to some decisions of the Thai Supreme Court, 'whether such work was an adaptation of a copyright work and was made without the consent of the copyright owner' is relevant to the interpretation of originality and creativity for the purpose of finding protection for a work of creation regardless of whether the creation is an original or a derivative work. It is noteworthy that this particular requirement is applied to every type of work of creation whether or not the creation is an original or a derivative work. It follows from the reasoning of the Thai Supreme Court that if a work was an adaptation of a copyright work and was made without the consent of the copyright owner, even though it has been made with skill and effort, it will not qualify for protection. The following recent decisions of the Supreme Court serve as examples:

(a) The work in this case was bas-relief clay wall sculptures. The Supreme Court held:

> Although the plaintiff does not need to prove that the work of creation of the plaintiff is a new job that nobody has never created before, because copyright protection on a work does not require novelty such as patent, *the plaintiff still has to prove that the plaintiff has created the work himself, without reproduction or modification, according to the definition of reproduction or modification as provided in Section 4*[98] *of the Copyright*

[98] Ibid s 4:

> 'Reproduction' includes any material method of copying, imitation, duplication, block-making, sound recording, video recording or sound and video recording from an original, a copy or a publication, whether in whole or in part, and, in the case of computer programs, means duplication or making copies of the program from any medium for a substantial part by any method, not creating a new work whether in whole or in part.
>
> 'Adaptation' means a reproduction by conversion, modification or emulation of an original work for a substantial part, not creating a new work whether in whole or in part, which
>
> (1) With regard to literary works, includes a translation, a transformation or a collection by means of selection and arrangement,
> (2) With regard to computer programs, includes a reproduction by means

> *Act, BE 2537 (1994)*. This means that the work is not a reproduction by copying, by any means, no matter via imitation, copying, or making mould from manuscripts or copies from the substantial parts, whether in whole or in part. Also the work is not modified by reproduction, alteration, or modification of the substantial part of the original work in any aspect. . . . And when the character of the work . . . There are reasonable grounds for suspicion that [those works] are reproduced or adapted from the works from the archaeological site. *Although the reproduction or adaptation from the sculptures in the archaeological site, may require some effort, it is just an effort in repetition or adaptation. This could not be considered as a sufficient effort in the creation of the work. Therefore this work is not protected by copyright.*[99]

(b) The work considered in this case is a musical work. The Supreme Court held:

> According to the appeal of the three defendants, there are problems that need to be identified. First, whether the three defendants committed the infringement by reproducing and modifying, by means of imitation, reproduction, and modification of the substantive parts of the melody and the lyrics of the song . . ., which is the copyrighted musical work of the plaintiff . . . without creating a new work. . . . Section 4[100] provides that the musical work means a work which is composed for playing or singing whether with rhythm and lyrics or rhythm only, including arranged and transcribed musical notes or musical diagrams. Therefore, the musical work which would be protected by copyright law requires melodies. The lyrics is not a significant subject matter. . . . *If the composer has initiated the work of the song itself with perseverance, without duplication or alteration of the copyrighted work of others without permission, . . ., the song is protect by copyright at the time it is created.* . . . It is believed that the third defendant used the melody of the song and the lyrics in the essence . . . in order to

---

of transformation, modification of the program for a substantial part, not creating a new work,

(3) With regard to dramatic works, includes the transformation of a non-dramatic work to a dramatic work or a dramatic work to a non-dramatic work, whether in the original language or a different language,

(4) With regard to artistic works, it includes the transformation of a two-dimensional work or a three-dimensional work to a three-dimensional work or a two-dimensional work or the making of a model from an original work,

(5) With regard to musical works, includes an arrangement of tunes or an alteration of lyrics or rhythm.

99 Supreme Court Decision No 7121/2552 (2009) (emphasis added).

100 Copyright Act 1994 (Thailand), s 4 ('"Musical work" means a work which is composed for playing or singing whether with rhythm and lyrics or rhythm only, including arranged and transcribed musical notes or musical diagrams').

> reproduce and modify, by means of imitation, reproduction and modification, without creating a new work. . . . Therefore, the third defendant's song which is a reproduction and adaptation of a copyrighted music of the plaintiff without the plaintiff's permission is an infringement of the copyrighted musical work of the plaintiff.[101]

(c) This case is about fabric design. The Supreme Court held:[102]

> *Work that is copyrightable must be a creative work that the creator has made or created by his or her own initiative, using knowledge, skill, and effort. The work must be completed as a creative work, without reproducing or altering the copyrighted work without permission of others.* The fabric of the plaintiff is just to change the size of the ancient pattern and to add some little more details of patterns in order to get a complete designs on the fabric which is suitable for weaving. It still keeps the main layout of the ancient pattern. This is just a reconstruction of an ancient style. The plaintiff does not use their ability and imagination to confine some new designs in the substantive parts. . . . The seven designs of the fabrics are the reconstruction of the ancient style which slightly change the pattern of the fabric in the sense that it will be popular to the customers. Elements and stripes are all ancient. Those ancient styles are merely reconstructed, reduced, expanded, or moved. This, in the sense of artistic work, is considered a reconstruction, not a new work. . . . The plaintiff's involvement in the design of the fabric, or the composition or change, or the addition of some small details onto the ancient patterns, is a copy, imitation, or reproduction of the pattern of the ancient fabric which is in the public domain. The plaintiff did not make or create a work by means of changing the form or modifying it in the substantive part. Therefore, this work is not an adaptation of an ancient work which was in the public domain to a certain degree that it would be qualified as a creative work of applied art, which would be considered a copyright work according to Copyright Act 1994, Section 4[103] and Section 6.[104]

---

[101] Supreme Court Decision No 9602/2554 (2011) (emphasis added).

[102] Supreme Court Decision No 14580/2557 (2014) (emphasis added).

[103] Copyright Act 1994 (Thailand), s 4 ('"artistic work" means a work of one or more of the following descriptions: . . . (7) work of applied art, which means a work which takes each or a composition of the works mentioned in items (1) to (6) for utility apart from the appreciation in the merit of the work such as for practical use of such work, decorating materials or appliances or using for commercial benefit, whether with or without artistic merit, and shall include photographs and plans of such works').

[104] Copyright Act 1994 (Thailand), s 6 ('Copyright work under this Act means a work of authorship in the form of a literary, dramatic, artistic, musical, audiovisual, cinematographic, sound recording, sound and video broadcasting work or any other work in the literary, scientific or artistic field whatever the mode or form of its expression. Copyright protection shall not extend to ideas or procedures, processes or systems or methods of use or operation or concepts, principles, discoveries or scientific or mathematical theories').

(d) In another case of copyright protection on the sculpture of Buddha, if, however, a work was not an adaptation of a copyright work and was original and was not made without the consent of the copyright owner it will be eligible for copyright protection. Therefore, when it was learnt by the court in this case that this sculpture had been created with the initiative and with perseverance of the author, the work was copyrightable. The Supreme Court held:

> From the provisions of Copyright Act 1994, ss 4 and 6, together with the philosophy of copyright protection, works of the sculptural arts which are copyright works which would be protected by copyright law according to the Copyright Act 1994 *is a work that the creator has made or created by their own initiative and originality without reproducing or altering the copyrighted work of others without authorisation. . . . Copyrighted work may or may not be similar to a copyrighted work. However, that similar works must originate from the creativity of the creator without reproducing or modifying the copyrighted work of others without permission. . . .* Despite the fact that the Central Intellectual Property and International Trade Court ruled that a sculpture was made by mimicking the nature or appearance of Buddha, or Buddha's image which has existed for thousands of years. *The sculpture of Buddha face on the leaves of the Bodhi Tree was created with initiative and with perseverance. The statue was not created by reproducing or modifying the copyrighted sculpture of Buddha face of others.* The plaintiff has registered the copyright information in the sculpture of Buddha face on the leaves of the Bodhi Tree in the name of 'Kumkrong'[105] and 'Bhodhipaktra'[106] to the Department of Intellectual Property. There is reason to believe that the plaintiff is the creator of the sculpture of Buddha face on the leaves of the Bodhi Tree. The plaintiff has, therefore, copyright in the sculpture.[107]

This decision of the Supreme Court No 19350/2557 (2014) could as well be compared with Decision No. 7121/2552 (2009) as mentioned earlier, where the court ruled that even though the reproduction or adaptation of the sculptures, according to the archaeological site, might require some effort, it was just an effort in repetition or adaptation. This could not be considered as a sufficient effort in the creation of the work. Therefore this work was not protected by copyright.

According to these decisions, the Thai Supreme Court has includes the idea of 'whether such work was an adaptation of a copyright work and made without the consent of the copyright owner' as one of the major conditions for whether such work would achieve the fundamental

---

105 Application No 186774.

106 Application No 186775.

107 Supreme Court Decision No 19350/2557 (2014) (emphasis added).

requirements as a creative work and therefore be eligible for copyright protection. As mentioned earlier, this particular requirement is applied to every type of work of creation, whether or not the creation is an original or a derivative work. This means that whether a creative work is a repetition, copy, reproduction, modification or adaptation of a prior work, whether that work was made with or without the consent of the copyright owner, is a very strong condition for whether the work receives protection. This approach is as important as the requirement of originality as the court use it as a condition to justify whether there is an original author of the work.

One important question is whether a work of creation which is a repetition, copy, reproduction, modification or adaptation of a prior work that is made without consent is non-original and therefore not copyrightable. Or is it because the whole work is non-original and therefore there is no consideration of whether there are distinguishable parts, or limitations and exceptions such as fair dealing, fair use, or transformative use that might be relevant to whether the work would be eligible for copyright protection? In such case would any derivative work be eligible for copyright protection? The definition of 'author' is relevant to this question.

B. Definition of Author under the Thai Copyright Act

The Thai Copyright Act provides '"author" means a person who makes or creates any work which is a copyright work by virtue of this Act' and 'copyright work' 'means a work of authorship in the form of a literary, dramatic, artistic, musical, audiovisual, cinematographic, sound recording, sound and video broadcasting work or any other work in the literary, scientific or artistic field whatever the mode or form of its expression'.[108]

Both sections indicate that a work will be protected by copyright if it is 'a work of authorship'. The next question is what is 'a work of authorship'? Is there any general concept for the criteria of 'originality and creativity',[109] or 'the author's own intellectual creation'[110] under Thailand's copyright regime? In fact, the concept of 'originality and creativity' or 'the author's' own intellectual creation' has not been specified under the current Copyright Act. Therefore, the meaning of 'a work of authorship' has been left to the interpretation of the court.

---

[108] Copyright Act 1994 (Thailand), s 4 and s 6.

[109] As appears in The Berne Convention, art 2(3), art 8 and art 11(2). See also Daniel J Gervais, 'The Compatibility of the "Skill and Labour" Originality Standard with the Berne Convention and the TRIPs Agreement' (2004) 26(2) EIPR 75.

[110] *Infopaq International v Danske Dagblades Forening* (n 10) 48.

As mentioned earlier, when the Thai Supreme Court had to clarify the meaning of 'a work of authorship' in order to grant copyright protection to a work of creation, the court adopted the idea of 'whether such work was an adaptation of a copyright work and made without the consent of the copyright owner' as one of the major conditions. The idea affects the result of the case considering whether a work of creation would be protected by copyright. Therefore, it is important here to look back on how the court has constructed the idea.

Historically, there was a major change to the definition of author under Thai copyright law. Under the previous Act,[111] the definition of author included the phrase 'by their own initiative', specifying that '"author" means the person who makes or creates a work by their own initiative'.[112] Later, the phrase 'by their own initiative' was removed.[113] Following the new law, Supreme Court Decision No. 6182/2533 (1990), which was handed down under the Copyright Act B.E. 2521 (1978) interpreted that

> [s]ection 6 of the Copyright Act, B.E. 2521 allows the author to hold copyright in the work he created, and Section 4 provides the definition of 'author' as the person who make or create a work by their own initiative. By definition, the person who will be named as the author must be the person who makes or originates the work from the initiative, not by imitation from the real thing, or by copying from the work of others, either appeared in shape or in photographs.

Later on, Supreme Court Decision No. 2750/2537 (1994), which was also handed down under the Copyright Act B.E. 2521 (1978), further extended such definition to 'skill and effort', providing that

> [a]ccording to Section 4 of the Copyright Act B.E. 2521 the 'author' means the person who make or create a work by their own initiative. This means that, in order to be the author of the copyright work, it does not matter whether the work was created as a new job or not. It is the person who made or produced the work, whether he had used his skill and effort, and whether the work originated or derived from that person without copying, reproducing, or adapting from another copyrighted work.

---

111 Copyright Act 1978 (Thailand).

112 Ibid s 4.

113 Since the repeal of the Copyright Act 1978 (Thailand), the Copyright Act 1994 has been in force. It is specified under section 4 of the Act that '"author" means a person who makes or creates any work which is a copyright work by virtue of this Act'.

IV. CONCLUSION

This chapter explains the issues of copyright protection granted to derivative works under the copyright law of Thailand in comparison to other jurisdictions. Thailand only provides copyright protection for derivative works which are made with permission of the copyright owner.

Since making derivative works without authorisation of the copyright owner is often done in the digital world and even though authorisation could prevent copyright infringement, searching for authorisation before creating an online digital derivative work is not an easy task. The requirement for authorisation under Thai law could create some problems in the internet environment.

APPENDIX: THE DEFINITION OF 'AUTHOR' IN SELECTED OTHER JURISDICTIONS

This appendix includes definitions of author, originality and copyright protection granted to unauthorised derivative works under the laws of some other Asian countries.

Japan Copyright Act No 48 of 6 May 1970[114]

Article 2(1): In this Law, the following terms shall have the meaning hereby assigned to them respectively:

(i) 'work' means a production in which thoughts or sentiments are expressed in a creative way and which falls within the literary, scientific, artistic or musical domain;
(ii) 'author' means a person who creates a work
. . .
(xi) 'derivative work' means a work created by translating, arranging musically, transforming, or dramatizing, cinematizing or otherwise adapting a pre-existing work;

Article 11: The protection granted by this Law to derivative works shall not prejudice the rights of authors of pre-existing works.

Article 28: In the exploitation of a derivative work, the author of the pre-existing work shall have the same rights as those the author of the derivative work has under the provisions of this Subsection.

---

[114] Copyright Law of Japan as translated by the Copyright Research and Information Center, Japan <http://www.cric.or.jp/english/clj/cl1.html#Chapter1> last accessed 31 December 2018.

The Copyright Act (Act No 432 of 28 January 1957) of the Republic of Korea[115]

Article 2 (Definitions)

1. 'Work' means the creation of a representation of the human spirit or emotion.
2. The 'author' shall mean the persons who created the work.

Article 5 (A Derivative Work)

(1) A creation produced by means of translation, arrangement, alteration, dramatization, cinematization, etc. of an original work (hereinafter referred to as 'derivative work') shall be protected as an independent work.
(2) The protection of a derivative work shall not prejudice the rights of the author of the original work.

The Copyright Law of the People's Republic of China[116]

Section 2: Ownership of Copyright.

Article 11: Except where otherwise provided in this Law, the copyright in a work shall belong to its author. The author of a work is the citizen who has created the Work.

Article 12: Where a work is created by adaptation, translation, annotation or arrangement of a pre-existing work, the copyright in the work thus created shall be enjoyed by the adapter, translator, annotator or arranger, Provided that the exercise of such copyright shall not prejudice the copyright in the original work.

---

[115] Copyright Act 1957 (Republic of Korea).

[116] Copyright Law of the People's Republic of China (as amended up to the Decision of 26 February 2010 by the Standing Committee of the National People's Congress on Amending the Copyright Law of the People's Republic of China).

14. The collective management system of copyright and related rights in Europe: competitive aspects

Maria Letizia Bixio*

I. INTRODUCTION

The collective management of copyright and related rights has become an economic, cultural and social need in order to ensure a proper remuneration to authors and artists for the exploitation of their works. However, several authors and artists have increasingly criticised the activities of collecting societies and the way efficiency and transparency are preserved. They have also questioned the legitimacy of collective management operating in a market characterised by increasing innovation and by the staggering development of technology used for exchanging and spreading digital content. It is therefore necessary to analyse the reasons behind this criticism.

The debate on the role of collecting societies in itself is not new. There are, however, new issues and aspects which require specific attention. Taking into account the role that Europe plays in relation to national sovereignty, and the (sometimes difficult) search for the harmonisation of certain national practices, we realise that it is only through their convergence in a consistent and non-contradictory way that a proper functioning of the internal market can be achieved. Moreover, the impact of Directive 2014/26/EU[1] should also be considered. Its transposition will likely prove

* All online sources were last accessed on 27 December 2018.

[1] Directive 2014/26/EU of the European Parliament and of the Council of 26 February 2014 on collective management of copyright and related rights and multi-territorial licensing of rights in musical works for online use in the internal market [2014] OJ L84/72, paves the way for a new form of multi-territorial licensing which is necessary in order to favour the digital market. For a broader analysis of the strategic role of such organisms see Victor Vincent Dehin, 'The Future of Legal Online Music Services in the European Union: A Review of the EU Commission's Recent Initiatives in Cross-border Copyright Management' (2010) 32(5) EIPR 220; Valeria Falce, *Copyright Societies Under Scrutiny: From*

to be problematic in such a fragmented scenario, characterised by different systems enclosed within the individual legislation of Member States of the EU. The regulation of practices such as those related to the granting of licences, since they affect not only copyright protection, but also the basic principles of free competition, and have a strong cross-border impact, is also necessary and urgent. Those principles currently appear to be based on uncertain practices and non-uniform laws.

This chapter, therefore, focuses on the analysis of the aims of collective management and of the ways in which it is progressing and changing. It also examines the related issues arising under EU competition law. Collective management is, in fact, not ascribable to a single model, structure or legal system. Indeed, heterogeneous systems continue to alter over time, ranging from mere representative groups of author's structures to public bodies responsible – pursuant to the law – for managing authors' rights, and from commercial companies to actual consortia.

All these organisations play a fundamental role in the international debate on the scope of the copyright system and its various implementations at the national level. Implementation has been interpreted and understood in different ways, depending on the country. In some systems, collective management organisations were considered as a threat which should be under the scrutiny of competition law. In others, they were regarded as a determining factor for the author's relatively weak bargaining position and as the only useful tool for guaranteeing authors balanced negotiations with the users of their rights.

II. HOW TO ENSURE THE PROTECTION AND EXERCISE OF COPYRIGHT

Following recent technological progress, enormous improvements have taken place in the communication field, particularly in sound techniques

the EU Approach to the Italian Solution (vol 37, Kluwer law International World Competition 2014) 121; Emanuela Arezzo, *Società di gestione collettiva dei diritti fra tutela della proprietà intellettuale e diritto della concorrenza: brevi note a margine della pronunzia International Confederation of Societies of Authors and Composers (CISAC) c Commissione europea* (Concorrenza e Mercato 2014) 673. For a first commentary see also Sylvie Nérisson, 'La directive 2014/26/UE du 26 février 2014 sur la gestion collective des droits d'auteur et des droits voisins: vol au-dessus de vaches sacrées inntouchables' (2014) 51 Proprétés Intellectuelles 135; Maria Letizia Bixio, 'Le sfide del recepimento della direttiva 2014/26 in materia di gestione collettiva. Ipotesi alternative tra innovazione e armonizzazione' (2016) 3 Diritto Industriale 425.

and image fixation, reproduction and distribution. These dramatic developments were accompanied by a facilitated access to intellectual property, making the interests of copyright and related rights holders more vulnerable.[2] In this regard, the advent of digitalisation has been emblematic. Among its merits, it has undoubtedly simplified the movement of works,[3] especially transnationally, and it has significantly reduced costs. However, through the use of digitalisation, the traditional copyright system has been dangerously put at risk.[4] The new volatility of the works, which means the deletion of physical traditional support and its substitution with digitalised technologies, represents a constant threat to the exercise of copyright.

The digitalisation of several types of works on the same support (such as flash drives, but also platforms) allows multiple uses from the same device, thus complicating any control procedure. Hence, the major risk is downgrading copyright to a mere 'agglomeration of information', which, as such, is likely to be reused and manipulated very easily, eventually causing disruption of the originality and integrity principles enshrined in the work. These principles, it is worth noting, are the pillars of the traditional author's system.

Based on the evolution of the digital era (it is evident that) intermediary organisations have a dual merit; on the one hand, providing authors with protection of their rights; on the other, providing users with a legal access to works.

---

2 Alberto Maria Gambino and Andrea Stazi, *Diritto dell'informatica e della comunicazione* (Giappichelli 2009) 1.

3 See Ariel Kratz, 'The Potential Demise of another Natural Monopoly: Rethinking Collective Administration of Rights' (2005) JCLE 541, introducing the three principal elements of the technological revolution: the Internet, DRM and Web-based control programs. In particular, with regard to the Web's potential, it states: 'The Internet, of course, could also be used for efficiently distributing the music files themselves, as demonstrated by the proliferation of unauthorized on-line music services since Napster and its progeny, as well as by the growth of new authorized on-line music services such as Apple's iTunes and its rivals. Yet the Internet *per se* does not provide copyright holders an efficient mechanism for effectively controlling the use of their music, and for collecting money for it. This could be achieved by implementing Digital Rights Management Systems, as authorized on-line music providers do.'

4 Thomas Paris, *Le droit d'auteur, l'ideologie et le système* (PUF 2002) 25, emphatically asking if we can still speak of copyright and of intellectual property in the Internet era ('Peut-on encore penser en termes de reproduction et de représentation à l'époque d'Internet? Peut-on encore parler d'auteur lorsque plusieurs personnes peuvent apporter, à distance et parfois à des siècles d'écart, leur contribution à une création? Peut-on encore parler d'oeuvre quand quiconque peut aujourd'hui collecter un ouevre et la rediffuser?').

With regard to EU legal novelties,[5] aimed mainly at incentivising cross-border exchanges, reducing fragmentation among national practices and favouring free competition, it should be possible to identify an actual balance with respect to the limits and advantages of the models of collective management, eventually achieving a valid assessment at the individual EU Member State level.

This chapter discusses how the recent technological evolution has forced the identification of new business models which aim at keeping efficient management. The competition principle, however, has led to a complete disruption of the traditional management models, advocating their substantial reorganisation based on a more efficient and lucrative approach.

III. IMMEDIATE RIGHTS, MEDIATED RIGHTS ON INTANGIBLE GOODS

In order to discuss the collective management of rights, we should first consider the nature of intellectual property rights and the object of their protection, thus exploring the peculiarities of intangible goods as compared to other *res.* Once we have become aware of the need for a monopoly system guaranteeing the full exercise of rights on these goods, the shortcomings of this system can be highlighted in order to identify the path to the most efficient dissemination and exploitation of knowledge. This leads to the central issue of the collective management of copyright.

It is important to understand the links existing between the author's exercise and enjoyment of his or her rights over a work, the dynamics relating to a work's exploitation, to the right to obtain fair remuneration, and the mechanisms leading to obtaining such remuneration. This bipartite aspect underlies the exercise of rights on intangible goods as a foundation of the author's system. Such bipartite nature is composed of an immediate right stemming from the creative act, and the mediacy of their enjoyment.

In order to discuss the systems that mediate the managing activity, which should be the concern of authors, we will first consider some of the intrinsic characteristics of intellectual works and thus of the larger category of intangible goods. By analysing the process that led to the

---

[5] Title III of Directive 26/2014, entitled 'multi-territorial licensing of online rights in musical works by collective management organisations', introduces cross-border licences.

development of these categories of goods, defined precisely as intangible,[6] we can identify goods that can be exploited, transferred, or bought differently from tangible property, such as land.

Intellectual property is capable of reproducing itself and of generating utility multiple times. This characteristic is in contrast with that of tangible goods on which the Italian Civil Code[7] was developed, which formed and enriched the intangible goods category for all purposes. These new types of property, stemming from economic activity, has implied a natural separation between the control and the use of these goods, and the formal ownership of the property right. For intangible goods, the distinction between control and formal ownership of the goods becomes a constant element.[8]

In order to exercise ownership more closely and thus the exclusiveness of their works, a protection system has been developed linked to the work aiming at dissociating entrepreneurial intermediation initiatives developed in the exercise of copyright. These intermediaries stem from types of voluntary aggregation of authors and publishers, often legitimised by national legal systems. On behalf of the author's community, they appoint trustees managing permissions to use the works entrusted to them, and the payment of the related fees.

The genesis of such structures is found in the establishment of the nation state.[9] In order to be legitimised they had to overcome the distrust of 1800s liberal states with respect to intermediate corporations placed between the

---

6 On the new types of ownership and on the new goods categories, see Pietro Rescigno, *Manuale di diritto privato* (Ipsoa 2000) 400 ('In reality, thanks to a technical and cultural progress, goods were emerging capable of being purchased, transferred and exploited differently than in ownership cases (which, in the code's vision, was intended as land ownership) that were often in conflict with the ownership, as in the case of implementing an economic activity through third parties' assets, whose value would increase').

7 It was enacted by Royal Decree no 262 of 16 March 1942. Book III concerns property: movable items, real estate, property rights and limits.

8 See Rescigno (n 6) 401 ('The two ownership aspects or "atoms" as a known doctrine calls them, are presented detached, and such dissociation has become a normal characteristic of the most impressive form of modern capitalism, i.e. share companies. In large share companies, the detachment of the two aspects, ownership of goods and power of control, indeed represents the rule').

9 On this issue, see Marco Ricolfi, 'Figure e tecniche di gestione collettiva del diritto d'autore e dei diritti connessi' in Paolo Spada (ed), *Gestione collettiva della domanda e offerta di prodotti culturali* (Quaderni di Aida 2006) 7; Adrian Sterling, *World Copyright Law* (Sweet & Maxwell 1998) 499; Valerio De Sanctis, *Le développement et la consécration internationale du droit d'auteur* (RIDA 1974) 221.

state and the citizen.[10] Based on the need to promote individual creativity and the shifting of cultural goods, almost all European states equipped themselves with national regulations aimed at ensuring the protection of copyright-related rights, and proceeded with the establishment of societies in charge of the collective management of rights. As has been observed,[11] collective management led to the loss of the peculiar characteristic of copyright as a property right. The proprietary model was in fact replaced by a more limited exclusive system. Collecting societies tend to transform, or even downgrade, authors' property rights into a mere right to compensation, and the fee due by users for exploiting their works into a tax on their activities.[12]

The desire of individuals to gain free access to information and the culture of their country or of any other country, which was transformed into a fundamental right of fair remuneration, will be limited by other fundamental rights of the individual to protect his moral and tangible interests for instance.

IV. COPYRIGHT AND COLLECTIVE MANAGEMENT

In order to actually involve the collective management role in the wider context of intellectual property protection, it is fundamental to identify the common element in the relationship between exclusive rights and collecting societies, namely copyright, which is the true reason for the collecting activity.[13] Such right embodies an author's subjective legal

---

[10] See Thierry Desurmont and Carole Guernalec, *Propriété littéraire et artistique* (SACEM 2000) 3; Jacques Boncompain, *La révolution des auteurs: Naissance de la propriété intellectuelle (1773–1815)* (Fayard 2001) 223.

[11] Thomas Streeter, 'Broadcast Copyright and the Bureaucratization of Property' (1992) 10 AELJ 567, claiming that copyright increasingly becomes a sort of legal foundation of an institutional bureaucracy that attempts simulating a market through statistical mechanisms.

[12] Ibid. Just as interesting is Marco Ricolfi, *Figure e tecniche di gestione collettiva del diritto d'autore e dei diritti connessi* (Giuffre 2006) 11, reiterating how non-individual management leads these rights to become 'credit for compensation'. The quote is also reminiscent of Paolo Spada, *Diritto industriale. Introduzione* (Giappichelli 1999) 55.

[13] The text of OMPI's 1967 Convention lists, among rights falling into Intellectual property under point 2 (viii), a series of disciplines, including copyright, related rights, inventions, trademarks, designs, protection against unfair competition, as well as all rights regarding intellectual activity.

position, indicating at the same time the recognition of the original and exclusive opportunity of spreading, exploiting and prohibiting the use of the author's work.[14]

If copyright[15] reflects the author's same personality as his emanation, making him the holder of moral and property rights in his work, in a current society which is rich in multiple mass communication systems, it is difficult for an author to individually exercise his rights since the sources for using his work are varied and keeping control over the possible uses becomes difficult.[16]

The mechanism for authorising the use of an individual work by users (i.e. radios, TVs, hotels, bars, etc) is very complex and it is impossible for users to obtain authorisation for any single work they intend to use. In this regard, the copyright crisis, caused by difficulties in the exercise of the same right, would seem to fall within the context that is opposed to the traditional closing of exclusive systems, reaffirming the social importance of knowledge.

Article 27 of the Universal Declaration of Human Rights (1948) is emblematic in this regard; in its first paragraph, on the importance of access to culture and information, it states: 'Everyone has the right to freely participate in the cultural life of the community, to enjoy the arts and to share in scientific advancement and its benefits.' In the second paragraph, just as emphatically, the extension of the right to authors, artists, producers and publishers of obtaining remuneration for the intellectual or material work they carry out is reiterated: 'Everyone has the right to the protection of the moral and material interests resulting from any scientific, literary or artistic production of which he is the author.' Within this context, the aim of this research is to identify a solution between the public interest of spreading 'culture', and the authors' and artists' private interest of obtaining a fair compensation for the use of their works and the efforts made in terms of time and energy for their creation.

The need to rationalise the quantity of online content, allowing users

---

[14] See Ferruccio Foà, 'Manuale del diritto d'autore' (1931) Flli Treves 35 ('copyright is an actual property right, even if this property concerns intangible and not tangible rights').

[15] Mario Are, *L'oggetto del diritto d'autore* (Cedam 1963) 2, made a clear distinction in the dual interpretation of copyright, objectively, as an organic complex of rules, and, subjectively, as a complex of prerogatives belonging to the author of the protected work.

[16] See Daniel Gervais and Alan Marushat, 'Fragmented Copyright, Fragmented Management: Proposals to Defrag Copyright Management' (2003) 15 Can J L & Tech 17.

– on the one hand – to access and then legally use the materials found and – on the other – allowing right-holders to obtain a fair remuneration based on the use of their works, calls for action by parties that are able to 'mediate' this type of complex market. Hence, the continuous call on intermediaries operating to the advantage of both categories of parties, managing their respective interests, can be understood. The expression 'rights management', therefore, refers to a way of managing copyright and related rights (licensing, transfer or pay-per-use).

To give a definition of the phenomenon underlying the term 'collective management', we have to start from its initial element, namely an organisation or a method that can meet requests from both right-holders and users. Copyright collection, the granting of licences for the exploitation of works, the distribution of compensation, and the implementation of measures for protecting rights are among the main activities of these societies.[17]

The role of collecting societies, however, goes beyond the simple management and administrative activities. In addition to the economic aspect, their role has a social and cultural nature. In particular, especially in traditional management models, the activity aimed at supporting and protecting the category's moral and property rights is reinvigorated by enhancing the managed repertoire and by better distributing it to the public.[18] In essence, this is an activity with a strong cultural nature in support of all the categories of associates. In more recent times, however, the collective management's function underwent a radical change. The need for finding useful tools to regulate the new methods of intellectual property exploitation most likely led national legislators to consider collective management as a relevant activity for them. There has hence been a proliferation of legal management systems, which were made mandatory by law. This activity, therefore, takes on a different meaning according to its function based on the social and cultural context.

There are several different reasons behind the foundation of collective management in its European form: social and cultural,[19] legal and

---

[17] Regarding the protection function for the category deemed as the weakest, namely that of creators compared to users, see Carine Doutrelepont, *Raison d'être des sociétés de gestion des droits, importance, essor et développements récents* (Yvon Blais Québec 1998) 472.

[18] See Fabrice Siiriainen, 'Théorie générale de la gestion collective – logique de droit exclusif de la gestion collective' in Fabrice Siiriainen (ed), *JCI – Propriété littéraire et artistique* (LexisNexis 2006) 1550; also Mihaly Ficsor, *Collective Management of Copyright and Related Rights* (WIPO 2002) 25.

[19] Regarding cultural use, see Adolf Dietz, *Cultural Functions of Collecting Societies* (CPRA 2010).

economic. Intermediaries' activities were considered as a *conditio sine qua non* to ease access to cultural property to the advantage of society. At the same time, based on the prevailing opinion among economists, these management activities were also considered as a useful remedy to the market's failure, in light of the fact that these societies represented the only way of reducing costs of negotiation for transactions that would have been unsustainable on an individual management level.[20] However, strong legal reasons contributed to the consecration of collective management activity: *inter alia*, collective management represented a valid protection tool to exercise copyright and related rights. Theoretically, right-holders can decide whether they want to personally manage their rights or use collective management. The latter option can, at times, leave the road open to choosing among the different bodies imposed by law.[21]

Management of rights, therefore, occurs on the basis of two different systems: individually, which means personally marketing the rights on behalf of each author to users; and through so-called 'collective' management, which utilises a system through which a third party jointly manages as a trustee its associates' rights such as recording, collecting and redistributing the income generated from copyright payments on behalf of different holders.[22] Due to the high number of users present on the market, the individual granting of authorisation proved to be complex and in practice unfeasible for certain types of rights, mainly for collecting fair compensation/equitable remuneration.[23] This is one more reason to conclude that the system of collecting societies is more practical and

---

[20] On this issue, see Martin Kretschmer, *The Failure of Property Rules in Collective Administration: Rethinking Copyright Societies as Regulatory Instruments* (EIPR 2002) 128, in underlining how collective management allows reducing transaction time, obtaining greater efficiency in transferring monopolies, monitoring and enforcement mechanisms. Obtaining scale economies, in addition to a collecting activity, favours both end users, who can choose from a wide catalogue of content managed by a single party, with a consequent reduction in transaction costs, and content rights holders who, thanks to contractual intermediation carried out by the society, generally obtain more favourable conditions.

[21] In most European countries, the management of rights for cable broadcasting is subject to mandatory collective management.

[22] In Council Directive 93/83/CEE of 27 September 1993, art 1 c.4, coordination of some provisions regarding copyright and related rights applicable to satellite broadcasting and cable rebroadcasting was defined as a 'collecting society', devoting attention to the principal nature of the activity carried out.

[23] Jay Fujitani, 'Controlling the Market Power of Performing Right Societies, an Administrative Substitute for antitrust Regulation' (1984) 72 Cal L Rev 106, underlines how the activity by collecting societies implies a reduction in transaction costs for identifying and localising the holder of rights.

economically suitable to solve the various problems and difficulties that authors and users face in adequately satisfying their interests.

In distinguishing possible typical cases within copyright management, four categories are found.[24] Despite the expression 'rights management' generally referring to the way of managing copyright and related rights,[25] objectively the first fundamental difference concerns voluntary and non-voluntary (mandatory) managements. In the voluntary case, reference is made to the right the author has to independently choose which type of rights management he prefers; in the opposite case, a type of management is chosen that is traced back to the legal provision's aim. The rationale behind the latter system is to highlight the superiority and the primacy of a general interest, which in turn implies that the regulatory function of collecting societies is enhanced.[26]

From a subjective point of view, within voluntary management, the author can decide whether to choose an individual or a collective right management type. In the first, individual authors personally market rights for commercial users; in the second, instead, a collecting society manages rights jointly, recording, collecting and distributing the income generated from copyright payment on behalf of various holders and upon their assignment.[27]

Once the reasons justifying each right-holder's choice of a specific system are understood, it is then clear why individually granting authorisations in relation to certain rights turned out to be much too complex. This is why most right-holders preferred relying on intermediaries rather than themselves, for the functions mentioned above.

A. The Economic Reasons for Collective Management

Economic reasons lie behind collective management, confirming that collective management represents an efficient means for both guaranteeing authors and right-holders market access and, for users, wide and facilitated

---

[24] Individual and collective management, collective-voluntary management and collective mandatory management.

[25] For the definition, see Commission of the European Communities, 'Communication of the Commission to the Council, the European Parliament and the European Economic and Social Committee' (2004) COM/2004/0261.

[26] In particular, Gunnar Karnell, *Les relations entre les auteurs et les organisme chargés de la gestion de leur droits* (RIDA 1986) 52.

[27] The Court of Justice highlighted how 'collecting societies pursue a legitimate effort when they attempt to protect the rights and interests of their members towards users'; Case C-395/87 *Public Prosecutor v Tournier* (1989) EU:C:1989:2521.

access to works.[28] Collective management therefore becomes part of the efficient process of economically regulating rights, where the movement of works is incentivised through their fair exploitation and right-holders are guaranteed fair remuneration.[29] Economic efficiency in managing rights related to copyright becomes a privileged way for ensuring the fulfilment of those authors' rights that are legally protected.

Based on a traditional economic assessment, the issue was reiterated of the capacity to reduce transaction costs through collective management, as well as of the role carried out in the face of possible market failures. More recently, however, the remedy that collective management provides, in rebalancing the power between authors and users, was emphasised.[30]

---

[28] In their conclusions, effectively Ruth Towse and Christian Handke, 'Economics of Copyright Collecting Societies' (2007) Rev of Intell Prop and Comp L 954 ('These cooperative membership organisations pool the costs of rights management and exploit economies of scale in the services of copyright administration. CCS thereby reduce the cost per member and make licensing cheaper for both copyright holders and users. They thus make some markets for copyrights more efficient and they can even assist the creation of markets for copyrights that would otherwise not exist').

[29] In Laurent Duvillier, *Le recours à la gestion collective* (Lègicom 2003) 83 ('Les sociétés d'auteurs sont comme un régulateur de l'économie des exploitations permettant de fluidifier la circulation des oevres, en facilitant une géstion équitable des droits dans un contexte de sécurité juridique') cited in Yvan Diringer, *Gestion collective des droits d'auteur et droit de la concurrence* (Presses Universitaires d'Aix-Marseille – PUAM 2011) 271. And again Diringer at 243 regarding collecting management, conclusions are very clear on its economic role ('elle favorise ainsi l'efficacité statique des droits de propriété intellectuelle dans le but de stimuler le arché des oeuvres de l'esprit. L'objectif d'une allocation optimale des ressources, en l'occurrence les oeuvres, surpasse alors toute autre considération. L'invention de la gestion collective en diminuant les coûts de transaction amoindrit l'opportunité de solutions radicales privilégiant les intérêts des investisseurs et des diffuseurs, . . . facilite l'échange, mais en retour elle augmente le revenue dés créateurs. Elle réalise les vertus incitatives du droit d'auteur; tout cela, et le point essential, au bénéfice premier des créateurs et non des seuls cessionnaires intermédiaires qui s'engagent dans la diffusion de l'oeuvre. Elle replace l'auteur au coeur du diapositive. . . . Elle est un instrument de protection des intérêts des créateurs. Les fondements économiques des sociétés d'auteurs ne se limitent pas à leur capacité à faciliter la concession des droits d'auteur. A la mutualisation des coutes, indispensable pour réaliser les économies nécessaires à une gestion efficace, s'ajoute la construction d'un rapport de forces pour garantir l'égalité contractuelle').

[30] See Gerd Hansen and Albrecht Schmidt-Bischoffshausen, *Economic Functions of Collecting Societies, Collective Rights Management in the Light of Transaction Cost and Information Economics* (SSRN 2007) 18 ('This imbalance of powers is certainly not solely to be attributed to information asymmetries. The predominance of one party vis-à-vis the other can also play a decisive role. One could argue though that "knowledge is power", this would however be too short-

Collecting societies in fact hold the necessary power to negotiate fair conditions with users. Therefore, in addition to preventing transaction costs from offsetting possible economic benefits and to filling the information gap, joint management brings in mutually supportive purposes. In this way, within the system, the respect for the principle of equal treatment is preserved; collective management, in fact, implies authors are not individualised but become collectivised. Equal fees and user conditions, as well as the application of the same management cost rates, are key to distributing risks and management costs so as to support smaller right-holders.[31]

By favouring a more functional approach, business and legal analysis demonstrates how collecting societies are natural intermediaries for authors and users, in spite of individual management forms.

V. NATURE AND FUNCTION OF MANAGEMENT BODIES WITH REGARD TO THEIR PURPOSES

For a long time, the promotion of national culture was a priority objective for governments, which meant that management bodies effectively conducted their functions carrying out mutualistic and redistribution objectives, typically useful for encouraging even smaller national repertoires.

Nowadays, with market globalisation, a reconsideration of allocation efficiency and transaction cost reduction, in an increasingly competitive context, is required. In comparing the different management models, with respect to changed needs and protected interests, aspects strongly linked to social and cultural reasons should also be considered.

As stated above, establishing organisations that aim at grouping category interests, based on corporatism such as collecting societies, prevailed when nation states were formed. It is no surprise then that some aspects, in the process of establishing these states, deeply influenced the nature and the purposes of these societies.

First of all, due consideration should be given to the origin of the territorial nature of collective management, which remains a stronghold with respect to Web challenges; the Internet is a virtual place of exploitation of

---

sighted and one would leave those aspects of power unconsidered, which could be based on the financial dependency of one licensor on his licensee. The fact that transaction cost – and information economics do not sufficiently take into account these aspects of power – and thereby the problem of disturbed contract parity, is one of the undeniable weaknesses of these approaches').

[31] See Towse and Handke (n 28) 38, arguing that the monopoly should be maintained if the transaction costs savings of the monopoly outweigh its costs.

the works without territorial boundaries. This peculiarity can doubtless be attributed to individual nation states' affirmation policies, aiming at promoting and spreading their culture.

In a context based on nationality-territoriality, management bodies primarily took on objectives having a mutualistic-redistribution-equalitarian and control nature, to the exclusive advantage of national authors. Features of a market economy required reassessing aspects such as allocation efficiency or reducing transaction costs, which collecting societies did not previously consider important.

With the advent of the Internet, the multiple opportunities offered by extraterritorial exchanges of intellectual property rights were considered, including their management. Conversely, for over a century of modern history, characterised by a cultural centralisation of each people's traditions,[32] the strictly national nature of collective management found its *raison d'être* in the so-called 'patriotic' spirit of spreading culture.

Meanwhile, traditional collecting societies would, in different ways, prioritise the pursuit of a 'subsidy function for the weakest individual economies'.[33] The historically recognised aim was to provide a tool allowing the full exercise of those rights envisaged by the legislator, to the benefit of persons whose talent would increase national culture. With this in mind, the pursuit of an activity mainly aimed at favouring some members (authors), with respect to others (publishers), can be explained. This was in addition to offering both authors and publishers the possibility of obtaining, when negotiating with users, a higher remuneration compared to the one that could have been obtained through individual bargaining.

The logic underlying the limiting of free individual bargaining is based on equity more than on efficiency. In fact, it was probably more risky leaving authors and publishers to bargain freely. In such a scenario, the former would surrender to the latter due to a lack capability to effectively protect their rights.[34] In this regard, imposing criteria for the allocation

---

32 'Universal curvature' was discussed in the doctrine, in other words prorated and limited to a specific national culture. Spada (n 9) 9.

33 Ibid 34 ('Gestione collettiva e modelli associativi').

34 Effectively on this concept see Ernst-Joachim Mestmäcker, 'Collecting Societies' (2005) European University Institute, Robert Schuman Centre for Advanced Studies EU Competition Law and Policy Workshop/Proceedings 17 ('Collecting societies are recognized worldwide as necessary for the efficient administration of copyrights and neighbouring rights. In relation to users, a blanket licence overcomes the complexity of fragmented copyrights aggravated by the duration of copyrights for 70 years post mortem autoris. From the perspective of members, the pooling of rights that make blanket licensing possible is predicated upon the Society's internal management').

of royalties was inspired by more equalitarian than meritocratic logic, and by more cultural than economic reasons. Income, in fact, does not directly match the works' economic success, but for the sake of protecting cultural diversity would be calibrated so as to compensate both less famous authors and those who devoted themselves to highly cultural works, despite their low commercial value.[35]

The solidarity and redistribution functions, described above, continue to emerge in other statutory provisions, which tend to impose, for example, the allocation of part of the income generated by the intermediary activity to solidarity funds for social security or subsidy purposes. By considering the solidarity function of traditional management bodies from the different angle of protecting the weakest interests, additional altruistic and equalitarian function, based on an equal treatment of members belonging to the same category, can be identified.[36] This confirms, on the one hand, a rebalancing of contractual relationships between authors and users and also between authors and publishers.[37] On the other hand, it confirms that the so-called equalitarian function also expresses society's commitment to avoid unfairly favouring the most successful authors' interests to the detriment of other authors, and to avoid favouring the interests of the major publishing groups to the detriment of independent ones.

---

35 In particular, see Spada (n 9) 11, naming strong intellectual property rights as the requirement for the establishment of institutions and for collective management, suitable to favour optimal negotiation modalities and allocation exchanges. Reference should be made to Robert Merges, 'Of Property Rules, Coase and Intellectual Property Law' (1994) Colum L Rev 2655; Robert Merges, 'Contracting into Liability Rules: Intellectual Property Rights and Collective Rights Organisations' (1996) 84 Cal L Rev 1293.

36 On the equal treatment obligations of companies having a dominant position with respect to collective management, see Marco Cassottana, *Antitrust e società di gestione dei diritti d'autore* (AIDA 1995) 125 and Roberto Mastroianni, *I diritti esclusivi delle collecting societies* (AIDA 2001) 220.

37 Among the advantages of traditional systems, described in the KEA study, *The Collective Management of Rights in Europe: The Quest for Efficiency* (2006) 33 ('Create solidarity between well off and poorer artists and between larger and smaller companies. There is a stronger bargaining position if the society represents a sizeable repertoire including the most successful bands or companies. This solidarity exists also in the fact that some rights may cross-subsidise the costlier collection of other rights').

VI. COMPARING MANAGEMENT MODELS: SOLIDARISTIC VERSUS CAPITALISTIC

The analysis of the main purposes attributable to the role of collecting societies reveals two opposing management models, expressing two different approaches: a traditional model, based on solidaristic purposes, and a capitalistic model, based on hyper-efficiency logics.

The first model is the traditional one, typical of collecting societies that were developed at the end of the 1800s, and which still exist. This collective management model's primary interest is in guaranteeing market access to the highest number of works, a characteristic which relates to the importance of enhancing each people's culture when national states were formed. Within this model, a joint negotiation by the highest number of creators is encouraged, even if this is done to the detriment of minimising intermediation costs for each work.

In traditional models, therefore, obtaining a high number of assignments on the part of the collecting society, especially by minor authors and publishers, implies the development diseconomies of scale. The increase in intermediation costs for each work represents the price that the system is willing to pay in order to finance the weakest parties, as well as to incentivise creative production. On closer inspection, by supporting the economically weakest parties, the traditional model fully represents the solidarity and altruistic functions, regardless of the actual demand for works. Generally these societies are non-profit-making.

Subsequently, pro-competition requests[38] led to traditional models wavering for the sake of allowing only more profitable products access to the market so as to achieve economies of scale. There was also the need for intermediaries to be specialised in certain types of works or right-holder categories. Moreover, technology made it possible to overcome national management limitations by extending their scope and facilitating cooperation and interoperability among collecting societies from different countries.

A second management model was thus developed. Supported by hyper-efficiency logic rather than by a solidaristic one, this system aims at preventing minor works from accessing the market, i.e. those works that are intended for a non-mass audience, by selecting and only favouring

[38] See Valeria Falce, 'Copyright Societies under Scrutiny: From the EU Approach to the Italian Solution' (2014) 37(1) World Compet 122 ('In such dis-intermediated environment, the collective administration of copyright and related rights as we know it becomes debatable as well as the uncritical persistence of systems based on single collecting societies acting under a monopoly regime at national level').

the most profitable contents.[39] The capitalistic approach favours the minimising of single costs for each transaction and the relative production of economies of scale. Furthermore, through a market-oriented approach, the incentive for a cultural production meeting the audience's demand, justifying a pro-competition policy, is highlighted.

Carrying out collecting activity in a capitalistic way entails a strong juxtaposition of the interests at stake. Indeed, the right-holders' primary interest of obtaining the highest possible income for their works is matched by the management society's equal and opposite interest of remunerating its own capital through the collected proceeds.

In order to be able to carry out an analysis of the two systems, we should verify whether cost reductions and the consequent economies of scale are sufficiently positive variables in a system that also reduces the availability of cultural products. Choosing either one of the models favours competition or otherwise.

VII. MONOPOLY AS A MODEL IN THE EUROPEAN TRADITION

One of the possible collective management systems available to artists, as a result of individual management's inefficiency, and one of the most favoured mechanisms in Europe, was that in which authors entrust rights management to one society only, even though they could alternatively choose to directly manage their rights.

The European Commission concluded that natural monopoly situations diffuse around a single collecting society.[40] Even if traditional microeconomic analyses tend to oppose the role of management societies

---

39 Collecting management organisations that adopt more competitive systems prefer repertoires of famous music, to the detriment of the niche repertoires.

40 See Josef Drexl, 'Collective Management of Copyrights and the EU Principle of Free Movement of Services after the OSA Judgement – In Favour of a More Balanced Approach' (2014) Max Planck Institute for Innovation and Competition Paper No 6, in the introduction of the essay devoted to the Court of Justice's verdict on the *OSA* case, where the verdict confirmed the legitimacy of monopoly, the author emphasises the presence of monopoly-based collecting management systems in Europe. The author explains '[t]he monopolistic character of CMOs is explained by the economies of scale that characterise collective rights management. CMOs incur large fixed costs caused by the machinery of collecting and distributing income and the need to build up monitoring systems, while the marginal costs of managing the rights of an additional rightholder are relatively low').

operating monopolies, since they have the power to impose prices without having to necessarily devote attention to costs reduction and service quality, it was often underlined that the negative effect of monopoly on society was significantly reduced when it is compared to the imposing market power of the large aggregators (as platforms).

According to an opinion in a Court of Justice decision,[41] its establishment is justified on the basis of the importance of protecting the authors' rights *vis-à-vis* any users' attempts at abuse of power. The intervention of a third party, holding all rights on large repertoires, creates an inevitable rebalancing of negotiations.[42]

A user's initial bargaining weakness *vis-à-vis* a monopolist right-holder is soon counterbalanced by a series of structural advantages to the end consumer.[43] Fees established by a single organisation are doubtless lower for users compared to the total costs and fees they would have to face through individual negotiations for works of interest, especially if the latter belong to different repertoires, with each work being managed by a different intermediary or by a powerful publisher.

With the prospect of a more competitive market, and thus with the presence on the market of multiple management organisations, the protection of authors' interests will be generally weakened and the royalties decreased for authors[44] will not be matched by the expected lowering of prices for consumers, as has been demonstrated.[45]

---

[41] Case C-351/12 *Ochranný svaz autorský pro práva k dílům hudebním os v Léčebné lázně Mariánské Lázně as* (2014) EU:C:2014:110.

[42] More and more generally on justifying monopolies based on rebalancing economic powers, see Mestmäcker (n 34) 344; in this sense also Louis Vogel and Pierre Sirinelli, 'Rapport de la commission sur la propriété littéraire et artistique et le droit de la concurrence' (2004) 26–28 <www.cspla.culture.gouv.fr>.

[43] Mihaly Ficsor, *Développement et objectifs de la gestion collective des droits des auteurs* (Dr Auteurs 1985) 304; in a more didactic way, see Deloitte & Touche, 'Ètude sur la gestion des droits dans l'Union européenne' (2000) Report for the European Commission 63.

[44] Ariel Katz, 'The Potential Demise of Another Natural Monopoly: Rethinking the Collective Administration of Performing Rights' (2005) JCLE 541, believing that management bodies, 'by granting blanket licences for their respective repertoires, achieve economies of scale and scope', where 'economies of scale' means the advantages offered by the presence of fixed administration costs spread over multiple managed rights, while 'economies of scope' means the advantages offered to users in having access to large repertories. In this sense, the justifying reasons for the trend to establish natural monopolies are reiterated.

[45] Francesco Parisi and Ben Depoorter, 'The Market for Intellectual Property: The Case of Complementary Oligopoly Developments in Research and Analysis'

The proposed scenario expresses a bilateral monopoly where the monopolisation of the offer is matched by a more dangerous monopolisation of the demand, a direct threat to the effective protection of authors' interests. Some economists believe that 'Negotiations in bilateral monopolies may even be the main mechanism through which prices approximate the socially efficient level . . . as a monopoly they (societies) are more efficient in the sense of having lower costs than if there were in competition'.[46] This opinion is shared by Posner in concluding that, in collective management, 'The monopoly price is probably lower than the competitive price'.[47] The European Parliament, in its Resolution 2002/2274,[48] reached similar conclusions, arguing that 'monopolies of collecting societies do not pose a problem for competition, since the increasing vertical concentration of the media is the real challenge in the area of access to works protected by copyright'.

In order to understand the reasons that justify the presence and permanence of monopolies in the sector of collective management of rights, efficiency is the starting point. Both the management organisations' cost structure and the network effects linked to the specific market, in fact, represent two unequalled barriers to the competitive expansion of the collective management market. By considering the delimitation of the collective management relevant market, the monopoly's dual value emerges, addressing the demands of two different customers: authors and users.[49]

According to a large part of the doctrine, this peculiarity of collective management corresponds to the phenomenon defined by economic analysis as a 'two sided market',[50] a concept that is reminiscent of

---

in Richard Watt and Wendy J Gordon, *The Economics of Copyright. Developments in Research and Analysis* (Edward Elgar 2003) 158–171, 165.

[46] Ruth Towse and Christian Handke, 'Economics of Collective Management of Copyright' (2007) Rev of Intell Prop and Comp L 937. This analysis was mentioned as grounds for the US Supreme Court in *BMI v Columbia Broadcasting* (1979) 441 US1 (SCOTUS).

[47] Richard Posner, *Antitrust Law* (University of Chicago Press 2001) 32.

[48] See Resolution 2002/2274 on a Community Framework for Collecting Management Societies in the Field of Copyright and Neighbouring Rights No 22 (January 2002) GUCE 92E/425.

[49] The most recent economic analysis defined this situation as a 'two sided market', particularly studied by David Evans, 'The Antitrust Economics of Two-Sided Markets' (2003) 20(2) Yale J Reg 325; David Evans and Richard Schmalensee, 'The Industrial Organization of Markets with Two-Sided Platforms' (2007) 3(1) Competition Policy International 29.

[50] The definition dates back to the early 2000's, following the study by Evans (n 49), a subject that was subsequently dealt with again by a group of French researchers that in 2007 re-proposed new studies in a conference on this issue.

intermediation, addressing various customers and carried out through a single platform. When faced with antagonist market interests, it is economically difficult to simultaneously provide a service that satisfies both. From a competition point of view, the management organisation cannot offer identical quality services in two different markets, where the potential satisfaction of one customer group is inversely proportional to the satisfaction of the other.

The particular case of the two-sided market does not, therefore, seem adaptable to collective management systems, as an actual demand on the part of users does not exist for a collective management service as it is currently provided by those organisations. Further the only existing competitive market is the one that offers services for authors.

Based on what we have seen so far regarding reasons for the legal and economic opportunity to link the monopoly's structure to collecting societies, this form clearly seems to be an equal condition for accessing the market. Establishing a 'one stop shop', allowing all of the protected works of a certain sector to be exploited from a single access point, is a clear advantage linked to collective management. This centralisation gives substance to the monopoly's economic and social value and it also represents the foundation of collective management.

The monopolistic market structure favours competition in terms of balanced market access. At the same time, it encourages creativity. Moreover, through management monopolies, exhaustive repertoires are created, thus optimising their fruition,[51] with a consequent enhancement of minor repertoires and of cultural diversity. Lastly, these monopolies offers a solution to the 'tragedy of the anti-commons' stemming from an excessive fragmentation of repertoires.

The analysis carried out so far shows how the monopolistic structure, even if extremely traditional, continues to keep its legal and economic relevance on the basis of the various advantages offered to authors and users, when compared to other systems.

See Jean-Charles Rochet and Jean Tirole, *Defining Two-Sided Markets* (Toulouse School of Economics 2004) 23–24 ('Two-sided (or more generally multi-sided) markets are roughly defined as markets in which one or several platforms enable interactions between end-users, and try to get the two (or multiple) sides "on board" by appropriately charging each side. That is, platforms court each side while attempting to make, or at least not lose, money overall').

[51] Josef Drexl, *Responses to the International Competition Network* (Unilateral Conduct Working Group 2007) 64 in considering the monopolist setup as an 'essential element for the flow of the competitive process'.

VIII. THE PROBLEM OF RIGHTS MANAGEMENT AT THE EU LEVEL, *DE IURE CONDENDO* ISSUES

From an EU law point of view, the position of most collecting societies is to be interpreted under paragraph 2 of article 106 of the Treaty on the Functioning of the European Union (TFEU). This provision also introduces a derogation from the general competition principle by establishing that:

> Undertakings entrusted with the operation of services of general economic interest or having the character of a revenue-producing monopoly shall be subject to the rules contained in the Treaties, in particular to the rules on competition, in so far as the application of such rules does not obstruct the performance, in law or in fact, of the particular tasks assigned to them. The development of trade must not be affected to such an extent as would be contrary to the interests of the Union.[52]

This provision demonstrates the propensity of competition law to open up to all markets and economic activities, including public sector ones. Therefore, even a state's action would seem to be subject to competition rules; this action benefits from a preferential scheme every time it aims at a general interest. On closer examination, the derogation as per art. 106 TFEU addresses not only public bodies, but also all the societies entrusted by a public authority with the managing of a service having a general economic interest.

In this respect, the Italian Authors and Editors Society – SIAE[53] – which operated under a monopoly until the recent liberalisation,[54] and its economic activity, like that of other European societies entrusted with similar tasks and carried out in the form of a monopoly,[55] generates an efficiency rate capable of overcoming the loss of potential competitiveness.

---

[52] Consolidated version of the Treaty on the Functioning of the European Union [2012] OJ C326 47–390.

[53] On SIAE, see Mario Fabiani, 'Voce Società Italiana Autori ed Editori' (1987) IV(XIII) Digesto Italiano 388.

[54] Albeit belatedly, several months after Decree Law 35/2017 implementing Directive 26/2014 in Italy came into force, the removal of the legal reserve which was originally envisaged fort the SIAE has been carried out. Thereby, at present, in Italy the market for the management of copyright is also entrusted to different subjects, which should comply with the following conditions: (1) be detained or controlled by its members; (2) be non-profit making.

[55] The legal monopoly in the intermediation of copyright, or even an exclusivity in the management of each category of rights, is also present in other European legislations, such as Austria, Hungary and the Czech Republic.

The common trend is to recognise the economic usefulness of the task carried out by copyright collecting societies, which allow authors, on the one hand, to benefit from significant remuneration for the use of their works, and users, on the other hand, to easily obtain licences in order to offer consumers large repertoires of the best possible quality. Within this context, the consolidated role of these societies as *de iure or de facto* monopolies strengthens their position,[56] leaving national and EU legislators hesitant to find alternative solutions based on free competition, because they risk failure.

Still in the EU context, it is interesting to examine the interpretations given by a Court of Justice judgment, preceding the implementation of the Directive by the Member States, particularly regarding the monopoly nature of management organisations and such activities being qualified as 'services' pursuant to Directive 123/2006/CE.[57]

In the *OSA* case,[58] the EU Court of Justice explored one of the most debated issues before the adoption phase of the Directive on collecting societies, that of interpreting art 16 of Directive 2006/123, concerning the free exercise on the part of the service provider of a service in a member state other than the state of establishment.[59]

Upon drafting of the proposal, the Commission, consistent with other EU policies, took the position that cross-border services provided by collecting societies had to be covered by art 16 of the Directive on services in the internal market[60] in order to ensure full freedom of establishment and the free movement of services among Member States. In considering the issue, in the light of the territorial nature of copyright, collective rights management services seem to be exempted from the scope of art 16 as they were subject to the derogation under art 17 of the Directive on services.

---

56 Silke von Lewinski, 'Copyright in Central and Eastern Europe: an Intellectual Property Metamorphosis' (1997) 8 Fordham Intell Prop Media & Ent 56, which emphasised how collecting societies usually are *de facto* or *de iure* monopolies, hence supervision is essential in order to prevent abuse of their position.

57 Directive 2006/123/EC of the European Parliament and of the Council of 12 December 2006 on Services in the Internal Market [2006] OJ L376 36–89.

58 Case C-351/12 (n 41).

59 Maria Letizia Bixio, 'Ancora una chance per il sistema monopolistico delle collecting societies. Osservazioni sulla decisione della Corte di Giustizia europea del 27 febbraio 2014 caso OSA' (2015) Rivista di diritto industriale 69–107.

60 Among the first analysis of the Directive Proposal, see Josef Drexl et al, 'Comments of the Max Planck Institute for Intellectual Property and Competition Law on the Proposal for a Directive of the European Parliament and of Council on Collective Management of Copyright' (2013) IIC 322.

The latter, however, does not make any specific reference to collective management activity.[61]

After a critical analysis of the Commission's Proposal, in the final text of the Directive on collecting societies, reference to the applicability of the Directive on services to collective management activity was entirely removed, while in the fourth Consideration a mild reference was kept to the opportunity for management organisations to benefit from freedoms laid down in treaties, among which the movement of services is implied.

In the *OSA* case, the Court of Justice reiterated the non-applicability of art 16 to services having as their object copyright, such as collective management; this exclusion seemed to be partially forced, considering the dual nature of collective management services, affecting both right-holders and users. Indeed, with regard to right-holders, the regime of the Directive on services would appear appropriate, where internal policies of various countries already favour the participation of authors in foreign collecting societies, with a consequent internationalisation of repertories. Reticence regarding the impact of art 16 *vis-à-vis* user protection, in situations of multi-territorial licensing, is more easily understood. Should a user be totally free to choose which management organisation to contact, even if this is in another EU country, in order to obtain authorisation for the use of protected works and for the related payment, serious problems would arise as regards the exercise of control over fees and royalties.[62]

The scope of art 16 in the current system is very complex, where the lack of competition law allowing Member States to operate *ex ante* controls on fees for licences granted in countries other than those in which management organisations are established makes the system incompatible with more competitive prospects. However, various Member States have already signed agreements and set specific regulation procedures for establishing royalties, at times creating control bodies, such as, for example, *Schiedsstelle* in Germany. This is a special arbitration committee in charge

---

61 The Court notes that the territorial monopoly granted to OSA, the Czech collecting organisation, constitutes a restriction on the freedom to provide services inasmuch as it does not allow users of protected works to choose the services of a collecting society established in another Member State. However, the Court emphasises that the restriction in question is justified since that system is appropriate and necessary for attaining the objective of the effective management of intellectual property rights. As EU law stands at present, there is no other method allowing the same level of copyright protection. The Court therefore concludes that the monopoly granted by the Czech legislation to OSA is compatible with the freedom to provide services.

62 See Josef Drexl, 'Collective Societies and Competition Law' <http://ip.mpg.de/shared/data/pdf/drexl_-_crmos_and_competition.pdf>.

of providing recommendations on the adequacy of royalties, should users disagree with the fees established by management organisations.

Mandatory mechanisms seem able to create uniform relationships among foreign and national management organisations, thus guaranteeing equal conditions among them. However, these systems appear to be totally in contrast with the principle of the free movement of services,[63] which does not establish any restriction in exercising activities through the obligation for the service provider to obtain authorisation from competent authorities.

Based on the current situation, the interpretation proposed by the Court for the very fragmented scenario of the EU would seem to be more adequate, especially for countries like the Czech Republic where legal monopolies still exist and the possibility is a priori excluded for foreign collecting societies to be established.[64]

Given the complex phase of transposition of the Directive on collective management,[65] what would had been desirable is a better link between the principle of free movement of services and the need to protect intellectual property, making sure that collecting societies be given the possibility to perform an effective control over royalties.

The Commission, however, did not carry out a policy of connection between the Directive on services and the Directive on the collective management of rights, thus allowing national legislators to reconcile the application and the implementation of said necessary control rules with the implementation of the principle of the free movement of services.

The *OSA* decision, then, remained in the background and provided little inspiration for following implementation of the Directive in the Member

---

[63] Directive 2006/123/EC of the European Parliament and of the Council of 12 December 2006 on Services in the Internal Market [2006] OJ L376, art 16(2)b.

[64] Article 98 of the Czech Copyright Law makes the collective management of copyright subject to the grant of an authorisation. Under paragraph 6(c) of that article, the relevant ministry may grant such an authorisation only if no other person already has such an authorisation for the exercise of the same right in relation to the same subject matter and, in so far as a work is concerned, for the exercise of the same right in relation to the same kind of work. The legislation such as that at issue in the main proceedings is liable to fall within the scope of Article 106(1) TFEU. That legislation grants exclusive rights to a collecting society such as OSA as regards the management of copyright relating to a certain category of works in the territory of the Member State concerned, thereby preventing other undertakings from exercising the economic activity in question in the same territory (see to that effect Case C-475/99 *Ambulanz Glöckner* (2001) ECR I 8089 [24]).

[65] The transposition of Directive 26/2014 was completed by every EU Member State between 2016 and 2017 (among the last countries, Italy transposed the text on 15 March 2017).

States. The vast majority of European countries, in fact, dismantled the legal monopolies, thus renouncing the entirety of national control over royalties.

Hence, at present, on the one hand the right-holders are allowed to:

> authorise a collective management organisation of their choice to manage the rights, categories of rights or types of works and other subject-matter of their choice, for the territories of their choice, irrespective of the Member State of nationality, residence or establishment of either the collective management organisation or the rightholder.[66]

On the other hand, all collective management organisations are also allowed to operate across borders. Nevertheless, the risks connected to such freedoms do not seem to be fully overcome.

As a matter of fact, if, as demonstrated, in traditional monopolistic systems with solidaristic purposes, the policy undertaken were justified by the protection of the general interest in cultural production, regardless of the actual market demand, in the new framework – inspired by a complete cross-border freedom of movement of services such as the collective management of rights – there is a danger of opening the intermediation market to subjects that will carry out a game of diminishing the cost of selling the service, with a consequent lowering of royalties and a related impoverishment of the right-holders.

---

[66] Directive 26/2014, art 5.

Index